THE HOSPITALITY INDUSTRY HANDBOOK SERIES

Legal Requirements

FOR HOSPITALITY BUSINESSES

Second Edition

Lisa Gordon-Davies
Peter Cumberlege

JUTA
AND COMPANY LTD

This book is the second edition of the book entitled *Legal Requirements for South African Students and Practitioners* (first published 2004). Copyright is reserved.

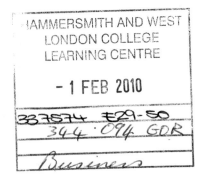

Legal Requirements for Hospitality Businesses

First published 2004
Second edition 2008
Reprinted October 2008

Juta & Company Ltd
Mercury Crescent, Wetton,
Cape Town, South Africa
© 2008 Juta & Company Ltd

ISBN 978 0 7021 7719 4

Project Manager: Marlinee Chetty
Editing & Indexing: Jennifer Stern
Proofreading: Rae Dalton
Design and typesetting: CBT Typesetting and Design
Cover design: Patricia Lynch-Blom
Printed and bound in South Africa by Formeset Printers Cape

Preface

The hotelier, restaurateur, licensee or catering manager will in the course of his or her work enter into many legal relationships with other parties. The owner or manager, for example, enters into a contract of employment with his or her employees. The business itself enters into many different contracts, both with suppliers for equipment and stores, and so on, and with customers for the provision of food, drink and accommodation. The business itself is regulated by a whole variety of Acts of Parliament that impose duties and standards of conduct that must be observed. Figure A below illustrates the various legal relationships that owners and their managers might find themselves in.

A sound knowledge of law is therefore as essential to the professional owner or manager as are knowledge of business management and the fundamental skills of the profession. The ways in which the manager is affected by the law are too numerous to mention, but this book provides information on:

- basic legal principles and how the law works in South Africa
- business law that pertains to running a legal business
- specific laws that affect operational aspects of the hospitality industry, and
- employment law

The primary market for which this book is intended is students who are studying for a career in the hotel, restaurant or catering sectors of the hospitality industry. However, this book will also provide hospitality managers in the industry with access to easily understandable and applicable information.

A primary function of this book is to consider the principles of law that relate to the hospitality industry in the context in which they arise. Simple legal examples relevant to the hospitality environment have been used throughout the text to illustrate legal principles.

Section 1 deals with the concept of law and defines and explores the basis of law in South Africa. It also deals with the concepts and requirements for the law of contract and the law of delict and various commercial contracts.

Section 2 deals with the application of the law to business, and covers the forms of business available for a commercial enterprise in South Africa, as well as the legal requirements for establishing a hospitality business – business licensing, naming the business, legal operational requirements and so forth.

Section 3 deals with laws that have particular relevance to hospitality operations, and includes liquor, tobacco, health and gaming laws.

Section 4 addresses issues pertaining to the employment of staff in the hospitality environment. The basic laws governing labour (Basic Conditions of Employment Act and the Labour Relations Act) are explained as well as the specific sectoral determination and bargaining councils applicable to the hospitality industry. Other legislative requirements that are dealt with include employment equity, occupational health and safely and skills development.

It is the hope of the authors that this book will be useful to the hospitality manager in creating an awareness of application of the law to their operations, and the duties and legal requirements that they must meet and fulfil. However, this text is not a substitute for professional advice from an attorney, and should never be used as such. This book is not intended to be a guide to legal practice, but is a simple and constructive guide to ensuring that the hospitality industries operate legally within the complex legal framework as encountered in South Africa today.

Figure A: The legal relationships of a professional hospitality manager

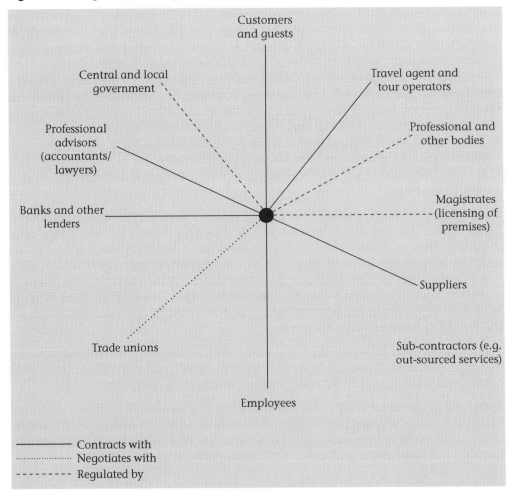

Acknowledgements

The authors would like to thank a number of people for their help and support in the writing of this book.

Firstly, we would like to thank our families and friends for their continued belief in and support of us.

Particular thanks go to Advocate Manie Moolman, National Convenor for Hospitality Management and lecturer of Hospitality Law at Technikon Free State School of Tourism, Hospitality and Sport for his professional and academic advice and guidance on Section 1.

In addition we would like to express our appreciation and thanks to the following people for their technical assistance and review of various topics and chapters:

Advocate Tlotliso Polaki, Board Secretary, National Gambling Board for input on the Gaming chapter.

Penny Campbell and Papiso Tshabalala from the Directorate of Food Control, Department of Health for review and input into the Hygiene chapter
Annie Baptiste from Franchising Plus for guidance on franchising issues.

Jinty Ainsworth, Hospitality Chamber Manager for THETA (Tourism, Hospitality and Sport Education and Training Authority) for verifying the chapter on skills development.

Thanks to all Juta's editing and technical staff for providing invaluable assistance in making this book a reality. Thanks in particular to Ute Späth.

Contents

Section 1: Introduction to Law

Chapter: 1 Introduction to South African Law

Chapter: 2 Law of contract

Chapter: 3 Law of delict

Chapter: 4 Commercial contracts

Section 2: Business and Hospitality Laws

Chapter: 5 Forms of business

Chapter: 6 Legal requirements for establishing a hospitality business

Chapter: 7 Liquor law

Chapter: 8 Food hygiene legislation

Chapter: 9 Tobacco legislation

Chapter: 10 Gambling legislation

Section 3: Law for Employment

Chapter: 11 The Labour Relations Act

Chapter:12 Introduction to labour law

Chapter:13 Hospitality employment law

Chapter:14 Occupational health and safety legislation

Chapter:15 Equal opportunities and anti-discrimination

Chapter:16 Skills development legislation

Table of Figures

Section 1

Introduction to Law

1

Introduction to South African Law

Objectives of this chapter:

By the end of this chapter the learner will be able to:
- Explain the process of creating laws in South Africa
- Distinguish between different legal professionals
- Describe the classification of law

The learner will know:
- The judicial system and hierarchy of courts in South Africa
- The sources of law
- Methods of settling disputes outside of court

1.1 Introduction

Every society has rules by which people live. These may be social rules (for example, manners and etiquette), moral rules (relating more to behaviour of a personal or sexual nature) and religious rules (such as the attendance of church).

Legal rules differ from social rules in that they are enforceable in courts of law. The law may be described as a set of rules used to control the behaviour of people in society. The purpose of these rules is to order society, and to create an environment in which people can interact on a basis of certainty. The law provides a form of guarantee that various parties, for example to a contract or relationship, will perform their obligations to each other, or they will be punished or made to pay by law.

Law can be defined as the following:
- The body of rules that governs the conduct of natural and artificial persons (for example, companies, close corporations, clubs, and societies).
- These rules tell you what you must do, what you may not do and what others may not do to you.
- These rules are recognised by the State as binding and enforceable.

The law is influenced by the environment in which it is applied, which is why different countries may have different legal systems. The law usually reflects or is influenced by the social, moral and religious rules within a country. In this way the laws of a predominantly Christian country such as South Africa will differ from a country where Hindu or Islam is the dominant religion.

In other words the law tells the individual about his or her legal rights and duties. Punishment is part of the set of rules; if the rules are not followed the guilty party can be punished by a decision made in a court of law.

Without laws there would be confusion, fear and disorder in society. However, this does not mean that all laws are always fair. Every society agrees that some laws are necessary, but these laws should be made in a democratic way, so that they will be just and fair to the population that they govern.

This chapter will explore the basic ways in which laws are classified, what law is and where it can be found, what courts are, how they function and how the legal profession in South Africa is organised.

1.2 History of South African law

Before the European settlers arrived at the Cape, the people of South Africa had their own laws and rules. Today these laws are called 'indigenous law' or 'customary law'.

When Jan van Riebeeck arrived at the Cape in 1652, the Dutch Settlers brought with them their legal system from the Netherlands. This is called 'Roman-Dutch Law'. For the next 150 years Roman-Dutch law was the official law of the Cape.

In the early 1800s the British took over the rule of the Cape from the Dutch. They brought the English legal system with them.

In 1910, the four colonies of South Africa joined together to become the Union of South Africa. This created one central government with the power to make all the laws of the country. However, as most people were not allowed to vote for this government, the laws were made by a government that was not elected in a democratic way. For the majority of the people of South Africa, many of these laws were unfair and did not protect their rights.

In April 1994, one central government was elected democratically for the first time in South Africa. Many changes have subsequently been made to the laws of South Africa by the democratically elected government.

Current South African law comes mainly from these cultures:
- the culture of the people who were here in the beginning
- the culture of the Dutch settlers from the Netherlands
- the culture of the British settlers
- the culture of the liberation movements

1.3 Sources of law

Sources of law refer to where laws may have originated or been found.

1.3.1 Constitutional law

In 1996 South Africa was given a new constitution in terms of the Constitution of the Republic of South Africa Act, 1996. Section 2 of the Constitution says that the Constitution is the supreme law of the land. No other law or government action can supersede the provisions of the Constitution. South Africa is thus a constitutional state and all legislation enacted by Parliament is subject to the Constitution.

The Constitution has a direct influence on legislation, which means that legislation that is in conflict with the Constitution can be struck down by the courts. Any legislation or other law that is in conflict with the Constitution is therefore of no legal force or effect.

Provincial governments can make their own constitutions, but these constitutions cannot contradict the national Constitution.

Chapter 2 of the Constitution contains the Bill of Rights, which is of particular importance to the people of South Africa. In the Bill of Rights certain fundamental or basic rights such as the right to equality, the right to human dignity, the right to life, the right to freedom of religion, belief and opinion, as well as the right to freedom of expression, are protected. An example of the impact of this on business practice and compliance, is that it is against this constitutional framework that the two main pieces of legislation aimed at achieving equality and eradicating discrimination within the workplace – the Employment Equity Act 55 of 1998, and the Promotion of Equality and Prevention of Unfair Discrimination Act 4 of 2000, – were developed. These Acts will be discussed in greater detail later on in this book.

Because the Bill of Rights is part of the Constitution, any legal rule (whether it is contained in an Act of Parliament or in any other source of law) that is in conflict with the Bill of Rights is void. It was, for instance, in terms of the Bill of Rights that the Constitutional Court declared the death penalty to be unconstitutional as it was in conflict with the right to life.

1.3.2 Statute law/legislation

Statute law is written law that has been made by the government. Laws made by Parliament are called statutes or Acts. They are published in a government newspaper called the *Government Gazette*. An example of a statute law is the Tobacco Products Control Act 83 of 1993. This means it was the 83rd law passed in 1993.

The Constitutional Court can declare any statute law invalid if it goes against the Constitution. Other courts can declare only less important laws invalid.

Parliament can give the power to make less important laws to other groups of people, or to a Minister. Sometimes a statute gives power to a person (for example a minister) or a body (for example the Department of Trade and Industry (DTI)) to make regulations. An example would be how the DTI promulgated the National Gambling Act, which makes provision for each province to have a provincial gambling authority that lays down the laws within that province using the national legislation as the regulatory framework.

Provinces, towns and cities are allowed to make their own laws that only apply only to them. Prior to 1994 the four provinces made ordinances. Now the nine provinces enact Provincial Acts. Towns and cities make bylaws. Examples of particular relevance to the hospitality industry are municipal health by-laws that expand on the national health regulations but have particular reference and application to a specific municipal area. Operators must always check with local authorities what their specific requirements are in addition to the national requirements. Section 1.6 of this chapter outlines in which fields provinces and municipalities have concurrent legislative and executive powers with the national sphere.

1.3.3 Common law

The common law is the set of laws that are not made by Parliament or any level of government. The laws against crimes like murder, rape, theft and treason are part of the common law. The common law has developed through the decisions of judges in the High Courts and the Supreme Court of Appeal. The Roman-Dutch and English law brought by the Dutch and British settlers is also part of the common law. The common law can be changed by new decisions of the courts.

Like England and the USA, South Africa follows a common law system. While some of its law is contained in legislative enactments – for example Acts of Parliament, Provincial Ordinances or Acts and local by-laws – much of South African law is not codified, but is based on common law sources that include case law and the decisions and writings of Roman-Dutch jurists. The decisions of the South African courts given over the years constitute precedents that generally bind courts in later cases involving comparable facts.

In the English tradition, law emanates primarily from legal practice. However, the writings of a number of legal academics (from between approximately 1200 to 1635 CE) played an important role in the early development of the common law. These days, however, there is an increasing tendency to refer to the writings of contemporary jurists.

In South Africa, the writings of the old (Roman-Dutch) writers are as authoritative in principle as court decisions, and in a sense even more so. A court decision that ignores the old authorities (or interprets or applies them wrongly) is in fact regarded as 'clearly wrong' and may be overturned.

Contemporary authors write about the law. They systematise the legal rules in particular branches of the law, discuss and sometimes criticise court decisions and legislation, and propose solutions to problems that may exist. Although they do not bind courts, the works of modern authors who are experts in their field are extremely valuable sources of knowledge of the law.

Lawyers often use those works to find the binding source of law that they can use in court. Because the authors are specialists in their field, their arguments and opinions are often used to persuade a court to come to a particular decision. One may thus say that, although the writings of modern authors have no binding force, they may have persuasive force and courts do in practice take notice of their opinions.

The common law applies to everyone equally in the whole country. Statutory law is, however, stronger than common law. It is only when no statutory law governing a matter exists that the common law will apply.

1.3.4 Precedent

Every day courts interpret and apply the law. It thus makes sense for a court to take note of decisions made in previous cases that are similar. This simple principle has led to the development of a doctrine that originated in England and is called *stare decisis*. This literally means 'to stand by previous decisions'. In terms of the *stare decisis* rule courts are bound by their previous decisions, and by the decisions of higher courts; previous judgments are therefore binding, and create precedents that must be followed. Courts must, therefore, take into account their previous judgments in similar cases because they are bound to the approach followed in the past. Previous judicial decisions are therefore also a source of law, and the way in which the law was applied is authoritative.

1.3.5 Customary law

It would be extremely short-sighted to claim that colonial settlers brought a legal system to South Africa. Before the arrival of the colonists in South Africa, there were in fact indigenous populations that had lived for generations according to their own distinctive laws.

Such an indigenous legal system has certain characteristics. As unwritten law it is passed on verbally from generation to generation and has strong ties with culture, tradition and the tribe.

Many South African communities live in accordance with indigenous law. Indigenous law consists of the customs of groups of people who live in accordance with their traditional, normally unwritten rules. Indigenous law is also customary law to the extent that it is not amended or abolished by legislation. It may be applied in cases where both parties to the dispute are black people who have maintained a traditional way of life and who respect the customary law in force in their area or in their community.

In terms of the Constitution, indigenous law, as customary law, is recognised if it is not in conflict with the Constitution or any legislation that specifically deals with customary law.

Indigenous law is applied in the ordinary courts, when the parties choose. The Law of Evidence Amendment Act 45 of 1988 stipulates that a court can take judicial notice of indigenous law, provided that it is not in conflict with the principles of public policy or natural justice. Judicial notice means that indigenous law does not have to be proved; the court may merely accept it. In some instances an expert will have to give testimony on the content of these rules.

There are chief's or headman's courts, but these can only deal with some cases between African people. In KwaZulu-Natal there is also the Code of Zulu Law. This code would apply in family matters, for example.

1.4 Classification of the law

The law, as it is found in the different sources, cannot be studied as an incoherent and disorderly mass of rules. The Romans started a tradition of classifying the law into different disciplines or branches, but no perfect or ideal classification of the law exists. Authors differ considerably as to where exactly some divisions of law fit into the whole classification. However, any classification of law at least has the advantage that it provides an overview of the different divisions or areas of law. To a large extent it also shows how the law fits together, and how it functions. The classification may be illustrated as follows:

Figure 1-1: Classification of law

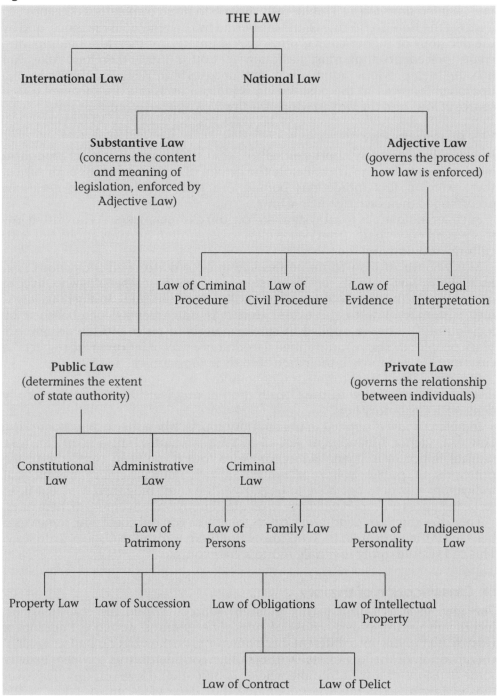

1.5 Types of law

There are various kinds of law in South Africa.

International and **national** law distinguish between the laws that operate between countries, such as diplomatic relations, international boundaries and airspace and the laws that operate within a country.

Within national law, there is **substantive law** and **adjective law**. Adjective law concerns the process of how law is enforced, and contains the laws for criminal and civil procedure, evidence and legal interpretation. For example, if a guest were to institute an action against a hotel for breach of contract, the rules of civil procedure would apply to how this is done. Substantive law is that part of the law that determines the content and meaning of the different legal rules. Substantive law is enforced through processes determined by adjective law.

Substantive law is then classified into **public law** and **private law**.

1.5.1 Public law

Public law determines the extent of State authority. It regulates the organisation of the state, the relation between the different organs of the State, and the relation between the State and its subjects. The law gives the state authority over individuals. This division of law includes constitutional law (the highest law of the land), administrative law and criminal law.

1.5.1.1 Criminal law

In a criminal case the state prosecutes the accused person for committing a crime or breaking the law. 'Prosecutes' means that the State makes a charge against someone. If the court finds the person guilty, the person can be sent to prison, fined, or punished in some other way.

Examples of different crimes and breaking the law:
* rape
* public violence
* assault
* theft
* trespassing

Usually the state is not the complainant (the one making a charge). The state prosecutes, but any person or individual can be the complainant and lay a charge against another person or against the state.

A criminal case can be brought against anyone who breaks the law, including a person who works for the state, such as a member of the police or defence force. If, for example, someone is unlawfully assaulted or shot by a member of the police or defence force, he or she can bring a criminal case against them.

1.5.2 Private law

Private law regulates the relationships between individuals where their relationship is on an equal basis, and where one party does not have authority over the other, as the State has over its subjects. The procedures of civil law apply in private law. Private law includes the law of persons, family law, the law of personality, indigenous laws and the law of patrimony. The law of patrimony regulates the relationships between persons with respect to their means – their assets and liabilities, i e their estate. A patrimonial loss would therefore be a loss to the estate of the individual. Patrimonial law includes property (ownership) law, law of succession, law of obligations (including law of contract and law of delict) and law of intellectual property.

1.5.2.1 Civil law
Civil law is the set of rules for your private relationships with other people. The state does not take sides in a dispute between private people.

Examples of what civil law deals with:
- marriage and divorce
- debt
- rent agreements
- evictions
- damage to property
- injuries to people
- disputes over a hire-purchase agreement

A civil case is usually brought by a person (called the plaintiff) who feels that he or she was wronged by another person (called the defendant). If the plaintiff wins the case, the court usually orders the defendant to pay compensation (money). Sometimes the court may also order a defendant to do, or stop doing, something – for example, to stop damaging the plaintiff's property.

The state may be involved in a civil case as a party if it is suing or being sued for a wrongful act – for example, if government property is damaged or a government official injures somebody without good reason.

1.5.2.2 Law of obligations
The law of obligations regulates the type of relationship between persons where one person has a right against another for performance, and the latter person has a corresponding duty to perform. Such a relationship is called an obligation. It is mainly contracts and delicts that create such obligations, both of which are important to the hospitality industry. These will be discussed in detail in the following chapters.

1.5.3 Criminal and civil actions
Sometimes a person's act may lead to both criminal and civil actions. For example, Mr Hotelier hits one of the waiters in his hotel. This is a crime of assault. The state will prosecute him in the criminal court if the waiter lays a charge against him. If there is enough proof to show that he is guilty, he may be punished by the state.

However, Mr Hotelier also causes pain to the worker. This is a damage that one person does to another person. The injured waiter could sue Mr Hotelier for damages and make him pay compensation for medical expenses, lost wages and pain and suffering. This will be a civil claim for damages through the civil court.

1.5.3.1 The South African legislative process

When a change in policy is being made, the government often first puts forward its proposals in a green paper, which is a discussion document on policy options. It originates in the department of the Ministry concerned and is then published for comment and ideas. A submission date is usually given for input from the public. This document forms the basis for a white paper, which is a broad statement of government policy. Comment may again be invited from interested parties.

Once these inputs have been taken into account, the Minister and officials within the State department concerned may draft Legislative Proposals. At this stage the proposals are also considered by the Cabinet. Occasionally this document may be gazetted as a draft bill, for comment by a defined date, or given to certain organisations for comment. Once all comments have been considered, the document is taken to the State Law Advisers who examine the proposals in detail and check their consistency with existing legislation. These proposals are printed by parliament and given a number. They are then tabled or introduced in either the National Assembly or the National Council of Provinces. The document is now no longer a draft Bill, it is now a Bill, and the introduction or tabling is called the first reading. After the reading it is put on the order paper and it goes to a committee for consideration.

Figure 1-2: South African legislative process

What	Action	Who
Green paper	Drafted and published for comment	Relevant Ministry
White paper	Drafted and published for comment	Relevant Ministry
Draft bill	Gazetted and published for comment	Relevant Ministry
Bill	Tabled in parliament and sent to committee for consideration, then returned to Parliament for discussion and approval	National Assembly, National Council of Provinces, committees
Act	Bill signed	President

The committee that discusses the Bill consists of members of the different parties represented in parliament. They sometimes call expert witnesses or invite submissions to help refine it, after which they may amend it. When the committee has approved the Bill, it goes for debate in the house in which it was tabled. Once that house has agreed to the Bill, it is transmitted to the other house and the same procedure is followed.

When both houses have passed the Bill it is allocated an Act number, and then goes to the President to be signed. It is then published in the *Government Gazette* as an Act, and it then becomes a law of the land.

Sometimes there are no green and white papers, and the process begins with the legislative proposals originating in the Ministry or Department.

South African legislation is constantly revised to meet changing circumstances in a dynamic and developing society. This is done on the advice of the legal sections of various government departments, and the South African Law Commission, in consultation with all interest groups.

1.6 The South African legal system

1.6.1 Parliament

Parliament is the legislative authority of South Africa and has the power to make laws for the country in accordance with the Constitution. It consists of the National Assembly and the National Council of Provinces (NCOP). Parliamentary sittings are open to the public.

1.6.1.1 The National Assembly

The National Assembly consists of no fewer than 350 and no more than 400 members elected through a system of proportional representation. The National Assembly, which is elected for a term of five years, is presided over by a Speaker, who is assisted by a Deputy Speaker.

The National Assembly is elected to represent the people and to ensure democratic governance as required by the Constitution. It does this by electing the President, by providing a national forum for public consideration of issues, by passing legislation, and by scrutinising and overseeing executive action.

1.6.1.2 The National Council of Provinces (NCOP)

The NCOP consists of 54 permanent members and 36 special delegates, and aims to represent provincial interests in the national sphere of government. Delegations from each province consist of 10 representatives. The NCOP gets a mandate from the provinces before it can make certain decisions. It cannot, however, initiate a Bill concerning money, which is the prerogative of the Minister of Finance.

1.6.2 The Presidency

1.6.2.1 The President

The President is the Head of State and leads the Cabinet. He or she is elected by the National Assembly from among its members, and leads the country in the interest of national unity, in accordance with the Constitution and the law.

The President:
* must select the Deputy President from among the members of the National Assembly
* may select any number of Ministers from among the members of the Assembly
* may select no more than two Ministers from outside the Assembly

1.6.2.2 The Deputy President

The President appoints the Deputy President from among the members of the National Assembly. The Deputy President must assist the President in executing government functions.

1.6.3 The Cabinet

The Cabinet consists of the President, who is head of the Cabinet, the Deputy President and Ministers. The President appoints the Deputy President and Ministers, assigns their powers and functions, and may dismiss them.

The President may select any number of Ministers from among the members of the National Assembly, and may select no more than two Ministers from outside the Assembly. The President appoints a member of the Cabinet to be the leader of government business in the National Assembly.

Departments and members of the Cabinet

- Agriculture
- Arts & Culture
- Communications
- Correctional Services
- Defence
- Education
- Environmental Affairs & Tourism
- Foreign Affairs
- Government Communications (GCIS)
- Health
- Home Affairs
- Housing
- Independent Complaints Directorate
- Justice & Constitutional Development
- Labour
- Land Affairs
- Minerals and Energy
- National Intelligence Agency
- National Treasury
- Provincial & Local Government
- Public Enterprises
- Public Service & Administration
- Public Service Commission
- Public Works
- Science & Technology
- Secretariat for Safety & Security
- SA Management Development Institute
- SA Police Service
- SA Revenue Service
- SA Secret Service
- Social Development
- Sport & Recreation South Africa
- Statistics South Africa
- The Presidency
- Trade and Industry
- Transport
- Water Affairs & Forestry

1.7 Provincial government

In accordance with the Constitution, each of the nine provinces has its own legislature consisting of between 30 and 80 members. The number of members is determined by a formula set out in national legislation. The members are elected in terms of proportional representation.

The executive council of a province consists of a Premier and a number of members. The Premier is elected by the Provincial Legislature.

Decisions are taken by consensus, as happens in the national Cabinet. Besides being able to make provincial laws, a provincial legislature may adopt a constitution for its province if two-thirds of its members agree. However, a provincial Constitution must correspond with the national Constitution as confirmed by the co-ordinating council.

According to the constitution, provinces may have legislative and executive powers concurrently with the national sphere over, among other things:

◆ agriculture
◆ casinos, racing, gambling and wagering
◆ cultural affairs
◆ education at all levels, excluding university and technikon education
◆ environment
◆ health services
◆ housing
◆ language policy
◆ nature conservation
◆ police services
◆ provincial public media
◆ public transport
◆ regional planning and development
◆ road traffic regulation
◆ tourism
◆ trade and industrial promotion
◆ traditional authorities
◆ urban and rural development
◆ vehicle licensing
◆ welfare services

An example of this is how the National Gambling Act sets out a national policy for gaming, while each province sets provincial legislation for the regulation of gambling activities in its province.

Provinces also have exclusive competency over a number of areas. The areas relevant to the hospitality industry include:

◆ abattoirs
◆ ambulance services
◆ liquor licences
◆ museums other than national museums
◆ provincial planning
◆ provincial cultural matters
◆ provincial recreation and activities
◆ provincial roads and traffic

1.8 Local government

The recognition of local government in the Constitution as a sphere of government has enhanced the status of local government as a whole, and of municipalities in particular, and has given them a new dynamic role as instruments of delivery.

National legislation therefore makes provision for regulations and laws to be made at local level, which is why establishments must adhere to by-laws and obtain licences at local level.

1.8.1 Municipalities

The Constitution provides for three categories of municipalities: category A (metropolitan municipalities), category B (district municipalities) or category C (local areas or municipalities). It also determines that category A municipalities can only be established in metropolitan areas.

The Municipal Demarcation Board determined that Johannesburg, Durban, Cape Town, Pretoria, East Rand and Port Elizabeth are metropolitan areas. Metropolitan councils have a single metropolitan budget, common property rating and service tariffs systems, and a single employer body. South Africa has six metropolitan municipalities (namely Tshwane, Johannesburg, Ekurhuleni, Ethekwini, Cape Town and Nelson Mandela), 231 local municipalities and 47 district municipalities.

Metropolitan councils may decentralise powers and functions. In metropolitan areas there is a choice of two types of executive systems: the mayoral executive system where legislative and executive authority is vested in the mayor, and the collective executive committee where these powers are vested in the executive committee.

Non-metropolitan areas consist of district councils and local (town) councils.

Figure 1–3: Illustration of levels of legislation

Level	Legislation	Example
National	National Acts and regulations	National Liquor Act and regulations
Provincial	Provincial ordinances and regulations	Provincial (retail) liquor Acts
Municipal/Local Authorities	By-laws	Municipal by-laws: liquor trading hours

1.9 Justice

1.9.1 The administration of justice

In terms of the Constitution, the judicial authority of South Africa is vested in the courts, which are independent and subject only to the Constitution and the law.

No person or organ of State may interfere with the functioning of the courts, and an order or decision of a court binds all organs of State and persons to whom it applies. The Department of Justice and Constitutional Development is responsible for constitutional development and the administration of the courts.

It performs these functions in conjunction with the judges, magistrates, National Director of Public Prosecutions (NDPP) and Directors of Public Prosecution (DPP), who are all independent.

The department's responsibilities include the provision of adequate resources for the proper and efficient functioning of the criminal and civil justice systems. It provides legislation, and gives administrative support for the establishment of institutions required by the constitution.

1.10 The judicial system and hierarchy of courts

In terms of its Constitution, South Africa has the following courts:

* the **Constitutional Court**
* the **Supreme Court of Appeal**
* the **high courts**, including any High Court of Appeal established by an Act of parliament to hear appeals from high courts
* the **Labour Court** which has jurisdiction on any constitutional matter not falling within the exclusive jurisdiction of the Constitutional Court or assigned to another court of a status similar to a high court, and the **Labour Appeal Court** which has exclusive jurisdiction to determine appeals from the Labour Court
* the **magistrates' courts**
* **any other court established or recognised by an Act of parliament**, including any court with a status similar to either the high courts or the magistrates' courts

Judicial powers are exercised by a formal court system. This comprises a hierarchy of courts, with each level in the hierarchy having a specified jurisdiction.

The small claims courts deal with claims with a monetary value of up to R7 000. Litigants appear personally with no legal representation and proceedings are relatively informal, providing swift and effective relief.

The lower courts are called magistrates' courts and these generally have jurisdiction over most criminal cases and civil cases where the amount in dispute is less than R100 000. Magistrates are officials of the Department of Justice and are appointed by an independent body, the Magistrates' Commission.

The superior courts are called the high courts. There are a number of provincial and local high courts. Judges, appointed by the Judicial Services Commission (an independent body), are usually chosen from the ranks of practising senior advocates, attorneys or academics, and they enjoy a high degree of autonomy and independence.

High courts have original jurisdiction in respect of criminal matters and civil matters, and have appellate jurisdiction in respect of matters originally heard in the magistrates' courts and matters heard by single judges in a high court.

The highest court in South Africa for non-constitutional matters is the

Supreme Court of Appeal. It is situated in Bloemfontein, and has appellate jurisdiction only. Its judgments are binding on all lower courts.

The Constitutional Court has jurisdiction throughout South Africa as a court of final instance over all matters relating to the interpretation, protection and enforcement of the provisions of the Constitution. Most constitutional disputes will first be heard by a high court. However, some constitutional matters fall exclusively within the jurisdiction of the Constitutional Court.

Although many commercial contracts are specifically made subject to the jurisdiction of the magistrates' courts (which can exercise that jurisdiction even though such cases would normally fall outside its jurisdiction), as a general rule commercial matters involving significant monetary value will be heard in a high court.

Commercial disputes in the area of jurisdiction of the Witwatersrand Provincial Division of the High Court, an area that includes Johannesburg, Pretoria and the Witwatersrand and which is the largest commercial centre of South Africa, may be referred to a commercial court that has been established as part of the High Court.

The commercial courts' judges have expertise in commercial matters, and special rules and procedures are available to facilitate and expedite the handing down of decisions.

Arbitration, mediation and other alternative dispute resolution procedures are widely used as an alternative to the courts. A non-governmental body, the Arbitration Foundation of Southern Africa (AFSA) in Johannesburg is often used, particularly in commercial disputes. Arbitration clauses are often incorporated in commercial contracts.

1.11 The legal profession in South Africa

1.11.1 Judges
Judges are appointed by the President. Judges hear and decide cases in the Constitutional Court, Supreme Court of Appeal and high courts. They often decide cases by themselves, but sometimes will hear a case in groups of two or more.

1.11.2 Assessors
In serious criminal cases in the high courts, two assessors are appointed to help the judge. Assessors are usually advocates or retired magistrates. They sit with the judge during the court case, and listen to all the evidence presented to the court. At the end of the court case they give the judge their opinion. The judge does not have to listen to the assessors' opinions but it usually helps the judge to make a decision.

1.11.3 Magistrates
Magistrates are appointed by the Minister of Justice. They hear and decide cases in the magistrates' courts.

1.11.4 Director of Public Prosecutions (Attorney-General)
At each high court there is a Director of Public Prosecutions (DPP) with a staff of assistants. (DPPs used to be known as Attorney Generals.) The DPPs are appointed by the Minister of Justice.

The DPPs are responsible for all the criminal cases in their province, so all the prosecutors are under their control. The police bring the information about a criminal case to the DPP. The DPP then decides whether there is good reason to have a trial, and if there is enough information to prove in court that the person is guilty. There is a National Director of Public Prosecutions who is in charge of all the DPPs.

1.11.5 Prosecutors

The prosecutor represents the state in a criminal trial against people who are accused of committing a crime. Before the trial, the prosecutor works with the South African Police Services to find out all the facts about the case, and to prepare state witnesses who saw what happened or who have other information.

The prosecutor then presents all this information in court, and tries to convince the judge or magistrate that the accused person is guilty. The prosecutor does this by asking the state witnesses to tell their stories. The prosecutor also cross-questions the witnesses that the accused person brings to court to try to disprove their evidence.

1.11.6 Advocates and attorneys

The legal profession is divided into two branches of lawyers:

- *Advocates* do mostly trial work (special litigators), especially in the high courts. They may not take work directly from the public, but must be briefed by attorneys. In addition, they may not form partnerships but must remain independent.
- *Attorneys* are the 'general practitioners' of the legal industry, who deal directly with clients and are entitled, if they so wish, to work in partnerships.

Advocates were previously the only lawyers entitled to appear in the high courts. However, attorneys who have been practising for more than three years may now obtain equal rights of appearance in all courts.

All advocates and most attorneys are university graduates. New attorneys are required to be university graduates. The legal profession is based largely on the British system, and the level of expertise and service is comparable to that found in Britain or the United States.

1.11.7 Public defenders

If a person who is accused in a serious criminal case cannot afford to pay for his or her own lawyer, his or her case will be taken by a public defender. Public defenders are lawyers who are paid for by the state.

1.11.8 Paralegals

Paralegals do not have any formal legal training and cannot act in formal legal procedures. They give advice to people and organisations on different aspects of the law, including advice on their rights, and ways of protecting their rights. They also provide basic legal education to communities or organisations.

1.12 Trials, appeals and reviews

1.12.1 Trials

A trial is a court hearing in a magistrate's court or a high court, called the trial court. The magistrate or judge listens to all the people who have information about the case. This information is called the verbal or oral evidence. The court also looks at the physical evidence, for example, a knife or a letter. These are called exhibits in the trial.

The magistrate or judge listens to the evidence from both sides. If it is a criminal trial, the magistrate or judge listens to the state and its witnesses. Then he or she listens to the story of the accused, and to the witnesses called by the accused. The magistrate or judge then makes a decision, which is called a judgment.

1.12.2 Appeals

The person who loses a trial has the right to appeal. This means that he or she can ask a higher court to change the decision of the trial court. Usually this appeal court will not listen to any new evidence. It will only read the report from the lower court to see what evidence was given. It is therefore very important that everything that needs to be presented is said in the first court that hears the case.

A case that was heard in a magistrate's court can go on appeal to the nearest high court, and then to the Supreme Court of Appeal. A case heard in a high court can go directly on appeal to the Supreme Court of Appeal. The Supreme Court of Appeal listens only to appeals – it does not hear any trials.

In a civil case, the person who loses the case must usually pay the costs of the person who wins. The person who loses the appeal must usually pay the legal costs of the other party for both the trial and the appeal. In a criminal appeal, the person making the appeal must pay his or her own legal costs, whether he or she wins or loses. It should be noted that it is very expensive to take a case on appeal.

1.12.3 Reviews

Review takes place in the case of a possible irregularity in the proceedings. Certain criminal cases heard by magistrates' courts, in which heavy sentences were imposed, are automatically reviewed by the high courts. In other cases, an application must be brought to the high courts for review.

1.13 Settling disputes outside courts

Many legal problems can be settled without going to court. Usually court procedures are slow and expensive, and require the services of a lawyer. A lawyer is not needed in the Small Claims Court, or for a labour dispute taken to the Commission for Conciliation, Mediation and Arbitration (CCMA).

There are a number of different ways to solve disputes without going to any of the courts:
◆ negotiation
◆ mediation
◆ arbitration

1.13.1 Negotiation

Negotiation means that people who have a problem talk to each other about their problem, and try to solve it by coming up with a solution that suits both sides. Negotiations can happen at a national level, for example, when political parties come together to negotiate how political prisoners will be released. At a local level, civic organisations can negotiate with the local authority about land rights in the area.

Sometimes people hire lawyers to negotiate for them. For example, a person involved in a motor car accident may hire a lawyer to negotiate for him or her with an insurance company.

The lawyers of people involved in a court case will often negotiate an agreement (also called a settlement) before the case gets to court. This saves time and money.

1.13.2 Mediation

Mediation happens when people with a problem agree to have a third person act as a go-between to help them settle their problem. For example, two neighbours are always fighting about the noise coming from each other's houses. A mediator will bring the neighbours together and try to make them talk about the problem. His or her aim will be to make both parties agree to compromise on the noise.

The mediator does not act as a judge. He or she makes no decision that the parties must follow. The mediator listens to both arguments, and tries to get the parties to compromise and come to some agreement. Mediation is often used in worker disputes, but is also used by community and church leaders to resolve disputes in a community.

1.13.3 Arbitration

Arbitration takes place when people who have a problem agree to have a third person (called an arbitrator) to listen to their arguments and work out a solution. The arbitrator acts like a judge and both sides usually agree to follow whatever decision the arbitrator makes. Arbitration is used mostly in disputes between workers and employers. It is usually quicker and more informal than a court case.

Questions and exercises

1. A provincial liquor Bill has been published. A restaurateur in that province has heard that certain provisions may be detrimental to his business, and is concerned about these provisions. Explain how the restaurateur can enter the public hearing process and ensure that his interests or concerns are heard before the Bill is enacted. Explain how to obtain a copy of such a Bill.
2. Explain why it is important for a hospitality manager to know the various levels of lawmaking and how it affects his or her business.
3. With reference to the Constitution, describe the various competencies assigned to each tier of government.

2
Law of contract

Objectives of this chapter:

By the end of this chapter the learner will be able to:
- Describe the elements required for the formation of the contract
- Distinguish between valid, void and voidable contracts
- Understand the rules applicable to breach of contract
- Identify and understand the remedies for breach of contract

The learner will know:
- The definition of a contract
- The elements for the formation of a valid contract
- Differences between a valid, void and unenforceable contract
- How to achieve consensus for the formation of a contract
- The requirements for offer and acceptance of a contract
- The remedies available for a breach of contract

2.1 Introduction

Many people think of a contract as a thick legal document. However, what most people do not realise, is that they conclude contracts almost every day – when they go to a shop and buy groceries, or when they go to a restaurant and order a meal. Contracts are a part of life, and in the hospitality industry, when providing goods and services to guests and customers, contracts govern most transactions. It is therefore, important for managers in the hospitality industry to understand the concepts of contract law.

A contract is an agreement between persons in terms of which a right and a corresponding duty to a performance come into existence.

When Mr Hotelier provides a room for Ms Guest, in terms of a contract, Mr Hotelier has a right against Ms Guest to claim payment for that room, and Ms Guest has a duty to pay for it.

Examples of contracts that are concluded in the hospitality industry include lease agreements (for example, where a restaurateur rents the premises of the restaurant from a lessor), a contract of sale (where the purchasing officer buys food for the hotel), or partnership agreements (where one or more people may establish a business together).

The relationship between an employer and an employee is brought into existence by contract. Labour law, as a subdivision of commercial law is therefore also a form of contract law. However, industrial relations are regulated quite extensively by legislation and by the Constitution. Labour Law will be discussed in Section 3.

The law of contract prescribes the requirements for the conclusion of a contract as well as the termination of contracts.

2.2 Meaning of contract

A contract is an agreement giving rise to legal obligations, and which is entered into between at least two persons with the intention of bringing into existence a legal relationship. The agreement must comply with the formalities provided for by the law for the formation of a valid contract. More simply, a contract is an agreement that is enforceable by law and creates rights and duties between the parties. The obligations arising from a contract entitle the parties to the contract to receive performance and/or require either or both to perform.

The intention of the contracting parties to create rights and obligations that are enforceable in law distinguishes a contract from any other agreement. The law of contract is therefore a part of the law of obligations.

2.3 Debtor and creditor

The legal relationship consists, on one hand, of a right to receive something or to have something done and, on the other hand, a duty to give something or to do something. The party who has the legal right to have something done for him or her, or receive something, is known as the creditor, and the party who has a duty to do or give something is the debtor (they are, in a manner of speaking, in debt to the other party).

A contract of sale gives rise to at least two legal relationships:
◆ A legal relationship to make the item that is bought available
◆ A legal relationship to pay for the item

In the first legal relationship, the seller has a duty to make the item available and the buyer has a right to receive the item. The seller is therefore the debtor and the buyer is the creditor. In the second legal relationship, the buyer has the duty to pay the purchase price and the seller has a right to be paid. In the second relationship, the roles are reversed, and the seller is therefore the creditor, and the buyer is the debtor.

2.4 Requirements for a valid contract

A contract comes into existence and gives rise to legal relationships only if certain requirements are met. If the contract is found to be invalid through lack of compliance with the requirements, the remedies provided by law to assist in the enforcement of the rights and obligations arising out of the contract will not be available to the contracting parties. When the following requirements are not met, it is said that the contract is 'void', meaning that it has never come into existence.

2.4.1 Consensus

This refers to the meeting of the minds of the contracting parties, and requires that all parties to the contract must have the serious intention of creating legally binding rights and obligations, and that they make this intention known to each other.

2.4.2 Contractual ability

This refers to the ability of each party to the contract to be legally capable of performing the act that gives rise to the contract.

2.4.3 Legal possibility of performance

To form a valid contract, the agreement must be permitted by law. In other words, it must not be illegal.

2.4.4 Physical possibility of performance

In addition to being legally possible, the agreement must also be physically executable. This means that the parties must be able to exercise their rights and duties in terms of the contract in practice.

2.4.5 Compliance with formalities

In some instances, the law may prescribe certain formalities that must be complied with before a valid contract is formed. When such formalities are prescribed, they have to be adhered to and observed by the contracting parties before a valid contract comes into existence.

2.5 Consensus as a requirement for the formation of a contract

Consensus as a legal concept can be defined as 'the meeting of the minds' of the contracting parties. It forms the basis for every contract. In South Africa, it is the most important requirement for the conclusion of a valid contract. Contractual commitment requires that the contracting parties achieve consensus on the rights and duties of their agreement. If the parties do not have coinciding intentions, then there is no consensus and therefore no contract.

2.5.1 Elements of consensus

Consensus comprises three elements, and each of these elements has to be present before consensus can said to have been reached:

2.5.1.1 The intention to be contractually bound

This element means that every contracting party must have the serious intention to be contractually bound. This serious intention entails a willingness to create specific rights and duties in law. Each contracting party's intention must extend to a willingness to be legally bound to perform his or her duties, as well as hold the other party or parties bound to perform their duties in turn.

2.5.1.2 Common intention

In addition to having a serious intention to be contractually bound, the contracting parties must share or agree on that intention. This sharing of an intention must extend to the rights and duties to which the parties will be bound.

Figure 2-1: Elements of contract

1. Consensus		**Elements:** Intention to be contractually bound Common intention Making the intention known
	Offer and acceptance	**Requirements:** ♦ complete offer and unconditional acceptance ♦ Clarity and certainty ♦ Intention to be legally bound ♦ Manner of offer and acceptance ♦ Identity of offeree ♦ Communication of declaration of intention **Termination/expiry:** ♦ Time ♦ Revocation ♦ Rejection ♦ Counter offer ♦ Death
	Moment and place of contract	Physical presence No physical presence: ♦ Telephone ♦ Post or telegraph ♦ Email ♦ Internet
	Consensus and defects in will	**Void:** ♦ Mistake: fact or law, rules or principles, reasonable **Voidable:** ♦ Misrepresentation: intentional, negligent, innocent ♦ Duress – 3 requirements ♦ Undue influence
2. Contractual capacity	Age	♦ Majority ♦ Minority
	Marriage	♦ In community of property ♦ Out of community of property
	Mental deficiency	
	Influence of alcohol and drugs	
	Prodigals	
	Insolvency	
3. Legal possibility	Contrary to common law	Legal execution is possible
	Contrary to good morals	
	Contrary to public policy	♦ Involving administration of justice ♦ Involving crimes and delicts ♦ Involving safety of the state ♦ Restraint of trade ♦ Wagering and betting
	Contrary to statutory law	

4. Physical possibility	Objective possibility to perform	Divisibility/indivisibility of performance
	Determined or ascertainable performance	
5. Compliance with formalities	Contracts where formalities required	◆ Alienation of land ◆ Suretyship ◆ Donation ◆ Ante-nuptial contracts
	Types of formalities	◆ Written ◆ Signatures
	Formalities required by contracting parties	

2.5.1.3 Making the intention known

This is the final element of consensus: until the contracting parties have declared the first two elements, namely the intention to be legally bound as well as the common intention to be so bound, consensus has not taken place. The law therefore requires a declaration of intent, and, as a result, consensus can only be said to exist once the parties are mutually aware of each other's intention. The mechanism by which the parties mutually declare their intention is by means of an offer and acceptance.

2.5.2 Offer and acceptance

Offer and acceptance are statements through which parties to a contract make their intentions known.

2.5.2.1 Meaning of offer and acceptance

2.5.2.1.1 Offer
An offer is a declaration made by a person, the offeror, in which the offeror indicates his or her intention to be contractually bound, and in which he or she stipulates the rights and duties to be created.

2.5.2.1.2 Acceptance
The acceptance is a declaration of a person, the offeree, receiving the offer, through which the offeree indicates that he or she agrees to the terms of the offer as stipulated by the offeror.

2.5.2.2 Requirements of offer and acceptance

The formation of a contract will only take place if the offer and acceptance fulfil certain requirements. The six requirements that have to be satisfied are the following:

2.5.2.2.1 Complete offer and unconditional acceptance
Completeness of the offer means that the offer must contain all the relevant terms by which the offeror is prepared to be bound, as well as the terms by which the offeror wants the offeree to be bound. The offer must be formulated in such a way that a mere agreement by the offeree will result in the formation of a

contract. In other words, on acceptance of the offer by the offeree, the parties must be committed to the same terms without reservation and condition. As a result, the acceptance of the offer by the offeree must be unconditional acceptance of all the terms of the offer.

2.5.2.2.2 Clarity and certainty

Both the offer and the acceptance must be clear and certain. The obligations intended to be created by the contract must be stated unambiguously and unequivocally so that the rights and duties arising from the obligations are easily determined. An offer that is vague and ambiguous cannot give rise to a contract as one of the requirements for the formation of a contract is that the performance required by the contract must be certain or ascertainable. In turn, the acceptance must also be clear so as not to create any doubt as to the offeree's intentions.

2.5.2.2.3 Intention to be legally bound

Every offer and the acceptance thereof must contain the undertaking to be legally bound by the terms of the offer.

Note: It is important to note that an advertisement is an invitation to do business, and not an offer to contract. Once a person responds to an advertisement, an offer is made to the advertiser to buy the advertised item. A contract thus only arises once the advertiser accepts the offer made by the person responding to the advertisement. For example, if a hotel advertises its facilities and services in a brochure, the brochure does not constitute an offer. Only once a potential guest contacts the hotel to enquire about a room, is an offer made. The potential guest is the offeror, and the hotel is the offeree. Consensus exists only once the hotel communicates its acceptance of the offer to the potential guest; that is, the hotel confirms its willingness to accommodate the guest.

2.5.2.2.4 Manner of offer and acceptance

The general rule regarding the form that the offer has to take is that there are no prescribed formalities. An offer can be made expressly in writing, or verbally, as well as tacitly (by means of conduct). For example, the owner of a guest house buys bread from the bakery. He takes a loaf of bread from the shelf and pays for it at the counter. There is no written contract and no words were spoken.

In some cases the law prescribes certain formalities with regard to the manner in which an offer must be made, and how it is to be accepted. An example of such an instance is the alienation (sale) of land where various legal require-ments must be met. When the law prescribes certain formalities with regard to the manner of the offer and the acceptance thereof, the parties are obliged to form a valid contract.

2.5.2.2.5 Identity of the offeree

An offer must be made to a particular person or persons or to a group of persons. Where an offer is addressed to a particular person or persons, only those persons can accept the offer. Even in cases where the offer is made to unidentified persons, the offer must be formulated in such a way that the group or class of offerees can be identified. In such cases, anyone falling into that group or class of person may accept the offer. For example, if Protea Hotels or Southern Sun Hotels make an offer to their 'frequent guests', only a person or persons falling into that category will qualify for acceptance of this offer.

2.5.2.2.6 Communication of the declaration of the intention

An offer is not complete until and unless the offeror has communicated his or her declaration of intent to be contractually bound to the offeree. Conversely, the acceptance of the offer is only complete once the offeree has communicated his or her acceptance of the offer to the offeror.

2.5.2.3 Termination or expiry of the offer

An offer on its own does not complete the formation of a contract. Acceptance of the offer is required to achieve consensus. This means that the offeror could change his mind about the offer in its entirety or about its individual terms before it is accepted by the offeree. An offer does not remain open indefinitely; in certain circumstances an offer will terminate:

2.5.2.3.1 Expiration of time limit

An offer that is subject to a time limit will fall away if it is not accepted by the offeree before the time limit expires. Examples may be special offers for accommodation at reduced rates during off-peak season. If the offeror did not attach a time limit to the offer, the offer will fall away if it is not accepted within a reasonable time period.

2.5.2.3.2 Revocation of the offer

If the offeror revokes or withdraws the offer before the offeree has accepted, the offer terminates.

2.5.2.3.3 Rejection by the offeree

An offer that has been rejected by the offeree is extinguished and cannot be revived.

2.5.2.3.4 Counter offer by the offeree

In some instances, an offeree will not reject the offer outright, but will indicate that he or she is prepared to accept the offer subject to certain changes in the terms or subject to certain conditions. This does not mean acceptance, it constitutes a counter-offer by the offeree. The result by implication is that the offeree has rejected the offer, and that the offer is now terminated. The counter-offer thus stands as a new offer in respect of which the original offeror is now the offeree and the original offeree becomes the offeror.

2.5.2.3.5 Death of the offeror or offeree

If one of the parties dies before the offer is accepted, the offer is extinguished, and no rights and duties in respect thereof can be transferred to the deceased's estate.

2.5.2.3.6 Insanity of the offeror or offeree

If one of the parties is declared insane before the offer is accepted, the offer is irrevocable, and no rights and duties in respect thereof can be upheld.

2.5.3 Moment and place of formation of a contract

Once it is established that consensus has been reached, it is important to establish where and when it was reached, and therefore where and when the contract was concluded.

Establishing the moment when consensus was reached is relevant to determine if the offer may still be revoked, whether the offer has expired and whether the contractual rights and duties have become enforceable. It is necessary to know where the contract was concluded as this determines the court jurisdiction for the hearing of claims and disputes that may arise from the contract. This means that if a contract was concluded in a particular magisterial district, such as Nelspruit, then any disputes to that contract would be dealt with in the Nelspruit magistrate's court. This has to be considered when signing contracts, as the logistical implications if this were not where the contract was executed, could be costly in terms of time and expense. An example would be where two friends sign a partnership agreement while on a weekend away in Dullstroom to negotiate and conclude their partnership. However, they both live and work in Johannesburg. Should any dispute arise from their partnership agreement, the courts in the magisterial district into which Dullstroom falls, would have to deal with the issue. This means that any party to a contract must understand the practical implications of where they sign the contract. Where the contract is signed is where it may be contested, and this may entail costly travel expenses and legal consultation in a place that is far away from either party's place of residence or business.

The place and date are provided for at the end of the contract, just above the signatories: 'Thus done and signed at (place), on (date).'

2.5.3.1 Formation of a contract with the parties being in each other's physical presence

When the parties are within each other's physical presence, it is usually easy to determine the time and the place of formation of the contract because *the contract arises at the place and time when the offeror learns of the acceptance of the offer by the offeree*. This is called the *ascertainment theory*.

2.5.3.2 Formation of the contract with the parties not being in each other's physical presence

In this instance the acceptance of the offer is not directly communicated to the offeror:

2.5.3.2.1 Conclusion of contracts over the telephone

In this instance, the parties are regarded as being in each other's presence, and it follows that the ascertainment theory applies, which means that the contract is concluded when and where the offeror learns of the acceptance of the offer.

2.5.3.2.2 Conclusion of contracts by post or telegraph

The rules that are applicable here are a deviation from the general rule of ascertainment theory. In this instance, the dispatch theory applies, and the contract is formed at the place where, and at the time when, the letter of acceptance is posted or dispatched. The question arises whether the offeree can undo the acceptance by means of a faster method of communication, for example fax or telephone, and instruct the offeror to ignore the letter of acceptance. In terms of the dispatch theory, the answer to this is negative, but since the dispatch theory aims primarily at protecting the offeree, the ascertainment theory will be applied in such an instance, and the offeree is entitled to undo his acceptance by means of a faster means of communication.

2.5.3.2.3 Conclusions of contracts by email

Contracts cannot be concluded by email as signatures are needed for contracts to be valid. Unsigned contracts may be sent by email, then must be printed and officially signed by the parties. Contracts may be faxed, but the original should be sent to the receiver as well.

2.5.3.2.4 Conclusions of contracts on the internet

Purchases and reservations made over the internet are binding because of the terms and conditions of sale that have to be checked by the party completing the reservation. There is usually a box that must be ticked that states that the person making the purchase or reservation agrees to abide by the terms and conditions of the sale. These terms and conditions are available on the internet site. The sale or reservations usually cannot proceed without this box being ticked – which protects both parties. Contracts of this nature made over the internet are therefore valid and binding.

2.5.4 Consensus and defects in will

If consensus is the basis for every contract, then it follows that any circumstance that affects the existence of consensus must also affect the formation of the contract. In other words, if for any reason consensus is absent, no valid contract arises and as a result, the contract is **void**. In instances where consensus exists, but has been obtained in an improper manner (for example, coercion), there is a valid contract, but it is **voidable** at the insistence of the innocent or prejudiced party. Voidable means that the aggrieved party has a choice to have the contract set aside (declared void). Void and voidable contracts are thus distinguished by the absence and presence of consensus between the contract-ing parties.

2.5.4.1 Void contracts: absence of consensus by virtue of a mistake

A mistake in contract occurs when one or more of the parties are mistaken about the identity of the other contracting party or about the content of the contract. As a result of this, the mistaken party does not direct his or her will at the facts or obligations of the contract, and consensus cannot arise at the time of concluding the contract. If only one of the parties is mistaken about an aspect of the offer, a unilateral mistake has occurred, which will nevertheless negate consensus. For example, Mr Guest reserves a room and pays a deposit to the

Ocean View Hotel assuming, by its name, that it has ocean views. When he gets to the hotel, however, he finds that it is in the middle of the city. Mr Guest is upset as he wanted to spend some time with his wife on holiday at a seaside hotel. As a result of his misconception he wants to declare the contract of reservation as void. Mr Guest may rely on lack of consensus due to material mistake.

A two-sided mistake occurs when both parties are mistaken about different aspects of the offer. A two-sided mistake may occur if, coupled with the fact that Mr Guest is unhappy about the location of the hotel, the Ocean View Hotel has made a reservation for a single room instead of a double room for Mr Guest and his wife.

2.5.4.1.1 Effect of mistake

If either one or both of the parties are under a mistaken impression that is material, a so-called material mistake, there is no consensus, and therefore no contract arises. The contract is therefore rendered void by the mistake. The parties are allowed to use/rely on the mistake that destroyed the consensus to avoid the consequences of the contract. Mr Guest and the Ocean View Hotel may render their contract void due to both parties having made a mistake in terms of consensus.

2.5.4.1.2 Conditions under which a mistake will render a contract void

In order to avoid parties using the mistake as a reason to escape contractual obligations, a mistake will only render a contract void under three particular instances:

The mistake must be one of fact or law. Before a mistake can render a contract void, one or both of the parties must be mistaken about a fact, or a legal principle or rule. A mistake in law or fact will only invalidate the contract if it is considered to be excusable in the circumstances.

The mistake must relate to a material fact or legal principle or rule. A material mistake can be any of the following:
* a mistake in respect of the identity of the person with whom the agreement is reached
* a mistake in the content of the intended contract – one or both parties must be mistaken about the time of performance, or the place and method of delivery, or the performance itself that is due
* a mistake in respect of the interpretation of the law attaching to offer and acceptance – this relates to the perception of one or both parties of the rights and duties created by the agreement, where the law attaches a different meaning to it

The mistake in fact or law must be reasonable. If the mistake is not a justifiable error, the contract will be enforced as it appears from the parties' declaration of intention, despite the fact that no consensus was reached due to mistake. A reasonable mistake is one where a reasonable person in the same circumstances would have been mistaken. The party relying on the mistake to deny the contract should have no fault in respect of the mistake. This means that the party trying to escape the contract on the basis of a mistake cannot rely on a mistake if he/she was negligent or careless and did not pay sufficient attention to the matter (a common example being not reading the fine-print and then wishing to escape from the contract). However, a person can rely on a mistake to escape the contract if the other party was to blame for his or her unreasonable mistake.

2.5.4.2 Voidable contracts: improper obtaining of consensus

In some instances the agreement of one of the parties to the contract is obtained in an improper way. The following ways qualify as improper means of obtaining the other party's consensus to contract:

2.5.4.2.1 Misrepresentation

This is a false representation made by one party to another, either in the form of a statement, by conduct or by keeping silent and not telling the other the true state of affairs. Such a false statement or representation is made with the aim of creating a contract and misleading the other party into concluding a contract.

The misrepresentation may relate to the characteristics or qualities of the subject matter of the contract. Misrepresentations can be made by an express statement or by conduct. Concealing the facts also constitutes misrepresentation, but only if the person misrepresenting has a duty to disclose the concealed facts. Offering an honest opinion or an estimate is not considered a misrepresentation of facts.

A contract would be voidable at the instance of the innocent or prejudiced party as a result of misrepresentation in the following circumstances:

- The misrepresentation must have been made by one party (or by his or her duly authorised representative) to the contract to the contracting party. A false representation made by an outsider is not a misrepresentation, but a misstatement, which is irrelevant to the parties' consensus.
- The misrepresentation must have been made during the negotiation preceding the formation of the contract.
- The misrepresentation must be unlawful. It is unlawful to mislead someone, even if it is done innocently.
- The misrepresentation must have induced the contract as it was concluded. This means that the contract would not have been concluded at all or on the same terms, but for the misrepresentation.

When Mr Hotelier advertises his hotel as a luxury bush lodge, and thereby gets reservations from tourists, when his 'luxury lodge' is in fact a number of rondavels in a bad state of repair, he is intentionally misleading the tourists, who could then insist that their contract for accommodation is declared void.

There are certain legal circumstances from which a contract will be voidable at the insistence of the innocent party. The instances in which a party may claim damages are those where misrepresentation is made intentionally (for example, fraudulent misrepresentation) or negligently. Where the misrepresentation is innocent, the aggrieved party is not entitled to claim damages. This is because fault is a requirement for delictual liability, and in the case of innocent representation there is no fault.

2.5.4.2.2 Duress

Duress can be defined as an unlawful threat of injury or harm made by one party to the contract that leads to the other party to enter the contract. In the case of duress, a person is forced to conclude a contract that they would not otherwise have concluded. For example, Mr Groom can tell Mr Hotelier to give him a 50% discount off his wedding reception, failing which Mr Groom will break Mrs Hotelier's legs.

Even though consensus is essentially reached, it is not done so willingly on the part of one of the parties. The contract is voidable on the instance of the innocent or threatened party as consensus was improperly obtained. The innocent party may also claim damages in delict from the other party who exerted the pressure or force.

A contract is voidable on grounds of duress when the following requirements have been fulfilled:

* duress must be exerted by one contracting party on the other party;
* there has to be actual violence or a reasonable fear of such violence;
* the fear has to be caused by a threat of considerable evil to the aggrieved party or a member of his or her family;
* the threat must be immediate or inevitable;
* the threat has to be unlawful;
* the threat has to cause damage;
* the threat must lead to the threatened party entering into the contract

2.5.4.2.3 Undue influence

In the case of undue influence the aggrieved party is influenced to conclude a contract by someone who has power over them. This is any improper or unfair conduct by one of the parties to the contract by means of which he or she convinces the other party to enter into the contract against the other party's will. Undue influence is not easily distinguishable from intentional misrepresentation or duress. Undue influence is often found where there is a special relationship between the contracting parties, for example between a doctor and patient, attorney and client, or a guardian and minor.

Elements of undue influence need to be proved before a contract is voidable on grounds of undue influence. The aggrieved party has to prove the following:

* The party allegedly exerting influence must have acquired an influence over the other party.
* This influence weakened the other party's resolve to exercise their own free will.
* The influence must have been used unscrupulously to convince the other party to enter into the contract.
* The contract was concluded to the detriment of the other party.

2.6 Capacity to act as a requirement for the formation of a contract

Not all persons have the capacity to conclude binding contracts. Certain persons have no contractual capacity at all. Others have limited contractual capacity.

Capacity to act is the capacity to perform juristic or legal acts and to conclude valid contracts. Juristic or legal persons such as companies and close corporations can never have the capacity to act, that is, to perform legal acts. Natural persons, namely human beings, have to act on behalf of a juristic person to conclude the contract on behalf of the juristic person. In other words, a company cannot physically sign a contract as it has no physical form or body. Therefore, a human being, a natural person with a physical body, must sign on behalf of company as humans *can* perform this physical act.

Although all natural persons have the potential capacity to act, they may not have actual capacity to act. This lack of capacity to act or diminished capacity to act is determined by the law's perception of that person's ability to form and declare his or her will and also of his or her ability to evaluate the rights and duties flowing from his or her acts. The general rule is that an unmarried person who has reached the age of majority has full capacity to act and may perform all juristic acts independently.

It is presumed that all people who fall into this category are capable of performing juristic acts. However, such a person may lose that capacity completely or partially, based on the following factors:

2.6.1 Age

2.6.1.1 Majority
Majority is reached at the age of 18. However, a minor can obtain majority through marriage.

2.6.1.2 Minority
A minor is a person who has not yet reached the age of majority. A distinction is drawn between minors under the age of seven years and minors between the age of seven and 18.

Minors under the age of seven years cannot enter into a contract at all, and a guardian is appointed (usually one or both parents) to conclude any contracts on their behalf.

Minors between the age of seven and 18 have limited contractual capacity as their ability to act is limited because the law accepts the assumption that minors do not possess the maturity to make sound judgements. They, therefore, need the assistance of their parents or guardian to complete valid contracts. A minor of this type may conclude contracts to their own benefit, such as making deposits and withdrawals from a building society or bank without assistance.

When a minor concludes a contract without the consent of his or her parent or legal guardian, this contract is known as a 'limping' agreement, which means that it is not enforceable against the minor. If the other contract to the party is a major, the contract is still enforceable against the major. The minor can repudiate or enforce the contract at his or her option.

The implications of this is that any major who enters into an agreement with a minor must be aware that the contract will be enforceable against them in the event of a breach, but that the contract may not be enforceable against the minor due to their limited contractual capacity.

2.6.2 Marriage

Where persons are married in community of property, their separate estates become one joint estate. The spouses have equal powers regarding the administration of the joint estate. In certain circumstances a spouse requires the consent of the other spouse for the conclusion of contracts pertaining to the joint estate.

There are two types of marriage property regimes in South Africa (regulated by the Matrimonial Property Act 88 of 1984). They are the following:

2.6.2.1 Marriage in community of property

All marriages in South Africa are in community of property unless agreed otherwise. The estates of the spouses are joined and one joint estate is formed. Each spouse owns half of the estate, which, however, would only be divided if the estate were dissolved through death or divorce.

2.6.2.1.1 Spouses' capacity to act

The general rule is that each spouse has full capacity to act with regard to the joint estate. They may, therefore, enter into a contract without the other spouse's consent. However, in marriage contracts concluded prior to 1 December 1993 the husband had the marital power to conclude contracts on behalf of the joint estate. Any contract concluded prior to that date by a wife subject to marital power without her husband's assistance would still be voidable at the instance of the husband.

2.6.2.2 Marriage out of community of property

To avoid being married in community of property, parties may agree by means of an ante-nuptual contract (to be concluded prior to the marriage) to be married out of community of property. An antenuptial contract is signed before a notary and registered with the Deeds Office. The contract usually stipulates that the marriage is out of community of property, and that each spouse therefore, retains his or her own separate estate, and the capacity to act in respect only of his or her own estate. The spouses will also be liable for their own debts, and not jointly with the other spouse, except in the case of household necessities. Spouses are required by the Matrimonial Property Act 88 of 1984 to make pro rata contributions according to their financial means to pay for the necessities of the common household.

Such marriages entered into after 1 November 1984 are subject to **accrual** (unless expressly excluded by the antenuptial contract), whereby the net value of each spouse's estate is declared before the marriage. The effect of the accrual system is that, at dissolution of the marriage by death or divorce, the spouse whose estate shows no accrual or a smaller accrual than the estate of the other spouse, acquires a claim against the other spouse or his or her estate equal to half the difference between the accrual of the respective estates. Therefore, each spouse retains what they brought into the marriage, and is entitled to half the value of the estate as accrued during the marriage.

2.6.2.2.1 Spouses' capacity to act:

Each spouse has full capacity to act.

2.6.3 Mental deficiency

A person who is mentally ill has no contractual capacity, unless that person concludes a contract in a lucid moment.

If a person's mental ability is such that he or she is not able to understand the consequences of his or her actions sufficiently to enable him or her to make rational decisions, that person does not form the required will to conclude a contract. Such a person is completely incapable of acting legally. Any contract concluded with such a person is void and without consequences. This means that no rights and duties are created by a contract concluded with a mentally deficient person. The burden of proof regarding mental deficiency lies with the party who wants to declare the contract void.

If a mentally deficient person concludes a contract after having being certified by the High Court as mentally deficient, he or she can still be held liable if he or she was of sound and lucid mind at the time of concluding the contract. However, the certification of mental deficiency creates a presumption that the person no longer has the capacity to act, and thus their full capacity at the time of contract has to be proved should the contract be contested.

2.6.4 Influence of alcohol and drugs

When a person is under the influence of alcohol or drugs to such an extent that he or she does not appreciate the nature and consequences of his or her actions, he or she is incapable of forming a will. Legally, he or she cannot perform juristic acts, and a contract concluded in such a state is void and unenforceable. If the person can still act despite being under the influence, he or she has capacity to act despite the fact that his or her judgement may be affected.

2.6.5 Prodigals

Prodigals are persons who have the propensity to squander money in an irresponsible manner. If this results in the person not being able to manage his or her affairs competently, the High Court, may, on application by an interested party, declare him or her a prodigal, and appoint a curator. Prodigal tendencies do not affect a person's capacity to act, but once a person is declared a prodigal, he or she has limited capacity to act, and requires the consent of his or her curator. Only a contract solely to the advantage of the prodigal may be entered into without the curator's assistance. A prodigal's position is thus similar to that of a minor with limited capacity to act.

2.6.6 Insolvency

The insolvent person loses his or her capacity to act in respect of the assets of the insolvent estate. Any attempt by the insolvent person to dispose of assets is futile and invalid.

An insolvent may not enter into agreements that have a detrimental effect on the insolvent estate without the trustee's consent, and in this regard, his or her capacity is limited. In such an instance the contract is voidable at the instance of the trustee. An insolvent has capacity to act with regard to other aspects. This means that the insolvent person's capacity to act is limited only as far as the Insolvency Act provides.

2.7 Legal possibility as a requirement for the formation of a contract

A requirement for possibility is that a contract must be permitted by law. This means that the contract must not be unlawful. A contract will be unlawful when

- its conclusion; or
- the performance to be rendered in terms thereof; or
- the reason for it or the object thereof,

is not permitted by common law or statute, or it is contrary to public policy or good morals.

2.7.1. Restraint of trade agreements

Agreements that are aimed at restraining a person's freedom to engage in commercial arrangements are called restraint of trade agreements. One can distinguish between two restraint of trade agreements:

2.7.1.1 Agreement prohibiting competition

This type of agreement entails the purchaser of a business enterprise or a professional practice insisting on concluding an undertaking with the seller that the seller will not, for a specified period of time, and in respect of a particular geographical area, practice his or her profession or carry on a business in competition with the purchaser. For example, an agreement of sale regarding the sale of a restaurant situated in Rivonia in Johannesburg, may contain a clause in terms of which the seller undertakes not to open another restaurant in competition with the purchaser in the Sandton area of Johannes-burg for a specified period of time after the transfer of ownership of the restaurant from the seller to the purchaser.

2.7.1.2 Agreements protecting trade secrets and commercial contracts

An example of this type of agreement is where an employer requires an employee to undertake not to render a similar service or provide trade secrets within a specified time period or area subsequent to leaving the employer's service. The employee's freedom to compete in the employment market is restricted by such an agreement.

These restraint of trade contracts bring two principles of public policy into conflict: namely, the right for everyone to participate freely in the market place on the one hand, and the public interest in executing contracts on the other. Both the principle of freedom of trade, as well as the principle of contractual commitment are in the public interest. So when these interests conflict, they have to be set off against each other. The law will grant precedence to the principle of contractual commitment, as it is regarded as the stronger of the two interests.

A person who maintains that he or she should not be bound by a restraint of trade agreement must prove that the clause is contrary to public policy. One of the factors the court will consider is whether the restraint is *reasonable* on both parties. Thus in principle, contracts in restraint of trade are valid and enforceable and the law permits the restraint of a person's freedom of trade if the parties freely enter into such agreements. The contract is therefore valid on the face of it but the court will refuse to enforce it, if it has been proven that the enforcement will be contrary to public policy.

The reasonableness of such a restraint may hinge on the nature of the restraint (what activity it prevents), the geographical size of the area that is covered by the restraint and the length of time of operation. For example, a restraint that a restaurateur may not open another restaurant in South Africa within 10 years will probably be regarded as unreasonable, as it unnaturally limits the person's ability to take part in the restaurant industry.

2.7.2 Wagering/betting contracts

In a wagering contract, one party undertakes to render a performance to another if some uncertain future event, the occurrence of which is dependent on chance or luck, occurs. At common law, a wagering contract is invalid. A contracting party may indeed render performance in terms of the contract, but the law will not assist in the enforcement of such a contract. This means that a wagering contract is not enforceable in a court of law.

However, section 18 of the Gambling Act, 33 of 1996 provides that any gambling debt lawfully incurred by a person in the course and scope of any gambling activity regulated by law, be enforceable by law. This means that gambling debts incurred at a licensed casino, for example, are within scope of the law, and the casino owner has the right to collect the debt through legal channels.

2.7.3 Contracts that are contrary to statutory law

A contract is regarded as illegal where either the conclusion of the contract, the performance in terms of the contract, or the purpose for which the contract is concluded violates a statute or common law. The effect of illegality is that a contract does not come into existence, and no claim can therefore be brought in terms of such a 'contract'.

For example, Mr Thug contracts Mr Hitman to kill Mr Victim. The terms of the contract are 50% of payment up front, and 50% on conclusion of the deed. If Mr Hitman does not kill Mr Victim and retains the deposit, then Mr Thug cannot enforce this illegal contract in a court of law.

2.7.4 Consequence of unlawful contracts

The general rule is that an unlawful contract is void, and none of the parties acquires any forceable rights and duties from that contract. Wagering contracts are the exception to this rule as they are valid, but not enforceable.

The maxim *ex turpi causa non oritur action* (no action arises from a shameful cause) applies here and results in no party being able to institute action to claim performance on such an unlawful contract. This rule is never relaxed. Even if one party has performed his or her part of the contract, the court will not consider a claim for reciprocal performance from the other party. Also, if one party suffers a loss or damage as a result of such a contract, he or she cannot claim damages from the other party, as the court does not recognise the contract.

Usually a party who has performed, but has not received performance from the other party, can also not claim on the basis of unjustified enrichment because of the *par delictum* rule: this means that when there is guilt, the possessor is in the stronger position (*in pari delicto potior est condition possidentis*). This rule is applicable only in actions that are based on unjustified enrichment. Courts have indicated that they may relax this rule where particular circumstances indicate that the public interest requires relaxation. In contrast, the *ex turpi causa* rule is never relaxed.

2.8 Physical possibility of performance as a requirement for the formation of a contract

Physical possibility means that the performance in terms of the contract must not only be possible, but that the performance must be certain or ascertainable at the time when the contract is concluded. This means that both parties must physically be able to perform the duties that they have committed themselves to in the contract.

There are two elements to physical possibility of performance:

2.8.1 Objective/absolute possibility to perform

Performance will be physically impossible if, at the moment of concluding a contract, it is objectively and absolutely impossible to render the performance. Only objective impossibility of performance causes a contract to void – this implies that it must be totally impossible for anyone to perform that function.

If performance by one of the parties to the contract becomes impossible before all the obligations of the contract can be met, then this is known as initial impossibility of performance. For example, Mr Hotelier enters into a contract with Mr Groom to provide a wedding reception for Mr Groom. However, when they enter into the contract, they cannot possibly know that the hotel will be destroyed by fire in the week before the reception is due to take place. Therefore, Mr Hotelier is unable to conclude his side of the contract – which is an impossibility of performance.

When the performance becomes impossible after the conclusion of the contract, the impossibility results in the obligation in terms of the contract becoming extinct. In other words, the legal relationship that was created in terms of the contract comes to an end. In the case of a contract of sale, the application of the risk rule determines who bears the risk of the impossibility. When Mr Groom concludes a contract as above, but the hotel burns down after the conclusion of the contract, the contract comes to an end. The hotel is no longer contractually bound to provide Mr Groom with a wedding reception, and Mr Groom is no longer responsible to pay for the reception.

An impossibility to perform only from the action of one particular person is subjective, and not objective. Inconvenience or difficulty in performing the required action does not qualify as objective impossibility to perform. Where performance is difficult or inconvenient, the validity of the contract will not be affected unless the parties agree otherwise. If one or both parties does not perform because it is too difficult or inconvenient to do so, this amounts to a breach of contract.

2.8.1.1 Divisibility of performance

Divisibility is a legal concept. Where performance is indivisible (that means it cannot be done in parts) no valid contract arises if the performance is objectively impossible. If however, the performance is divisible into separate parts, and only a part cannot be delivered, then a valid contract will arise in respect of the part that has been performed.

Whether a performance is divisible or not depends on the type of performance and the intention of the parties. An indivisible performance is a performance that can only be rendered in one way – completely. An example of this would be the delivery of a car. A divisible performance can be broken into separate parts, such as a 1 000 kg load of coal being delivered in parts. In addition, the contracting parties should intend to regard this performance as divisible, and therefore expect it to be delivered in parts.

As divisibility is a legal concept, the law cannot convert a physically indivisible performance into a divisible one. However, the opposite is possible in law; something that is physically divisible can be regarded as indivisible. For example, items packaged and sold in quantities such as dozens or sets are usually regarded as indivisible by the law, and not as individual items. For example, a set of wine glasses would be treated by the law as an indivisible item, and not as individual glasses. Whether a performance is seen as divisible or indivisible will always depend on the subject matter and on the intention of the parties. A purchase price on the global amount is usually an indicator that the performance is meant to be indivisible.

Conversely, where the purchase price is stipulated as a price per unit, the law will usually regard this as an indication of divisibility of performance. For example, if one party agrees to sell two vehicles, one for R50 000 and one for R70 000 to another party, this is regarded as divisible unless the parties agree that the delivery and payment of the vehicles must be made in one act. This means that two vehicles are delivered and R120 000 is paid for them, irrespective of the individual value of each. In determining the intention of the contracting parties, the courts will ask whether the contracting parties would have entered into separate contracts in respect of each distinct part of the performance.

2.8.2 Determined or ascertained performance

The terms of the contract must appear clearly and unambiguously for their performance to be physically possible. This means that the performance must either be determined or ascertainable.

2.8.2.1 Determined performance

Determined performance refers to a situation where the parties have clearly stated their respective performance in the contract. For example, a contract of sale on a house or vehicle will clearly stipulate the selling price, and the item to be purchased. In this case, both the subject matter and the price have been specified and the required performance is clearly identified. As a result, the performance is determined from the beginning and neither party can claim or deliver a different performance than that stipulated in the contract.

2.8.2.2 Ascertainable performance

A performance is ascertainable when, at the time of concluding the contract, the parties agree on criteria to identify when performance has taken place. For example, Simba chips may enter into a contract to buy a potato crop from a farmer, but the market price of the potatoes, and the size of the crop cannot be determined at the time the contract is concluded. These will be determined at the time the performance is required. A condition may be that the price is in line with current market prices at the time of delivery.

2.9 Compliance with formalities as a requirement for the formation of a contract

The final requirement for the conclusion of a valid contract is compliance with any prescribed formalities. Formalities are those requirements relating to the outward, visible form in which the agreement must be cast in order to result in a valid contract. As a general rule, there are no formal requirements for contracts. A verbal contract is therefore, in most instances, perfectly valid. A written contract is, however, preferred as it creates proof of the terms and conditions of the agreement, and contains the signatories of both parties as further proof of their consensus.

However, formalities can be prescribed by law (statutory formalities) or can be agreed by the contracting parties themselves. The most common formality is that the contract is reduced to writing and/or signed by both parties.

Whether the formalities are statutory or agreed between the parties, the contract is not valid unless these formalities are complied with.

In most cases, a contract is valid and binding without any formalities having to be complied with. For example, many contracts of sale occur verbally or through conduct, such as a normal purchase of meals from a restaurant. As a general rule, the parties are free to choose the way in which they create the contract, that is either tacitly (by their actions) or verbally or in writing.

2.9.1 Contracts where formalities are required

2.9.1.1 Formalities required by law

The prescription of formalities is the exception to the rule. No formalities are required by common law for the formation of a valid contract. The law has laid down certain requirements that must be complied with in a number of cases in order to create a valid and binding contract. The main aims for such requirements are the prevention of fraud, the reduction of uncertainty, and the prevention of evidentiary problems. Examples of contracts that must be put in writing and signed by both parties are the following:

2.9.1.1.1 Contracts for the alienation of land

Contracts regarding the alienation of land include contracts for the sale, donation and exchange of land, and also include the option to buy land and the conferring of the right of first refusal on land.

2.9.1.1.2 Contract of suretyship

A contract of suretyship is an agreement by which one party (the surety) agrees to be liable for a debt owed to a party (the creditor) by a third person (the debtor) in the event of the debtor defaulting in his or her obligations to the creditor. Such a contract is valid only if it is in writing and signed by, or on behalf, of the surety.

2.9.1.1.3 Contracts of donation in terms of which performance is due in the future

The contract under which performance is due in future is valid only if the terms are in writing and signed by the donor and by someone acting on his written authority.

2.9.1.1.4 Antenuptial contracts

An antenuptial contract must be registered in the Deeds Office in order for it to be valid and binding. It must therefore be in writing.

2.9.2 Types of formalities imposed

2.9.2.1 A written record

If an agreement is written, then two rules have to be applied:
- The writing must contain the essential terms of the type of contract in question.
- The wording must indicate the identity of the parties and the force and effect of the basic terms of the agreement.

2.9.2.2 Signature by one or both parties

A signature must appear to have been intended to cover the whole document. The basic rule is to place the signature at the end of the agreement, but to reinforce the signature with the initials of the signatories on every page of the document.

2.9.2.3 Formalities required by the contracting parties

Sometimes the contracting parties stipulate their own formalities. Examples of formalities agreed on between the parties are:
- If the acceptance of the offer must be in writing – as determined by the offeror.
- If the parties agree that their agreement is valid only if it is recorded in writing, the contract comes into effect only once it is put in writing. But, if the written version is intended as proof of a verbal contract, then the contract comes into being the moment that consensus is reached verbally.

2.10 Terms and conditions of contracts

2.10.1 Essential, residual and incidental terms

Terms of contracts may be divided into essential terms, residual terms and incidental terms.

The essential terms or *essentialia* characterise a contract as a particular type of contract, for example a contract of lease or sale. The essential terms of the contract of lease refer to the thing to be leased, the rental, and an undertaking that the lessee is to have temporary usage and enjoyment of that thing. The essential terms of a contract of sale refer to the thing to be sold, the price and an undertaking to transfer ownership of the thing. If any of these essential terms are missing, the contract is not necessarily invalid, but it is not a contract of sale or lease. The significance of whether a contract is one of sale or not lies in the so-called residual terms or *naturalia*.

The residual terms apply by operation of law or, in other words, automatically. In the case of the contract of sale, the warranty against latent defects is a residual term. This means that it does not have to be included in the contract, it applies automatically. The residual terms may be excluded by the parties. Those terms are also referred to by some writers as implied terms in that they are implied by law.

The incidental terms or *incidentalia* are those added by the parties. Parties may use those incidental terms to add further provisions or to exclude residual terms.

2.10.2 Express and tacit terms

Express terms are terms that the parties have agreed to – either verbally, in writing, or by some other means of conduct such as nodding the head. It is advisable to commit agreements to writing to ensure that consensus is reached, and that both parties are clear about the content of the contract. For example, the express terms to be found in a commercial contract for the supply of goods will normally include the following:

◆ date of delivery
◆ cost of delivery
◆ terms of payment
◆ lost or damaged goods
◆ limitation or exclusion of liability
◆ price
◆ cancellation and variation of contract

Tacit terms, on the other hand, derive from the common intention of the parties but are not expressed by them. Those terms are inferred from the surrounding circumstances. The phrase 'implied terms' is sometimes used to refer to tacit terms. An example of implied terms in a supply contract with a greengrocer is that the fruit and vegetables to be supplied, are fresh.

2.10.3 Conditions and time clauses

The words 'condition' and 'term' are often used synonymously. In the legal sense of the word, a condition is a specific type of term, namely one that qualifies the operation of a contractual obligation in such a way that it is dependent on whether an uncertain future event takes place or not. In other words, not only is it not certain *when* the event will take place, but it is also not certain *whether* the event will take place. There are two types of condition.

2.10.3.1 The suspensive condition

The operation of the obligation is suspended until an uncertain future event actually takes place. For example Mr Hotelier undertakes to cater for the wedding reception of Mr Groom if Ms Bride accepts Mr Groom's proposal of marriage.

2.10.3.2 The resolutive condition

The obligation comes into operation immediately, but the obligation is terminated once the condition is fulfilled. For example, the contract of accommodation is terminated once the guest has been accommodated and has paid for the accommodation.

A time clause is a contractual term that qualifies a contractual obligation by making it subject to a certain future event taking place. In this instance, it is certain that the event *will* take place; it is just not certain *when* it will take place.

A distinction is drawn between suspensive and resolutive time clauses. In the case of a suspensive time clause, the operation of the obligation is suspended until the event takes place (Mr Hotelier will cater for Mr Groom's wedding when it takes place). In the case of a resolutive time clause, the operation of the conclusion commences immediately, but lapses upon the taking place of the event in question (Mr Guest stays in the hotel until his reservation of the room expires).

2.11 Breach of contract

When a party does not do what he or she is expected to do in terms of a contract, that party is in breach of contract. Where somebody suffers loss as a result of another party's breach of contract, that party has certain remedies at his or her disposal.

There are five different forms of breach of contract:
- breach by the debtor
- breach by the creditor
- positive malperformance
- repudiation
- prevention of performance

Some forms of breach can be committed by both the debtor and the creditor, while others are unique to the obligations of either the debtor or the creditor. The terms 'debtor' and 'creditor' are used in relation to a specific obligation of the contract, and not the contract as a whole.

The debtor is the party who has to perform a specific obligation. The creditor is the party who is entitled to performance of the obligation in question. Therefore, where a contract creates obligations for both parties, each will in turn be the debtor or creditor, depending on the obligations involved. For example, in a contract of sale, the seller is the debtor in respect of the delivery of the sold item, and the purchaser is the debtor in respect of the obligation to pay the purchase price for the item.

2.11.1 Default by the debtor

A debtor commits a breach of contract if he or she fails to render a performance on time and the delay is due to his or her fault.

Two requirements have to be met before a breach of contract by the debtor can be proved:

2.11.1.1 Performance must be delayed:

In the case of default on the part of the debtor, he or she is late only with his or her performance. The performance must already be claimable or due, otherwise there can be no question of late performance. Where a specific date or time of performance has been stipulated in the contract, the debtor is automatically in *mora* if he or she fails to perform. The debtor is then in *mora ex re*. Where no date for the performance is specified, the creditor can determine the date by demanding that the debtor perform before or on a certain date. Such a demand may be verbal, but it is advisable to put it in writing. The creditor must allow a reasonable time for the debtor to perform. This depends on the circumstances in each case. For example, if Mr Hotelier calls Mr Plumber in an emergency plumbing call, then the reasonable time is a very short time, whereas in a less urgent situation, a longer period would be considered reasonable performance. If the debtor fails to perform by the stipulated time, he or she will be in *mora ex persona*.

2.11.1.2 The delay must be due to the debtor's fault

The breach only exists if a party culpably does not honour his or her obligation. Where bad fortune or circumstances beyond the debtor's control prevent performance, the debtor is not in breach. For example: the resort that Mr Vacation wanted to stay in burns down; an incident of terrorism or outbreak of contagious illness prevents travel to the country specified by Mr Vacation; or Ms Travel Consultant is in an accident and cannot perform. In all these cases non-performance is not the debtor's fault.

2.11.1.3 Consequences of debtor's default

The debtors default entitles the creditor to the remedies for breach of contract. As a general rule, if it is impossible for the debtor to perform the duty, then this releases the debtor from the performance because the obligation no longer exists. For example, late payment of money due for services rendered such as food or accommodation constitutes a debtors' breach of contract due to late payment. If Mr Guest does not pay Mr Hotelier for food and accommodation by the time required of the contract, then Mr Hotelier is entitled to the remedies of breach of contact against Mr Guest.

2.11.2 Default by the creditor

A default by the creditor occurs when the creditor causes the debtor's performance to be delayed. This means that a creditor's co-operation is required for the debtor's performance. For example, in a contract for service, the creditor (Mr Hotelier) would need to allow the debtor's (Mr Painter) workmen access to the premises. If the creditor fails to allow the workmen timeous access to the premises, and thereby delays the debtor's performance, the creditor is guilty of a breach of contract.

There are certain requirements to prove breach of contract by the creditor. A number of elements have to be present before a case of breach of contract by the creditor can be proved:

- The creditor must be late in accepting performance. Where a deadline is set for performance, the creditor is automatically in breach if he or she fails to co-operate by that deadline. Where there is no deadline for performance, and the creditor refuses to act on a letter of demand for co-operation from the debtor, then the creditor is in breach of contract.
- The debtor must tender performance and must call on the creditor for co-operation.
- The performance must still be possible.
- The creditor must fail to give his co-operation.
- The delay must be due to the fault of the creditor.

For example, a hotel purchases new beds for the hotel. The supplier wants to deliver, but the rooms' division manager refuses to accept delivery. In terms of the contract the supplier is entitled to payment within 30 days from delivery date. The supplier will then send a letter of demand to place the rooms' division manager in *mora*.

2.11.2.1 *Consequences of creditor's default*
In this instance the creditor is in breach of the contract in his or her capacity as creditor, and not as a debtor in terms of a reciprocal performance. A creditor has a duty in certain instances to co-operate with the debtor when the latter performs. In such cases, the creditor commits breach of contract in his or her capacity as creditor if, due to his or her failure to co-operate, the debtor cannot render performance on time. The creditor is then in *mora creditorus*.

The debtor's duty of care is diminished if the creditor is at fault. If the debtor's performance becomes impossible, then the debtor is released from the obligation, but the creditor remains liable for counter-performance. For example, in the case of the example above, if the bed factory burns down due to lightning, the hotel has to pay even though delivery has not taken place

2.11.3 Positive malperformance
This type of breach of contract is also known as incomplete or defective performance, and occurs where the debtor does perform, but the performance is either incomplete or defective, or the debtor commits an act that is contrary to the terms of the contract. Two situations can be distinguished in this type of breach:

2.11.3.1 *When the debtor renders defective or improper performance*
For example, if the wedding reception for Mr Groom does not meet the standards expected of a five-star hotel.

2.11.3.2 *The debtor does something that the terms of the contract prohibit*
For example, when an employee carries on a business in competition with the former employer in breach of a restraint of trade agreement, as discussed in paragraph 2.7.1.1.

2.11.4 Repudiation

Repudiation consists of any behaviour by a party to a contract that indicates that he or she does not intend to honour his or her part of the contract. For example, if the party denies the existence of the contract, refuses to perform, or tries without justification to withdraw from the contract, that party repudiates that contract. A contractant also commits repudiation where he or she cancels a contract under circumstances where he or she has no cancellation right.

Failure to perform does not constitute repudiation. Repudiation constitutes a breach, which entitles the innocent party to the usual remedies for breach of contract.

Repudiation is proved if the person alleged to have repudiated the obligation has behaved in such a way as to lead a reasonable person to believe that they do not intend to fulfil their part of the contract.

2.11.5 Prevention of performance

Prevention of performance entails that the performance is made impossible by either the debtor or the creditor. In the case of prevention of performance, the impossibility is therefore the fault of one of the parties.

2.11.5.1 Prevention of performance by the debtor

The debtor commits breach of contract by prevention of performance when he or she culpably renders his or her own performance impossible. The debtor is not then released from performance. For example, if a seller (debtor) in a contract crashes the vehicle he or she is supposed to deliver to the purchaser (creditor), and as a result can no longer deliver as per the contract, then he or she has prevented his or her own performance.

2.11.5.2 Prevention of performance by the creditor

The creditor commits breach of contract by prevention of performance if he or she culpably renders the debtor's performance impossible. This is different from the delay in performance discussed previously. Where the creditor makes performance by the debtor impossible, the debtor is released from his or her obligation. The debtor will still be entitled to the creditor's performance, but will have to calculate any expenses saved by not having to perform.

An example of this is when an airline passenger (who is the creditor to the performance by the airline) misses his or her flight, thus making it impossible for the airline (the debtor) to fulfil its obligation to transport the passenger in terms of the contract between the two parties.

2.12 Remedies for breach of contract

The law recognises three different remedies for breach of contract. Which remedy is available depends on the type of breach that was committed, the terms of the contract and how serious that breach was. When one party to the contract commits a breach of contract, the innocent party has three remedies at his or her disposal:

◆ execution of the contract (specific performance)

- cancellation of the contract
- a claim for damages

2.12.1 Execution of the contract
This remedy attempts to fulfil the contract with the same result as was intended originally by the parties, or achieve a result as close as possible to that. Execution, or specific performance can be applied in one of three orders:
- an order for specific performance
- an order for reduced performance
- a prohibitory interdict

2.12.1.1 An order for specific performance
A court order that requires the defaulting party to render the performance he or she is obligated to do in the contract – provided that the person is not in sequestration, and that the performance is still possible.

When a party to a contract (A) sues the other contractant (B) for specific performance, but he or she has not yet performed, contractant B has a right to withhold performance, until A has performed in full. This is known as the defence of *exceptio non adimpleti contractus.* This right to withhold is not absolute. In certain circumstances, the courts would relax the application of this defence and allow A to claim reduced performance (referred to as a reduced contract price). The discretion of the courts to relax this defence arises where B has received a partial performance and has used it.

2.12.1.2 An order for reduced performance
This is a court order to render partial or reduced performance – usually to match the amount of performance already tendered by the other party. Full performance is not required, but it is enough for the debtor and creditor to equal out the differences between their levels of performance in terms of the principle of reciprocity.

2.12.1.3 A prohibitory interdict
Where a party does something contrary to the terms of the contract, or threatens to, the innocent party may apply for an interdict to prevent this. For example, where an employee conducts business contrary to a restraint of trade agreement, the former employer can obtain an interdict preventing him or her from doing so.

2.12.2 Cancellation of contracts
This is an abnormal way to remedy a breach of contract, as the parties do not achieve what they originally intended to do. The general rule of our law is that parties should be bound by their contracts. As a result, this remedy is not always available. The parties can expressly agree that one or both of them will be entitled to cancel the contract if the other party commits a breach. The cancellation clause will determine under which circumstances the remedy would be available.

2.12.2.1 Cancellation and default by the debtor

If the debtor defaults, the creditor will have the right to cancel only in the following cases:
◆ Where there is a specific date, as well as a tacit term that timely performance is essential.
◆ Notice of intention to cancel – the creditor can send the defaulting debtor a notice of intention to cancel the contract, and thereby acquires the right to cancel the contract. The notice must allow a reasonable time for the debtor to perform, and must state the intention that the creditor will cancel if the debtor does not perform.
◆ Cancellation clause – if the parties have agreed that the creditor can cancel the contract in the event of the debtor's default, then the creditor can cancel the contract even if the debtor is not in material (serious) breach of contract.

2.12.2.2 Cancellation and default by the creditor

If the debtor defaults, the creditor will have the right to cancel only in the following cases:
◆ Where there is a specific date, as well as a tacit term that timely performance is essential – it is essential that the creditor co-operates with the debtor to allow timely performance.
◆ Notice of intention to cancel – the debtor notifies the creditor that he or she will cancel the contract if the creditor does not co-operate to receive the debtor's performance.
◆ Cancellation clause – if the parties have agreed that the debtor can cancel the contract in the event of the creditor's default, then the debtor can cancel the contract even if the creditor is not in material (serious) breach of contract.

2.12.2.3 Cancellation and defective performance

The creditor will be entitled to cancellation in the following circumstances:
◆ Cancellation is allowed where the breach is of such a serious nature that the creditor cannot reasonably be expected to abide by the contract. This is known as material breach of contract.
◆ If the parties agreed on a cancellation clause, the creditor will be able to cancel even if the performance is not materially defective.

2.12.2.4 Cancellation and repudiation

In cases of breach of contract by repudiation, cancellation is available in the following circumstances:
◆ The repudiation must be of a materially important obligation before the innocent party can cancel the contract.
◆ If the parties agreed on a cancellation clause, the innocent party will be able to cancel even if the repudiation was not of a materially important obligation.

2.12.2.5 Cancellation and prevention of performance

Prevention of performance always entitles the innocent party to cancel, since execution of the performance in terms of the contract is no longer possible.

2.12.2.6 *The act of cancellation*

Where the innocent party is entitled to cancel the contract, he or she must make a choice between cancelling or enforcing the contract. The innocent party always has a choice as to whether or not to cancel the contract, unless the other party has made performance impossible. The right to cancel must be exercised within a reasonable time after the innocent party has become aware of the other party's breach, failing which, it would appear that he or she waives his or her right to do so.

The innocent party has to notify the defaulting party of the cancellation. This may be in any form, but is preferred in writing to provide proof of notification. If the contract stipulates written notification of cancellation, then this must be complied with if the cancellation is to be valid. The party who has the right of cancellation can give the defaulting party the chance to rectify his or her performance.

2.12.2.7 *Consequences of cancellation*

The result of the cancellation of the contract is that all contractual obligations in terms of the cancelled contract are terminated. If either or both of the parties has performed, then whatever has been performed must be returned to that party. This return of performances is called restitution. If restitution becomes impossible, the party who is cancelling the contract is relieved of his or her duty to return the performance, as long as the impossibility is not his or her fault. If the defaulting party cannot return performance, the innocent party need not return performance.

2.12.3 Damages

The underlying idea is that the innocent party's estate (patrimony) should not be allowed to diminish as a result of the defaulting party's breach. The aggrieved party can claim damages provided that he or she has suffered patrimonial or monetary loss. The idea is to place the innocent party in the position where he or she would have been if the contract had been met. Whenever an innocent party has suffered loss, and whether or not he or she has cancelled or claimed execution, he or she is entitled to damages as a remedy.

2.12.3.1 *Patrimonial loss:*

The mere fact that one of the parties has committed a breach does not mean that the other party has suffered a loss of any kind. The innocent party must prove that the breach negatively affected the value of his or her estate. If not compensation cannot be claimed on the basis of contract, or in delict.

The loss of the plaintiff (in this case the injured or innocent party) can be the amount by which his or her estate would have increased if the contract had been fulfilled. The loss is determined by comparing the financial position of the plaintiff, if the contract had been met, with his or her actual financial position. The difference is the plaintiff's loss. For example, if the plaintiff were to make a profit through the contract that was cancelled, he or she can claim this profit in damages. The innocent party has to be compensated to the amount of his or her positive interest.

However, before damages can be claimed for breach of contract, the loss must be shown to be a result of the breach. Also, the defendant's liability for damages is limited to such loss as would normally result from the kind of breach in question.

Proof of the loss being a result of the breach, as well as the amount of the loss in question, must be provided by the plaintiff.

Questions and exercises

Find three examples of legal action to do with breach of contract in the newspapers. Determine the following:
- if the debtor or creditor was in breach
- what the breach was, and
- the remedies that were used by the plaintiff

3

Law of delict

Objectives of this chapter:

By the end of this chapter the learner will be able to:

- Define and explain the term delict
- Distinguish between a delict and a crime
- Explain the difference between intention and negligence as elements of fault
- Outline possible defences to a delictual claim

The learner will know:

- The definition of delict
- The elements of delict
- Application of the law of delict to the operation and management of a hospitality enterprise
- Identification and understanding of the remedies available to an injured party

3.1 Introduction

Private law is the part of the law that governs relationships between citizens in their dealings with each other. Public law consists of the rules that regulate the relationships between the state and its citizens. The law of obligations forms part of private law, and consists of the law of delict and the law of contract.

An obligation arises when a personal right comes into existence between legal subjects. For example, if Mr Groom owed Mr Hotelier money in respect of a wedding reception provided by Mr Hotelier, the bond or legal relationship between the legal subjects (citizens or people) is referred to as an obligation. In the example, the personal right of Mr Hotelier to receive a sum of money from Mr Groom has come through a contract (in this case a contract of sale). Personal rights may also come about through delict and a number of other causes, the most important being unjustified enrichment.

- In a **contract**, the legal object is the performance that must be delivered (namely the payment of the amount of money).
- In the case of **delict**, the legal object is the payment of compensation.
- In the case of **enrichment**, the legal object is the payment of an amount equal to the amount by which one person has been enriched by another.

3.2 Law of delict

Every person is exposed to some extent to the possibility of suffering damage or loss. This damage or loss may be caused by natural disasters or factors beyond the control of humans or their actions. Where the damage or loss has been caused by human action, the law of delict provides for the recovery of compensation by the injured person from the person who inflicted the damage. However, such compensation may only be recovered from the other person if there are legally recognised grounds for recovery.

The law of delict sets out

◆ when an act causing damage qualifies as a delict (that is, when the recovery of damage is legally allowed), and
◆ which remedies are available to the party suffering the damage

3.3 Definition of delict

A delict may be described as the unreasonable behaviour of a person who acts either negligently or intentionally, and thereby causes someone else to suffer damage or loss. A delict is an unlawful culpable act whereby a person (the wrongdoer) causes the other party (the injured or wronged person) damage or an injury to personality, and whereby the injured or wronged person is granted the right to damages or compensation, depending on the circumstances.

3.4 The elements of delict

It is apparent from this definition that the mere fact that one person has caused another to suffer damage is not enough to render that person liable in delict. Further requirements have to be met. These requirements, the five elements of delict, can be identified from the definition:

◆ an act/conduct
◆ unlawfulness
◆ fault
◆ causation
◆ damage

In South African law a victim is entitled to claim compensation from the wrongdoer if he or she can prove the elements of delict. Therefore, before a wrongdoer can be held responsible for the harm he or she has caused, all these elements must be proved. The following examples apply:

Example 1: An employee who washes dishes in a restaurant has bad diarrhoea and does not wash his or her hands after going to the toilet. He or she, therefore, transmits bacteria onto all the plates handled. The food dished onto the plates becomes infected, and in turn gives guests food poisoning. They become ill and require medical attention and hospitalisation. The elements can be proved as follows:

An act/conduct	Failure to wash hands after using toilet
Wrongfulness/unlawfulness	Contravenes Health Regulations R918
Fault	Unlawfulness
Causation	Food poisoning resulting from careless food handling
Damage	Illness, medical costs, loss of earnings for victim

Example 2: A cleaner in a hotel fails to put out warning signs for slippery floors when cleaning the foyer of a hotel. A guest enters, slips and falls and breaks his or her leg. The elements can be proved as follows:

An act/conduct	Failure to put out warning signs
Wrongfulness/unlawfulness	Contravenes OHS Act Regulations
Fault	Unlawfulness
Causation	Broken leg resulting from omission of warning signs
Damage	Medical costs, loss of earnings for victim

3.4.1 An act/conduct

A person can only be held responsible in delict if he or she has committed some kind of act or displayed some kind of conduct. This conduct may even constitute an omission or failure to act when a person should have acted to prevent damage or injury to another person.

In the law of delict, the concept of conduct is often defined as a voluntary act or omission. This implies that only human beings can act in the eyes of the law, and secondly, that any human conduct that can be controlled by human will is, legally speaking, an act.

An example of this would be where a restaurateur makes derogatory remarks about another restaurant, which may have a beneficial effect on his own restaurant and a detrimental effect on the other restaurant. Negligence in applying kitchen hygiene practices that result in food poisoning of guests may also constitute an act of delict.

If a person has acted in a state of automatism (without control of his or her body movements, or involuntarily), his or her conduct will not be considered as legal conduct. Examples of this from case law include cases where an act is committed by someone during an epileptic fit, while asleep, as an act of reflex, or when in a state of serious intoxication. However, in the last instance, a person is still capable of acting, even though he or she lacks accountability for his or her actions, or lacks the necessary mental capacity to appreciate the actions due to intoxication.

It is important to note that when someone drinks alcohol while he or she knows or should reasonably foresee that he or she will later drive a vehicle, and then injures another person while subsequently driving under the influence of alcohol, that person *will be held responsible* although he or she may not have acted voluntarily due to intoxication.

Conduct includes an act and/or an omission. In legal terms, an omission describes a situation where a person fails to take precautions against the occurrence of damage and such failure is not an integral part of or linked to positive conduct (an act).

Examples of omissions in the legal sense are:

- The staircase of a hotel does not have a rail and a child falls from the fourth floor staircase and dies.
- A game lodge does not provide lighting between chalets and the main lodge. A guest falls in the dark and hurts him or herself.
- Failure to apply lawful food hygiene practices results in guests getting food poisoning.

As a general rule, liability for an omission will arise only where a legal duty rests on the person to act to prevent harm or damage from occurring.

3.4.2 Wrongfulness/unlawfulness

An act that causes damage to another is in itself not enough to give rise to delictual liability. For liability to follow, prejudice must be brought about in a way that is wrongful, unreasonable or unacceptable in the eyes of the community.

Every person has certain subjective rights, such as the right to a good name, physical integrity, honour, privacy, and identity. It is wrongful to infringe on these rights, and where infringement does take place, the law restores the balance between individuals by granting the injured or wronged party a right of action in civil law.

If, for example, a newspaper publishes a report about a hotel in which it is said that the hotel makes use of guest transport busses that are not roadworthy, the reputation of the hotel has been infringed. If the report is true, the infringement will not be wrongful. However, if the report is false, the infringement could be wrongful.

An act is therefore, unlawful when it infringes the rights of another, or if the wrongdoer owed the injured person a duty of care and this duty is breached.

If the wrongdoer has a ground for justification (or legal defence) for his or her conduct, he or she cannot be held liable in delict. Grounds of justification are special circumstances that reveal that conduct that appears to be unlawful, is in reality, lawful. In order for justifiable grounds to apply, certain individual requirements have to be met. The following grounds for justification are generally recognised in South African law:

3.4.2.1 Necessity

A state of necessity empowers a person to infringe on the right of an innocent third party; for example, a fire breaks out in a busy restaurant and a guest breaks a window to escape. The purpose of an act of necessity is to protect the interests of the wrongdoer or of a third party against a dangerous situation.

There are no definite rules in our law with regard to assessing whether necessity is present in a particular case. However, there are a number of guidelines that can assist in determining whether necessity is present in a particular case. For example, apply the following guidelines to the example of the guest breaking the window of the restaurant to escape a fire:

- The existence of a state of necessity must be determined objectively. This means that the state of necessity must actually have existed and must not just have been a belief in the defendant's mind. *Reference to example: The fire created a necessity to break the widow*
- It is not clear whether a person may rely on a state of necessity that they have caused themselves. In some cases the courts allow it, and in some cases not, depending on the situation. *Reference to example: If the guest started the fire him- or herself, this would have to be examined more closely*
- The necessity must in fact be imminent or present, and not only be a threat in the future. *Reference to example: The fire is imminent*
- A person must act out of necessity not only to protect his or her own interests, but also to protect the interests of other people from the danger. *Reference to example: The broken window allowed for many guests to escape*
- A person may act out of a state of necessity to protect life, physical integrity and property. *Reference to example: The escape from the restaurant fire protected the lives of the guests and their immediate property such as clothes, personal effects, etc*
- A person may not rely on necessity where he or she is required by law to endure the danger. *Reference to example: If the guest is a fire-fighter, he or she would be required to remain and assist others to escape*
- The general rule is that the interest, that is sacrificed must not be more valuable than the interest that is being protected. *Reference to example: Human life is more valuable than property (the broken window)*

3.4.2.2 *Self-defence*

An act of defence is lawful conduct directed against an actual or imminent unlawful attack by a person on the rights of the defendant or some other person. Self-defence as a ground of justification differs from necessity in that it is a defence against an unlawful threat or attack.

For example, a thief enters a coffee shop, points a gun at the cashier and demands all the cash in the cash register. The cashier grabs a knife and stabs the thief in the arm. The thief runs away, but sues the cashier for medical costs of R10 000. The cashier can claim that he or she acted in self-defence.

A number of requirements must be met before the accused can successfully rely on self-defence. The first category of requirements relates to the attack against which the accused was defending him- or herself.

- The attack must consist of a human attack. If the attack is not human (for example a fire or flood) it is out of necessity, not self-defence. *Reference to example: The attack was by the thief with the gun.*
- The attack must be wrongful and must therefore violate or threaten a legally protected interest without justification. *Reference to example: The attack is a criminal act.*
- The attack must already have commenced or be imminently threatening, but must not yet have ceased. *Reference to example: The cashier reacts to the immediate danger of being threatened with a gun.*

The second category of requirements relates to the actual act of self-defence: The defence must be directed against the aggressor himself or herself. *Reference to example: The cashier, in her defence, stabs the thief, the aggressor.*

- The defence must be necessary to protect the threatened right. If the interest can reasonably be protected by some other, less harmful means, the defensive act is wrongful. *Reference to example: The cashier uses a knife against a gun, which is possibly more harmful.*
- The act of defence must not be more harmful than is necessary in order to ward off the attack. The act of self-defence must therefore be reasonable. *Reference to example: The stab-wound to the arm was sufficient to deter the attacker. Had the cashier shot the attacker dead with a gun, it would possibly have constituted unnecessary force to deflect the attack. The stab was sufficient.*

3.4.2.3 Consent by injured party

If the wrongdoer or injured person consented to the injury, the wrongdoer is not liable in principle. For example, medical procedures performed by a doctor are not wrongful because the other person has consented to the procedure.

However, consent must be given freely and voluntarily, and must not be contrary to good morals. Also, consent given without the consenting party being aware of the nature or seriousness of possible consequences is also invalid.

3.4.2.4 Voluntary assumption of risk

Consent may also exist when one party realises that the defendant's act will entail a certain risk, but that he or she nevertheless and with full knowledge of the danger involved, voluntarily assume the risk of injury. Examples are when a person engages in activities such as sky-diving, boxing and bungee jumping. In each case, the injured party has given the defendant the right to act in these circumstances, even if such action has the effect of causing injury. In this sense, the person has waived the right to physical integrity. For example, Mr Hotelier employs Mr Fixit to repair the roof of a hotel building that has four floors. Mr Fixit fully understands the risk involved in working on the roof of such a building, and the use of scaffolding and other devices for such work, and accepts the job. During the course of his work, Mr Fixit falls from the scaffolding and injures his back.

All the requirements for valid consent (the action is not against good morals, it is freely and voluntarily done with the required knowledge of the risk involved) must be present before the wrongfulness of the infringing action falls away. Mr Fixit has voluntarily assumed the risk attached to the job, and therefore cannot hold Mr Hotelier liable in delict in the case of his injury. Two requirements in particular are important here:
- The person who acts must act within the limits of consent. *Reference to example: Mr Fixit consented to the risk.*
- The consent must not be contrary to good morals; for example, consent to serious bodily injury is generally considered contrary to good morals unless it is clearly permitted in terms of the organised sporting code. *Reference to example: Carrying out a contract to paint a building is not contrary to good morals.*

It is important to draw a distinction between consent and *pactum de non petendo in anticipando*. In the case of the former, the element of wrongfulness is not present and hence there is no delict. In the case of the latter, delictual liability may arise, but the victim and the wrongdoer conclude a contract in terms of which the victim undertakes not to sue the wrongdoer.

Reference to example: Mr Fixit undertakes not to sue Mr Hotelier in the case of any injury sustained during the repairs to the roof of the hotel.

3.4.2.5 Provocation

Some doubt exists as to whether provocation constitutes a ground for justification, but it is generally accepted that it may constitute a ground in respect of a claim for impairment of personality but not against a claim for patrimonial damages. Provocation as a complete defence does not apply when verbal provocation is followed by physical assault. However, if provocation takes the form of a physical assault, it may in fact constitute a complete defence against an action on the basis of the subsequent retaliatory physical assault, provided that two requirements are met:

- The provocative conduct itself must be of such a nature that a reaction thereto is reasonable and therefore excusable.
- The conduct of the provoked person must constitute an immediate and reasonable retaliation against the other person – the action of revenge must therefore not only follow the provocation directly, but must be objectively reasonable as well – reasonable means that the physical assault by the second person is not out of proportion in its nature and degree to the assault by the first aggressor.

3.4.2.6 *Pactum de non petendo in anticipando.*

It is important to draw a distinction between consent and *pactum de non petendo in anticipando*. In the case of the former, the element of wrongfulness is not present and hence there is no delict. In the case of the latter, delictual liability may arise, but the victim and the wrongdoer conclude a contract in terms of which the victim undertakes not to sue the wrongdoer.

Reference to example: Mr Fixit undertakes not to sue Mr Hotelier in the case of any injury sustained during the repairs to the roof of the hotel. This also relates to indemnities. For example, guests at a resort hotel or game lodge indemnifying the hotel against injury during water sports or game viewing.

3.4.3 Fault/blameworthiness/culpability

Once it has been established that there has been conduct, and that this conduct is wrongful, it is necessary to prove fault in the form of either negligence or intent. Fault refers to the legal blameworthiness of a person – it can be said to be a subjective element of delict because it refers to the wrongdoer's attitude or state of mind when displaying the wrongful conduct.

Fault can only exist when someone has acted wrongfully – one cannot blame someone who has acted lawfully. Fault can exist in two forms: intention (*dolus*) and negligence (*culpa*).

3.4.3.1 Accountability

Prior to making an inquiry into fault, it has to be established whether the wrongdoer is accountable. Accountability means that the wrongdoer has the necessary mental capacity to distinguish between right and wrong and, in addition, is capable of acting according to that understanding. One cannot blame someone who does not have the sufficient mental capacity to know any better. The legal requirement for intent or negligence is that the wrongdoer must have reached a sufficient level of mental development to be able to comprehend or appreciate the nature and consequences of his or her actions. The basic principle is constituted in the requirement that a person must have the capacity to have a blameworthy state of mind before he or she can be held responsible in delict. As a result, insane persons and children under the age of 7 years are not capable of having a blameworthy state of mind (they are *doli and culpa incapax*).

A wrongdoer could be regarded as not being accountable under the following circumstances:

◆ youth
◆ intoxication
◆ mental illness
◆ provocation

Once it has been established that a wrongdoer is accountable by establishing mental capacity, fault in the form of intent or negligence may be proved.

3.4.3.2 Intent

A person acts intentionally when he or she directs his or her will toward bringing about a certain result, which he or she causes while being conscious of the wrongfulness of his or her conduct. Intention contains two elements:

◆ direction of will
◆ knowledge of wrongfulness of the conduct

3.4.3.2.1 Direction of will

In order to prove intent, it is necessary to establish that the wrongdoer has 'directed his or her will' to a particular consequence. This can mean one of the following:

◆ The wrongdoer actually wants his or her conduct to result in a specific consequence (this is known as direct intent).
◆ The wrongdoer wants his or her conduct to have a result, but knows that another consequence will inevitably take place (indirect intent).
◆ The wrongdoer wants a consequence, and also foresees that another consequence could take place and reconciles himself or herself with that fact (this is known as *dolus eventualis*).

Here are examples of the above:

◆ Mr Hotelier advertises his hotel as a luxury resort in the heart of the African bush in a malaria-free area. He is aware, however, that there have been a few incidents of malaria in the area. The 'luxury hotel' actually consists of a few rondavels and is dirty and in disrepair. Mr Hotelier has direct intent to defraud his guests.
◆ Mr Hotelier advertises his hotel as above, and is fully aware that his advert will be seen by foreign tour operators who may make bookings at his hotel on behalf of their clients. In this case, Mr Hotelier also has the indirect intent of defrauding the tour operators.

- Mr Hotelier advertises his hotel as above while foreseeing that his guests may possibly contract malaria while staying in his hotel. In this case he has *dolus eventualis*.

3.4.3.2.2 Knowledge of wrongfulness

Direction of will is not enough to establish wrongfulness. The wrongdoer has to know that what he or she is doing is wrongful; that is, that his or her conduct is regarded as unacceptable in terms of the legal conviction of society. If the wrongdoer does not realise that his or her conduct is wrongful, there will not be 'knowledge of wrongfulness' and hence no intent, and no delictual liability.

3.4.3.3 Negligence

In the case of negligence, a person is blamed for a careless attitude or conduct, thoughtlessness or imprudence, because, by giving insufficient attention or thought to his or her action, he or she failed to adhere to the standard of care legally required of a person. The criterion used to determine whether a person has acted negligently is the criterion of the reasonable or ordinary person. A wrongdoer is therefore negligent if the reasonable person in the same position as the wrongdoer would have foreseen harm to another and so probably would either not have acted or would have taken precautions to prevent damage before acting.

The test for negligence is therefore the so-called 'reasonable person' test. The reasonable person is an average person who is put into the position of the wrongdoer. He or she is not extremely knowledgeable, but is also not totally ignorant. The test involves the following questions:
- Whether the reasonable person in the position of the wrongdoer would have foreseen the damage arising from his or her wrongful conduct.
- Whether the reasonable person would have taken precautions to prevent damage from arising.

Where the wrongdoer did not act as the reasonable person would have acted in his or her position, he or she is regarded as having been negligent.

3.4.3.4 Innkeeper's liability

A hotel or establishment offering accommodation has a duty of care towards its guests' property. A judgment handed down in our courts in 2002 has serious implications for the small-scale accommodation sector of the tourism industry

The case concerned the plaintiffs, Mr and Mrs Gabriel, who visited Cape Town on holiday in March 2001 and booked in at the Enchanted Bed and Breakfast in Sea Point, owned and operated by the defendant. One evening, the plaintiffs retired to bed with the outside door of their first floor room open (it being summer), but the security door locked. On waking up the next morning, Mr Gabriel was unable to find his watch and wallet. Mrs Gabriel's watch and jewellery were also missing, as well as certain items of clothing. The plaintiffs further noticed that the security door was open with its key in the lock on the inside, while the outside door had been closed.

Gabriel and Another v Enchanted Bed and Breakfast CC 2002 (6) SA 597 (C)

The Summary

Liability of innkeepers in respect of goods brought on to their property by guests: Under the Praetor's *edict de nautis cauponibus et stabularis* innkeepers can be held strictly liable for goods which their guests bring onto their property.

Gabriel and Another v Enchanted Bed & Breakfast CC 2002 (6) SA 597 (C) dealt with a claim under the edict flowing from the theft of a wallet, watch, jewellery and clothes to the value of R252 000 from Gabriel's room in the defendant's B&B establishment.

In his judgment, the judge first confirmed that this edict still applies in our law, and that it has not been replaced by a simple test of negligence. However, there are certain defences which could be relied upon in order to defeat strict liability. Here the defendant first sought to prove that the loss was unforeseen, unexpected and irresistible. However, this defence failed since the loss was occasioned by simple burglary.

Secondly, the defendant relied on a (contractual) exclusion of a notice stating that 'the owner and staff will not be held liable for loss or damage sustained by whatsoever cause'. However, the notice was not prominently displayed, the plaintiffs' attention was not drawn to it, and it could therefore not be accepted that they agreed thereto.

Finally, it was agreed that the Gabriels were negligent in leaving their watches and jewellery next to their bed and in failing to place the keys in an otherwise safe or secure place. However, negligence was not proven on the facts.

Judgment was consequently handed down in favour of the Gabriels in the sum of R252 000, plus costs.

The Case

The Court held that the Roman edict *de nautis cauponibus et stabularis*, confirmed as part of South African law in Davis v Lockstone 1921 AD 153, 'remained unaffected by the passage of time'. In terms of the edict, innkeepers are liable for the loss or damage to the property of travellers brought onto their premises even in the absence of fault or negligence on their part. As a result, there existed a *prima facie* case for the defendant to be held liable for the loss suffered by the plaintiffs.

The defendant raised four defences, which it bore the onus of establishing:

Firstly, the defendant argued that the loss was unforeseen, unexpected and irresistible. The Court stated that 'any event which is unforeseen, unexpected or irresistible and which human foresight cannot guard against, such as burglary with violence or unavoidable accident, can be raised as a special defence'. However, it was clear in this case that the burglary had not been accompanied by violence. Furthermore, the incident was clearly not unforeseeable since 'thefts from houses in the area were common at the time'. It should be noted that in this particular case the defendant's argument hinged on the claim that the loss was unforeseen, unexpected and irresistible. The judge ruled however that the incident was neither unforeseen nor unexpected as thefts were common in the area and that as there was no violence involved it could not be ruled to have been irresistible. As a result of the ruling, the argument could not be accepted by the court as a special defence.

Secondly, the defendant argued that it was exempt from liability on the ground that a notice reading: 'The owner and the staff will not be held liable for any loss or damage sustained by whatsoever cause', was exhibited on the front door as well as in a brochure left in the room. However, the Court accepted the plaintiffs' evidence that they were not aware of the notices and, as a result, there could be no question of them ever having agreed to the terms of the notice.

Thirdly, the defendant argued that the plaintiffs' negligence caused the loss. This was the aspect that received most attention during the course of the evidence. The Court concluded that, 'on a balance of probability, access was gained through the bathroom window' that had been left slightly open. The Court also held that the plaintiffs had not been negligent in leaving the key of the security door as well as other valuables on a glass table, a dresser or a kitchenette counter.

Fourthly, the defendant argued that it was entitled to an apportionment of the loss resulting from contributory negligence by the plaintiffs. Here the Court replied that it was 'strictly speaking not correct to speak of contributory negligence in cases of this nature' since 'the defendant's liability flowed from the Praetor's edict and not from negligence'. The Court added that, 'if anyone was negligent, it was the defendant' because its failure 'to secure the bathroom window properly was inadequate to prevent the foreseen danger'.

The defendant having been unsuccessful, judgment was entered for the plaintiffs in the sum of R252 000 and costs, the latter including the travel costs of the plaintiffs on the grounds that it was necessary for them to give evidence at the trial.

Source: De Rebus and Professor Patrick Vrancken

In respect of this decision, the owner of a B&B is assumed to be an innkeeper, even though there are significant differences between a hotel consisting of tens of rooms, operated by a substantial number of professional staff and with a turnover of millions of rand, and a B&B offering a couple of rooms and operated by a single person, possibly assisted by a domestic, with a turnover of a few hundred thousand rand. Both therefore have the same innkeeper's liability.

The implications of this decision for small accommodation establishments are quite serious. It is suspected that many individuals operating B&Bs in South Africa are unaware of the liability that they could incur on the basis of the edict. As the amount involved in this case illustrates, such liability could well cripple a business to such an extent that no option is left but to close down.

3.4.3.5 Liability without fault

There are instances in delict where fault is not a requirement for delictual liability at all, and the person will be held liable irrespective of whether or not he or she acted intentionally or negligently. One such instance of liability without fault is vicarious liability. Instances such as this are where one party holds liability for another. This implies a relationship between the parties. There are three relationships where liability is held by a party who might not in fact cause the fault:

3.4.3.5.1 The relationship of employer-employee

The applicable principle here is that where an employee, acting within the scope of his or her employment, commits a delict, his or her employer is fully liable for the damage. However, the principle applies only if three requirements are satisfied:

◆ There must have been an employer-employee relationship at the time when the delict was committed.
◆ The employee must have committed the delict.
◆ The employee must have acted within the course and scope of his or her employment when he or she committed a delict.

Examples include the following: where laundry staff burn a shirt while ironing it; when a valet parking a guest's car dents or scratches it; where a chef has not acted in accordance with hygiene practice and guests become ill with food poisoning; or where a guest gets mauled by a lion because the warden forgot to close the gate of the compound.

An employer will be held liable for any actions that the employee undertakes to further the employer's business, even if the employer has prohibited specific actions. For example, an employer is responsible, particularly under the law, if an employee sells liquor or tobacco products to an underage person.

A further example is if Mr Hotelier employs Mr Groundsman to maintain the grounds of his resort hotel. Mr Groundsman illegally hires some children from the local community to collect litter on the grounds. One of the children cuts himself when picking up a broken bottle. Mr Hotelier can be held responsible for the action of Mr Groundsman, and is therefore responsible for damages towards the child. So, although the hiring of children was prohibited, Mr Groundsman hired them to promote Mr Hotelier's business. Mr Hotelier is thus still responsible for this illegal action of Mr Groundsman.

It is, therefore, extremely important that both industry managers and their staff are fully aware of the responsibilities and risks taken with regard to their actions within the normal scope of their work.

3.4.3.5.2 Principal-agent

A relationship of agency is characterised by the granting of authority by one person (the principal) to another person (the agent) to conclude a legal act, usually a contract, with a third party on behalf of the principal. Thus, if during the execution of his or her authority, the agent commits a delict, the principal will be fully liable therefor. In order to establish liability on the part of the principal, three requirements have to be fulfilled:

◆ There must have been a relationship of agency in existence at the time the delict was committed.
◆ The agent must have committed the delict.
◆ The agent must have acted within the scope of his or her authority or mandate when the delict was committed.

Mr Hotelier acts as an agent for Mr Timeshare, and sells the same unit of timeshare to two different buyers. Mr Timeshare is then responsible for the actions of Mr Hotelier.

Mr Resort acts as an agent for a scuba-diving company. He sells diving trips to guests and provides sub-standard and unsafe diving equipment to the divers. The scuba-diving company can be held liable in the case of any diving accidents or incidents.

3.4.3.5.3 Motor vehicle owner-motor vehicle driver

In this instance the motor vehicle owner is held vicariously liable for the drivers' delict if three requirements are met:

- The owner must have requested the driver (who is not his or her employee) to drive the vehicle or supervise his or her driving.
- The vehicle was being driven in the interests of the owner.
- The owner retained control over the manner in which the vehicle was driven.

Mr Hotelier asks Ms Friend to take his vehicle to collect some supplies for the hotel. Ms Friend collides with another vehicle on the way there, due to faulty brakes on the vehicle she is driving. Ms Friend cannot be held liable for the damage caused to the other vehicle; Mr Hotelier will be held vicariously liable.

3.4.4 Causation/causal connection

Once conduct, wrongfulness and fault are established, it becomes necessary to see if there is in fact a connection or a link between the conduct and the damage. Before a person can be held liable in delict, a causal connection must exist between the act/conduct and the damage that results from that action. The word 'causation' is used to describe that link.

In order to establish causation in the law of delict, it is necessary to prove two elements: factual and legal causation. *Factual causation* is present if there is a factual link between the act and the damage. This is determined by considering the available evidence. The question asked is 'would the damage still exist if the act had not occurred?' If the answer is no, then there is factual causation.

A single act can sometimes give rise to a number of harmful events. But, the *legal causation* is determined as to how far down the chain of events the liability lies. The approach followed in the determination of legal causation by South African courts, is a flexible approach in terms of which factors such as reasonableness, equity and fairness are used to establish whether or not the wrongful, blameworthy conduct of the wrongdoer may be connected to the damage suffered by the victim, or whether his or her conduct is regarded as too far removed from the damage.

An example of legal causation is when Mr Barman supplies liquor to a 16-year-old, Mr Young. Mr Young gets drunk, and while in this state he breaks into a car and slashes his arm badly. His mother claims damages from the owner of the bar, because the barman provided him with the liquor that made him drunk and caused him to break into the car, which in turn caused the injury.

Another example is when Ms Guest breaks a leg by slipping on a wet floor in a hotel, and the hotel insurance pays for medical expenses. If the leg is broken again later on due to slipping and falling from crutches, is the insurance company still liable for the medical costs resulting from the second fracture? Clearly the events are linked, but the legal view is that the connection between the second fracture is too remote for the insurance company to have to cover these medical costs as well.

3.4.5 Damage

The purpose of the law of delict is to compensate a victim for damage incurred through the wrongful, blameworthy conduct of the wrongdoer. Where there is no damage, there can be no delictual liability. Damage therefore has to be assessed or established and quantified to determine the actual financial damage. Damage refers to harmful consequences of the delict, and can take place in two ways:

3.4.5.1 Patrimonial (material) loss – damage

Damage is deemed to be financial or pecuniary where the person suffers some kind of loss that can be expressed in money – for example, loss of income, medical or hospital costs. The injured party can claim actual damages, that is, an amount of money in order to restore his or her financial position to its previous state.

3.4.5.2 Injury to personality

Loss that cannot be expressed in monetary terms is non-patrimonial loss, and refers to the infringement of a person's personality rights; for example, his or her right to dignity, physical integrity and good name. Such loss includes pain and suffering, reduced life expectancy, disfiguration, loss of amenities of life and any other damage to a person's body or mental health. The courts grant sentimental or moral damages in compensation referred to as 'satisfaction'. This is also an amount of money and it is determined after the court has weighed up all the facts, and has made a decision on what is fair and reasonable in the circumstances.

Note: An infringement of a person's personality rights can also lead to actual damages being granted, because financial loss was suffered at the same time; for example, where a person's reputation or good name is tarnished (in the case of defamation), the person may suffer an injury to his or her personality, (good name) but may also suffer in his or her business relations as a result.

3.4.5.3 Assessment of damage

In order to assess damage, a comparison is made between the position the victim would have been in had the delict not been committed and the position in which the victim finds himself or herself after the commission of the delict. The victim's actual present situation is therefore compared with a hypothetical position he or she would have been in had the delict not been committed.

If the victim has received some form of compensation as a result of the damage suffered (for example, an insurance payout, or donations from sympathetic persons) this may or may not be deducted from the amount of damages claimed by the victim.

The victim must also take reasonable steps to control the amount of damage suffered where possible. For example, Mr Hotelier has a minibus that he uses for airport transfers for his guests. One day, Mr Public crashes into Mr Hotelier's minibus, rendering it out of commission while being repaired. Mr Hotelier hires another minibus to continue with his (charged for) transfers, and therefore does not lose all the income from the provision of the transfer service. Mr Hotelier can claim some loss of income and the cost of the hired vehicle from Mr Public. Mr Hotelier should not in fact suspend the transfer activity, thereby claiming loss of earnings, without trying to remedy (control the losses incurred) the situation.

3.5 Remedies

The purpose of the law of delict is to set right the balance between the wrongdoer and the injured person. For this purpose, two basic types of remedies are granted to the injured person.

3.5.1 Interdict

This is a court order that prohibits a person or persons from acting in a wrongful way or that orders him or her to stop his or her wrongful conduct. It is a method of preventing a future delict. Unlike with a claim for damages, which can only be instituted once the damage has been done, an interdict can be obtained before the wrongful act is committed. The aim of an interdict is thus prevention rather than compensation.

For example, the hotel's employees strike and threaten to burn down the hotel. The manager can apply for an interdict to deny access to the premises and thereby prevent them setting fire to the hotel.

3.5.2 Claim for damages

If the wrongful act has already resulted in harm or damage to the injured person, the injured person has a claim for compensation against the wrong-doer. The injured party has several possible actions at his or her disposal:

3.5.2.1 Actio legis Aquiliae (Aquilian Action)

This action is available where the injured party has suffered financial or patrimonial loss, and thus aims at restoring the person's estate to its previous state.

3.5.2.2 Actio iniuriarum (action for pain and suffering)

If the person has not suffered patrimonial loss, but an injury to personality, the claim for damages will be based on the *actio iniuriarum*. This action is thus aimed at recovering sentimental damages.

3.6 Distinction between delict and crime

The law of delict and criminal law have a common factor: both fields of law are concerned with situations where a wrongdoer causes harm or damage to another person or property. Beyond this common factor, there are a number of differences between the two areas of law.

It has been established that the law of delict forms part of the law of obligation, which in turn forms part of private law. Criminal law, however, forms part of public law, and this is where the key difference between the law of delict and criminal law lies: how the wrongdoer is held accountable.

- In the law of delict, the wrongdoer is accountable to the private individual, the injured party
- In criminal law, the wrongdoer is accountable to the state.

Figure 3-1: Differences between crimes and delicts

Crime	Delict
1. Is part of public law	1. Is part of private law
2. Is directed at public interests	2. Is directed at private interests
3. Is applicable only if there is a rule forbidding the conduct and providing for punishment	3. Is applicable if the damage is caused in a wrongful and blameworthy manner regardless of whether the conduct is prohibited or not
4. The state is the prosecuting authority	4. The injured party, the private citizen, institutes action
5. Purpose is to punish the offender	5. Purpose is to compensate the person who suffered the damage
6. The parties involved in the proceedings are the public prosecutor or state advocate, the accused and witnesses	6. The parties involved in the proceedings are the plaintiff (who is the claimant and institutes the action) and the defendant and witnesses
7. The result or outcome is a sanction by way of the imposition of punishment in the form of imprisonment or a fine. All fines are paid to the state	7. The remedies available to the plaintiff are aimed primarily at compensating the plaintiff, and take the form of an interdict or damages – any damages ordered to be paid, are paid to the plaintiff (the injured party)
8. The state controls the action: the state is entitled to prosecute irrespective of the injured party's wishes	8. The private individual has a choice: the injured party can choose to institute an action for damages or apply for an interdict, or not
9. The rules of criminal procedure apply	9. The rules of civil procedure apply
10. The burden of proof to prove the crime against the accused rests with the state and has to be discharged 'beyond a reasonable doubt'	10. The burden of proof to prove the defendant is liable for the injury inflicted or damage caused rests with the plaintiff, and has to be discharged 'on a preponderance or balance of probabilities'

3.7 Examples of delictual liability in hospitality

The South African law of delict works with general principles. In other words, South African law does not only grant relief in the case of certain pre-defined situations. Therefore, if a guest or hospitality service provider suffers loss, and can prove this within the elements of delictual liability, he or she should be able to claim for that loss.

The following are examples of situations where delictual responsibility may occur in the hospitality context.

3.7.1 Misrepresentation

Where misrepresentation results in a party suffering patrimonial loss, that party could make use of the *actio legis Aquiliae* to claim damages. It does not matter whether the misrepresentation was fraudulent or negligent as long as some form of fault is proven. It also does not matter whether the misrepresentation occurs within a contractual setting or not. An example of misrepresentation is when Mr Hotelier advertises his luxury bush lodge, which in fact is a miserable collection of rondavels in a bad state of disrepair.

3.7.2 Loss of personal effects

Personal effects represent property, which include that which the guests bring onto the hospitality premises in the form of luggage, vehicles, jewellery, camera equipment, and so on. Should they suffer loss, the *actio legis Aquiliae* is available, and it is necessary to prove all the elements of delict, including negligence.

3.7.3 Personal injuries

A victim who suffers personal injuries can claim for all or some of the following:
- compensation for hospital or medical costs
- loss of income and loss of future income (depending on the seriousness of the victim's injury, as well as the profession of the victim)
- future medical costs (depending on the seriousness of the injury)
- pain and suffering

Injuries may occur very easily, and should be prevented if at all possible with sound operational, safety and maintenance practices. Examples include the following: a guest slips on a wet floor that does not have safety warnings posted on it; a guest falls down garden steps where the light bulb has blown and not been replaced; guests become ill with food poisoning due to poor food hygiene practices; and a guest is bitten by an animal (wild or domestic) on the premises.

Questions and exercises

1. Which elements do you feel are important to prove a delictual crime: conduct, wrongfulness, fault, causation or damage?
2. Explain the concept of contributory negligence and provide your own example, which you think will be suitable for this concept.
3. Define the concept of strict liability and vicarious liability and provide an example of each.

4

Commercial contracts

Objectives of this chapter:

By the end of this chapter the learner will be able to:

◆ Define various contracts encountered during the course of business
◆ Explain the basic requirements pertaining to a range of relevant commercial contracts

The learner will know:

◆ The *essentialia* of various types of commercial contracts
◆ The basic rights and duties to the parties of various types of commercial contracts
◆ The advantages and disadvantages of operating a franchise

4.1 Introduction

All owners and managers of businesses in the hospitality industry, in offering their professional services to their customers, rely on other business organisations in order to provide their services. Restaurateurs, for example, will enter into supply contracts with butchers, grocers and other suppliers for food and beverages with which to supply their guests, and also enter into contracts either for the purchase or the hire of equipment for their kitchens. Hoteliers may enter into service contracts with a laundry to provide clean linen for their guests' rooms, or with a security company to provide for the security of guests and premises.

Hotels, restaurants and other hospitality establishments may retain the services of professional advisors such as lawyers and accountants. Some may also use the services of architects, advertising agencies, or rent their premises from a landlord. All of these facets of the hospitality enterprise involve commercial contracts between the hospitality establishment and other businesses.

This chapter will explore the requirements for various contracts that the hospitality operator is likely to encounter in the industry. This provides a guide for operators of what to keep in mind when entering into various contracts, but does not serve as a comprehensive analysis of such agreements. For further advice consult a professional legal consultant or lawyer.

4.2 Contract of sale

Certain kinds of contracts are concluded more often than others; for example, contracts of sale, lease and employment. Of these, the contract of sale is probably the most common kind of contract. It is virtually impossible to live or carry on any kind of business without either purchasing or selling goods from time to time. Although all contracts must comply with the general requirements for valid contracts, certain special principles have evolved concerning the most commonly concluded kinds of contract. These contracts are known as specific or named contracts. For a contract to qualify as a specific contract certain additional characteristics or requirements (*essentialia*) must be present.

The reason for classifying a contract as a specific contract is that certain *naturalia* could flow from that contract. These natural consequences regulate the relationship between the parties on certain aspects, even if the parties do not regulate it themselves. For example, if the parties to a contract of sale have not agreed when payment shall be made, it is assumed that payment must take place simultaneously with delivery of the thing to be sold (the *merx*); that is, it will be a cash sale, not a credit sale. As is also evident from this example, it is fairly easy for parties to make other arrangements. For example, they can arrange that payment will take place only at the end of the month.

A contract of sale may be defined as a contract in which one party (the seller) undertakes to deliver the *merx* to another party (the buyer or purchaser), and the purchaser, in exchange for this, agrees to pay the seller a certain sum of money (the purchase price).

A contract of sale must, of course, comply with those requirements that need to be satisfied for all contracts. In addition to this, the parties have to agree on the above-mentioned two essential characteristics, that is, the *merx* and the purchase price, before the contract can be described and treated as a contract of sale. The existence of consensus regarding the purchase price and the thing sold shows that a contract of sale has been concluded, and distinguishes it from other types of contract. They are, therefore, the *essentialia* of a contract of sale.

4.2.1 The *merx*

A valid contract of sale can come into existence only if there is agreement regarding the *merx*. The *merx*, therefore, must be definite or ascertainable.

The *merx* is definite if it is mentioned by name in the agreement; for example, 'Homeleigh Restaurant, in the district of Rustenburg'. It is also definite if it is clear that the parties were in agreement about the thing being sold. In the case of a generic sale, that is a sale of a quantity of a particular type of thing, the *merx* is not definite, but ascertainable, since the number, weight or measure is mentioned together with the type of thing, for example 'ten double beds', or 'fifty litres of milk'.

Nearly anything may be sold, provided that it can form part of one's patrimony; that is, it can be owned by someone. The *merx* may consist of movable or immovable goods, or may even be an incorporeal thing such as a claim or a patent. In keeping with the general requirement that contracts should be lawful, no contract will come into being where the law prohibits the sale of the *merx*, for example in the case of illegal drugs.

4.2.2 The purchase price

An essential requirement for a contract of sale is that a price for the *merx* must be agreed upon. Like the *merx*, the purchase price must be definite or ascertainable. Therefore, the parties have to agree on an amount, stipulate a price per unit, or determine a method by which the purchase price can be determined without reference to the parties themselves.

It often happens that goods that are in free supply in commerce are bought and sold without any explicit reference being made to their price. For example, when a person enters a shop and takes and buys an article without a price tag. A valid contract nonetheless comes into being and the parties are deemed to have agreed on the customary price for the *merx*.

4.2.3 The rights and duties of the purchaser and the seller

The classification of a contract as a contract of sale has important practical legal consequences:

◆ It determines certain legal consequences that cannot be excluded by the parties. The delivery of the *merx* and the payment of the purchase price are consequences that cannot be excluded by the parties.
◆ It determines the legal position of the parties in respect of certain matters that were not arranged by them. It often happens that the parties to a contract of sale agree on only the two essential characteristics of a contract of sale. They might not even consider all the matters that are potentially relevant; for example, whether or not the price has to be paid in cash, in what way delivery has to take place, or what would happen if the *merx* were destroyed before it could be delivered to the purchaser. Our common law provides a legal framework for contracts of sale, and if the parties do not make arrangements to the contrary, these natural consequences (*naturalia*) will apply.

It is important to realise that a substantial number of contracts are not concluded on this common-law basis, but on the basis of a comprehensive set of terms contained in a printed document that is signed by both parties. This document then constitutes a contract of sale.

4.2.4 The common-law rights of the purchaser

4.2.4.1 The purchaser is entitled to delivery of the merx

This means that the *merx* must be made available to the purchaser, and that he or she is entitled to free and undisturbed possession of the *merx*.

4.2.4.2 The purchaser is entitled to preservation of the merx pending delivery

One of the duties of the seller is to preserve the *merx* until it is delivered to the purchaser. If the *merx* is damaged or destroyed owing to the negligence or intentional conduct of the seller, he or she will be liable.

4.2.4.3 *The purchaser is entitled to be protected by the seller against eviction*

In our law it is not an automatic consequence of a contract of sale that the seller has to transfer ownership in the *merx* to the purchaser. The seller merely undertakes that the purchaser will not be disturbed in his or her enjoyment and possession of the *merx* by another person claiming legal title to the *merx*.

The undertaking so implied by our common law is known as the seller's warranty against eviction. It entails that, if the purchaser is disturbed in his or her possession and enjoyment of the *merx* by someone claiming legal title to it, it is the seller's duty to come to the purchaser's assistance after being notified by the purchaser.

4.2.4.4 *The purchaser is entitled to a* merx *free from latent defects*

An implied warranty against latent defects is read into every contract of sale, unless it has been excluded by the parties. This warranty entitles the purchaser to certain legal remedies, should the *merx* contain a latent defect. The seller is liable for latent defects despite the fact that he or she was unaware of the defect, and did not act in bad faith. A purchaser who wishes to institute a claim because of latent defects in the *merx*, must prove that:

- there is or was a material defect in the *merx*
- the defect was present when the contract of sale was concluded
- the defect was latent. Defects are regarded as latent if the purchaser could not have readily noticed it during a reasonable inspection of the *merx* at the time of the sale
- the purchaser was unaware of the defect at the time of the sale

The remedies for breach of the implied warranty against latent defects are the so-called *aedilitian* actions, namely the *actio redhibitoria* and the *actio quanti minoris*. When a latent defect is discovered, the purchaser will, depending on the degree of the defect, be entitled to the *actio redhibitoria* and in the alternative the *actio quanti minoris*, or to the latter only. A legal practitioner will be able to provide further advice in this regard.

4.2.4.5 *'As is' sales*

The warranty against latent defects may be excluded by the parties. This can be achieved in any way from which the intention to exclude the warranty can be deduced, but the usual way is to state that the article is sold 'voetstoots' or 'as is'. The purchaser then has no legal remedies if the *merx* has a latent defect, except where the seller knew of the defect – in which case the purchaser will be entitled to claim damages.

4.2.4.6 *The* actio empti

The *actio empti* is not a separate common-law right of the purchaser, but a remedy the purchaser can use to enforce his or her rights against the seller. The purchaser may rely on the *actio empti* in the following instances:

- **Defective performance:** Where the *merx* is delivered without the good qualities guaranteed by the seller or with defects, the absence of which was guaranteed by the seller, the purchaser may claim damages and, if the *merx* is seriously defective, cancellation. This is known as

♦ **Misrepresentation:** Where the seller is aware of defects in the *merx* but does not disclose this to the purchaser, or if the seller induces the contract by making false representations about good qualities of the *merx*, the purchaser may rely on the *actio empti* to claim damages.

♦ **Manufacturer's liability:** Where the seller is the manufacturer of the *merx* or a specialist dealer with expert knowledge of the *merx*, he or she can, if the *merx* is defective, be held liable for damages, including damages for consequential loss.

♦ **Breach of the warranty against eviction:** This aspect has already been discussed.

4.2.5 The common-law rights of the seller

The seller is entitled to payment of the purchase price by the purchaser. This is the most important obligation of the purchaser and cannot be excluded by the parties. The payment of a sum of money is one of the essential characteristics of a contract of sale.

4.2.6 The transfer of ownership

When a contract of sale is executed in full and without hitches, the purchaser acquires ownership of the *merx*. The transfer of ownership is usually the primary purpose of the parties to a contract of sale, yet it is not an automatic consequence of the execution of a contract of sale.

The transfer of ownership is regulated by the rules of the law of property. One of the ways in which a person can obtain the ownership of a movable corporeal thing, is by its transfer to him by another person. Four requirements are set:

♦ The transferor must deliver the thing to the transferee. In the case of immovables delivery is not possible. Immovables are transferred by way of registration in a deeds office.

♦ Both parties must have the intention that ownership should pass from the transferor to the transferee.

♦ The transferor must be in a position to transfer ownership, that is, he must be the owner of the thing.

♦ In the case of contracts of sale the purchase price must be paid, or security given for the payment thereof, or credit must have been granted. If it is a cash sale, ownership will pass only once the purchase price is paid or security given. In the case of a credit sale, that is, where the seller has given extension for the payment of the price, ownership will pass upon delivery.

4.2.7 Delivery

Movable property has to be delivered to the transferee. There are different forms of delivery:

4.2.7.1 Actual delivery

This is the most common form of delivery and entails the physical handing over of the *merx* by the seller to the purchaser.

4.2.7.2 Symbolic delivery

Here the *merx* is not physically handed over to the purchaser, but something else is delivered to the purchaser that enables him or her to obtain control of the *merx*; for example, the seller of a restaurant hands the keys of the premises to the purchaser.

4.2.7.3 Delivery with the long hand

This entails the pointing out of the *merx* and its being made available to the purchaser. This method is used where the *merx* is too large or heavy to be handed over physically; for example, cattle in a kraal.

4.2.7.4 Delivery with the short hand

This form of delivery occurs where the purchaser is already in possession of the *merx*, but does not hold it as owner, and then subsequently holds it as owner. For example, Missy borrows a car from Billy, and while she has it, they agree that she may buy it from him. She therefore does not take delivery of the vehicle as she already has it in her possession.

4.2.7.5 Constitutum possessorium

This form of delivery is the opposite of delivery with the short hand. The seller retains possession of the *merx*, but on behalf of the purchaser; for example, because he or she rents it from the purchaser for a period of time.

4.2.8 Registration

Immovables, for example land, are transferred by way of their registration in the name of the purchaser. As soon as the transfer is registered in a deeds office, transfer of ownership takes place.

4.2.9 The intention that ownership be transferred

Both parties must have the intention that ownership be transferred by delivery of the *merx*. The parties can, of course, explicitly or tacitly agree on the moment when ownership will be transferred, for example only once the purchase price is paid.

4.2.10 The seller must be the owner

If the seller is not the owner of the *merx*, he or she cannot transfer ownership to the purchaser, because one cannot transfer more rights than one has. If the seller is not the owner of the *merx*, but still delivers the thing to the purchaser, the purchaser can acquire only the same rights in respect of the merx that the seller had. The real owner can claim back the thing from the purchaser with the owner's action, even if the purchaser obtained the thing in good faith and paid for it. An example is when Daisy buys a car from Bob in good faith, but the car was in fact stolen from Stuart. Stuart, therefore, can claim the car back from Daisy.

4.2.11 Payment of the purchase price

In the case of contracts of sale, it is a further requirement for the transfer of ownership that the purchase price must be paid, or that the seller must have given the purchaser credit for the payment thereof, or that the purchaser has given security for the payment thereof. If there is nothing to indicate the contrary, it is accepted that a contract of sale is concluded on a cash basis, that is, ownership will pass only once the purchase price is paid. Delivery and payment have then to be made simultaneously. In the case of a credit sale, ownership will pass immediately when the *merx* is delivered.

4.2.12 The passing of the risk

When property is destroyed, it is normally its owner who bears the loss. It is also the owner who is entitled to any benefit or profit accruing to the thing. If performance accidentally becomes impossible after conclusion of a contract, the general rule is that both parties are released from their respective obligations.

However, it is one of the consequences of a contract of sale that the risk of accidental damage to, or loss of, the *merx*, as well as the right to any potential benefit or profit accruing to the *merx*, passes from the seller to the purchaser as soon as the contract is *perfecta;* that is, even before the purchaser has become the owner. This consequence can be excluded from the contract by the parties agreeing on another risk arrangement.

4.3 Credit agreements

A credit agreement is not one of the specific or named contracts like sale or lease, but is any contract in terms of which the parties agree that payment will take place at a future date. The creditor thus extends credit for the contract price. In this sense, a credit agreement is merely the opposite of a cash transaction.

The supply of credit enables the consumer to obtain goods or services immediately, while delaying payment or spacing it over a period.

4.3.1 The National Credit Act

Legislation has been introduced to protect the consumer in certain credit agreements. The National Credit Act 34 of 2005 (NCA) came into effect in June 2007. The Act is designed to better regulate all players in the credit market and to improve customer protection. All personal loans granted by banks and in some cases some business loans, are governed by the act.

The National Credit Regulator (NCR) was established as the regulator under the NCA and is responsible for the regulation of the South African credit industry. It is tasked with carrying out education, research, policy development, registration of industry participants, investigation of complaints, and ensuring enforcement of the Act.

The Act requires the Regulator to promote the development of an accessible credit market, particularly to address the needs of historically disadvantaged persons, low income persons, and remote, isolated or low density communities.

The NCR is also tasked with the registration of credit providers, credit bureaux and debt counsellors; and enforcement of compliance with the Act.

4.3.1.1 Reckless Credit

Reckless credit is prohibited under the NCA and is defined as lending money to customers without first:

- ensuring they have enough income to pay it back
- assessing a customer's debt repayment history
- ensuring a customer understands the costs, risks and obligations of the credit agreement

4.3.1.2 The contract

- Documents should be written in plain understandable language so all customers can understand them.
- Customers will receive a pre-agreement quote that will list all costs when borrowing money. This quote is valid for a minimum of five days.

4.3.1.3 Fee structure

The NCA specifies that customers may be required to pay the following as part of the principal debt:
- an initiation fee, connection fees, levies or charges
- the cost of any extended warranty agreement
- service fees, default and collection fees
- taxes, licence or registration fees
- credit insurance

The NCA also lays down maximum initiation and service fees and interest rates depending on the type of credit agreement.

4.3.1.4 Interest rates and charges

The NCA states that:
- A credit provider may charge a customer an interest rate that varies during the term of the agreement, but only if the variation is linked to a reference rate.
- Customers should be notified in writing five days in advance of any changes to the interest rate or fees.

4.3.1.5 Insurance matters

Credit providers may require customers to take out credit life insurance for the duration of the credit agreement, however:
- The amount of insurance may not exceed the total outstanding debt owed to the credit provider under the agreement.
- Insurance must not exceed the full replacement value of a property or the outstanding amount on a vehicle agreement.
- Customers must be informed of their right to waive a proposed policy from the credit provider and provide a policy of their own choice.
- Where the credit provider arranges insurance for a customer, the credit provider may not charge any additional amount over and above the actual cost of the insurance.

4.3.1.6 Complaints

The National Consumer Tribunal was launched on 1 September 2006. It acts as an informal court to resolve problems that customers experience with credit transactions, credit bureaux and credit providers.

4.1.1.7 Demographic reporting

Credit providers will have to report to the National Credit Regulator the volume and type of credit extended. The NCA seeks to inform customers on the major issues.

Quotations must disclose:
- the full cost of the credit applied for including all fees
- interest rate payments and the effect of not paying a deposit
- the cost of skipping payments and 'free for the first six months' offers
- penalties, hidden costs and implications of compound interest on long-term loans

4.3.1.8 Why does SA need the Act?

The NCA will ensure that:
- credit providers lend money in a responsible manner
- customers don't borrow more than they can afford to repay
- if customers are over indebted they can apply for debt counselling
- customers are protected from unfair discrimination

4.3.1.9 Credit Bureau information

Credit providers must:
- Ensure that the information submitted is accurate, up to date, relevant, complete, valid and not duplicated.
- Give the customer 20 business days' notice before they submit their name to a Bureau.

The Bureau must:
- Ensure that the information they hold is accurate, up to date and remains confidential and secure.

Any person may question the validity or accuracy of his or her credit record.

4.3.1.10 Can customers afford the loan?

- Credit providers are obliged to make sure customers can afford to repay their debt.
- Customers will need to provide details on income and expenses when applying for credit.

4.3.1.11 Advertising and marketing

The NCA aims to stop misleading or deceptive advertising:
- Words like 'no credit checks required', 'free credit' and 'guaranteed loans' cannot be used.
- Negative option marketing where the credit provider enters into a credit agreement is not allowed without a customer's express consent.

The NCA specifically prohibits credit providers from:
- harassing customers to apply for credit or to enter into a credit agreement
- increasing the limits on a customer's credit card, overdraft or any other credit facility without their consent

4.3.1.12 Spousal consent

If spouses are married in community of property, the NCA requires all customers applying for credit to obtain their spouse's consent.

4.3.1.13 Parties to agreements in terms of the NCA

The Department of Trade and Industry has formed a team of credit regulators to regulate the new Credit Act. For more information visit its site at http://www.ncr.org.za.

The NCA generally does not apply where the state or a government body is the creditor.

The parties to a credit agreement are the credit grantor and the credit receiver. The credit grantor is the seller, dealer, service provider, lessor, or a person to whom the rights of one of these parties have passed. A credit receiver is the purchaser, a person to whom a service is rendered, lessee, or a person to whom the rights of one of these parties have passed.

4.3.1.14 The NCA in general

The NCA is a large and significant document that categorises types of credit agreements into small (e.g. pawn transactions), intermediate and large (e.g. mortgages) credit agreements with specific thresholds for each.

If you are entering into credit agreements, or wish to extend credit to customers or clients, it is advisable to seek legal advice on setting up your credit agreements, or getting your legal advisor to check any credit agreements you enter into to ensure that they are compliant with the Act. Your legal advisor will also ensure that all formalities are met and all clauses and extensions of credit are lawful. Do not try and do this on your own – this is a specialised and complex field where you will need advice and guidance on all the provisions of the Act befor extending credit in your business.

4.4 Lease agreements

Many hospitality establishments, especially restaurants, rent their premises from a landlord, who is the legal owner of the property. The lease granted by the landlord to the tenants gives the tenants exclusive possession of the premises for a fixed period of time, at the end of which the property reverts to the landlord. The tenants will normally be answerable to the landlord for the use they make of the property, and certain restrictions are normally agreed on and contained in the lease agreement.

The legal relationship between the lessor and the lessee may fall within the ambit of the Rental Housing Act 21 of 1999 (RHA).

South African law recognises three forms of the contract of letting and hiring. There is the letting and hiring of a movable or immovable thing, the letting and hiring of services, and the letting and hiring of work to be done (for example, a house to be built). This section concerns mainly the letting and hiring of immovable property, including a building or part of it. It is concerned with what is also described as a contract of landlord and tenant.

A contract for the lease, or a contract for the letting and hiring of a thing is a reciprocal contract in terms of which one party (the lessor, or landlord) undertakes to make temporarily available to another party (the lessee, or tenant) the use and enjoyment of a thing, wholly or in part, in return for the payment of a sum of money.

4.4.1 The essentials of a contract of lease

Three essential elements are apparent from the definition above. They are:

- an undertaking by the lessor to give the lessee the use and enjoyment of a thing
- an agreement between the lessor and the lessee that the lessee's use and enjoyment is to be temporary
- an undertaking to pay rent, in other words an undertaking by the lessee to pay a sum of money in return for the use and enjoyment that he or she will receive

In principle, any corporeal thing, movable or immovable, can be let. It is not required that the contract should confer the full use and enjoyment of the thing. A partial letting and hiring is allowed; for example, a room in a house may be let.

The parties must agree on the object that is to be the subject of the lease. The thing, or part of it, that is let must be identified or identifiable.

There is no requirement for the validity of a lease that it be entered into for a definite time. A contract of lease may stipulate that it will run until the occurrence of an event that is bound to occur, although the time for its occurrence is unknown. The duration of the contract of lease may also be indefinite, and it may also be expressed to be at the will of either the lessor or the lessee.

4.4.1.1 The rent

The lessee must undertake to pay rent. The rent must be in money.

The amount of rent that is payable must be certain. Parties to a lease normally agree on a specific amount of money, but they can also create a valid lease by agreeing to a method or formula by which the amount of rent is to be determined.

The amount of the rent does not have to be market-related, but the RHA forbids it to be exploitative. As far as the deposit is concerned, it is not a requirement of the contract. However, the parties usually agree on a deposit to be used by the lessor, if necessary, to cover arrear rental, the replacement of lost keys and damage that may have been caused by the lessee. The amount of the deposit may not exceed an amount equivalent to the amount specified in the agreement or otherwise agreed to between the parties. Any such deposit must be invested by the landlord in an interest-bearing account with a financial institution, interest accruing to the tenant. The tenant may request the landlord to provide him or her with written proof concerning accrued interest during the lease period.

4.4.1.2 Inspections

The RHA compels lessors and lessees to undertake two joint inspections of the premises. The first one must take place prior to the tenant moving into the premises. The purpose of that inspection is to determine that the premises are in sound condition. The second inspection must take place at the end of the lease period to determine if any damage was caused by the tenant during the duration of the lease. Lessors' failures to inspect the premises in the presence of the lessees are deemed to constitute acknowledgements by the lessors that the premises are in a good state of repair. In such cases, the lessors do not have the right to retain the deposit or any part thereof. If deductions are made from the deposit, receipts indicating the costs incurred must be available to the tenant for inspection.

4.4.2 The formation of a contract of lease

No formalities are required for a valid contract of lease to come into being. A lease, including a lease of land, may therefore be entered into informally. The Rental Housing Act, however, provides that a landlord must, if requested thereto by a tenant, reduce a lease to writing.

4.4.3 The rights and duties of the lessor and the lessee

Contracts of lease are often embodied in standard-form contracts. The lessor and lessee may not exclude any of the essential elements of this type of contract. They must, for example, specify an object that is to be the subject of the lease as well as the rent that will be payable. But they may exclude some consequences of the contract of lease that would otherwise have resulted according to common law. The following paragraphs set out the position according to common law, that is in the absence of any contrary contractual terms.

4.4.3.1 The duties of the lessor

4.4.3.1.1 The duty to deliver the thing let to the lessee
The lessor must put the use and occupation of the subject leased at the disposal of the lessee in such a manner that the latter is able to enter into undisturbed occupation of it. In the case of a lease of fixed property (for example, a restaurant property) the lessor must, for instance, ensure that the property is not occupied by someone other than the lessee.

The lessor must deliver the thing let in a condition that will enable the lessee to use and enjoy it. Accessories that are essential to the proper use of the thing (for example, the keys to the property), must be delivered with the thing.

4.4.3.1.2 The duty to maintain the thing let in proper condition
The thing let must not only be delivered in a condition that is reasonably fit for the purpose for which it is being leased. It must also be maintained in that state. The contract of lease normally gives rise to obligations of a continuing nature. The lessor must therefore, allowing for normal wear and tear, continue to maintain the subject of the lease in the condition in which he or she was obliged to deliver it. Failure to do this constitutes a breach of the lessor's contractual duties.

4.4.3.1.3 The duty to ensure the lessee's undisturbed use and enjoyment
The terms of the lease may warrant that the lessor is the owner of the property let. If they do not, no such warranty exists. In principle a lease may be valid even though the lessor is not the owner of the property let and had no right to let

it. All the lessor warrants is that no one has the right in law to disturb the lessee's use and enjoyment of the property.

4.4.3.2 The duties of the lessee

4.4.3.2.1 The lessee's duty to pay the rent

The payment of rent is an essential element of a contract of lease. It may therefore not be excluded, not even by agreement between the parties. Certain common-law rules relating to the payment of rent may, however, be altered by agreement between the parties. For example, the time of payment is usually determined contractually. In the absence of any specific provision, the general rule is that the rent will be payable at the end of the term of the lease. Unless the parties have agreed otherwise, a lessor is entitled to insist on being paid in South African currency.

A lessee can commit a breach of the duty to pay rent in two ways. The lessee can default in payments, or can repudiate liability for rent. If the lessee does commit a breach, the remedies for repudiation or *mora debitoris* are available to the lessor.

4.4.3.2.2 The lessor's tacit hypothec for unpaid rent

As soon as the lessee of immovable property falls into arrears with the rent, the lessor or landlord acquires a hypothec over all movables situated on the property. This is known as the landlord's tacit hypothec, and serves as security in respect of such rent. The hypothec is operative only when, and for as long as, the rent is in arrears. Although it arises immediately when the lessee falls in arrears with his or her rent, it is of no force and effect until the lessor makes an attachment of the goods in respect of which the hypothec is operative. Thus, if the goods are removed from the leased premises before the lessor has made the attachment, the lessor will lose his or her tacit hypothec unless the goods can be pursued and 'arrested' before they arrive at their new destination. The lessor may, however, not seize the moveable property, without a court order from a magistrate's court.

The lessor may only rely on the hypothec when and while the lessee is in arrears with rent.

4.4.3.2.3 The lessee's duty of proper use and care of the thing let

The lessee may not use the object of the lease improperly or unreasonably. The lease object must be maintained in a good condition and may only be used for the purpose for which it has been leased. If the lessee breaches his or her duty to use the thing let in a proper manner, the usual contractual remedies will apply.

4.4.3.2.4 The lessee's duty to restore the thing let on termination of the lease

Upon termination of the lease, the lessee must return the lease object or evacuate the premises. This obligation flows from the essential characteristic of a contract of lease that the lessor binds him- or herself to make the temporary use and enjoyment of a thing available to the lessee. The thing must be returned in the condition in which it was received, deterioration as a result of reasonable wear and tear excepted.

Should the lessee return the thing let in a damaged condition, or should it have been destroyed, he or she is obliged to make good the damage unless the lessee can show that the damage was not due to any fault either on his or her own part or on the part of anybody for whose actions the lessee bears responsibility (for example, an employee of the lessee).

If the lessee fails to comply with this duty, the normal remedies apply.

4.4.3.3 Rights of the lessor

The most important right of the lessor is the right to payment of the rent. Failure by the lessee to do so constitutes a breach of contract. The lessor then has the usual remedies for breach of contract as well as a hypothec.

The lessor also has the right, upon termination of the lease, to regain full control of the property in a good state of repair, save for fair wear and tear. If the property is damaged, the lessor is entitled to compensation. The lessor also has the right to demand that the lessee use the premises only for the purpose for which they were let and in the manner in which the premises would be used if the lessee were the owner ot the premises. The lessor also has the right to terminate the lease under certain circumstances.

4.4.3.4 The rights of the lessee

The most important right of the lessee is the right to the use and enjoyment of the leased premises. While doing so, the RHA confirms that the lessees, the members of their household and their visitors have the right to privacy that includes the right not to have their person, property or the premises searched, as well as the right not to have the privacy of their communications infringed. In this regard, the lessor only has a right of inspection performed in a reasonable manner after reasonable notice has been given to the lessee.

The lessees also have the right to demand that the lessor maintains the leased premises in good condition unless agreed otherwise.

4.4.3.4.1 Subletting

In most cases, in the absence of an agreement to the contrary, the lessee is entitled to sublet the property. This is done by means of a contract of sublease entered into between the lessee of the property and someone eIse. In terms of the sublease the normal relationship of lessor and lessee is established between the original lessee and the sublessee. The relationship between the original lessor and lessee remains unaffected and no rights and duties are constituted between the original lessor and the sublessee. The original lessor can, however, evict the sublessee if he or she stays in occupation of the premises after the original lease has terminated.

If the lease contains a clause forbidding the lessee to sublet the property, the lessee commits a material breach of contract if he or she does sublet the property. Such a breach entitles the lessor to cancel the lease immediately.

Subletting in breach of a prohibition against so doing, constitutes so serious a breach of the lease that it entitles the lessor to justify cancellation even in the absence of a cancellation clause.

4.4.3.4.2 The lessee's relationship with successors of the lessor: the maxim 'huur gaat voor koop'

This maxim can be translated as 'hire takes precedence over sale'. It arose from considerations of equity, and is relevant to contracts pertaining to the lease of immovable property (for example, a house). It refers to the principle that the person to whom such property has been sold is bound by any contract of lease existing in respect of the property at the time of its sale. The purchaser therefore cannot evict the tenant, but is obliged to abide by the terms of the lease, provided that the tenant continues to pay the rent due under the lease.

4.4.4 The termination of a lease

Apart from the normal termination of contracts, there are various ways of terminating a lease contract:

4.4.4.1 Termination by effluxion of time

If a lease is for a fixed period, or until the occurrence of a specified event, the obligations arising from it automatically come to an end when the period ends or the event occurs.

4.4.4.2 Termination by notice

If the contract of letting and hiring is for an indefinite time, but with rent payable periodically (for example, monthly), the obligations flowing from it can be terminated by notice given by the lessor or the lessee. If there is no agreement on the period for such notice, reasonable notice must be given.

4.4.4.3 Termination by extinction of the lessor's title

As was stated above, it is not a requirement for a contract of lease that the lessor should have a valid title to the property let. Therefore the expiry of the lessor's title does not normally terminate the obligations created by the lease. But it does so if the parties intended that it should, or if it must be taken that this was their intention.

4.4.4.4 Termination by death

A lease is terminated by the death of the lessor or the lessee if the contract so provides. In other instances the rights and duties of a deceased lessor or lessee pass to the heirs of that party on his or her death.

4.4.5 The lessee's right to compensation for improvements

Improvements can be
- useful (if they improve the property and increase its market value)
- luxurious (if they satisfy the fancy of an individual, whether or not they increase the market value)
- necessary (if they are required for the preservation of the property)

The parties to a contract of letting and hiring should agree on the rights of the lessee to remove improvements and on his or her claim to compensation if improvements are not removed. If they have not agreed otherwise, the lessee may remove annexures constituting luxurious or useful improvements before the lease terminates, provided the property will not be left in a worse condition than when it was received. After termination everything annexed belongs to the lessor.

4.4.6 Renewal of a lease

A contract of lease may be renewed, that is a new contract of lease is concluded between the same lessor and lessee and commences immediately upon the expiration of their existing lease. The agreement to enter into a new lease may be express or tacit.

4.5 Insurance agreements

Hospitality service providers need to insure their businesses against risks such as theft, fire and liability to third parties that may arise as a result of a breach of contract or a delict. Hospitality managers must assess the problems that they might face and decide whether or not the probability of these problems occurring is sufficiently high for them to insure themselves against such occurrences. These problems could include a function being cancelled at the last minute, an accident causing injury or death, or luggage or money being stolen or lost. By insuring themselves against these dangers, the managers are transferring the risk, or at least a portion of that risk, to an insurer.

They may not be able to prevent the event from happening, but if it does occur they will at least be provided with the finances to enable them to replace items, apply for any damage to be repaired or ensure that adequate medical attention is received. If they elect not to insure, then they will have to bear the whole financial burden themselves should such an event occur.

Insurance is an essential aspect of any business. Owners should consider it crucial to conducting business, and ensure that they are always covered. It is no good to discover after a fire or robbery that the business was underinsured. Policies must be reviewed annually, and any shortfalls addressed with additional coverage.

Business owners must be careful when buying insurance with regards to whom they purchase insurance from. Brokers should preferably be members of professional insurance associations such as The Insurance Brokers Council (IBC) or The South African Insurance Brokers Association (SAIBA). Members of these institutions are obliged to insure themselves against professional negligence, which, in turn, gives the insured party protection in the case of negligence or misconduct on the part of the broker. These institutions are bound by a strict code of ethics.

4.5.1 Liability

It is possible for hospitality establishment owners to be held liable for the claims made against them by their guests under a delict or public liability. The following are examples of instances in which the establishment can be held liable:

◆ When the food or drink supplied to guests causes them bodily injury or illness. There is an implied condition that the food and beverages supplied on the premises are reasonably fit and safe for human consumption. The establishment can therefore be held liable if the food and beverages supplied do not meet this implied condition.

◆ When accidents cause bodily injury or damage to guests' property, owing to defects on the premises of the hospitality establishment. An example of when the establishment may be sued is if a guest slips on a slippery floor.

◆ For the loss of a guest's property brought into the hospitality establishment.

◆ For any wrongful act committed by an employee, provided that the employee acts in the course and within the scope of his or her employment. The establishment can therefore be held liable for the damage to a guest's clothing should an employee damage a garment while laundering it.

The impact of the cost of insurance premiums can be reduced if a hospitality establishment uses proper disclaimers, which are approved by insurers.

Disclaimers can take various forms, and usually appear in notices at swimming pools and parking areas. It is very important to bring the contents of a disclaimer to the guests' attention. This may be achieved by incorporating properly drafted wording on registration forms, invoices, safe-deposit forms and key cards.

The various types of insurances needed by hospitality establishments are discussed further in chapter 5.

4.5.2 Insurance contracts

Insurance is a contract between an insurance company (the insurer) and a person (the insured) whereby the insurer agrees, in return for the payment of a premium, to pay the insured a sum of money, or its equivalent, on the happening of an uncertain event in which the insured has some interest.

An insurance contract is a contract that exposes the insurer to identified risks of loss from events or circumstances occurring or discovered within a specified period, including death (in the case of an annuity, the survival of the annuitant), sickness, disability, property damage, injury to others and business interruption.

The contract is usually formed when an insured completes a proposal form and submits it to an insurer for consideration. The contract is completed when the insurance company accepts the proposal unconditionally, and this is communicated to the insured.

There must be agreement on all the material terms of the contract. These terms include the person or property to be insured, the risk that is being insured against, the amount payable on the occurrence of the event, the premium to be paid by the insured and the period of cover.

Once the insurer agrees to insure, a document setting out the terms of the contract of insurance is issued by the insurer. This is known as an insurance policy. The proposal form is an extremely important part of the insurance contract as it forms the basis on which the insurer agreed to insure.

4.5.3 The nature and basis of the contract of insurance

The principle of the formation of an estate serves as the basis of the concept of insurance that is manifested in the insurance contract. An insurance contract serves to protect the formation, preservation and development of the insured's estate against risks. In practice, one effects insurance by contributing to a fund to which other persons who are exposed to the same risks, contribute as well. The risks that endanger the formation, preservation and development of the insured's estate are thus distributed amongst a group of people who are equally at risk. The law recognises two types of insurance contracts, namely indemnity insurance and non-indemnity insurance contracts.

4.5.3.1 Indemnity insurance
In indemnity insurance the insurer undertakes to make good the damage that the insured may suffer through the occurrence of the event insured against. Common examples of indemnity insurance are fire, theft and motor vehicle insurance. The insurer is obliged to compensate the insured for the actual loss that has been suffered, provided the insured is adequately covered. In this case, the insured is not compensated for the consequences such as inconvenience and sentimental loss.

4.5.3.2 Non-indemnity insurance
In the case of non-indemnity insurance, the insurer undertakes to pay the insured or the beneficiary a fixed sum of money if the event insured against takes place. Non-indemnity insurance includes life and personal accident insurance.

4.5.4 Essentialia of the insurance contract
The *essentialia* of a contract are those characteristics of a particular contract that distinguish it from other types of contracts. In this regard, it is not easy to identify the *essentialia* of an insurance contract since the courts have as yet given no comprehensive definition. For the present the following will suffice:
- an undertaking by the insured to pay a premium
- an undertaking by the insurer to pay a sum of money or its equivalent
- a particular uncertain future event upon which the insurer's obligation to pay depends (the risk)
- an insurable interest

4.5.4.1 The premium
The insured undertakes to pay a premium. The premium is usually a sum of money. Although the actual payment of the premium is not a requirement for the creation of the contract, payment is usually a condition for the policy to take effect.

4.5.4.2 An undertaking by the insurer to pay a sum of money
In the event of a claim by the insured, the insurer will pay out a sum of money as specified in the contract

4.5.4.3 Determination of the amount payable (non-indemnity insurance)
In the case of non-indemnity insurance, the sum payable will be a predetermined amount. Where, for example, a person insures his or her life for R250 000 (the insured amount), the insurer will have to pay that amount to the estate of the insured or the beneficiary.

4.5.4.4 Determination of the amount payable (indemnity insurance)

In the case of indemnity insurance, the insurer's obligation is to pay a determinable sum of money. The exact amount of the payment is determined after the occurrence of the event insured against, by determining the extent of the damage.

The value of the claim, or the measure of indemnity in respect of the loss of the risk-object is determined, not by its cost, but by its value at the date and place of the loss. The insured must be placed in the same financial position he or she was in – but not a better financial position – before the occurrence of the event insured against. The sentimental value of the object is thus ignored and only the present value of the object is considered, irrespective of whether its value has appreciated or depreciated since the conclusion of the contract.

For example, if an item valued at R200 000 is insured against fire and at the time of its subsequent destruction by fire it is worth R250 000, then the insured's loss, which he or she may recover from the insurer is R250 000. Normally, however, a maximum value of compensation is stipulated in the insurance contract.

Where the object has only been damaged, the insurer will be liable for the amount of the partial loss suffered. The extent of partial loss is usually taken to be the cost of repairing the risk object. Other principles that are applicable to indemnity insurance contracts include:

4.5.4.5 The insurer's right to repair

An insurer often reserves the right in an insurance contract to have the damaged risk-object repaired, instead of compensating the insured.

4.5.4.6 Insuring with several insurers

An insured has the right to insure the same risk-object with as many insurers as he or she wishes. In the event of a loss occurring, the insured may, however, only recover the full amount of the loss and no more.

4.5.4.7 Over- and underinsurance

There is nothing to prevent an insured from insuring for a larger amount than is necessary to secure full compensation in the event of loss of the insured risk-object. In the case of indemnity insurance, however, the insured may recover no more than the total value of the loss.

Where an insured insures for an amount less than the actual value of the insured object, he or she is underinsured. For example, if Helen's car, valued at R200 000, is insured for R150 000, and the car is damaged to the value of R60 000, Helen will be able to recover only R45 000 because, as she insured for only three quarters of the value, she can recover only three quarters of her loss.

4.5.4.8 Excess clauses

In motor vehicle and liability insurance, so-called excess clauses are common. In terms of these clauses the insured must bear a specific proportion of the loss himself or herself, for example the first R100 of the loss.

4.5.5 The risk

The uncertain event insured against is known as the risk. Description of the risk in the contract is important, because the insurer must know precisely the nature of the risk and the insured, the extent of his or her cover. The parties always agree to insure against the occurrence of a specific (or determinable) event. The insurer's obligations are always coupled with some event that must cause the result mentioned in the contract, for example a fire that damages the insured's house.

The description of the risk must include:

◆ the object insured, for example a motor car, or a person's life
◆ the hazard insured against, for example theft
◆ circumstances affecting the risk, for example, limitation of the insurance to theft of a motor car while it is parked in a specific place

It is very important for hospitality service providers to ensure that their policies cover the risks that they wish to insure against. In this regard, exclusion and excess clauses are vitally important as insurers always limit their liability, and an insurer will only accept liability for a loss that falls within the limits of the policy. For example, it is possible for a policy that provides cover for medical expenses not to cover injuries caused in a boating accident at a resort hotel.

4.5.6 Parties to the contract

Apart from the insurer and the insured other parties may also be involved when an insurance contract is concluded. These include, for example, insurance brokers and insurance agents.

An insurance broker is an independent intermediary who mediates insurance contracts between his or her client, the insured, and insurers. Brokers are not tied to any insurer, in the sense that they are compelled to sell the products of one insurer only, but may choose the best insurer depending on their client's needs. An insurance broker is primarily the agent of an insured and is mandated to obtain insurance coverage for him or her.

Insurance agents also mediate insurance contracts but unlike insurance brokers they are primarily agents of the insurer.

4.5.6.1 Insurer

The insurance industry is regulated by the Long-term Insurance Act 52 of 1998, and the Short-term Insurance Act 53 of 1998. This legislation aims at protecting the interests of those who invest in the insurance industry. It stipulates that only companies registered in accordance with the acts are entitled to carry on the business of insurance. In order to obtain such a registration, various require-ments need to be complied with.

4.5.6.2 Insured

It is a basic requirement of a valid insurance contract that the insured must have an insurable interest in the subject matter of the insurance. This is because insurance is about compensation for loss and it is only when a person has an insurable interest that he or she will suffer loss when the risk insured against occurs. If there is no insurance interest, the policy is illegal or unenforceable. In the case of indemnity insurance, the test is whether the insured will suffer financial loss if the event insured against occurs. Usually the person who owns the property is the one who should insure it.

As far as non-indemnity insurance is concerned, an insurable interest is one's own life and the life of one's spouse. In all other cases an insured would have to show that the death, injury or permanent disability of the person who is the subject of the insurance has affected him or her financially.

4.6 Employment contracts

The contract of employment can be defined as follows:

An agreement between two parties, in terms of which one party (the employee or worker) places his or her labour potential at the disposal and under the control of the other party (the employer), in exchange for some form of remuneration.

From this definition, it is clear that the *essentialia* of the contract of employment are work and remuneration. The contract is reciprocal in nature: the employee works in exchange for remuneration from the employer. A distinguishing feature of the employment relationship is the element of subordination and control. The employer generally has the right to control the employee, and the relationship is essentially one of inequality. The employer generally has greater bargaining power, unless the employees increase their power by forming and joining trade unions and bargaining collectively with the employer.

4.6.1 The parties to an employment contract

There must be two parties to a contract of employment – the employer and the employee.

4.6.1.1 The employer

The employer may be a natural person or a juristic person, such as a company or a close corporation.

4.6.1.2 The employee

The other party to the contract, the employee, will always be a natural person.

There are certain statutory limitations on who may be employed. For example, the BCEA provides that no employer shall employ a person under the age of fifteen years.

Before recruiting employees who will be required to work in designated public smoking areas, it would be wise to ensure that exposure to smoke is noted as a condition of service that is unavoidable, and that the contract of employment covers the requirement, and that employment is therefore agreed to on this basis.

4.6.2 The duration of an employment contract

It is up to the parties to the employment relationship to agree on the nature of their relationship and the duration of that relationship. In this regard, it is possible to distinguish between indefinite employment contracts and fixed-term employment contracts. Many employees are appointed on an indefinite (permanent) basis – in this case, termination of the employment contract is subject to the rules discussed below. Sometimes, employees are appointed for either a specific period or to perform a specific task. In these cases, the contract of employment terminates automatically on completion of the task or expiry of the period.

4.6.3 The content of an employment contract

Typically, an employment contract will provide for a number of issues. This includes:

- the job description of the employee
- the hours of work (including possible overtime work, work on Sundays and work on public holidays)
- the remuneration, and how and when it will be paid
- the amount of leave (vacation, sick, maternity and family responsibility leave) the employee will be entitled to
- whether the employer will pay for relocation expenses (if any)
- restraint of trade
- the duties of the employee in relation to the employer and the like

For the most part, employment contracts are rather brief – the parties simply include all the existing policies of the employer by reference into their contract. It is important to bear in mind that although parties, as a general rule, can decide what to put in the contract, they are not entirely free to do so. This is because of two principles. First, certain principles of the common law are automatically part of the contract, unless specifically excluded. Secondly, legislation dictates and limits the freedom of the parties not only to decide on what rights and duties will be part of their contract (an employer, for example, has to give female employees maternity leave), but also what the level of certain rights in the contract should be (an employer has to give female employees four months' maternity leave).

4.6.4 The duties of an employer

4.6.4.1 The payment of remuneration

Generally speaking, there is nothing in any law that lays down how much an employee is to be paid. However, collective agreements and sectoral determinations (in terms of the BCEA) may establish minimum standards in this regard, and the parties will then be bound by contract to pay the minimum wage or may agree to pay more.

- *The 'no work, no pay' rule*: In terms of the common law, the general rule is 'no work, no pay'. If the worker has not performed in terms of the contract, the employer does not have to pay the employee. Consequently, the common law does not make provision for any form of paid leave.
- *Unjust enrichment*: If an employee has worked for part of a month and terminates the contract, the employer must generally pay for the services already rendered, based on the principle that one person may not be unjustly enriched at the expense of another. This principle does not apply if the employee has deserted the employer.

◆ *The payment of the remuneration*: Wages or salary are normally paid in cash, but may be paid in kind, by providing the employee with a benefit such as accommodation.

4.6.4.2 To receive the employee into service

The employer must honour the contractual obligation to enter into the employment relationship with the employee: failure to do this will constitute a breach of contract.

The employer does not have a general duty to provide the employee with work, as long as the employee is paid in terms of the contract. Exceptions to this rule include the situation where the employee is paid on commission, and this commission depends on the provision of work, or where an apprentice requires work in order to develop skills.

4.6.4.3 To provide safe working conditions

The employer has a common-law duty to provide the employee with safe working conditions, safe machinery and safe tools. The Occupational Health and Safety Act also places further responsibility on the employer in this regard.

4.6.4.4 Not to victimise the employee

The LRA, the BCEA, the EEA and the Occupational Health and Safety Act 85 of 1993 all contain provisions outlawing victimisation by an employer of an employee for exercising a constitutional or statutory right, such as that of freedom of association, or the right to strike.

4.6.4.5 Vicarious liability

As discussed in Law of Delict, it is important to mention that, in terms of the common law, an employer can be held liable by a third party for the unlawful or delictual acts performed by its employees during the course and scope of their duties.

There are, however, various prerequisites for vicarious liability:
◆ *A contract of employment*: There must be a contract of employment between the employer and the employee at the time of the act or omission.
◆ *Unlawful conduct*: The employee must, by the act or conduct, have committed an   unlawful act. The act or omission must comply with the requirements of delict, which are discussed in chapter 3.
◆ *Employee acted in the course or scope of employment*: The employee must have acted in the course or scope of his or her duties, not merely on the business of the employer. But if the employer is vicariously liable and the employee has been negligent, for example, the employer may have a right of recourse against the employee.

4.6.5 The duties of an employee

Although the employee has freedom to contract, the provisions of the common law play a significant role in setting out his or her duties.

4.6.5.1 To enter into the service of the employer

The primary duty of an employee is to actually place his or her labour potential at the disposal of the employer. In terms of the 'no work, no pay' rule, if the employee does not work, there is generally no entitlement to remuneration.

4.6.5.2 To work competently and without negligence

The employee implicitly guarantees that he or she is capable of doing the work for which he or she contracted. There is a further duty to exercise due care and diligence. A failure to perform the work competently, and without negligence, will result in a breach of contract and a possible termination of the employment relationship.

4.6.5.3 To obey all reasonable and lawful commands

The employee, as stated above, is under the control and authority of the employer. The employee, therefore, has an implied duty to obey all reasonable and lawful commands of the employer. Serious insubordination may amount to a breach of contract. The interpretation of 'reasonable command' will depend on the circumstances of each individual case.

4.6.5.4 To act in good faith

The common-law duty to act in good faith is implied in every contract of employment: it exists even if it is not an express term of the contract of employment.

- *Confidential information:* The unauthorised use or divulging of confidential information amounts to a breach of good faith, if it occurs during or even after the period of employment has terminated. An employee is entitled to use general knowledge acquired during employment, but not knowledge that is confidential in nature. The distinction between the two may not always be easy to make.
- *The employee must promote the business of the employer:* The employee must devote his or her hours of work to furthering the employer's business. The employee may not, therefore, work for another employer if there is a conflict of interest with the original employer.
- *The employee may not compete with the employer:* For example, by providing the same product or service in their own time for their own profit.
- *The employee must act honestly:* Any dishonest behaviour, on the part of the employee, such as theft, fraud or the procurement of secret commissions (kickbacks), will be a breach of good faith. If the breach is serious, the employer may dismiss the employee summarily.

4.6.5.5 Restraint of trade

Clauses in restraint of trade are not allowed under the Competition Act and therefore may not be included in any contract.

4.6.6 Termination of the contract of employment

Some of the most common ways in which a contract of employment may be terminated lawfully are briefly discussed below:

4.6.6.1 Termination on completion of the agreed period or task

A contract of employment is often concluded for an indefinite period and may be terminated lawfully by giving the required notice. Sometimes, a contract of employment, called a 'fixed-term contract' is for a specified period or for a certain project. The contract of employment will usually state expressly that a contract is for a fixed term, but in some cases this may be implied. Normally, the fixed-term contract expires automatically and no notice need be given to effect its termination. The contract may, however, be expressly or impliedly renewed.

4.6.6.2 Termination by mutual agreement of the parties

The parties to the contract must have consensus prior to the contract coming into existence, and the agreement of the parties can also terminate the contract. The agreement must, however, be mutual and it must be freely given.

4.6.6.3 Termination by notice

A contract of service for an indefinite period may be terminated by one party giving the other notice of intention to terminate the contract. The period of notice usually is stipulated in the contract. Note that the BCEA sets out statutory minimum notice periods. If the contract does not specify the notice period, the period of notice will be that provided for by the BCEA.

4.6.6.4 Termination on grounds of impossibility of performance

If one of the parties is no longer able to perform in terms of the contract, for a period that is considered to be unreasonable, the other party is entitled to terminate the contract in terms of the common law, unless the impossibility is caused by a party to the contract. If the impossibility is temporary, the performance does not fall away altogether but is merely suspended. An example of supervening impossibility is the death of the employee. The employee is no longer able to perform in terms of the contract, and the contract is automatically terminated.

4.6.6.5 Termination on insolvency

Although not in terms of the common law, it is important to note that the Insolvency Act 24 of 1936 provides that the contract of employment of all employees will terminate automatically on the sequestration or liquidation of the employer. The employees will be entitled to claim unpaid wages, leave pay and bonuses from the insolvent estate. The insolvency of the employee, on the other hand, does not generally affect the employment contract.

4.6.6.6 Termination as a result of breach of contract

As already discussed in chapter 2, if a party to a contract fails to carry out the obligations in terms of the contract, he or she is guilty of breach of contract and the relevant remedies apply.

4.7 Franchises

Franchises are a popular business form in the hospitality industry, especially in the restaurant and fast food sector. The term 'franchise' refers to a situation where a person who has developed a complete (and successful) business package grants another person the right to use that package in exchange for the payment of royalties. The person who grants the right to use their business package is the *franchisor*, and the person who pays for it is the *franchisee*.

When deciding on a franchise, the franchisee has to accept that he or she will have to run the business according to the franchisor's business plan. The franchisee uses the franchisor's marketing system to attract and keep customers. The franchisee receives the right to use the franchisor's trademark, logo, trade name and advertising. Franchising allows a number of people to use the same brand identification and a successful method of doing business with approved marketing and distribution systems.

Under the franchise agreement the franchisor grants the right to sell the product in a particular territory. If the premises are a fast-food outlet, the territory is delimited by limiting or excluding other outlets within a certain distance of those premises.

4.7.1 Advantages

The franchisee gains the following advantages from a franchise:

◆ The franchisor provides training and ongoing support so that the franchisee does not normally need previous experience.
◆ All the information and training that is needed for setting up and running the franchise is provided by the franchisor.
◆ The franchisee receives a complete operating manual on how to manage the business.
◆ The business format has been tried and tested. Teething problems normally encountered in starting a business have been overcome and, as a result, a franchise is usually up and running faster than a completely new business.
◆ It is a proven way of doing business, although it is not a guarantee of success.
◆ Because of the scale of the business, the franchisor has considerable negotiating power with suppliers. The benefits of these cost savings can be passed on to the franchisee.
◆ The franchisee develops a customer base faster.
◆ The franchisor usually undertakes continued product development and research, which is made available to the franchisee.
◆ Franchising provides the franchisor a continuous supply of income through royalties paid by the franchisee.

4.7.2 Disadvantages

◆ An initial fee is payable to the franchisor, as well as a percentage of the annual profits.
◆ The franchisor controls and therefore limits the scope of the franchise and the methods of business operated.
◆ The franchisor may supply certain branded products to the franchisee, which limits the scope of the franchisee to find more competitive suppliers.
◆ The sale of the franchise may not always be easy.

4.7.3 Franchise agreements

Franchisors are obliged by the code of ethics and business practice for franchises, to provide all prospective franchisees with a disclosure document and a copy of the franchise agreement. When a franchisee signs a franchise agreement, there is a seven-day cooling-off period during which the franchisee cannot be required to pay any money or sign any binding document. The potential franchisee is given the opportunity to make a decision about the franchise and may decide not to go ahead with the agreement without being in breach of contract.

The franchisor must assist in determining where the business will be located when the franchise agreement has been entered into. The franchisor must provide advice on the design and décor of the premises, such as the shopfitting, signwriting, furnishings and other specific requirements of the franchise.

Advertising is a major cost in any business; with a franchise the franchisee hopes to capitalise on the franchisor's resources to raise the profile of the franchise and the product it sells. The media coverage available to a large franchise operation is vastly different from that available to a small restaurant or hotel. It is normal for the franchisor to charge the franchisee an advertising levy for promoting the product and the brand of the franchise.

A franchise comes into being through a contract of franchise between the franchisor and the franchisee. The franchise agreement contains clauses covering the following aspects of the business:

◆ The business name and the use to which the name can be put.
◆ The territory within which the franchisee can operate.
◆ The period of time for which the franchise is granted.
◆ The initial fee to be paid by the franchisee for the franchise, the service fee and the advertising levy.
◆ The limitations on the scope of the business, including the franchisee's right to sell or transfer the franchise.
◆ Terms that put the agreement into effect, including sales targets, the purchase of supplies from the franchisor, quality control, training and franchise support, and management and advisory services.

Although the contracts of the various franchise networks may differ, many of them have certain terms in common. On the whole, franchise contracts are standard-form contracts that leave little room for negotiation. The reason for this is that successful franchise networks require internal uniformity and the maintenance of set standards. The franchise contract is thus used as a tool to enforce uniformity and the maintenance of standards within the franchise network. It places obligations on both parties to their mutual advantage.

4.7.4 The duties of the franchisor

The franchisee needs to be successfully assimilated into the franchise network. The franchisor is, therefore, not only obliged to disclose the business system to the franchisee and to make available the intellectual property licensed to the franchisee in terms of the franchise agreement, but also to advise the franchisee on matters relating to the establishment of the franchised business, such as a suitable building, the design and decor of the premises, shopfittings, electrical wiring, signwriting, sources of supply for equipment and furnishings, and other requirements specifically related to the particular franchise.

The franchisor usually provides the franchisee with training. The franchisor determines, in consultation with the franchisee, which of the franchisee's employees will undergo training in the business system. The franchisor must provide or supply the franchisee with the same services and facilities that the franchisor supplies or provides to its other franchisees.

The franchise contract obliges the franchisor to provide continuous support services after the conclusion of the contract. These services include marketing, development of the business system to adapt to the changing demands of commerce, and advice and training. The franchisor is also obliged to disclose all improvements and developments in the business system to the franchisee and, as a result, to provide further training to the franchisee.

4.7.5 The duties of the franchisee
The franchisee is obliged to conduct the business strictly according to the operations manual. The franchisee also undertakes to meet any requirements that the franchisor may issue from time to time. These may be, for example, special offers, changes to a standard menu, or special attractions and events.

The franchisee and/or his or her employees are obliged to undergo training by the franchisor in the business system. The franchisee may not induce employees of fellow franchisees to leave their employment and take up employment with the first mentioned. It is not in the interest of the development of a franchise network to allow franchisees to lure trained employees away from fellow franchisees.

The franchised business is usually conducted from premises that were approved by the franchisor. The premises must be maintained in a good and clean condition. The franchisor may require the franchisee to redecorate or refurbish the premises to ensure that the premises are in the same condition as those of other franchisees. Also, the franchisee is required to observe minimum business hours.

The franchisee is not allowed to advertise or conduct promotional marketing activities without the prior written approval of the franchisor, but is obliged to use and display the franchisor's point-of-sale, advertising, or promotional material.

The franchisee is also obliged to allow the franchisor at all reasonable times to carry out such inspections or investigations that may be considered necessary for the purposes of ascertaining whether the provisions of the agreement between them are complied with. The franchisee must ensure that he or she and all employees co-operate fully in such inspections.

4.7.6 The protection of the franchisor's intellectual property
A franchisee obtains a right or licence to use the intellectual property of the franchisor but does not become its owner. The franchisee may not do, cause, or permit anything that may adversely affect the franchisor's rights to the intellectual property.

The franchisee not only obtains the right to use the franchisor's trademarks but also is obliged to do so. The franchisee does not, however, become the owner of the trademarks. The use of a well-known and distinctive trademark obviously benefits the franchisee. To maintain the distinctiveness of the trademark, the franchisee is obliged, when using the trademark, to reproduce it exactly and accurately and in accordance with specifications and directions laid down by the franchisor from time to time.

The franchisee may not divulge, or allow to be divulged, to any person any aspect of the business system, the know-how, or the trade secrets other than for the purposes of the franchise agreement. In this regard, the franchisee and his or her employees may be required to sign a confidentiality undertaking.

The franchisee undertakes to protect and promote the goodwill associated with the   franchised business. All goodwill generated by the conduct of the franchised business will endure for the benefit of the franchisor.

4.7.7 Restraints of trade

The Competition Act 89 of 1998 prohibits any restraints of trade and promotes a free market and competitive economy. Therefore, by law, a franchisor may not place restraints of trade on its franchisees. This includes any restraints of exclusive territories, products or sales, suppliers, prices and so on.

A franchisor may *recommend* certain suppliers, prices or products to the franchisee. It is usually in the best interests of the franchisee to follow these recommendations as it promotes uniformity of the franchise product and is ultimately in the best interests of the brand and his or her own business.

If you are setting up your own franchise, you are not allowed to include any restraint clauses in your franchise agreements. It is recommended that you seek professional advice from the Franchise Association of South Africa (FASA) or a specialist company such as Franchising Plus to assist with the legal conditions of such contracts.

If on the other hand you are considering buying into a franchise as a franchisee, be aware that the franchisor may not include any restraints on you in the franchise agreement.

4.7.8 Payment obligations

The franchisee usually pays the franchisor an initial lump sum once the contract has been finalised. Thereafter, royalties are paid throughout the period of the contract. The royalties may be fixed amounts that are payable periodically or may be calculated as a percentage of turnover or sales within a set period of time – such as a month, quarter or year.

The lump-sum payment is usually an initial payment for the rights granted in terms of the agreement and for the equipment, advice, assistance, and training provided by the franchisor to enable the franchisee to establish the business.

In addition to the royalties, the franchise agreement may also provide for additional levies related to specific services by the franchisor. The franchisee may, for example, be obliged to pay the franchisor an amount for marketing or advertising campaigns, which are also calculated as a percentage of the net sales.

4.7.9 Termination of the agreement

Franchise agreements may provide for the termination of the contract after a fixed period or on the death, insolvency, or incapacity of the franchisee.

The contract may also provide that on the death of the franchisee, the franchisor may approve the transfer of the franchised business to any of the beneficiaries of the deceased franchisee, who will be required to sign a new contract with the franchisor.

Upon termination of the agreement, the franchisee must immediately cease any further use of the trademarks and other intellectual property that was licensed to him or her. The franchisee must, therefore, hand over all dies, blocks, labels, advertising material, and printed matter featuring the trademarks that were obtained from, or which he or she was authorised to use, to the franchisor.

Franchise contracts often oblige franchisees upon termination of the contract not to participate directly or indirectly in the management or control of a similar business to the franchised business for a certain period of time. The former franchisee is also obliged not to disclose confidential information or other trade secrets of the franchisor.

Questions and exercises

1. Under what circumstances, and for what purposes, would a hospitality establishment enter into lease contracts?
2. Write an article for a hospitality magazine explaining the need for, and types of, insurance available to the hospitality industry.
3. Discuss the benefits and disadvantages of restraint of trade agreements.
4. Draw a flowchart that will enable a franchisee to understand the process of applying for a franchise, from initial contact with the franchisor, to opening and operating the establishment.

Section 2

Business and Hospitality Laws

5

Forms of business

Objectives of this chapter:

By the end of this chapter the learner will be able to:
- Choose the most appropriate form of business for a new enterprise
- Compare the different types of business enterprise and evaluate these according to his or her business needs

The learner will know:
- The minimum legal requirements of various forms of business entities for registration, membership, filing and disclosure
- The advantages and disadvantages of various business entities that may be chosen as the form of business for an enterprise
- Statutory auditing requirements for companies

5.1 Introduction

This chapter introduces the various options from which an entrepreneur can choose when establishing a business. When starting a business it is very important to consider the type of entity that one wants to utilise for the business because every entity has different legal requirements and implications. The Companies Act 61 of 1973 and the Close Corporations Act 69 of 1984 are the two most important acts that govern business entities. They affect their formation and accounting practices, and have numerous other implications for the owners of businesses.

There are many important factors that need to be taken into account when choosing a suitable form of business. However, as a result of the finer details, the various forms of business, the related legal requirements and the particular procedures applicable to each form of business, it is not possible to cover the topic comprehensively in this book. It is recommended that an accountant, auditor or attorney is approached when decisions are taken as to what form the business should take.

5.2 Forms of enterprise for a business

Entrepreneurs can choose from four forms of enterprise:
- sole proprietorship
- partnership

- close corporation
- company

Figure 5-1: Comparison of different business structures

	Sole proprietor	Partnership	Close corporation	Companies
Number of Members or Shareholders and Directors	One – the owner.	Two to 20 partners.	One to 10 members. Does not need separate board of directors	One to 50 shareholders.Minimum one for private company, seven for public company Minimum one director for private company, two for public company
Capital contributions	Limited to the contribution of the owner.	Limited to the contribution of the separate partners.	Limited to the contribution of the members.	Limited to the contribution of the founders.
Formation	Simple. No formal requirements.	Simple. Partnership agreement recommended.	A founding statement should be registered and a certificate of incorporation issued.	Memorandum and articles of association are registered and certificate of incorporation is issued.
Legal personality	The business is not a separate legal entity.	The business is not a separate legal entity.	The business is a separate legal entity.	The business is a separate legal entity.
Liability	Unlimited.	Unlimited.	Limited.	Limited.
Distribution of profits	The profits belong to the owner.	Partnership agreement stipulates the distribution of profits.	Resolution should be passed approving distribution or it should have been validated by the association agreement.	Shareholders become entitled to a share of the net profit when dividends are declared.

	Sole proprietor	Partnership	Close corporation	Companies
Taxpayer	The business is not a separate taxpayer. The owner includes income from the business in his or her own gross income.	The business is not a separate taxpayer. Partners include profit share from the business in their own gross income.	The business is a separate taxpayer.	The business is separate taxpayer.
Tax losses	Losses from the business can be offset against any other income.	Each partner's share of losses from the business can be offset against his or her other income.	Losses retained within the close corporation cannot be offset against members' other income.	Losses retained within the company cannot be offset against shareholders' other income.
Audit	Not required by law.	Not required by law.	Not required by law. The appointed accounting officer performs an accounting review.	An independent audit of the financial statements by a registered auditor is required by law.

Adapted: Source Adv M Moolman

Factors to be considered when choosing a suitable form of enterprise include the following:

◆ Whether you need to involve third parties from a financial point of view. How great are the financial needs of the company? If they are high, then investors may well be required.
◆ Legal requirements in respect of establishing the enterprise and complying with regulations.
◆ The ability of the enterprise to exist independently of its owners. How long is the organisation expected to last?
◆ The liability of the owners of the enterprise for debts and their share of the profits. In some cases, the owner's assets are at risk if the enterprise should fail.
◆ The continuity of the enterprise, including the extent of direct control.
◆ The tax position of the various forms of enterprise and how this will affect the owners.

5.3 Registration of business entities

In addition to meeting the registration requirements of the Companies Act (and/or the Close Corporations Act, where applicable) a business generally has to register with the authorities that regulate value added tax (VAT), employees' tax, workmen's compensation and the unemployment insurance fund. Companies and individuals must also register for income tax purposes. Business licences are required for certain activities and are generally easily obtainable from the licensing authorities, subject to compliance with the relevant requirements.

5.4 Formation procedures for businesses

Different business entities have different statutory requirements regulating their formation and registration. All South African companies are governed by the Companies Act, which was originally based on English Company Law. The Act prescribes the procedures to be followed to form a private or public company. The Companies Act is administered by the Company's Registration Office which forms part of Companies and Intellectual Property Registration Office of South Africa (CIPRO), based in Pretoria.

All South African Close Corporations are governed by the Close Corporations Act. There are no formal procedures relating to the formation of partnerships and sole proprietorships.

5.5 Sole proprietorship

A sole proprietorship is an enterprise that belongs to only one person and has no partners or co-owners. The owner can appoint people to work for him or her. He or she provides the capital, takes all the decisions alone, manages the enterprise and accepts all the responsibility for profits and debts. The lifetime of the enterprise is linked to that of the owner and there is no difference between private and business property.

All loans taken out and debts incurred for this type of business are in the owner's name, so the owner stands to lose everything, including his or her private estate if the business fails.

There are no formal requirements for the establishment and auditing of a sole proprietorship but you may be required to register for all or some of the following:
- Provisional Tax
- Employees Tax
- Income Tax
- Value Added Tax
- Trading licences
- Unemployment Insurance Fund
- Workman's Compensation Insurance

5.5.1 Advantages of sole proprietorships
- From a legal point of view, it is easy to start and to close down a sole proprietorship.
- All income belongs to the owner.
- The functioning of the enterprise is simple and can easily be adapted to changing circumstances.

5.5.2 Disadvantages of sole proprietorships
- The creditworthiness of the enterprise is limited to the assets of the owner.

- The owner is fully responsible for losses, and can lose his or her private possessions if the enterprise should fail.
- There is uncertainty regarding the continued existence of the business if the owner dies.
- If it is sold or taken over the enterprise will no longer exist. It must legally be re-founded from scratch.
- The future of the enterprise is limited not only in terms of its establishment, but also in terms of expansion. A sole proprietorship can develop to a level where it exceeds the owner's capital means. If more capital is to be secured, it could mean changing the form of the enterprise in order to raise the additional funding.

5.6 Partnership

A partnership is formed when two or more people conclude an agreement in order to conduct a business by combining their capital, labour, know-how and experience contractually with the aim of making a profit.

This agreement or contract, which should preferably be drawn up by an attorney, will contain the names of the partners, the name and nature of the enterprise, the contributions (financial or otherwise) of the partners, remuneration of the partners, division of profits and other aspects. Partners must therefore be chosen carefully and the partnership agreement must be drawn up very carefully.

The Companies Act limits the membership in a partnership to 20 persons, who (except for partnerships of certain recognised professions, including accountants and attorneys) may be either natural or juristic persons.

No other statutory provisions (such as auditing requirements) govern the partnership but they are subject to the general principles of the law of contract, and to various special principles of common law applicable particularly to partnerships. They are not separate legal entities and no registration formalities exist.

All partners are required to include all income from the partnership in their personal tax returns and the partnership may also be required to register for some if not all of the following:
- Provisional Tax
- Employees Tax
- Income Tax
- Value Added Tax
- Trading licences
- Unemployment Insurance Fund
- Workman's Compensation Insurance

5.6.1 Advantages of partnerships
- The management techniques, judgement and special characteristics and expertise of a number of people are pooled.
- Opportunities for obtaining capital are usually favourable and each partner can contribute to the capital of the enterprise.
- The legal requirements, such as a partnership agreement, can easily be dealt with.

- In a partnership, the partners are taxed in their personal capacity and not collectively. The profit is shared and each partner's share is taxed separately.

5.6.2 Disadvantages of partnerships

- It is not always easy to find suitable and trustworthy partners with appropriate expertise and funding capabilities.
- Partners are jointly liable for the debts that other partners may incur on behalf of the partnership.
- Each partner is both a principal and an agent of the enterprise and can commit the partners by his or her actions, for example by incurring debts.
- The partnership is dissolved by any change in its composition, and the life expectancy of a partnership is therefore uncertain.
- It is sometimes difficult for a partner to withdraw from an agreement should he or she wish to do so or if there happens to be a fall-out between the partners.

5.7 Close corporation

Since the Close Corporations Act 69 of 1984 was promulgated in June 1984, the Close Corporation (CC) has become a popular form of business entity. It has a more simplified and flexible business format than a company, but still provides a corporate status and a legal identity distinct from its members.

The managerial and administrative requirements for Close Corporations are less formal than for companies. In contrast to a company, the CC Act has been designed so that the ordinary person would be able to draft the papers and register the corporation by her/himself.

A close corporation is formed by filing a founding statement with the Close Corporation Registration Office which forms part of CIPRO. Private companies with qualifying members can be converted into close corporations and close corporations may be converted into private companies. A close corporation indicates its status by the letters 'CC' or the words 'Close Corporation' at the end of its name and the word 'company' may not appear in the name. The close corporation's name, registration number and the names of the members must appear on all business documents.

A close corporation does not have shareholders, only members who all have an interest in the enterprise. This interest is expressed as a percentage of all the interests in the corporation. The total interest must be 100% at all times. Instead of share capital, close corporations therefore have members' interests, the distribution of which is arrived at by agreement with the other members.

At the time of founding the close corporation, each member must make a contribution either in the form of money, movable or fixed assets, or provision of services.

The extent of a member's interest does not have to be in proportion to that member's contribution. Unless otherwise agreed in an association agreement between the members, a sale of a member's interest requires the consent of the other members, failing which the member can sell his or her interest back to the corporation.

Close corporations may give financial assistance for the acquisition of members' interests and may themselves acquire members' interests from any member. However, if the close corporation does not remain both solvent and liquid immediately after giving that assistance or acquiring that interest, the members will have personal liability to creditors prejudiced as a result.

A close corporation may be formed by at least one but not more than 10 members. The only persons qualified to become members are:

Natural persons, including non-residents. A juristic person such as a company may not directly or indirectly hold an interest in a close corporation.
- A trustee of a testamentary trust. A trustee of an *inter vivos* trust (a trust created by contract) is specifically excluded from membership.
- A trustee, administrator, executor or curator for a member who is insolvent, deceased, mentally disordered or otherwise incapable of managing his or her affairs.

Natural persons may not hold members' interests as nominees for persons who are disqualified from being members. Companies, partnerships, societies and clubs are therefore excluded. Close corporations are managed by their members. There is no separate board of directors or management body, and each member is entitled to participate in the management, unless the members agree to the contrary.

Each member stands in a fiduciary relationship to the corporation, and may become liable to the corporation for losses suffered as a result of breach of fiduciary duties. The members may enter into an association agreement to govern their relationship. However, if no such agreement is concluded, the Close Corporations Act contains provisions regulating the relationship of members.

The close corporation is largely self-regulating. Relatively few provisions of the Close Corporations Act are linked to criminal sanctions. However members may lose their limited liability status by transgressing certain provisions of the Act.

5.7.1 Advantages of close corporations
- The law is simple and easy to comply with.
- The close corporation has a simple management and decision-making structure. Most decisions are taken informally by the members.
- All members are part of the management, and have a direct interest in the success of the enterprise.
- The close corporation has a legal personality (it can act in its own name) with all the benefits this involves. This gives the enterprise continuity.
- The proprietor or member is not personally liable for the debts of a CC.
- CCs may become shareholders in other companies.
- The members are not taxed personally for the dividends they receive.
- An auditor does not have to be appointed, only an accounting officer.
- No annual returns are currently required.
- Annual general meetings are not mandatory.
- Any addendum to the original founding document can be added simply by registering the addendum.

5.7.2 Disadvantages of close corporations

◆ The fact that a close corporation may have only 10 members can have a restricting effect on the enterprise if it wishes to expand. It could eventually require that the close corporation to be converted to a company.
◆ Because members have limited liability for debts, it can make it difficult for the close corporation to raise funds or to obtain credit.
◆ If a member wishes to sell his interest, all the other members of the corporation must give their consent.

5.7.3 Registration of close corporations

Registration of a close corporation (CC) is a relatively simple and quick process. However an application for the reservation of the name of the CC must be made first. Information on how to reserve the name can be found in chapter 6. The only constitutional document required is a founding statement, which must be filed with the Close Corporation Registration Office which forms part of the CIPRO of South Africa. Registration takes about four to six weeks and costs around R200 to R300.

A private company that meets the requirements of a close corporation may convert to a close corporation, and a close corporation may convert to a private company.

5.7.4 Statutory auditing requirements for close corporations

For a CC, the requirements relating to the maintenance of accounting records are similar to those of a company. A CC's annual financial statements must be drafted within nine months after its year-end. The annual financial statements must be approved and signed by, or on behalf of, members holding at least 51% of the members' interest in the CC and must consist of:

◆ a balance sheet and notes
◆ an income statement or any similar financial statement (if such alternative is appropriate)
◆ a members' net investment statement

The financial statements must fairly present the state of affairs, and the result of the operations of the CC, in conformity with Generally Accepted Accounting Practice (GAAP) as appropriate to the business of the CC.

Close corporations are not subject to a compulsory audit. However, the corporation is required to appoint an independent accounting officer, who is responsible for the preparation of the financial statements, and who must be a member of one of the recognised professional accounting bodies.

Under the Close Corporations Act, a close corporation's accounting officer is required to ensure that the annual financial statements accord with the books and records of the corporation.

The disclosure requirements for a close corporation are subject to the overriding requirement of fair presentation. The complexity of the financial statements would depend on the needs of the members, who, as owners and managers of the corporation, are the primary recipients of the financial information.

5.8 Company

The company is a legal person in its own right. In other words, it has a 'life' independent of the shareholders. There are various kinds of companies, such as the private company, the public company and the company limited by guarantee (such a company does not issue shares and is not profit-orientated). A private company is the most suitable form of company for a small business.

The Companies Act 61 of 1973 makes provision for two types of companies, namely:

- A company having share capital, which can be either a public company or a private company.
- A company that has no share capital (this company is also referred to as a company limited by guarantee).

5.8.1 Limited liability company

The most common form of business entity in South Africa is the limited liability company. Companies can be limited by guarantee or limited by shares. Companies limited by guarantee are generally 'not-for-profit' organisations that primarily promote religious, charitable, educational or other similar interests.

The names of companies limited by guarantee must end with the words 'Limited (Limited by Guarantee)'. Companies having share capital may be public or private companies. The names of public companies must end with the word 'Limited', whereas those of private companies must end with the words '(Proprietary) Limited'.

A private company is one which by its articles:

- restricts the right to transfer its shares
- limits the number of its members (other than employees of the company) to 50
- prohibits any offer for the subscription of any shares or debentures to the public

All other companies are public companies and, as such, are not subject to the above restrictions. A public company may be listed or unlisted. Listed companies are subject to the rules and regulations laid down by the Johannesburg Securities Exchange of South Africa (JSE).

For a private company, the minimum number of shareholders and directors is one, while a public company must have at least seven shareholders (unless it is a wholly-owned subsidiary of another company) and two directors. Directors need not own shares in the company, and need not be resident in South Africa but a South African resident must be appointed as a public officer of the company to handle income tax matters. The company secretary of a public company must be a South African resident. The board of directors is responsible for the daily management of the company for the benefit of its shareholders, and acts for the company in transactions entered into by it. The shareholders exercise their powers in general meetings. The annual general meeting must be held within nine months of the financial year-end and not more than 15 months after the last such meeting. Shareholders may be individuals or corporate bodies, and any or all of the company's shares may be held by non-residents.

Shares can be in any denomination, and no-par value shares are permitted. There is no minimum amount of share capital required (other than the requirement that on subscription each subscriber must subscribe for at least one share), nor is there any prescribed ratio between share capital and borrowings.

Since par value, more or less means the price to be paid for the shares when purchased from the corporation, no-par value stock is stock for which no fixed price is set. This is usually the case in small corporations where the owners issue themselves a number of shares, and simply infuse money into the corporation when needed.

A private company, with a maximum of 50 shareholders, must be registered with the Registrar of Companies and is identified by the word '(Proprietary) Limited' after its name. The company may commence operations only after registration with the Registrar of Companies to which an annual levy is payable.

A private company is required by law to prepare audited financial statements annually. Appointing a chartered accountant is, therefore, mandatory. The company may be established by either an attorney or a chartered accountant. All prescriptions relating to authority, liability, management, the sale of shares, remuneration or dividends, are indicated in the Memorandum and Articles of Association. The chartered accountant or attorney assists by ensuring that annual tax returns and so on are submitted. Directors can be prosecuted if legal requirements are not strictly met.

The principle that a company is a separate entity, and exists separately from its shareholders, applies to both private and public companies. A company can enter into contracts and can sue or be sued in its own name. A shareholder's liability for the debts of the company is limited to the amount of capital invested in shares. Partly paid shares are not permitted. A director may be required to indemnify the company and/or its shareholders against losses suffered by them in the following circumstances, among others:

◆ unauthorised loans to directors or companies controlled by directors
◆ breach of trust or faith, or wrongs committed, by the director
◆ reckless trading or fraud
◆ untrue statements contained in a prospectus
◆ failure to repay monies received in respect of a share offer within a specified period.

Private companies may not offer shares to the public. 'The public' is widely construed. Offers of shares to the public by public companies are controlled by statutory restrictions.

Prior to the Companies Amendment Act 37 of 1999, a company was not entitled to provide any financial assistance to any person (other than an employee) in connection with the purchase of, or subscription for, its shares – and a company could not purchase its own shares. The amendment allows a company to reduce its capital by acquiring its own shares.

A subsidiary company is entitled to acquire shares and be a shareholder in its holding company to a maximum of 10% of the issued share capital of the holding company. Such acquisition is, however, subject to liquidity and solvency provisions protecting the creditors of the companies.

5.8.1.1 Advantages of companies
- The company is a legal person on its own and therefore exists independently of its shareholders. In this way, some of the disadvantages of a sole proprietorship and a partnership are overcome.
- Its shareholders have a limited liability for the debts that it incurs.
- Shares, and therefore ownership, can be transferred.
- The private company is free of many of the formalities required of a public company.
- The company and its members are taxed separately.

5.8.1.2 Disadvantages of companies
- Various extra costs must be met – such as the founding costs, annual subscriptions, and the cost of issuing shares.
- There are extensive prescriptions for establishing and managing the company.
- The company's business is, as a result of the compulsory publication of its statements, constitution, and so on, known to everyone, including its competitors.

5.8.2 External company and branch operations
Instead of operating through a South African subsidiary, a foreign company may operate through a branch in South Africa. A company incorporated outside South Africa that establishes a place of business in South Africa is classified as an 'external company'. The definition of an external company has been amended to deem a foreign company, which acquires immovable property in South Africa, to have established a place of business in South Africa. An external company is obliged to register with the Registrar of Companies and must comply with the provisions of the Companies Act, including the submission of statutory returns and the filing of annual financial statements for its entire operations (and not only its South African operations) with the Registrar of Companies, where they are open to public scrutiny.

Exemption from the obligation to file those accounts can be applied for, and is fairly readily granted.

The external company is required to appoint a South African resident who is authorised to accept notices served on the company. Once registered, the external company will effectively be treated under South African law like a South African incorporated company; for example, it may be sued in South Africa.

5.8.3 Unlimited liability companies
Members of certain organised professions, such as attorneys, medical practitioners and accountants, are allowed to incorporate. Their companies are private companies but do not confer limited liability on the members, who are jointly and severally liable for the debts of the company. These companies are

identified by the word "Incorporated" at the end of their names instead of '(Proprietary) Limited'.

5.8.4 Registration of companies

Incorporation of a company entails the following steps:
* reserving a company name
* filing the memorandum and articles
* filing the written consent of auditors to act for the company

A company name must be reserved with, and approved by, CIPRO. It is advisable to suggest alternative names in case the first name is deemed unsuitable by the Registrar.

The memorandum and articles must also be filed with the Registrar of Companies, and then completed in the form prescribed in the Companies Act. Both documents have to be signed by each subscriber to the memorandum. The persons signing the memorandum and the articles must state their full name, occupation and residential, business and postal addresses.

5.8.4.1 The memorandum

The memorandum of a company is the document that deals with the external structure of the company. The memorandum must state the purpose for which the company is formed; it must describe the main business that the company will conduct. The memorandum must also indicate, among other things:
* the name of the company
* the company's main objective, although there may be any number of secondary objectives.
* the amount of authorised share capital (not all of which is required to be issued)

There is no minimum capital requirement.

5.8.4.2 Articles of association

The articles of association determine the internal structure of the company. Schedule One to the Companies Act contains an example of articles for a public company in Table A and for a private company in Table B. However, a company is not compelled to follow one of those examples when drafting its articles. The Companies Act prescribes the content of the memorandum, but not the articles. The only requirement is that the articles do not conflict with the law or with the provisions of the Companies Act.

When a memorandum and articles that comply with the requirements of the Companies Act, together with two certified copies, are lodged with the Registrar, the latter must, upon payment of the prescribed fee, register the memorandum and articles. The Registrar will allocate a registration number to the company on registration of the memorandum and the articles. The Registrar will also issue a certificate of incorporation. This certificate is documentary proof that the company has been duly incorporated in terms of the Companies Act. From the date of incorporation stated in the certificate of incorporation, the entity is regarded as a legal person with the name as stated in the memorandum.

Incorporation takes about four to six weeks to complete, and costs approximately R3 000 (excluding VAT and disbursements). Once the company has been incorporated, it must display its name on the outside of its registered office and every other office or place where the company carries out its business. A company is not allowed to commence business until the Registrar issues a certificate that entitles the company to do so.

5.8.5 Shareholders and directors

For a private company, the minimum number of shareholders and directors is one (the sole shareholder may also be the sole director), while a public company must have at least seven shareholders (unless it is a wholly-owned subsidiary of another company) and two directors. No residence or nationality restrictions apply to either shareholders or directors.

5.8.6 Statutory auditing requirements for companies

5.8.6.1 Accounting principles

Statements of Generally Accepted Accounting Practice (GAAP) were drafted by the South African Institute of Chartered Accountants and approved by the Accounting Practices Board (APB). The APB consists of representatives from the accounting profession, commerce and industry.

The provisions of GAAP must be followed in the preparation of the financial statements of companies subject to the Companies Act. They are also relevant to the financial statements of other entities purporting to achieve fair presentation.

Form and content of financial statements

The Companies Act does not require a company to specify how its net profit for the year is made up, but does require certain items of income and expenditure to be detailed, for example turnover, depreciation, directors' remuneration, interest paid and provision for taxation. If a company or group is involved in more than one type of business, the directors' report must indicate the proportion of profit attributable to each type of business. Notes to the financial statements usually provide details of all significant items shown on the balance sheet.

In addition to the Companies Act requirements, GAAP requires the disclosure of information concerning the company's accounting policies, details of taxation, details of extraordinary items and prior-year adjustments in the income statement.

Additional disclosure requirements apply to companies listed on the JSE. These requirements call for the disclosure of directors' interests in the share capital of the company, employee share incentive schemes and borrowing powers, and also require interim and preliminary reports to the members. The Second King Report on Corporate Governance has also recommended disclosure of directors' remuneration and benefits on an individual basis.

5.8.6.2 Accounting records

In terms of the Companies Act, all companies must keep accounting records in one of the 11 official languages. At a minimum, these records must include:

- the assets and liabilities of the company
- a fixed-assets register
- cash receipts and payments
- details of goods purchased and sold
- annual stock-taking (inventory) statements

The accounting records must fairly present the state of affairs and business of the company, and explain the transactions and financial position of the trade or business of the company.

5.8.6.3 Annual financial statements

In terms of the Companies Act, the directors of every company must prepare annual financial statements and present them to the annual general meeting of the company. At a minimum, the annual financial statements must consist of:
- a balance sheet and notes
- an income statement and notes
- a directors' report
- an auditors' report
- a cash flow statement

The annual financial statements must fairly present the state of affairs of the company as at the financial year-end, and its profit or loss for that year in conformity with GAAP. Both the company and group financial statements must set out certain additional information prescribed by the Companies Act, must be approved by the directors and must be signed by two directors or, if there is only one director, by that director.

Every company that is not a wholly-owned subsidiary of another company incorporated in South Africa must submit a directors' report, which must cover such matters as:
- the state of affairs of the company
- a description of the company's business
- the profit or loss of the company and its subsidiaries

Any material matters in any of these areas and certain other matters specifically identified in applicable legislation must be addressed in the directors' report.

5.8.6.4 Interim reports

Public companies and branches of foreign companies (external companies) are required to send all members and debenture holders a half-yearly interim report, fairly presenting the business and operations of the company (or, if applicable, the group). It is not required that such interim reports be audited, but they must be approved by the directors and signed on their behalf by two of the directors. Private companies are not required to provide an interim report to members.

5.8.6.5 *Provisional financial statements*

If a public company has not issued annual financial statements within three months after its year-end, it must (within the three-month period) issue provisional financial statements to its members and debenture holders. These must fairly present the business and operations of the company or, if applicable, the group.

The requirements for private companies are less stringent. If a private company has not issued its financial statements within six months after its year-end, the Registrar of Companies may, on application by a member and for good cause shown, require that provisional financial statements be submitted to that member. It is not necessary that such provisional annual financial statements be audited but they must be approved and signed by the company's directors.

5.8.6.6 *Annual audit requirement*

The financial statements of both public and private companies are subject to an annual audit in terms of the Companies Act. Only chartered accountants registered with the Public Accountants and Auditors Board may be appointed as auditors for the purposes of the annual audit.

5.8.7 Filing and disclosure requirements

Copies of a company's annual financial statements and group annual financial statements (if any) must be sent to the shareholders and debenture holders of the company not less than twenty-one days before the date of the company's annual general meeting. Public companies and external companies are required to file a copy of their annual financial statements with the Registrar of Companies within six months from the end of their financial year. Private companies are not required to do so, although the Second King Report on Corporate Governance has recommended that the Companies Act be amended to require this. In the case of an external company it must also file a copy of its annual financial statements as prepared in terms of the requirements of the jurisdiction in which it is incorporated. External companies can apply for exemption from this and other requirements and such exemption is fairly readily granted.

The annual financial statements of companies must comply with the disclosure requirements set out in the fourth schedule to the Companies Act and as prescribed by GAAP. It should be noted that listed companies must also comply with the requirements of the JSE.

5.9 The business form and the effects of taxation

The effect or impact of income taxation often determines the choice of the most suitable business in many cases. The taxation policy changes frequently; for example, when the Minister of Finance announces certain tax increases or concessions in the budget speech each year, or when the South African Revenue Services (SARS) makes amendments to existing legislation. Such changes have specific tax implications and it is therefore, important for the business owners to know how the tax policy affects them.

A close corporation and a company possess their own legal personality, which is not the case with a sole proprietor or a partnership. This means that the persons in a sole proprietorship and the persons in a partnership are usually responsible for tax, debt obligations and the commitments of the business. This is termed an *unlimited liability*. The shareholders of companies and members of close corporations have what is termed *limited liability* in respect of the commitments of the particular business form. The person can therefore be held responsible to a limited extent for the commitments of the company or close corporation.

To encourage business investment and development, the tax rate for companies and close corporations was reduced to 35% in 1995. This is less than the maximum personal tax of 43%. Sole proprietors and partnerships do not qualify for the reduced rate, and can pay up to the maximum rate of 43% or more.

A company that has shareholders and pays dividends is subject to secondary tax on companies (STC). The tax rate on dividends was raised from 15% to 25% in 1995.

These are a few examples of changes in income tax that play a role in the choice of the business form. The entrepreneur must keep abreast of changes or consult tax experts on these matters.

Questions and exercises

Choose the most appropriate form of business for each of the following enterprises:

- A restaurant being established by a well-known chef and a successful restaurateur.
- A hotel bought by a man and woman and their son, who is a Hotel School graduate.
- A Bed and Breakfast in a private home in Soweto.
- An exclusive game lodge planning to establish another private game reserve and lodge in another province as part of their portfolio.
- A cultural village established by a community for the purposes of tourism and hospitality activities as a generator of income for the community.

Motivate your answer and outline the process to be followed. Include the length of time the steps of the process will take.

6

Legal requirements for establishing a hospitality business

Objectives of this chapter:

By the end of this chapter the learner will be able to:

* register a business
* license a business
* apply for tax registration
* insure the business according to legal requirements

The learner will know:

* the legal requirements applicable to setting up a hospitality business
* the procedures to be followed for the establishment of a specific type of business
* the licences needed for a hospitality business
* the levies and taxes payable by a hospitality business

6.1 Introduction

This chapter has been structured to take a prospective hospitality establishment owner through the complex process of starting up a business. There are many requirements that have to be met: some pertain to any business, and some only to hospitality businesses. This chapter makes reference to all of these requirements and, in most cases, will refer you to additional material and, where appropriate, advise you to seek professional help and guidance.

The table below lists the various requirements in sequential order, relative to the approximate time it will take to complete a particular undertaking, before starting a hospitality business.

The following guide will give you an excellent overview of what the legislative requirements are for setting up a hospitality business. Although the following sections are not exhaustive, they cover a good 90% of what should be considered when planning to start up a business.

Figure 6-1: A guide to opening a hospitality establishment

Checklist	Appropriate authority
1. Naming the business	Registrar of Companies
2. Registration of the business	Registrar of Companies
3. Land and zoning requirements	Provincial and/or local
4. Business and directional signage	Various
5. Access to and from a public road	Local/Provincial and or National Roads Authority
6. Establishment of freedom from a land claim	Provincial Land Claims Commission
7. Establish liability to register in terms of the National Water Act	Provincial Dept of Water Affairs
8. Submission of environmental scoping report if required	Provincial Department of Environmental Affairs and Tourism
9. Submission of building plans	Local Authority
10. Licence to carry on a business	Local Authority
11. Application for a liquor licence	Provincial Liquor Board
12. Application for a gaming licence (if applicable)	Provincial Gambling Board
13. Employee benefits – pensions	Various
14. Employee benefits – medical aid	Various
15. Register for Unemployment Insurance Fund	UIF Department of Labour, Pretoria
16. Register for Workmen's Compensation Fund	Department of Labour, Pretoria
17. Register for company tax, VAT, PAYE	SARS – nearest office
18. Licences and insurance for company vehicles	Local licensing/insurance broker
19. Acquire fire certificate	Local Fire Department
20. First aid requirements	Local Dept of Labour
21. Register under the Skills Development Act	THETA, Sandton
22. Register with chosen optional grading scheme	SANGC, AA Travel Guides, SABS
23. Prepare employment equity plan when/if number of employees exceeds 50	Department of Labour, Pretoria

Checklist	Appropriate authority
24. Register with South African music rights organisation (SAMRO) for the provision of piped or live music	SAMRO office, Johannes-burg
25. Apply for television licences	SABC, Auckland Park
26. Ensure all insurance policies in place prior to opening (fire, public liability and so on)	Insurance brokers
27. Register with provincial local tourism authority	Provincial or local tourism authority
28. Apply for health certificate	Local authority

6.2 Naming the business

Figure 6-2: Naming a business

Requirement	Authority	Location
Register the name of the business	Registrar of Companies	Pretoria

The law governing business names limits the choice of names. The trading name of a business must be approved to protect existing businesses, and to avoid duplication. The names of companies are approved by the Registrar of Companies. The registration protects the company so that other businesses do not use the same name.

The choice of a name must comply with the Business Names Act 27 of 1960. The letters 'CC' must, for example, appear at the end of a close corporation. (Proprietary) Limited/(Eiendoms) Beperk or (Pty) Ltd/(Edms) Bpk must appear at the end of the name of a private company.

As mentioned above, the name chosen for the business must comply with the Business Names Act 27 of 1960. The Registrar may order a person to cease using a specific name for a business if he or she is of the opinion that the name might deceive or mislead, cause annoyance or offence, or is suggestive of blasphemy or indecency.

According to the Business Act, the following particulars have to appear on all business correspondence, orders for goods or statements of accounts pertaining to the business:

◆ The name, title or description under which business is conducted.
◆ The physical address of the business.
◆ The name under which the business was registered or established if the business is conducted by a corporate body under a name other than the name by which it was established or registered.
◆ The name of every partner if the business is structured as a partnership.
◆ The current or, where applicable, previous given names, initials and surnames of every person carrying on the business.
◆ The nationality of the persons carrying on the business, should they not be South African citizens.

Contravention of the above renders a person, on conviction, liable to a fine of R200.

6.3 The registration of a business

Figure 6-3: Registering a business

Requirement	Authority	Location
Register the business	Registrar of Companies	Pretoria

Numerous factors are important when choosing a suitable form of business. The forms of business and processes for registration have been comprehensively discussed in chapter 4. It is recommended that an accountant, auditor or attorney is approached when decisions in respect of business form are taken.

6.4 Land and zoning requirements

Figure 6-4: Locating a business

Requirement	Authority	Location
Zoning and consent for use of land	Local council or municipality	Local

It may be an infringement of local planning regulations or by-laws to start a business from a residence. A visit to the local municipality to find out whether the town planning scheme permits such a business on the site is recommended before starting a business from a residence.

If an individual is looking to purchase a property specifically for the purpose of opening a business, he or she must ensure that the zoning of the land permits the opening of such a business prior to concluding the purchase.

If there is a restrictive condition (for example, that the land may be used for residential purposes only) in the title deed of the land intended for use for business purposes, an application for the removal of the restriction or rezoning must be submitted. The Removal of Restrictions Act 84 of 1967 empowers provinces to alter, suspend or remove certain restrictions on land. The zoning requirements, charges and procedures thus differ from region to region, and it is therefore necessary to contact the local municipality and provincial government for the exact details.

If the land is situated in the area governed by a local authority, the application for rezoning should be lodged with this authority. Simultaneously, a copy of the application should be forwarded to the director-general of the province in which the land is located.

If the land is not situated in an area governed by a local authority, ie a council or municipality, the application for rezoning should be lodged with the director-general of the province in which it is located.

The written consent of the bondholder should accompany an application if a bond is registered against the business property.

On receipt of the application, the director-general will require that a notice be placed in both official languages in the council of the province. The director-general will also require that a notice be placed twice (with an interval of one week between placements) in a newspaper widely circulated in the area in which the business is to be located. This notice will state that an application for the removal of a restriction on the land of the business has been made, and that objections against the application may be lodged with the director-general on or before a specific date. This date should not be less than 21 days after the date of the last publication of the notice.

The director-general will also require that a copy of the notice be sent by registered post to every owner of land who is, or may be, directly affected by the application; this is usually the immediate neighbours. In such an event it would be wise to first canvass the support and acceptance of the neighbours.

A copy of every objection received by the director-general will be sent to the applicant by registered post.

Some municipalities expect submission of the following documentation together with the application for the alteration, suspension or removal of the restriction on the land on which your business is to be located:

◆ the title deed to the property (this is registered with the deeds office when the application is submitted)
◆ proof of having placed the advertisements in the provincial gazette (as outlined above)
◆ prints of the locality plan and a plan indicating the proposed rezoning. (A locality plan is available from the local municipality and indicates the position of the business stand in the town or city)

In some instances, the applicant may be required to give reasons as to why the restriction on the land use should be altered, suspended or removed.

It is important to take the following factors into account when applying for rezoning:

◆ the rate base after rezoning will usually change, so this must be budgeted for in the business plan
◆ if the premises of the business are leased, it might constitute a breach of the lease agreement to use it for business purposes or to make any additions or alterations thereto. The lease agreement must provide for the establishment of a business and/or alterations should they be required
◆ an application for special consent use, in terms of the Planning and Development Act 5 of 1998, will have to comply with the requirements and procedures as outlined in the Act

6.5 Business and directional signage

Figure 6-5: Signage

Requirement	Authority	Location
Application for business and road directional signage	Various	Various

If the business is appropriately zoned, it is usually not necessary to get approval from your local municipality if you wish to erect signs on the property.

Directional road signage concerning the business will need to be in line with the existing character of the locality. Signage policy and any other regulations in this regard will have to be followed.

For permission to erect directional road signage, the applicant will probably need to make application to the local authority responsible for roads management and/or the local tourism authority. As the method of application differs across the provinces and from region to region, it is best to either contact the local authority or the local tourism authority in order to ascertain the exact application procedure.

In terms of the National Roads Act 7 of 1998, no signage (neither directional nor informative) may be located in such a manner that it becomes visible from a national road unless it complies with certain requirements in terms of section 50 of the act. The requirements cover the permissible location, size and contents of the signs. Failure to do so will result in a letter from the National Roads Agency requiring the removal of the sign. Failing that, the agency will remove the sign, costs will be recovered and/or a fine will be imposed under the act.

6.6 Access to and from a public road

Figure 6-6: Access

Requirement	Authority	Location
Planning permission for access to and from a public road	Local/Provincial and or National Roads Authority	Local

There are various limitations as to what is, or is not, permissible in terms of access to and from a public road. Most of the limitations are concerned with public safety so the type or classification of road (local, provincial or national) will play a significant role, as will the distance between the proposed entry point and potential danger points such as blind corners, traffic lights and pedestrian crossings.

Road access plans are usually drawn up by the architects together with the building plans, and will be approved or declined as the case may be by the local authority.

It is important to note that local by-laws and even provincial requirements will differ so it is important to get permission from the appropriate authority before the finalisation and building of the proposed access.

6.7 Freedom from a land claim

Figure 6-7: Claims against property

Requirement	Authority	Location
Establishing freedom from a land claim	Department of Land Affairs and the Land Claims Court	Pretoria and Randburg

The government introduced land reform in 1994, and this is further derived from section 25 of the Constitution of South Africa, 1996. When considering buying either land or an existing business, it is important to ensure that there is no outstanding claim against the property.

The objectives of the South African land reform policy are to

◆ redress the injustices of apartheid
◆ foster national reconciliation and stability
◆ underpin economic growth
◆ improve household welfare and alleviate poverty

The Land Reform Programme consists of:

◆ **Land restitution**, which usually involves returning land lost because of racially discriminatory laws, although it can also be effected through compensation.
◆ **Land redistribution**, which enables disadvantaged people to buy land with the help of a settlement or land acquisition grant.
◆ **Land tenure reform**, which aims to bring all people occupying land under one legal system of landholding. It will provide for diverse and secure forms of tenure, help resolve tenure disputes, and provide alternatives for people who are displaced in the process.

The Land Restitution Programme, which could impact on the sale or purchase of a particular property, originates from the Constitution and was established by the Restitution of Land Rights Act of 1994. The purpose of the programme is to assess the validity of claims, restore land, and/or pay financial compensation to people who were dispossessed of their land rights as a result of racially discriminatory laws and practices after 19 June 1913.

The Land Claims Court, situated in Randburg, is responsible for determining restitution and compensation for those who lost land as a result of forced removals. The court is required to be accessible to everyone and to establish processes that will enable it to make speedy decisions. Enquiries can be made through the court or directly with the Department of Land Affairs in Pretoria.

6.8 The environmental scoping report

Figure 6-8: Environmental conservation

Requirement	Authority	Location
Adherence to the various environmental conservation requirements	Local and/or Provincial Authorities	Various

The Minister of Environmental Affairs and Tourism has identified a number of activities that may have a detrimental impact of the environment, and has therefore made provision for specific procedures that must be followed before starting any of these activities. These provisions are contained in the Environmental Conservation Act 73 of 1989 as amended.

The more severe the impact on the environment, the more comprehensive the application procedures to be followed will be. The felling of one or two trees may only require a phone call and a visit from a representative of the local authority whereas the building of a road will undoubtedly require the applicant to follow every condition of the Act. It is important to note that it is the authorities, and not the applicant, who will decide on whether or not an activity may or may not have an impact on the environment. There is no protection on the grounds of ignorance or error.

It is more than likely, should rezoning of land have taken place, that the applicant will be required to follow the complete procedure. It is recommended, however, that pre-consultation takes place before any application as, under certain circumstances, an exemption from the Act may apply.

Legal requirements will usually require the applicant to complete the following:

- a pre-consultation process with the local authorities to ascertain what level of application is likely to be required relative to the proposed undertaking
- a plan of study for scoping report
- a scoping report
- an environmental impact assessment report

The process is relatively complex, so it is suggested that either an environmental specialist or legal consultant be approached, or that confirmation is received from the appointed builder or architects that they are fully conversant with the requirements of the act.

6.9 Registration in terms of the National Water Act

Figure 6-9: Water

Requirement	Authority	Location
Registration requirements in terms of the National Water Act	Local Department of Water Affairs and Forestry	Various

South Africa's scarce water resources are under increasing pressure and will need to be wisely managed in the coming years. In order to achieve this, the Department of Water Affairs and Forestry needs to know how much water is being used, by whom, and where. The department can then ascertain how much water is actually available for use, and effectively manage the future sustainability of the country's water resources.

The National Water Act 36 of 1998 gives the Department of Water Affairs and Forestry the wherewithal to gather the required information for the optimal management of all of the country's water resources. The registration of water use is one of these tools.

6.9.1 Registration

All water users instructed to register have a statutory obligation to do so and there are strict penalties, prescribed within the act, for those who do not comply. The following water users must register their water use:

All surface and ground water users who do not receive their water from a service provider, local authority, water board, irrigation board, government water scheme or other bulk supplier and who are using water for

- irrigation
- mining purposes
- industrial use
- feedlots
- in terms of a general authorisation

Other uses, which must be registered, include:

- diversion of rivers and streams
- discharges of waste or water containing waste
- storage: any person or body storing water for any purpose (including irrigation, domestic supply, industrial use, mining, aqua culture, fishing,

water sport, aesthetic value, gardening, landscaping, golfing and so on) from surface runoff, groundwater or fountain flow in excess of 10 000 cubic meters or where the water area at full supply level exceeds one hectare in total

If water is received from a local authority, a water board, an irrigation board or any other bulk water supplier, registration is not required.

All persons or bodies required to register can contact any regional office of the Department of Water Affairs and Forestry for the relevant forms, information and assistance. For additional information access the website (http://www-dwaf.pwv.gov.za) where most of the information regarding the implementation of the Act is available.

6.10 Submission of building plans

Figure 6-10: Building plans

Requirement	Authority	Location
Submitting building plans for approval	The local authority in the area in which the building activity is to take place	Various

Building plans are required to conform with national, provincial and local laws and by-laws, so it is important to ensure that the appointed architect or builder is totally familiar with these requirements, and makes the necessary submissions to the appropriate council or municipality.

Many aspects relevant to the building plans will be of concern to the local authorities. These could include the parking layout, turning, loading facilities and street access. Bear in mind that parking facilities must be adequate and correspond with the number of guest rooms/restaurant seats planned for the establishment.

In many cases, local by-laws differ from one council or municipality to another so it is wise to ensure that the architect or builder knows the specific local requirements, thereby reducing the potential for delays. Examples of items covered by statutory requirements would include the provision of toilet facilities, fire escapes and so on.

Formal approval will be required from the local authorities if extensions, changes to frontages and structural alterations are to be made.

6.11 A licence to carry on a business

Figure 6-11: Trade licence

Requirement	Authority	Location
Application for a trade licence	Local council/municipality	Municipality or council

In terms of Schedule 1 to the Businesses Act 71 of 1991, a business is required to apply for a licence if it intends selling or supplying any foodstuffs in the form of meals for consumption on or off the business's premises.

The Act provides for the deregulation of trading licences in South Africa. In terms of the Act, only businesses dealing in the following require a licence:

- **The sale or supply of meals or perishable foodstuffs.** Any form of foodstuffs whether on or off consumption (consumed on the property or taken away and consumed elsewhere).
- **Certain types of entertainment.** In terms of the hospitality industry this would include those establishments keeping three or more snooker or billiard tables, keeping a night club or discotheque or three or more devices for the purposes of playing any game for the purposes of recreation or entertainment and which involves the payment of any valuable consideration (that is, monetary payment).

All other types of licence are governed by legislation as published by the councils from time to time and the requirements, charges and renewal procedures differ from province to province. It is therefore advisable to check the requirements. Further details can be obtained from the local authority (municipality or council) in which the business is located. In other words, each province is required to provide for the licence categories mentioned above as well as any other licence type assented to by the Provincial Premier.

In all regions, an application for a trading licence has to be completed and submitted to the licensing department of the local authority. The local council or municipality then circulates the application to the health, fire and building inspectors, the town planning department and, in some cases, the development service board. These bodies will evaluate the plan before the application is approved. The waiting period for a business licence is usually between three and eight weeks.

6.12 Application for a health permit

Figure 6-12: Health permit

Requirement	Authority	Location
Apply for a permit	Local authority: Johannesburg	Local: Johannesburg

Unlike other local authorities, the City of Johannesburg Metropolitan Council requires all types of accommodation establishments to make application for, and obtain, a health permit. This permit is over and above the health requirements in terms of the Certificate of Health Acceptability covered in Chapter 8. All accommodation establishments located in Johannesburg must obtain and complete form R.P.1 which can be obtained from the council, or from www.joburg.org.za.

6.13 Liquor licence

Figure 6-13: Liquor licence

Requirement	Authority	Location
Application for a liquor licence	Provincial Liquor Authority	Major city within the province

Any business that desires to sell liquor will have to apply for a liquor licence. Liquor legislation in South Africa remains a little confusing at present with both the National Liquor Act 59 of 2003 and certain parts of the National Liquor Act 27 of 1989 as amended in 1993 and 1995 still in force, together with the Gauteng Liquor Act 2 of 2003 and the Eastern Cape Liquor Act 10 of 2003. All of the requirements are dealt with comprehensively in chapter 7.

6.14 Gaming licence for limited payout machines

Figure 6-14: Gaming licence

Requirement	Authority	Location
Application for a gaming licence	Provincial Gaming Authority	Various

Should an establishment want to provide for limited payout machines on its premises, it will have to apply to the provincial gaming board for a site operator licence. The full details and requirements are comprehensively discussed in chapter 10.

6.15 Employee benefits – pensions

Figure 6-15: Pension Schemes

Requirement	Authority	Location
Employee benefits – pension schemes	Various private sector organisations and companies	Various

There is at present no national pension scheme, but a government-appointed committee is examining the issue at present. Apart from those pension schemes operated for civil servants, the government provides social pensions, old-age pensions, pensions for the blind, disability pensions and war veterans' pensions.

Private sector pension schemes are usually administered by industry associations, or insurance companies, and offer varying products and services. Pension funds are subject to statutory regulation and contributions to the various schemes are invariably made by both employer and employee.

6.16 Employee benefits – medical aid

Figure 6-16: Medical aid

Requirement	Authority	Location
Employee benefits – medical aid schemes.	Various private sector organisations and companies	Various

South Africa does not have a national medical insurance scheme. Medical aid schemes are operated by various private companies and cover most types of medical expenses in accordance with scales of benefits (tariffs) established by each scheme, which are revised from time to time.

These expenses include the costs of private medical and dental services, prescribed medicines, hospital and nursing home fees. Contributions are usually made by both employer and employee in equal shares. However, the scales of benefits usually do not equal the charges actually levied. The excess must be borne directly by the patient. A number of insurance schemes are available to cover the excess, and other medical expenses that are not provided for by the medical aid schemes.

Medical schemes are increasingly establishing and operating managed health care programmes, in an effort to control steeply escalating claims and abuses of the benefits provided by them.

The Medical Schemes Act 131 of 1998 provides for the establishment of a council and registrar of medical schemes, and contains provisions relating to the registration and control of certain activities of medical schemes and the protection of the interests of medical scheme members. The Act also seeks to extend the ambit of medical aid cover to less advantaged South Africans.

6.17 Registration with the Unemployment Insurance Fund (UIF)

Figure 6-17: UIF

Requirement	Authority	Location
Registration in terms of the Unemployment Insurance Act	Unemployment Insurance Fund (UIF)	UIF offices – Pretoria

The main purpose of unemployment insurance is to ensure that employees who are contributors have access to the Unemployment Insurance Fund and to financial aid under certain circumstances.

A full explanation of the Unemployment Insurance Act is covered in Chapter 11.

6.18 Registration with the Workmen's Compensation Fund

Figure 6-18: Workmen's compensation

Requirement	Authority	Location
Registration for the Workmen's Compensation Fund	Compensation commissioner	Pretoria

The objective of workmen's compensation is to provide compensation for disablement caused by injuries and diseases sustained in the workplace, and as a result of the work or working conditions under which the person is placed.

Workmen's compensation, and the requirements for registration and payment, are discussed fully in chapter 14.

6.19 Company and individual taxation

Figure 6-19: Taxation

Requirement	Authority	Location
The registration for company, PAYE and personal taxation	The South African Revenue Services	Pretoria or branch offices located throughout South Africa

Taxation is a complex and evolving subject, and business owners are advised to make use of specialist accountants or tax consultants. This section will give you a broad understanding of primary taxation as it applies to a business, but it is by no means exhaustive.

The primary purpose of paying income tax is to assist the state in funding its expenditure. Income tax is charged in terms of the Income Tax Act 58 of 1962 as amended from time to time. Most taxes in South Africa are levied by the central government but the Constitution gives some taxation powers to the provinces. These mainly involve assessment rates and other taxes based on immovable property.

Every individual, partner in a partnership, company or close corporation in South Africa that derives a taxable income is liable to pay tax to the Receiver of Revenue. A business owner who derives a taxable income from a business, will be regarded as a taxpayer and will therefore have the same duties and responsibilities as all other taxpayers in South Africa.

Tax is collected and administered by the South African Revenue Services (SARS) who have offices in all major centres. SARS is also known as the Receiver of Revenue.

Income tax returns are submitted annually to the Receiver of Revenue. If the entity is a sole proprietor or a partner in a partnership, the individual and the entity or business are regarded as one taxpayer and will therefore have to declare all other forms of income, as well as the taxable income from the business, on the same return.

If the business is a close corporation or company, the individual is required to submit a personal income tax return, as well as one for the company or close corporation. Business owners are strongly advised to appoint a tax consultant or an accountant for tax purposes.

6.19.1 Company taxation

Company tax is essentially an annual tax on the income of companies and close corporations.

Secondary tax on companies is a tax imposed on dividends declared by companies and distributions made by close corporations, payable and borne by the companies and close corporations.

A tax on dividends from foreign-registered, or incorporated, companies, including retirement funds and insurers, was announced by the Minister of Finance in his budget speech in February 2000.

Before 1 January 2001, companies were subject to income tax only on their income from South African sources excluding capital gains. Since 1 January 2001, South African residents have been taxed on their world-wide income for years of assessment.

6.19.2 Secondary tax on companies (STC)

The secondary tax on companies is a tax on dividends declared by a company (or a distribution declared by a close corporation). The tax liability is based on the net amount calculated by subtracting dividends accruing to the company from those declared by it. That net amount is taxed at the rate of 12,5%, and the tax is borne and paid by the company. Dividends paid by distributing capitalisation shares do not give rise to a secondary tax liability. Secondary tax is also payable on amounts distributed by companies to shareholders that are deemed to be dividends, like loans to shareholders.

Secondary tax was previously imposed on dividends declared by foreign companies, to the extent that the dividend was paid out of profits generated from a South African source. The tax does not apply to those dividends declared in respect of years of assessment ending on or after 1 April 1996.

Pursuant to the introduction of a tax on foreign dividends, a South African resident company will not be able to claim a foreign dividend as a credit in the determination of its liability for STC.

6.19.3 Employee taxation

Each time an employer pays an employee, and dependent on the amount paid over, the employer will be required to deduct an amount known as employees' tax from the remuneration. This tax is then paid over to SARS at the end of each month.

Employees' tax comprises the following two elements:
1. Standard Income Tax on Employees (SITE). SITE is calculated only on the net remuneration of an employee which, when annualised, does not exceed the amount specified under the Act and amended year by year.
2. Pay-as-you-earn (PAYE). After having allocated a portion of the employees' tax to SITE, the balance of any employee's tax paid over will be classified as PAYE.

6.19.3.1 Employees' tax – PAYE

Employees' tax is an amount of tax that an employer deducts from all regular or periodic payments, which are made to an employee. The purpose of employees' tax is to ensure that the taxpayer's income tax, which is due in respect of remuneration received, is settled at the same time that it is earned.

The PAYE system is not based on a calendar year, but on a year of assessment within which there are tax periods. A year of assessment commences on 1 March and ends on 28 (or 29) February the following year. A tax period commences on the date the employee commences employment and ends on either 28 (or 29) February of a year of assessment or, if an employee leaves employment before 28 (or 29) February, on the date of cessation of employment.

In terms of the PAYE system, an employer is obliged to deduct 'employees' tax' on a regular basis from remuneration paid to employees.

The employer must pay the deducted amount to the local Receiver of Revenue within the prescribed period. To enable employers to meet their obligations, each employee must furnish employers with personal particulars, which are taken into account when the employer calculates the employee's PAYE deduction.

With effect from the 1996 year of assessment, the income tax liability of individuals (natural persons) has been determined without reference to gender or marital status. The only factor of importance is the age of the taxpayer, that is, if the taxpayer is under or over the age of 65 years. The taxpayer must provide the employer with a declaration stating whether he or she is under or over 65.

The declaration is important as it enables the employer to deduct the correct amount of employee's tax, and also ensures that a correct SITE (see below) calculation is made at the end of a tax period or the year of assessment. In certain circumstances, an employee may be entitled to have either no tax deducted, tax deducted at a rate less than that shown in the prescribed tax deduction tables, or tax deducted at a fixed percentage. However, a tax directive must be obtained from the Receiver of Revenue.

An employer is obliged to issue an IRP 5 certificate within the prescribed period to each employee to whom remuneration has been paid or has become due and from which employees' tax has been deducted. This certificate serves as an acknowledgement of payments of employees' tax. If there is a valid reason for employees' tax not being deducted, the employer must provide the employee with an IT 3(a) return.

6.19.3.2 *Standard income tax on employees (SITE)*

A system of standard income tax on employees or SITE was introduced with effect from 1 March 1988. SITE is an alternative method of determining liability for normal tax, and is not a separate tax payable in lieu of normal tax. Thus, where reference is made to SITE being deductible from certain remuneration and PAYE being deductible from other remuneration, this is done for convenience only as both deductions represent payments towards liability for normal tax. The main objective of SITE is to ensure that the tax deductions made by employers are, as far as possible, equal to an employee's normal tax liability. This obviates the need for certain employees to submit tax returns at the end of the tax year. Under the SITE system, a taxpayer is relieved of the obligation to submit an income tax return if:

◆ The taxpayer's taxable income consists solely of net remuneration. For example, salary, allowances, wages, overtime pay, bonus emoluments and pension.
◆ The taxpayer's remuneration for the tax year does not exceed the amount specified and provided for under the act as amended from time to time.
◆ The prescribed amount of SITE has been deducted from the remuneration.

SITE does not apply to all types of income, but only to net remuneration received from standard employment, or from an annuity payable by a pension fund, provident fund or benefit fund during a tax period. In terms of this system, employees' tax is deducted from all remuneration that has been paid or has become due to an employee during a year of assessment.

At the end of the tax period (and not at the end of every pay period), the employer makes a calculation to determine what amount of the employees tax deducted represents SITE. If an employee's net remuneration is subject to SITE only, the employer is obliged to refund any amount of tax deducted that exceeds the employee's liability. This provision eliminates the necessity of an employee having to apply to his or her local Receiver of Revenue for a refund.

However, under the following circumstances, the local Receiver of Revenue will recalculate the employee's SITE liability and refund any overpayment:

◆ if the employee's medical expenses exceed a certain percentage of his or her taxable income, subject to a minimum claim as determined by the Act, or if the medical expenses are more than the prescribed amount in the case of a handicapped person, or in the case of an employee of 65 years or older who incurred medical expenses that were not taken into account by the employer on the determination of SITE

◆ if the employer did not take the employee's retirement annuity fund contributions into account or if the employer did not take the employee's pension fund contributions into account

To enable a person to claim a refund of over-deducted SITE, an IT 11 return must be completed and returned, together with the relevant IRP 5 certificate(s), as well as proof of payment of contributions expenses where required, to the local Receiver of Revenue. The IT 11 returns are obtainable from the Receiver of Revenue offices. If the employee's net remuneration is subject to SITE and PAYE, the local Receiver of Revenue will refund any overpayment when an assessment is issued.

As mentioned above, taxable income is determined for a specific period referred to as the 'year of assessment'. The Income Tax Act 21 of 1994 as amended lays down various rules as to how taxable income and tax liabilities should be calculated.

Figure 6-20: Basic framework for the calculation of income tax liability

Gross income	XXX
Less exempt income	XXX
Equals income	XXX
Less deductions	XXX
Less tax allowances	XXX
Equals taxable income	XXX
Plus taxable capital gain	XXX
Equals total taxable income	XXX
Calculate tax payable on your taxable income	XXX
Less rebates	XXX
Equals tax liability for the year	XXX
Less tax paid (employees' tax and provisional tax)	XXX
Equals outstanding tax liability or refund	XXX

6.19.4 Provisional tax

Provisional tax forms part of the PAYE system of tax collection. It is not a separate tax, but simply a provision for the final tax liability for a year of assessment, which will be determined on assessment. The payments, which are made in August and February, represent tax on the income that has already been earned during the year of assessment. Therefore, this tax can be compared to employees' tax deducted from remuneration before it is paid to an employee. The payments are made under cover of IRP 6(i) returns, which are posted to taxpayers approximately a month before the date on which the provisional tax for the relevant period is due.

A taxpayer must register as a provisional taxpayer if he or she:

- derives income from sources other than remuneration (for example, business or farming income, interest, rental income and building society dividends) where the taxable income from such other sources will exceed that amount specified under the Act and amended from time to time
- is notified that he or she is a provisional taxpayer

Taxpayers who are 65 years and older and whose taxable income for the relevant year of assessment does not exceed the amount specified under the act and amended from time to time, are relieved of the obligation of making provisional tax payments. However, this concession will not apply where an individual derives income otherwise than from remuneration pension, interest, building society dividends or rental from the letting of fixed property.

A provisional taxpayer with a taxable income exceeding that amount specified under the Act and amended from time to time, is required to settle his or her total income tax liability within seven months after the end of the year of assessment, if the tax year falls on the last day of February. If the year of assessment of the taxpayer ends on another date, the taxpayer is required to settle the total income tax liability within six months after the end of the relevant tax year. Failure to do so will, unless reasonable grounds for such failure can be submitted, result in interest being charged on any underpayment. In the case of an overpayment, interest is paid on such overpayment. To facilitate this final settlement, a provisional taxpayer is allowed a third voluntary payment within the six or seven months following the end of the tax year.

6.20 Valued-added taxation

Figure 6-21: VAT

Requirement	Authority	Location
Registration for value-added taxation (VAT)	The South African Revenue Services	Pretoria or branch offices located throughout South Africa

The invoice-based value-added tax (VAT) was introduced on 30 September 1991. The value-added tax system is similar to those used in Western Europe and New Zealand. The tax is levied on the value added in each transaction, including gambling.

VAT is levied on all supplies made by registered vendors in the course or furtherance of their enterprises. Only a registered vendor may levy VAT. A vendor providing exempt supplies or who is not registered may, therefore, not charge VAT and may not claim back any VAT borne by the enterprise.

If a business's taxable turnover exceed or is likely to exceed R300 000 over a twelve-month period, the business will be required to register for VAT at the local Receiver of Revenue office. If a vendor makes taxable income of less than R300 000 per annum he or she is not obliged to register as a VAT vendor, but may as a business decision and in order to assist his or her clients, nevertheless apply for voluntary registration.

A particular category of tax period will be allocated once the business has been registered. Businesses are required to complete a VAT 201 return, which must be submitted within the prescribed period. Should the business fail to submit a VAT return, or fail to pay VAT within the prescribed period, it will be liable for penalties and interest.

In terms of the Value-Added Tax Act 89 of 1991, a business is required to subtract the VAT charged (input VAT) from the VAT the business charges their clients (output VAT) in order to calculate the VAT payable to the Receiver of Revenue. If the output tax exceeds the input tax, the difference is VAT payable to the Receiver. If the input tax exceeds the output tax, the difference is VAT receivable from the Receiver. An input tax credit can only be claimed as a deduction if the input tax was paid and invoiced by a registered vendor and if the business is in the possession of a valid tax invoice.

When a registered vendor is supplied with goods or services by another registered vendor, the supplier of those goods or services will levy VAT. A vendor subtracts his or her input tax (VAT borne by him or her on the acquisition of goods and services) from his or her output tax (the VAT charged by him her on the supply of goods and services). The difference is VAT payable to the Receiver of Revenue. The effect of this is that VAT is borne by the end consumer of goods and services.

The current rate of VAT is 14%. This means that a registered business is required to add 14% to the price of nearly all its sales, and must make sure that prices quoted to clients always include VAT.

In the accommodation sector, if a guest stays for longer than 28 days, only 60% of an all-inclusive charge for accommodation and domestic goods or services (for example, meals, telephone, television, radio, cleaning and maintenance) will be subject to VAT. If a guest stays for longer than 28 days at an accommodation establishment and the business does not charge an inclusive tariff, the full tariff for domestic goods and services – or other goods and services charged or supplied separately – will attract VAT at 14%. Only 60% of the charge for accommodation will attract VAT at 14%. VAT will be calculated on the full tariff only if the person stays for 28 days or less.

A registered business is required to keep adequate records in order to comply with the Act. Invoices, credit notes, bank statements, deposit slips and paid cheques must be maintained. The following information should appear on a VAT invoice:
- The words 'tax invoice' printed on the invoice in a prominent place.
- The name, address and VAT registration number of the business.
- The date of the tax invoice.
- An individual serialised invoice number.
- A description of the goods and services supplied.
- The amount of VAT charged for the goods or services (for example, R54.00) and the rate at which it was charged (that is, 14%), or a statement that VAT of 14% has been included in the price.

The following additional information is required if the supply exceeds R1 000:
- The name and address of the recipient.
- The quantity and a description of the goods or services supplied.

If a business supplies its employees with free meals, no input tax deduction is available and an apportionment of tax is required. However, if the business supplies meals to its employees from the surplus of food not consumed by the clients, an input tax deduction is available.

6.20.1 Items subject to the zero rate

The following goods and services are subject to VAT at the zero rate:
◆ goods exported from South Africa
◆ brown bread
◆ brown wheaten meal
◆ maize meal
◆ samp
◆ mealie rice
◆ dried mealies
◆ dried beans
◆ rice
◆ lentils
◆ fruit and vegetables
◆ pilchards and sardines in tins or cans
◆ milk, cultured milk and milk powder
◆ cooking oil
◆ eggs
◆ edible legumes and pulse or leguminous plants
◆ dairy powder blends
◆ petrol and diesel
◆ certain supplies made for farming, agricultural or pastoral purposes, provided that certain requirements are met
◆ certain gold coins issued by the South Africa Reserve Bank (including the Kruger Rand)
◆ international transport
◆ state subsidies and donations to welfare organisations
◆ transfer payments made by public authorities to vendors
◆ services supplied outside South Africa

A zero-rating implies that VAT at zero percent is levied on supplies and all VAT borne by the vendor for purposes of making such supplies, is claimable as an input tax deduction.

6.20.2 Goods and services exempt from VAT

An exemption implies that the supplier of services bears VAT on its purchases but does not levy VAT on its sales. The following goods and services are exempt from VAT:
◆ passenger transport by road and rail
◆ the rental of residential accommodation
◆ educational services in crèches, nursery schools, primary and secondary schools, after-school centres, universities and technikons
◆ interest, pension and life insurance benefits

- medical services and medicines supplied by state and provincial hospitals and local authority clinics
- the supply of any goods or services by an employee organisation to its members to the extent that the consideration consists of membership contributions

6.20.3 VAT and the tourist

VAT borne by foreign tourists may be refunded by the VAT Refund Administrator (VRA) upon departure from South Africa. The tourist must be in possession of a tax invoice and have the goods available for inspection upon departure from South Africa. A small commission is levied by the VRA for processing the refund.

The refund only covers VAT paid on goods that are bought to be exported and consumed outside of South Africa, so VAT paid on accommodation is not refundable.

6.21 Application for a vehicle operating licence

Figure 6-22: Vehicle licence

Requirement	Authority	Location
Public transportation licence	Local council or municipality	Local

If a business owner wants to render a transport service to guests for a fare, reward or any other consideration, an application for the necessary permit or operating licence in terms of the National Land Transport Transition Act 22 of 2000 should be made. Application for the transportation of guests within a specific province should be made to the public transport licensing board of the province in which the guests will be transported.

An operating licence is not necessary if the owner provides a courtesy service for guests using his or her own vehicle, or a vehicle provided by an operator, in terms of a contract with that organisation. However, should the business provide a dedicated vehicle for transport services it will need a licence and, equally importantly, should ensure that public liability insurance has been taken out to protect both the clients and the business.

Professional driving permits are required for any person who is paid for or takes responsibility for driving members of the public. This would include the provision of airport transfers and the like for guests. The permits are obtained from the traffic authorities and are subject to a police clearance report, a medical test and a driving test. Permits are renewable every second year.

6.22 Fire regulations and requirements

Figure 6-23: Fire and safety

Requirement	Authority	Location
Fire and safety regulations	Local authority – fire division.	Various

6.22.1 Building regulations and safety provisions

Occupational health and safety is not just to do with safe work practices; it is also applicable to buildings and the safety provisions built into premises. Should an accident happen or fire break out, legislation also provides for the means of dealing with an emergency, or for the evacuation and escape of both employees and guests. The safety of premises and practices should be viewed as a single safety responsibility by hospitality managers.

Section 33 of the Standards Act 30 of 1982 makes provision for the South African Bureau of Standards (SABS) to apply for incorporation of codes of practice into legislation. The codes of practice listed below have all been incorporated into law, so adherence to the provisions made in the codes of practice is thus mandatory.

The National Building Regulations are applied through SABS 0400, and are the basis for architectural design in South Africa. The SABS 0400 is quoted extensively in relation to provision for fire escapes and fire fighting equipment. All of these documents are available from any branch of SABS.

6.22.2 Fire clearance certificate

The establishment is required to comply with the regulations as contained in the SABS 0400 document. Once the building is complete or the establishment is ready for inspection the owner or manager is required to contact the local fire department and ask for the fire prevention section to inspect the premises in terms of 0400. If all is well they will issue a FIRE CLEARANCE CERTIFICATE.

6.22.3 Relevant codes of practice or SABS documents

These are as follows:

SABS 543:	Fire hose reels (with hose)
SABS 810:	Portable rechargeable dry powder fire extinguishers
SABS 889:	Portable fire extinguishers (water types)
SABS 1128:	Fire fighting equipment
SABS 1151:	Portable fire extinguishers of the halogenated hydrocarbon type
SABS 1186:	Symbolic safety signs
SABS 0105:	The classification, use and routine maintenance of portable fire extinguishers
SABS 0139:	Fire detection and alarm systems
SABS 1475:	Service and maintenance of portable fire fighting equipment
SABS 0400:	The application of the National Building Regulations incorporated in the National Building Regulations and Building Standards Act 103 of 1977

International hazard signs, photoluminescent and approved by the SABS 1186: Symbolic Safety Signs, must be displayed where deemed necessary by the local authorities. The most important fire, evacuation and first aid requirements are briefly outlined below.

6.22.4 Fire and emergency services

The fire and emergency services work within the parameters of the National Building Regulations and Building Standards Act 103 of 1977, also found in SABS 0400: The application of the National Building Regulations. If in doubt about any fire or emergency information or requirements, the local fire authority will be of assistance in this regard. There are, however, a few regulations that are easy to understand and apply.

Many fire authorities have their own specific by-laws, so ensure that these authorities have been consulted with regard to mechanisms such as approved locking devices and any other pertinent local issues.

Gas installations must be inspected annually by the fire department. At the same time, they will check for the required amount of extinguishers, maintenance thereof, and any other fire hazards in the establishment. Not meeting their requirements could lead to failure to receive the gas permit, which could stop trading for a while. It is recommended to be on the safe side and ensure that regulations are complied with.

6.22.5 Provision of fixed fire fighting equipment

All buildings exceeding $1\,000\,m^2$, must have one fire hydrant for every $1\,000\,m^2$ of floor area, or part thereof.

Hose reels must be provided for as follows in Building Regulation: SABS 0400: TT34:

◆ hose reels for the purposes of fire-fighting shall be installed in any building of two or more storeys in height or in any single-storey building of more than $250\,m^2$ at a rate of 1 hose reel for every $500\,m^2$, or part thereof, of floor area of any storey
◆ any hose reel installed in such a building shall comply with the requirements contained in SABS 543

6.22.6 Portable fire fighting equipment

SABS 0400: TT37 stipulates that any building must contain one 4.5 kg fire extinguisher per $200\,m^2$ of floor area. Many fire authorities will recommend dry powder extinguishers, as they are effective for all types of fires.

Fire extinguishers must be kept in approved, accessible positions, and must be routinely inspected and maintained by an approved service engineer. Please consult your fire department for advice on positioning and number of extinguishers required. The maintenance of portable fire fighting equipment is governed by SABS: 1475.

Fire blankets are not stipulated in the regulations, but they are highly recommended by the fire authorities, especially for use in kitchens.

6.22.7 Provision for means of escape

Evacuation routes have to be provided for in terms of SABS 0400: TT 16–21. When planning or converting a building as a place of entertainment, ensure that your architect is highly conversant with the relevant safety building codes. All plans have to be approved by the local fire authorities, so it will be in your favour to have all the requirements provided for during the planning phase.

A place of entertainment must have at least two means of escape, which, with the approval of the fire authorities, may include the front door. Doors have to be within a certain width for a certain number of people, so, when submitting plans for a place of entertainment, ensure that provision is made for exit doors.

The locking mechanisms on fire escape doors must be approved by the local fire authority. Some fire departments will not allow break-glass key boxes, but locking devices that are secure and operated from the inside will be approved. If in doubt, consult the authorities.

6.22.8 Detection and alarm systems

In terms of SABS 0400: TT 31, establishments and restaurants shall have a manually activated audible alarm system that is approved in terms of SABS 0139. There is no regulation for fire or smoke detectors in smaller establishments, but they are also highly recommended by the fire authorities.

6.22.9 Disaster management

By law, all local authorities (for example, municipalities) must have a division that regulates disaster management. This may be the local fire department, the town clerk, or the traffic police. Investigate who the authority is, and consult with it when determining escape routes, evacuation procedures, or any such matters.

6.23 First aid requirements

Figure 6-24: First aid

Requirement	Authority	Location
First aid requirements	Local Authority – Fire and Safety division	Various

The General Safety Regulation R1031 in terms of the Occupational Health and Safety Act 85 of 1993 makes the following stipulations with regard to the mandatory provision of first aid supplies and equipment:

Taking into account the type of injuries that are likely to occur at a workplace, the nature of the activities performed and the number of employees employed at such workplace, the employer shall make sure that the first aid box or boxes contain suitable first aid equipment, which includes at least the equipment listed hereunder;
and that such an employer shall make sure that only articles and equipment or medicines is kept in the first aid box or boxes.

6.23.1 Minimum contents of a first aid box

In the case of shops and offices, the quantities stated for items 1, 8, 9, 10, 14, 15, 17, and 18 may be reduced by half.

Item 1: Wound cleaner/antiseptic (100 ml)
Item 2: Swabs for cleaning wounds
Item 3: Cotton wool for padding (100 g)
Item 4: Sterile gauze (minimum quantity 10)
Item 5: 1 pair of forceps (for splinters)
Item 6: 1 pair of scissors (minimum size 100 mm)
Item 7: 1 set of safety pins
Item 8: 4 triangular bandages
Item 9: 4 roller bandages (75 mm × 5 m)
Item 10: 4 roller bandages (100 mm × 5 m)
Item 11: 1 roll of elastic adhesive (25 mm × 3 m)

Item 12: 1 non-allergenic adhesive strip (25 mm × 3 m)
Item 13: 1 packet of adhesive dressing strips (minimum quantity: 10 assorted)
Item 14: 4 first aid dressings (75 mm × 100 mm)
Item 15: 4 first aid dressings (150 mm × 200 mm)
Item 16: 2 straight splints
Item 17: 2 pairs large and 2 pairs medium disposable latex gloves
Item 18: 2 CPR mouth pieces or similar devices

6.24 Registration under the Skills Development Act

Figure 6-25: Skills development

Requirement	Authority	Location
Registration under the Skills Development Act	The Tourism and Hospitality Education and Training Authority (THETA)	Johannesburg

The payment of levies in accordance with the Skills Development Act 97 of 1998 is discussed comprehensively in chapter 16.

6.25 Optional grading and classification schemes

Figure 6-2: Grading

Requirement	Authority	Location
Grading	Tourism Grading Council of South Africa	Johannesburg

The decision to grade an accommodation establishment is entirely up to the owner, and is not a statutory requirement. The organisations dealing with the grading of establishments offer various marketing and promotional activities of benefit to those members whose businesses conform to specific product and service criteria and standards as prescribed.

If a business is in the process of design and establishment, the owner should decide if the business is aiming to acquire a certain level of grading with any scheme. If this is the case, the grading criteria can be planned for during the design phase of the establishment.

The Tourism Grading Council of South Africa (TGCSA), which offers a star rating, currently grades accommodation establishments as well as restaurants and conference venues.

6.26 Employment Equity Act

Figure 6-27: Employment equity

Requirement	Authority	Location
The completion and submission of an employment equity plan	Department of Labour	Labour offices located around South Africa.

The purpose of the Employment Equity Act 55 of 1998 is to eliminate employment discrimination, and to ensure equity in the workplace. The objective of the Act is to be achieved through the promotion of equal opportunity, fair treatment and the elimination of unfair employment practices.

The requirements for reporting on equity are extensively discussed and outlined in chapter 15.

6.27 Registration with the South African Music Rights Organisation

Figure 6-28: Music rights

Requirement	Authority	Location
Registration with the South African Music Rights Organisation	The South African Music Rights Organisation (SAMRO)	Johannesburg

If an owner of a guest house, hotel or restaurant chooses to play music of any kind by means of a radio, television set or tape recorder or sound system, he or she will be required to apply for a licence from the South African Music Rights Organisation (SAMRO) in Johannesburg. This organisation is a section 21 company (that is, it does not operate for profit) and controls the performing rights in music throughout South Africa. All fees collected by SAMRO are distributed to the composers concerned, after allowing for administrative expenses.

6.28 Application for a television licence

Figure 6-29: Television licence

Requirement	Authority	Location
The application and payment of a television licence	SABC TV	Various

Unlike homeowners who pay a single fee per household, the owner of a commercial business is required to pay a television licence fee for each of the televisions sets located within his or her establishment.

Under certain circumstances the SABC is prepared to negotiate a bulk discount with industry associations and organisations. The discount is based on the number of television sets represented by the Association. The Federated Hospitality Association of South Africa (FEDHASA) has in the past negotiated discounts of up to 25% for their members.

It is against the law not to pay your television licence fee. The Television Licences Department has implemented several strategies aimed at cutting the piracy rate, and substantially increasing the revenue from television licences. These strategies include employing the services of a countrywide tracking company to crack down on pirate viewers, the implementation of stricter credit control measures and an intensified legal action plan.

6.29 Insurance for hospitality establishments

There are certain risks inherent in operating a hospitality establishment. No hospitality establishment can afford *not* to have adequate insurance. The future of the hospitality establishment is put at risk, as a disaster can shut down the business permanently.

Contingencies against which the business owner can insure can be divided into two main categories:

* property and financial (including motor insurance)
* liability

The property and financial sector deals with coverage of losses incurred in the event of fires and allied perils, and for losses incurred through interruption of business. This division also covers office contents, glass on business premises, money insurance, theft insurance, insurance of electronic equipment, coverage of goods in transit, business all-risks insurance and motor vehicle insurance.

Fire and allied perils insurance covers the policy holder for damages to the business premises and to its contents, including stock, raw materials, finished products and machinery, in the event of a fire. The policy can be extended to cover the material damages as a result of lightning, explosions, earthquakes, earth tremors, storms, water, wind, snow, subsistence and malicious damage.

Business interruption insurance, also known as loss of profits or consequential loss, operates alongside the fire and allied perils insurance and covers the operator for loss of income as a result of being unable to resume normal business activities. Cover provides for payment of outstanding charges like rent, salaries and lease payments and operates at the same level as before the loss, continuing until the business is up and running again. Extensions are available to protect against loss of profits arising from the failure of public utilities such as electricity or water supply interruptions, which prevent the business from operating as normal.

Office contents insurance, also called office comprehensive, caters for commercial or office type risks. Most of the fire perils are also covered, as is theft preceded by forcible and violent entry into the premises.

A glass insurance policy covers the cost of replacing glass on the business premises. An extension to the policy will cover replacement costs of any signwriting or decoration that was on the glass. In the case of rented premises, the landlord may carry glass insurance but many do not. This must be checked in the lease agreement.

6.29.1 Types of insurance required

The following types of insurance are available as cover for hospitality establishments:

* **Personal accident and life insurance:** By taking out life and accident insurance policies, the hospitality establishment can be protected against the death or injury of the owner, manager, key personnel and other investors in the business. Partnership insurance, which often forms part of a partnership agreement, covers partners in the event of the death of one of the partners. It is recommended to take out life insurance if there is a family or other dependants requiring financial security. This life insurance policy can also benefit the hospitality establishment – for example, it may be usable as collateral for a business expansion loan from the bank.
* **Fire and general property insurance:** This provides coverage for the hospitality establishment in the event of loss or damage suffered as a result of fire, vandalism, hailstorms, windstorms, explosions, rioting, lightning,

malicious mischief and stock losses. It is important to ensure that the policy covers the current rather than historical replacement costs of assets.

- **Homeowner's policy:** A homeowner's policy is required when a bond is registered on the property. Analyse the policy to see exactly what it includes: these policies typically cover damage caused by fire, lightning, wind, vandalism or the weight of snow on your roof. Note that some natural disasters such as earthquakes and hurricanes are often excluded.
- **Burglary insurance:** This type of insurance usually goes together with fire insurance. Burglary insurance may be procured as protection against the theft of stock, cash and assets.
- **Office contents insurance:** This covers the hospitality establishment for the loss of, or damage to, property inside the building – for example, files, office furniture, inventory, materials and so on. Analyse the policy and ensure it includes computers and telephone systems. Some insurers consider these items to be specialised equipment that require additional coverage.
- **Public liability insurance:** Liability insurance covers the injuries and losses suffered by members of the public on the premises of the hospitality establishment. This type of insurance will cover the business in the event of bodily injury or damage to someone's property that occurs on its premises.
- **Product insurance:** Product liability insurance is designed to protect the hospitality establishment from claims occurring as a result of injury to guests caused by the use of the products and services that the hospitality establishment offers. For example, this type of insurance will provide protection from a lawsuit by a guest who is admitted to hospital due to food poisoning caused by food consumed at the hospitality establishment.

Insurance companies are able to tailor-make policies to suit individual needs. A few policies are designed especially for the needs of hospitality establishment owners.

Ensure that you have the right cover for your needs, and that you have the right amount of cover. Ask yourself whether the cover is worth the premium. Try to manage as much of the risk as you can yourself – for example, install a proper security system and take precautionary steps to safeguard your guests from injuries and losses.

6.30 Registration in terms of a provincial tourism Act

Figure 6-30:Tourism

Requirement	Authority	Location
Registration with the provincial tourism authority	Provincial tourism authority	In each of the nine provinces

At the time of writing, only the Kwa-Zulu Natal Tourism Authority required statutory or compulsory registration for tourism establishments. The remaining tourism authorities offer varying opportunities to list and advertise your business. It should be noted that certain provincial tourism authorities require that your establishment be officially graded by the TGCSA prior to them agreeing to list or advertise your business.

Tourism business owners are advised to contact their provincial tourism authority from time to time in order to ascertain whether or not a provision for registration has been established, or has become compulsory.

The registration or listing process differs from province to province. Some of the authorities have provided a facility online, while others require that you to forward all of the relevant information by post of fax. In most cases, you will be required to pay a small joining fee and in the case of Kwa-Zulu Natal you will be required to pay a joining fee and an annual renewal fee.

The objective behind registration is to create a comprehensive provincial tourism establishment database whilst, at the same time, ensuring that all tourism businesses adhere to the minimum standards of health, safety and security, and that they adhere to all the national, provincial and local authority laws, and applicable by-laws.

6.31 Certificate of health acceptability

Figure 6-31: Health certificate

Requirement	Authority	Location
Certificate of health	Local health authority	Various

The provisions and processes for food hygiene regulations are discussed in chapter 8.

6.32 Immigration Act

Figure 6-32: Register of guests

Requirement	Authority	Location
Register your lodgers	Department of home affairs	Pretoria

In terms of section 40 of the Immigration Act 13 of 2002, accommodation establishment owners are required to record specific information relating to their clients.

The person in charge of any premises, whether furnished or unfurnished, where lodging or sleeping accommodation is provided for payment or reward shall, if those premises fall within a **prescribed class**, in the prescribed manner keep a **register** of all persons who are provided with lodging or sleeping accommodation thereon, and every person shall sign the register and furnish therein the prescribed particulars regarding himself or herself.

The prescribed classes are:
- hotels
- boarding houses and lodges
- guest houses
- apartment buildings

Furthermore, according to the Act, the register must be safeguarded by a duly authorised person for a period of six months; and, in respect of a lodger, contain:

- his or full names and surname
- the number of his or her identity document or passport
- his or her residence status in the Republic
- his or her normal residential address
- his or her signature

Every person in charge of such premises shall, when required to do so by an immigration officer or police officer, produce the register for inspection.

Any person who:
- contravenes or fails to comply with the requirements
- gives false or incorrect particulars
- hinders any officer in the performance of his or her functions

shall be guilty of an offence and liable, on conviction, to a fine or to imprisonment for a period not exceeding 12 months

Neither the Act nor the regulations state specifically how, and in what form, this information should be collected, collated or filed. It is suggested, as most if not all accommodation establishments have a guest register of some form, that the required information be incorporated within the existing registers, filed and kept for a minimum period of six months. This is unlikely to cause any additional work as most if not all accommodation establishments keep their guest registers for longer than that.

Questions and exercises

You plan to open a pub in the Knysna Forest.
Draw up a list of all the requirements that you would have to meet for your local, provincial and national authorities when establishing the business, categorising the legal requirements into the following categories:
- land/premises
- business
- operational
- employment
- other

7

Liquor law

Objectives of this chapter:

By the end of this chapter the learner will be able to:

- Describe the changes being affected to liquor legislation
- Define key aspects related to the sale and consumption of liquor in the hospitality industry
- Describe the authorities that are responsible for liquor governance

The learner will know:

- Restrictions placed on the serving of alcohol
- Who is eligible to obtain a liquor licence, and who is not
- The process of application for a liquor licence

7.1 Introduction

Liquor is a controlled substance and may not be sold or provided to the public without a relevant licence issued by the appropriate government authority. The provision of liquor to the public is an important element of the hospitality industry, and therefore all hospitality operations and establishments that are licensed to sell liquor should have a working knowledge of the regulatory framework that governs this activity.

However, it is important to note that liquor legislation in South Africa has undergone significant changes over the last few years and continues to do so at present. Although the Liquor Act 27 of 1989 is currently in force in some of the provinces, Gauteng and the Eastern Cape have now promulgated their own Provincial Liquor Acts.

7.2 Current legislative framework

Liquor legislation in South Africa remains a little confusing with both the National Liquor Act 59 of 2003 and certain parts of the National Liquor Act 27 of 1989, as amended in 1993 and 1995, still in force. Added to these are the Gauteng Liquor Act 2 of 2003, and the Eastern Cape Liquor Act 10 of 2003. At time of writing, the other provinces had not promulgated their own liquor legislation, so the sale and consumption of liquor in those provinces is regulated in terms of the Liquor Act 27 of 1989, as amended in 1993 and 1995.

What is important to note is that the Liquor Amendment Act 57 of 1995 replaced the existing National Liquor Board with separate liquor boards for each province in South Africa. The liquor boards are statutory bodies and have the authority to administer the provisions of the 1989 National Liquor Act. In terms of the functions and powers granted to the liquor boards by the National Liquor Act, the boards may:

- Consider applications for liquor licences, and either refuse or grant such licences.
- Suspend any licence or right or privilege attaching to that licence for an indefinite or a fixed period of time.
- Impose any further conditions on a liquor licensee.
- Rescind a suspension of a licence or any right or privilege that is attached to the licence.
- Take any other steps that the boards may deem fit with respect of licences and their conditions.
- Advise the Member of the Executive Council (MEC).
- Furnish reports or recommendations to the MEC.
- Perform such other functions as are assigned to it in terms of the Act.
- Advise the MEC, and report and make recommendations on any matter referred to the board for consideration.

7.3 National Liquor Act

In April 2004 the national government promulgated the national Liquor Act 59 of 2003 which essentially deals with the manufacture and wholesale distribution of liquor in South Africa. This Act does not apply to retail on or off consumption liquor licensing.

The objectives of the Act are to reduce the socio-economic and other costs of alcohol abuse. The Act sets out to achieve this by regulating the manufacture and wholesale distribution of liquor, by setting essential national norms and standards for the regulation of the retail sale and micro-manufacture of liquor and by providing for public participation in the consideration of applications for registration.

In addition, the Act seeks to promote the development of a responsible and sustainable liquor industry in a manner that facilitates the entry of new participants into the industry, diversity of ownership in the industry, and an ethos of social responsibility throughout the industry.

The Act makes provision, amongst others, for:

- a national liquor policy
- the regulation of manufacture and distribution of liquor
- the regulation of methylated spirits
- prohibitions regarding employment in the liquor industry
- advertising restrictions
- prohibition of supply of liquor or methylated spirits to minors
- manufacturer and distributor registration requirements
- compliance
- offences and penalties
- the National Liquor Policy Council

- regulations and notices
- general provisions
- transitional provisions
- the repeal of laws

7.4 National Liquor Act 27 of 1989 as amended

It should be noted that the following comments provide a broad outline of the contents of the act. This outline is not exhaustive and it is not intended that it should replace the Liquor Act 27 of 1989 as amended. All licensees and applicants are advised to obtain a copy of the Liquor Act 27 of 1989 from either the National Liquor Board, the Government Printer or the State Library. Unfortunately it is not available on line.

This Act deals with the retail sale and consumption of liquor, both on and off the licensed premises, in the following provinces:
- Western Cape
- Northern Cape
- Limpopo Province
- Free State
- Kwazulu Natal
- Mpumalanga
- North West Province

Although this Act has essentially been replaced by the National Liquor Act 59 of 2003 certain provisions dealing with retail liquor licensing have remained in force. The Liquor Act 27 of 1989 came into operation on 2 April 1990 together with the regulations contained in *Government Gazette* 12382. The regulations however were replaced in June 1992 by a notice published in *Government Gazette* 13997.

Since its inception, the Liquor Act has been amended twice by Amendment Acts: first by the Liquor Amendment Act 105 of 1993, and then by the Liquor Amendment Act 57 of 1995, which came into operation in October of that year. It was also amended by the Airports Company Act 44 of 1993 and by the Liquor Products Act 60 of 1989.

The liquor regulations cover issues relating to the sale of liquor on licensed premises, as well as the off-premises sale or consumption of liquor.

7.4.1 Applications for licence

Chapter three of the Act in the main deals with applications, kinds of licences, contents of licences and considerations in terms of application.

7.4.2 Licence types

Liquor licences fall into two categories, based on where the liquor that is sold is to be consumed. On-consumption licences allow the liquor to be consumed where it is bought, but not taken off the premises. Off-consumption licences govern liquor outlets that sell liquor that is consumed elsewhere, such as the buyer's home, but not on the seller's premises.

Examples of on-consumption licences are as follows:

- hotel liquor licences
- restaurant liquor licences
- wine house liquor licences
- theatre liquor licences
- club liquor licences
- sorghum beer licences
- special liquor licences
- temporary liquor licences
- occasional liquor licences

Examples of off-consumption licences are:
- wholesale liquor licences
- brewers licences
- biquor store licences
- grocers wine licences
- wine farmers' licences
- sorghum beer brewers' licences
- special licences
- producers' licences

Before going into one or two of the specific on-consumption licence types, it is important to note the general conditions attached to the sale of liquor.

7.4.3 General conditions applicable to on-consumption licences
- Any restricted area must be clearly indicated as such at the entrance, for example staff areas.
- No person under the age of 18 is permitted to be served in any restricted part of the licensed premises or be allowed to sit or stand there.
- No bottling of liquor is permitted to take place on the licensed premises.
- Adequate guest toilet facilities for males and females must be provided on or near the licensed premises.
- A register of accommodation sold to each lodger must be maintained on the licensed premises.
- No pin-table, grab-table, machine or instrument known as a 'one armed bandit' or a similar device is permitted to be installed or operated on licensed premises unless the premises are entitled to do so under the National Gambling Act 33 of 1996 as amended.
- Ordinary meals shall be available on the licensed premises during the hours that liquor is sold.
- Liquor may be sold on any day between 10h00 and 02h00, provided that on 'closed days' liquor may only be sold to a person taking an 'ordinary meal' on the licensed premises. Closed days are defined as Sundays, Good Friday and Christmas Day.

Approval will be granted to a licence holder to conduct the following business:
- a *bona fide* hotel providing accommodation and facilities in the case of a hotel liquor licence
- an establishment providing accommodation and facilities in the case of a special licence (accommodation)

- *a bone fide* restaurant, including incidental entertainment and where applicable, accommodation and related facilities in the case of a restaurant liquor licence
- a *bona fide* eating house, including incidental entertainment in the case of a special licence (eating house)
- any game, match, competition or social activity normally taking place on the licensed premises or any objective pursued according to the rules, in the case of a club liquor licence

7.4.4 Location of consumption of liquor

Every holder of an on-consumption licence must ensure that liquor sold under that licence is consumed on the licensed premises only. The only exception is the holder of a wine house licence to whom an off-consumption approval has been granted. This provision does away with the requirement of designating a specific place for the consumption of liquor. Consumption of liquor may now take place anywhere upon the licensed premises.

7.4.5 Bars

Although there is no definition of the word 'bar' in the Act itself, the Act defines a 'restricted part' as a bar on on-consumption licensed premises in which liquor is served over the counter and which does not form an integral part of a room where ordinary meals are taken continuously on a daily basis. A bar counter located in a restaurant for example, is not a 'restricted part'. A bar of this nature will also be open to the public on closed days.

The licence conditions applicable to on-consumption licences provide that no person under 18 may be served at a bar counter or be allowed to sit or stand thereat.

7.4.6 Corkage

Whereas the Act is 'silent' on corkage, and it is therefore not illegal to allow a customer to bring his or her own liquor onto the licensed premises, and to consume that liquor thereon, great care must be taken in this respect. The Liquor Act provides that the licensee shall ensure that liquor sold under the licence shall be consumed on the licensed premises only.

It goes without saying that a customer who has brought liquor onto the premises may legally remove that liquor from the premises when he or she leaves. The burden of proving, however, that the liquor removed has not been sold under the licence and therefore that the licensed holder is not in contravention of the Liquor Act, will fall upon the holder of the licence.

It is within the discretion of the licence holder to decide whether he or she will allow a guest to bring liquor onto the premises, whether he or she will charge corkage (a charge for support services rendered) in respect thereof, and whether he or she will allow the guest to remove unconsumed liquor from the premises.

7.4.7 Drunkenness

The Act provides that it will be an offence for the holder of an on-consumption licence to allow drunkenness or licentious conduct on the licensed premises. The licence holder may not sell or supply liquor to a person who is drunk, as to do so is an offence.

7.4.8 Types of licence conditions

7.4.8.1 Hotel liquor licences

It is a condition that a holder of a hotel liquor licence shall, at all times, maintain on the licensed premises a *bona fide* hotel. If a hotel is a member of the TGCSA's voluntary grading and classification system referred to in section 18 of the Tourism Act 72 of 1993, it may sell liquor at all times, and to any person, irrespective of whether such person is a guest or orders a meal on the premises.

The trading hours of a hotel that is not a member of the aforesaid system, are as follows:

- Liquor may be sold and supplied to a lodger or his guests at any time and on any day except that on a closed day liquor may not be sold to a lodger or his guests in a restricted part of the licensed premises. A restricted part is a bar that is not contained in a room in which meals are regularly served.
- Liquor may be served on any day between 10h00 and 02h00 of the following day to a person other than a lodger, but on a closed day liquor may not be served in a restricted part of the licensed premises and may only be sold to a person taking a meal purchased on the premises, and who consumes the liquor during or immediately before or after that meal.

7.4.8.2 Restaurant liquor licence

In terms of the Liquor Amendment Act of 1993, restaurants may now sell all types of liquor. It is a condition of a restaurant licence that the holder must maintain a *bone fide* restaurant on the premises at which meals are regularly supplied to guests. On Sundays, a restaurant may only sell liquor to a person for consumption before, during or after a meal.

The holder of a restaurant licence may sell liquor on any day between the hours of 10h00 and 02h00.

7.4.8.3 Club liquor licence

A club liquor licence may be granted only to a *bona fide* club that has a constitution complying with the requirements of the Act. Among the requirements for a club constitution are the following:

- The club must consist of at least 35 ordinary members and the management, who must be elected by the members, must hold regular meetings at which proper minutes are recorded and kept.
- Only the members of the club are permitted to pay for facilities, liquor or refreshments supplied on the premises. If the rules make provision for guests to make use of the facilities of the club, a guest register in the prescribed form must be kept in which particulars of the guests are recorded.
- No profit from the sale of liquor by a club may go to any individual.
- No member who has not paid his subscriptions within three months after they become due, is permitted to remain a member while the subscriptions remain unpaid.

The holder of a club liquor licence may sell liquor for on-consumption purposes between the hours of 10h00 on any day and 02h00 on the following day irrespective of whether or not any one of the days is a closed day.

7.4.8.4 Occasional licences

An occasional licence may be granted to the holder of a hotel liquor licence, a restaurant liquor licence, a wine house licence, a club liquor licence and a special licence for on-consumption. The purpose of the special licence is to enable the holder of the licence to operate, in terms of the licence, outside the normal trading hours for the purposes of a special occasion, such as New Year's Eve.

7.4.9 New licences

Applications for new licences are made through the agency of a magistrate in triplicate on the prescribed form. The application must be accompanied by a Notice of Intention to Apply, published in the *Government Gazette* on the first Friday of every month.

The application must be supported by a plan of the premises, a separate document containing a written description of the premises, written representations in support of the application, and numerous other documents.

The application lies for inspection with the magistrate during which time a police report is produced. During this period, objections may be lodged, and the applicant will be given an opportunity to reply to the police report and/or any objections.

The documents are then forwarded to the Liquor Board of the province concerned, who, on receipt of the application, will consider it and either grant or refuse the application.

The board will not grant a licence:
- unless it is satisfied that the premises are or will be suitable for the purposes of the licence
- if the premises are situated in the vicinity of a church, a school or residential area so that those institutions and residences will not be prejudiced
- unless the applicant is of good character and fit to hold the licence
- if the granting of the licence is not in the public interest
- if by the granting of the application it will cause a harmful monopolistic condition to arise

7.4.10 Objections

Objections, petitions or representations by various parties, in respect of an application for a liquor licence, may be lodged with the magistrate within 28 days of the lodgement of the application. A copy of the objection must also be forwarded to the person who applied for the licence, as well as to the police officer concerned. Proof of these copies being forwarded must also be provided.

No provision is made for an objection to an application for a temporary or occasional licence. If any person wants to object to such a licence, he or she should bring this to the attention of the police officer, asking that the objection be placed on record.

The Liquor Board will be convened (unless the chairperson feels that it is not warranted) for the consideration of any objections to a licence from:
- a person who is a resident in the district in which the licensed premises are situated

◆ a holder of a licence whose licensed premises are in the same district as the application licence

7.4.11 Management

A company, close corporation, partnership or trust may not conduct business under a liquor licence unless it has appointed a 'natural person' to manage and be responsible for that business. That person may not be disqualified from holding a licence. The regulations provide for the licence holder to give notice of the appointment to the secretary of the Liquor Board and the designated public officer. A form is available for this purpose.

It is important to note that the holder of a licence is responsible for the acts and omissions of the manager unless he/she can satisfy the court that:
◆ he/she neither connived nor permitted the act or omission by the manager
◆ he/she took all reasonable steps to prevent the act
◆ the act or omission did not fall within the scope of employment of the manager

The fact that the holder of the licence issued instructions prohibiting the act will not in itself be sufficient proof that he/she took all reasonable steps to prevent the act or omission.

Despite the fact that the holder of the licence is responsible for the acts of his/her managers, agents, employees and family members, these individuals are also liable as if they were holders of the licence concerned.

7.4.12 Disqualifications

A liquor licence may not be granted or transferred to a person who is disqualified from holding a licence. The following persons may not be granted a licence although exceptions may be made in suitable circumstances.
◆ a person who has in the preceding 10 years been sentenced for any offence, to imprisonment without the option of a fine
◆ a person who has in the preceding 10 years been convicted of an offence in terms of the Liquor Act of 1989 or its predecessor and was, within five years after that conviction again convicted of an offence in terms of the Act or its predecessor, and was then sentenced to a fine of not less that R200 000 or to imprisonment without the option of a fine
◆ a person who is an unrehabilitated insolvent
◆ a minor on the date of consideration of the application
◆ the husband or wife of any of the above persons

A company, close corporation, partnership or trust is similarly disqualified if any one of the persons referred to above has a controlling interest in the company or close corporation, or is a partner in that partnership or is the main beneficiary of that particular trust.

7.5 The Gauteng Liquor Act

The Gauteng Liquor Act 2 of 2003, promulgated in April 2004, deals with the retail sale and consumption of liquor, both on and off the licensed premises. It should be noted that the following provides a broad outline of the contents of the

Gauteng Liquor Act 2 of 2003, the Gauteng Liquor Amendment Act 9 of 2003 and the Regulations in terms of section 141 of the Gauteng Liquor Act, 2003.

The Act makes provision for:
- definitions
- the liquor board
- applications for licences
- issue of licences and permits
- general conditions of licences
- special conditions applicable to licences
- validity of licences and permits
- transfer of licences and permits
- enforcement and judicial proceedings
- prohibited and controlled substances
- exemptions
- offences
- miscellaneous matters
- transitional arrangements

It should be noted that the following comments provide a broad outline of the contents of the Act and regulations. This outline is not exhaustive and it is not intended that it should replace any one or more of the above listed enactments.

All licensees and applicants are advised to obtain a copy of all three of the documents listed above from either the Provincial Liquor Board, the Regional Liquor Offices, the Government Printer, the State Library or on line at www.gpg.gov.za – click on Legislation & Documents.

7.5.1 Chapters one and two
Chapter 1 deals with definitions and Chapter 2, sections 2 to 22, deals with the establishment, powers, administration and functions of the Gauteng Liquor Board, six local committees of the board and six regional offices. Essentially the main board will, together with other functions, give final approval on all liquor licence applications, transfers and the amendments of licensing conditions. The only exception to the above will be applications for catering or occasional permits, which are handled from start to finish by the local regional offices.

Committees of the board
The six local committees are responsible for considering all applications for licences, transfer of licences and amendments of conditions, received from the local regional office and they, in turn, make recommendations to the main board.

Regional Liquor Licensing Offices
In terms of the act all new applications, transfers and renewals will, unlike in the past, no longer be lodged at the local magistrate's office but must now be lodged at one of the six regional liquor licensing offices. Applicants will be required to deal with the regional liquor licensing office in the area in which their establishment is located. The regional licensing offices are located in –
- Johannesburg
- Tshwane

- Ekurhuleni
- Sedibeng
- West Rand
- Metsweding

7.5.2 Chapter three

Chapter 3, sections 23 to 36, deals with applications, the various types of liquor licences, objections, and the conditions attached to each licence type. Section 31 deals specifically with the application for a catering or occasional licence.

7.5.2.1 Licence types and conditions – The Act makes provision for the following types of liquor licences:

- hotel
- restaurant
- rub
- tavern
- gaming premises
- catering or occasional permit

In addition to the licence categories listed above, the Gauteng Liquor Act makes further provision for the following:
- club liquor licences
- dance hall liquor licences
- grocers' wine licences
- liquor store licences
- micro-manufacturer liquor licences
- night club liquor licences
- pool club liquor licences
- sorghum beer licences (on or off)
- sports ground liquor licences
- theatre liquor licences
- wholesale liquor licences

The Act specifically defines each licence category. For example a hotel is described as premises wherein the business of supplying lodging and meals for a reward is conducted, and includes a motel, inn, bed and breakfast, caravan and camping park, farmhouse, guest house, a lodge, boatel, boat and house boat.

7.5.2.2 Application process

With the exception of the catering or occasional permit all applications are lodged at the regional liquor licensing offices in the area in which the applicant's establishment is located. An application for a catering or occasional permit is made to the regional liquor licensing office in the area in which the event is to take place.

Applications for new licences must be lodged on the first Friday of the month (or second if the first is a public holiday) between the hours of 08h00 and 16h00 at the regional offices in the metropolitan area in which the licence is sought.

It is important to note that seven days before lodging an application for a new licence with one of the regional offices, applicants must ensure that they place an advertisement in two newspapers circulating in the area in which the establishment is located. The advertisement must provide certain details including the address of the regional liquor licensing office and must invite interested persons to lodge any objections with the appropriate licensing office.

The specific requirements for the application of a liquor licence, which are fairly lengthy, are provided for under the Act in section 23(1)(a) to (j) together with various forms set out in the regulations. Broadly speaking the Act requires an applicant to –

◆ motivate an application
◆ provide plans
◆ provide colour photographs
◆ provide a written description
◆ provide proof of publication in the newspapers
◆ provide a certificate of suitability of both the person and premises from the SAPS
◆ provide the usual company registration, addresses, identity numbers, etc
◆ attach proof of affiliation to an association
◆ provide proof of payment of the prescribed fees
◆ provide a tax clearance certificate from SARS

If the premises are incomplete, being built or alterations are taking place, an application may still be made for as long as all the information mentioned above is made available. It is important to note that the licence will, however, not be issued until the building or renovations have been completed.

7.5.2.3 Objections

As mentioned above, the applicant must place an advertisement in two newspapers circulating in the area in which the premises are located. As a result, any person wishing to make comment or object to the licence may do so by writing to the appropriate local committee within 21 days of the date that the application for the licence was made.

7.5.3 Chapter four

Chapter four, sections 37 to 102, deals with matters such as membership to the Gauteng Liquor Traders Association, general conditions attached to the various licence types, building alterations, management, employees and the maintaining of records.

7.5.3.1 Gauteng Liquor Traders Association

An important provision in the Act deals with the Gauteng Liquor Traders Association (GLTA). This provision requires that all associations within Gauteng who are active in the liquor trade must become members of the Gauteng Liquor Traders Association. An example would be FEDHASA, the Federated Hospitality Association of South Africa, whose members primarily operate licensed accommodation establishments and restaurants. This section also requires that all applicants who are not members of an association must become direct members of the GLTA.

The role of the GLTA is to promote an organised trade in liquor, ensure compliance with all laws, and assist with policies relating to the regulation and responsible consumption of liquor.

7.5.3.2 Employees

This section restricts the employment of persons under the age of 18 for the purposes of handling and/or serving liquor. In addition it deals with the restriction of the selling of liquor to persons under the age of 18 and not permitting minors, under the age of 18, to enter a restricted part on the licensed premises.

7.5.3.3 Licence conditions

The Act provides very specific conditions that apply to each licence type.

Some examples follow.

The holder of a hotel liquor licence must maintain an establishment where accommodation and meals are regularly supplied to guests. A record of the lodgers must be kept. The holder of the licence may sell liquor to a lodger or guest for consumption by the lodger or guest in the hotel room or to any person taking a meal purchased on the premises and consuming the liquor at or immediately before, during or after the meal.

The holder of a restaurant licence must maintain a restaurant at which meals are regularly supplied to guests and they may sell liquor on any day during the prescribed times set out in the regulations being from 10h00 to 02h00. Liquor may only be served to persons taking a meal purchased on the premises.

It is important to note that each licence type has very specific conditions attached to it.

7.5.3.4 General conditions

Some of the more significant general conditions contained in the act are –

Section 39. It is important that licensees and applicants for licences understand the provisions contained in section 39, as it deals with holders of certain types of licence not being permitted to hold a financial interest in various other types of licences.

Section 40 deals with management. If the licence holder is not the person managing and administrating liquor on the property, the licence holder is then required to ensure that a lawfully qualified person is appointed and that the liquor board is notified of the appointment. The licence holder is required to complete Form 4 which is contained in the regulations.

Sections 103 and 104 deal with the transferring of a licence. In the event that a licensee is looking to transfer a licence to another qualified person, the Act and regulations provide for the manner in which the process should be carried out.

7.5.4 Chapters five to ten

Chapters 5 to 10, sections 105 to 144, deal with the administrative processes such as the appointment and functions of liquor inspectors, and also matters such as offences under the Act.

7.5.5 Regulations

The regulations attached to the Act deal primarily with the manner in which applications, transfers, etc, are carried out, and provide copies of the various forms to be completed as required under the Act. In addition they make provision for the cost of licences and the trading hours associated with each licence type. The Act must always be read in conjunction with these regulations.

In addition and under each licence type, the regulations provide information on the following:
- times of business
- cost of application for such a licence
- cost of licence (once granted)
- annual renewal fee for the a licence
- cost of transferring the licence
  The following forms are provided for within the regulations:
- application for a licence
- notice of application
- information relating to an applicant
- information relating to the procurer of a financial or controlling interest
- application for the appointment of a natural person to manage the business
- application for the transfer of a licence.

7.6 The Eastern Cape Liquor Act

The Eastern Cape Liquor Act 10 of 2003 was promulgated in April 2004. The Act deals with the retail sale and consumption of liquor, both on and off the licensed premises, throughout the Eastern Cape. The objective of the Act is to provide for the registration of establishments concerned with the retail sale and micro-manufacturing of liquor.

Published in April 2004 *Gazette* 1143, the Act makes provision for the following:
- definitions
- application for registration
- notice requirements for applicants
- liquor board notification requirements
- representations and objections
- certificate of registration
- application for temporary registration
- transfer and removal of registration
- public access to application
- notices and summons
- payment
- annual renewal

- penalties, compliance and appeals
- various forms

It should be noted that the following comments provide a broad outline of the contents of the Eastern Cape Liquor Act 10 of 2003 and the Eastern Cape Liquor Regulations published under Notice 1143 of 2004. This outline is not exhaustive and it is not intended that it should replace any one or more of the above listed enactments.

All licensees and applicants are advised to obtain a copy of both of the documents listed above from the Provincial Liquor Board, the Government Printer, the State Library or on line at http://www.ecprov.gov.za (go to departments and click on Department of Economic Development & Environmental Affairs, then click on documents, then click on Acts or regulations).

7.6.1 Chapter one

Chapter one deals with definitions, and the objectives and application of the Act. It paves the way for the management and reduction of the socio-economic and other costs of excessive alcohol consumption. The Act also introduces several new processes and procedures, including the lodgement of applications directly with the board and no longer with magistrates, the lodgement of applications on any week day, involvement of municipalities and ward committees through relevant by-laws, and the regulated time frames of 60 days for consideration of application by the board.

7.6.2 Chapter two

Chapter two deals with provincial structures and functions, and covers the establishment, composition, financial matters and powers of the Eastern Cape Liquor Board, and the panel of appeal, together with provisions covering meetings and general provisions. The function and role of the board is to:
- consider and approve or refuse applications for the various categories of registration contemplated in the Act
- cancel, suspend or vary any registration
- determine conditions applicable to the various categories of registration
- publish in the *Provincial Gazette* applications received for registration, transfers or removal
- exercise any other power and perform any other duty conferred or imposed on it in terms of the Act

The role and function of the panel of appeal is to consider appeals against decisions made by the board.

7.6.3 Chapter three

It is important to note that no person may sell liquor unless that person is registered in terms of the Act to sell that liquor. Chapter three therefore deals with the registration of persons who qualify and who are permitted to sell liquor and the categories of registration. These are:
- the retail sale of liquor for consumption off the premises where the liquor is being sold

- the retail sale of liquor for consumption on the premises where the liquor is being sold
- the retail sale of liquor for consumption on and off the premises where the liquor is being sold
- the retail sale and consumption of liquor at a special event
- micro manufacturing

In addition, the chapter deals with the application process, time frames, appeals, certificates, commencement and cancellations, controlling interests, the register and payment for registration.

When making application, the specified form must be completed by providing the following:

- a natural person must include his or her full name, identity number and residential address, and a statement that he or she is not disqualified for registration
- a company or close corporation must include its full name, registration number and the address of its registered office together with the names, identity numbers and residential addresses of all shareholders and a statement that none of them is disqualified from registration
- a trust must include the names, identity numbers and residential addresses of all its trustees and known beneficiaries, and a statement that none of them is disqualified from registration
- an association or partnership, must include the names, identity numbers and residential addresses of all its members or partners, and a statement that none of them is disqualified from registration

In addition the applicant must provide the following information:

- the physical address and the erf, street or farm number and a description of the premises from which the applicant intends to sell liquor, including a plan
- the category registration that is being applied for
- whether the premises concerned are in existence or have not yet been built
- other information that may be required by the board to enable the board to determine whether or not the applicant meets the requirements of registration
- payment of the prescribed fee
- proof that he or she has notified the local ward committee and the governing body of every education institution or place of worship within the prescribed radius

The board will then follow the various procedures as laid down in sections 3 to 9 of chapter 3, and notify the applicant as to whether or not the application was successful, whether the applicant is required to meet any additional criteria, or if the application was unsuccessful.

If the board has not approved an application for registration, transfer or removal of a particular term or condition, an appeal against the decision may be made to the panel of appeal within 30 days of having received the notification.

If the board approves the application then it will register the applicant and issue a certificate of registration covering the registration number, the premises in respect of which registration has been granted, the conditions upon which registration was granted, the category of registration, and the period for which registration has been given.

It is also important to note that a registered person must not allow any other person to obtain a controlling interest in the business unless the liquor board has, on application by the registered person, agreed that the other person may purchase that interest.

7.6.4 Chapter four
Chapter four deals with terms and conditions applicable to the sale of liquor, and covers aspects such as the persons to whom liquor may or may not be sold, management of the business, special events, trading hours, public health and limitations on employers.

Section 38, for example, states that no registered person may sell liquor to any person who is under the age of 18 years or to an intoxicated person.

Section 40 deals with management. If the licence holder is not the person managing and administrating liquor on the property, the licence holder is then required to ensure that a lawfully qualified person is appointed and that the liquor board is notified of the appointment.

Section 42 deals with trading hours and states that a person registered to sell liquor may sell liquor only during the hours determined by the municipality in whose area of jurisdiction the premises are situated. Therefore all registered persons should check with their local authority in order to ascertain the exact trading hours permissible.

Section 44 states that no registered person may employ any person in connection with the sale of liquor who is under the age of 18 years. This, however, does not apply to a person 16 years or older who is undergoing apprenticed training in catering services, and who is employed on the premises of the registered person.

7.6.5 Chapters five, six and seven
These chapters deal with inspections, prohibited and controlled liquids, law enforcement, judicial proceedings, offences and penalties, general provisions, transitional arrangements and conversions.

7.6.6 Regulations
The regulations attached to the Act deal primarily with the manner in which applications, transfers, etc, are carried out, and provide copies of the various forms to be completed as required under the Act. In addition they make provision for the cost of licences. The Act must always be read in conjunction with these regulations.

The following forms, amongst others, are provided for within the regulations:
◆ application for registration
◆ notice to the ward committee, educational institutions and places of worship
◆ notice of lodgement of application for registration
◆ application for temporary registration
◆ application for transfer of certificate of registration
◆ application for removal of a certificate of registration

- application for a natural person to manage the business to which the registration relates
- application to procure a controlling interest in the business to which the registration relates

Questions and exercises

1. Diagrammatically portray the process of application and granting of a liquor licence.
2. Explain the difference between a hotel liquor licence and a restaurant liquor licence.
3. Draw up a corkage policy for the Buffalo Bill Restaurant.
4. Find and summarise the relevant provisions of the latest liquor legislation in your province.

8
Food hygiene legislation

Objectives of this chapter:

By the end of this chapter the learner will be able to:

◆ Identify which laws and regulations govern the handling of food for public consumption
◆ Use relevant SABS Codes of Practice in the handling and storage of food where applicable

The learner will know:

◆ Why it is important to comply with health and hygiene legislation
◆ How SABS codes of practice interface with health and hygiene legislation
◆ The duties and responsibilities of the person in charge of food premises
◆ The requirements for health certification by the health authorities
◆ The relevance and enforcement of municipal health by-laws on hygiene operations in a hospitality establishment
◆ The facilities required by law for food premises

8.1 Introduction

In South Africa, there are two main governmental food control authorities, namely, the Department of Health (DoH), and the Department of Agriculture (DoA). Other authorities are the Department of Trade and Industry (DTI) represented by the South African Bureau of Standards (SABS).

The collaborative activities and aims of all these departments are:

◆ to protect public health by reducing incidences of food-borne diseases
◆ to protect consumers from unsanitary, unwholesome, contaminated, misla-belled or adulterated foods
◆ to support economic development by maintaining consumer confidence in the food system
◆ to provide a sound regulatory foundation for domestic and international trade in food

The Department of Agriculture, among others, regulates and promotes the safety of animal products, as well as agricultural products, and controls the import and export of animal and agricultural products. The Animal Diseases Act 35 of 1984 ensures that imported food products are not likely to introduce diseases such as foot and mouth disease and bird flu, which also have public health implications. It also controls the importation of honey, which, if not monitored and controlled, may introduce pests that can spread, and affect the local industry and animal populations.

The Department of Health, through the promulgation of regulations in terms of the Foodstuffs, Cosmetics and Disinfectant Act 54 of 1972 (Foodstuffs Act) has developed legislation that governs the importation, manufacture and sale of certain foodstuffs. It has also promulgated regulations regarding foodstuffs offered for sale.

These regulations are enforced by the local authorities. They govern the handling, transportation, storage and sale of unpacked foods to the general public of South Africa by food-producing establishments. This legislation serves to protect the food industry from legal action, by giving them rules within which to operate. It is both the legal and moral responsibility of people who trade in food to protect the consumers from potential illness. This responsibility, combined with good hygienic practices, should keep businesses in good health.

8.2 The food control framework in South Africa

8.2.1 Hygiene regulations

It is intended that food regulations that were provided for under the Health Act 63 of 1977 will be incorporated into the Foodstuffs, Cosmetics and Disinfectants Act 54 of 1977 through the publication of an amendment to the Foodstuffs Act. These are Regulations R918 of July 1999 (to which small corrections were made by the R723 Regulations of 12 July 2002). These R918 Regulations govern: General Hygiene Requirements for Food Premises and the Transport of Food.

In addition to the text of all the relevant legislation, the Department of Health's Directorate of Food Control has a number of useful documents on its website, such as *'Guidelines for the Management and Health Surveillance of Food Handlers'*. There are also various pamphlets and posters that can be obtained from the department, and distributed or displayed on the food preparation premises. The directorate's website address is: www.doh.gov.za/department/dir_foodcontr-f.html

8.2.2 HACCP regulations

The Department of Health has made provision for the implementation of the Hazard Analysis and Critical Control Point (HACCP) system for, *inter alia,* the further strengthening of food hygiene management.

These regulations, published under the Foodstuffs Act, govern food processing and production operations and food vendors in South Africa. While these regulations are not yet applicable to the hospitality industry, the Minister of Health may decide to enforce the implementation of this system within the industry in future, if it is deemed to be in the interest of pubic health. However, this will be done in consultation with the industry. The regulations make provision for individual industries or sectors of the industry (such as contract catering) to apply to the Minister for mandatory application of HACCP in that particular industry or sector, should they wish to do so.

8.2.3 Microbiological standards and other national regulations

Although the regulations governing microbiological standards are not directly applicable to the hygiene requirements for food premises, these regulations provide some microbiological specifications for certain foodstuffs, such as milk and other dairy products, fruit juices, and herbs and spices, which are indicators of the hygiene conditions under which the food was handled or processed. The two sets of regulations available at present for this purpose have been published under the Foodstuffs, Cosmetics and Disinfectants Act 54 of 1977 and are the following:

◆ Regulations Governing the Microbiological Standards for Foodstuffs (R692 of 16 November 1997).
◆ Regulations relating to Milk and Dairy Products (R1555 of 21 November 1997).

A national guideline regarding the interpretation of microbiological analysis results is available on the Directorate's website. It includes microbiological standards other than those contained in the regulations, and covers, *inter alia,* prepared foods found in catering operations.

Other regulations that address aspects related to unhygienic practices applicable to regarding processed foods include the regulations governing processed foodstuffs (R723 of 10 August 2001). These regulations prohibit the food industry from either using foodstuffs that have been already offered for sale to the consumer as raw materials for other products, or reselling them after cleaning and repackaging.

8.3 Municipal by-laws

Apart from being responsible for the enforcement of, among others, all the regulations referred to under point 8.2, each municipal authority is allowed to create specific by-laws for governing health and hygienic practices in its area. These are usually developed to address a particular problem in a particular area. These by-laws will further assist the hospitality operator in the safe handling and preparation of food. Most municipalities have these by-laws for their particular area of jurisdiction, and they are responsible for their enforcement.

An example of this would be if the municipal area includes animal farming, or a racecourse that might encourage the breeding of flies. Extra protection regarding the control of flies in the area may then be included in by-laws. Health testing of food handlers may be compulsory in some municipal areas, so this needs to be checked with the local authorities.

It is the responsibility of the owner, or person in charge of each individual establishment, to contact the local health authority to ascertain what special provisions and by-laws are specific to his or her municipal area.

8.4 SABS codes of practice

The South African Bureau of Standards (SABS) has compiled codes of practice that apply to food handling, and chilled and frozen food storage. These codes are not legislated, but are merely references or guidelines for good practice, and may be used by anyone in the food preparation industry.

◆ Code of Practice for Food Hygiene Management, South African Bureau of Standards SABS No 049–1989. (Please check the status of this document as at the time of publication, it was under revision).

◆ Code of Practice for the Handling of Chilled and Frozen Foods, South African Bureau of Standards SABS No 0156–1979.

Compliance with these codes of practice is required only if the establishment would like to acquire SABS certification.

8.5 Additional detail on the regulations governing general hygiene requirements for food premises and the transport of food

The R918 Regulations Governing the General Hygiene Requirements for Food Premises and the Transport of Food are enforced by municipal health inspectors or environmental health officers. They, *inter alia,* process applications for health certificates, inspect premises and issue certificates.

The content of the regulations is summarised below. For further information on the application of these regulations, please refer to them directly, or contact the environmental health officer at the local authority concerned.

Note: the official name for a health inspector is an *environmental health practitioner*, and they have professional status and are registered with the Health Professions Council

8.5.1 Certificate of acceptability

These regulations govern the certification and inspection of food premises by environmental health officers operating at local government (municipal) level. The food operator must apply to the local authority for a Certificate of Acceptability for Food Premises. Upon receipt of the application, the authority will inspect the premises, and if they are satisfied that they meet the provisions of the regulations, they will issue a certificate, or will grant an extension to the person in charge to make any necessary adjustments to comply with the regulations.

The certificate must be on public display on the premises, or a copy must immediately be made available on request.

The certificate is issued in the name of the person in charge of the food premises. Therefore, if this person is replaced, the authorities must be informed in writing within 30 days so that they can issue a new certificate. The certificate is therefore not transferable from one person to another. This certificate will expire if various provisions of the regulations regarding prohibitions are not met.

The health inspectors have their own regulations governing how they inspect food premises, so these are consistently applied throughout South Africa.

8.5.2 Prohibitions

If the premises, activities or circumstances constitute a health hazard, the inspector will issue a notice containing the reasons for the prohibition, and the conditions under which (compliance) the notice will be removed. The inspector must inspect the premises within 72 hours of a request for the removal of the prohibition it issues, and can charge the person in charge of the food premises for non-compliance of the food premises.

8.5.3 Standards and requirements for food premises

Food premises must be located, designed, constructed and finished without creating a health hazard, and must enable food to be handled hygienically and prevent any spoilage or contamination of food.

The interior surfaces (walls, ceilings, floors) have specific requirements to ensure that they can be easily cleaned, and will not contaminate food. Each room must be ventilated effectively by either natural or artificial ventilation. Adequate lighting, either natural or artificial, must be provided.

Food premises must

- have a wash-up facility with hot and cold water for cleaning of facilities
- be rodent-proof in accordance with the best available methods
- be provided with effective means of preventing the access of flies or other insects to the area where food is handled
- have a waste-water disposal system approved by the local authority

The following must be available in respect of the food premises:

- handwashing facilities for staff and guests must be provided with cold and/or hot water
- liquid-proof, easy-to-clean refuse containers with close-fitting lids
- storage space for the hygienic storage of food, facilities and equipment, with a separate area for the hygienic storage of refuse and refuse containers
- a separate changing area with storage facilities for clothes
- an adequate supply of water
- sufficient latrines, urinal stalls and washbasins to meet the combined maximum number of staff and guests in accordance with the table in figure 8–1

Figure 8-1: Annexure C (Sanitation Regulation 5(3)(d)(i)):

Population	Number of sanitary conveniences to be installed in relation to the population as given in the first column				
	Men			Women	
For a population up to:	Latrines	Urinal stalls	Hand wash-basins	Latrines	Hand wash-basins
10	1	1	1	1	1
20	1	2	2	2	2
40	2	3	2	3	3
60	3	3	2	4	4
80	4	4	3	6	5
100	4	4	3	8	6

Population	Number of sanitary conveniences to be installed in relation to the population as given in the first column				
	Men			Women	
120	5	5	4	9	7
140	5	5	4	10	8
180	5	6	5	11	8
	Add 1 latrine, 1 hand washbasin and 1 urinal for every 70 persons in excess of 180 persons			Add 1 latrine and 1 hand washbasin for every 35 persons in excess of 180 persons	

Further, premises must not have direct connection with any area from which gases, odours or vapours can enter and contaminate food. This includes direct connection with toilets, unless these are equipped with self-sealing doors and special ventilation.

8.5.4 Standards and requirements for facilities on food premises

Working surfaces or food preparation equipment (crockery, cutlery, utensils) must be clean, smooth, rustproof, and not chipped, split or cracked. Disposable service ware must be stored in dust-free containers until used, and may not be used more than once.

Surfaces must be cleaned and washed before they come into contact with food for the first time of every shift, and must be washed/cleaned immediately after food handling.

'Clean' means that the surface will contain no more than 100 viable micro-organisms per cm^2 upon analysis, and no residue of cleaning materials or disinfectants.

Chilling and freezing facilities used for food must have a thermometer to reflect the temperature inside the facility. Likewise, heating equipment used for food must also have a thermometer to reflect the temperature inside the facility or equipment.

8.5.5 Standards and requirements for food containers

Cans or tins that bulge or are blown, rusting or leaking, may not be sold and must be removed and destroyed by an environmental health officer. Containers must be clean and free of any contaminants that may spoil food stored in them. Repacked food (for example sandwiches or salads on display for purchase and take-away consumption) must be packed in dust- or liquid-proof containers to protect it from contamination, and must be sealed so that food cannot be removed without the wrapper or seal being damaged.

8.5.6 Standards and requirements for the display, storage and temperature of food

These provisions govern the management and organisation of food stores, such as dry storage, cold-rooms and so forth. Food must not come into direct contact with a floor or any ground surface. Shelves or racks must be clean and free of dust or any other impurity.

Non-packed, ready-to-eat food such as meals or foods displayed in open containers must be protected against droplet contaminations (for example if someone sneezes nearby) or contamination by insects such as flies.

In general, the temperatures in figure 8–2 apply to the storage of frozen, chilled and hot-held foods. Exceptions to these general provisions apply to various items such as venison that has been hunted, or during delivery of foods, with a maximum of one-hour delivery time.

Figure 8-2: Annexure D – Food temperatures (Regulation 8(4))

Category	Type of Food	Required core temperature of food products
Frozen products	Ice cream and sorbet, excluding sorbet which is used for soft serve purposes	−18°C
	Any other food that is marketed as a frozen product	−12°C
Chilled products	Raw, unpreserved fish, molluscs, crustaceans, edible offal, poultry, meat and milk	+4°C
	Any other perishable food that must be kept chilled to prevent spoilage	+7°C
Heated products	Any perishable food not kept frozen or chilled	+65°C

The regulations provide for a code of practice for the measuring of the temperature of food (Annexure E).

8.5.7 Standards and requirements for protective clothing
No person is allowed to handle unpacked food without wearing protective clothing (including head covering and footwear) that conforms to the following:
◆ be clean and neat when the person begins to handle the food
◆ be clean and of such a design and material that it cannot contaminate food
◆ be designed so that the food does not come into contact with any part of the body except for the hands

8.5.8 Duties of the person in charge of the food premises
The regulations place the burden of compliance on the person in charge, as he or she has the authority to ensure the following:
◆ effective pest control
◆ training of food handlers in food hygiene
◆ regular and frequent refuse removal
◆ hygienic refuse storage
◆ cleaning and disinfection of refuse bins
◆ effective waste-water disposal
◆ cleanliness of food premises, vehicle compartments and food containers
◆ food handlers not wearing jewellery that will come into contact with the food that is being handled

- no animals being allowed in the food handling areas, except a guide dog for a blind person, or live shellfish awaiting preparation, or animals awaiting slaughter in a separate room
- no condition, act or omission that contaminates food being allowed on the premises
- compliance with the food regulations
- all staff handling food meeting the regulations
- Food handling areas not being used for sleeping, laundry of clothes, or anything else that may contaminate food
- not handling foods unless it is strictly necessary and in accordance with good practice
- reporting diseases and recording conditions for perusal by an inspector

8.5.9 Duties of a food handler

While the person in charge has organisational responsibilities, the food handler has a duty to ensure that his or her own actions do not cause contamination and/or spoilage of food. Therefore, food handlers must comply with the following:
- fingernails, hands and clothes must be clean
- wash hands thoroughly with soap and water
  - immediately before each shift
  - at the beginning of the day's work or after a rest period
  - after going to the toilet
  - after blowing their noses, or coming into contact with perspiration, or their hair, nose or mouth
  - after handling a handkerchief, money, refuse container or refuse
  - after handling raw vegetables, fruit, eggs, meat or fish, and before handling ready-to-use food
  - after smoking or on return to the food premises
  - after their hands have become contaminated for any other reason.

Food may not be handled by any person
- who has an abscess or sore or cut unless this is covered with a moisture-proof dressing to prevent contamination of the food
- who is suffering from, or is suspected of carrying, a contagious disease or condition that may be transmitted by food
- whose hands or clothing are not clean

Furthermore, the regulations prohibit the following actions:
- spitting in the area where food is handled
- smoking or use of tobacco in the area where food is handled
- Handling food in such a way that it brings it into contact with any body part other than the hands
- coughing or sneezing over non-packed food
- spitting on any food equipment, or inflating sausage casings or food wrappings by mouth (or any such activity)
- walk, stand, sit or lie on food
- use of a hand washbasin for cleaning of facilities
- any other action that could contaminate or spoil food

8.5.10 Standards and requirements for the handling of meat

All meat handled on the food premises must conform to the requirements of the Meat Safety Act 40 of 2000. If a species of animal not covered by the mentioned Act is slaughtered on premises where food is handled, the carcass must be properly bled, and gutted within 30 minutes after the animal is killed. Unskinned carcasses must be handled so that the skin does not come into contact with any other food or contaminate food premises or equipment. Further, no animal may be killed or dressed in any room other than one set aside for that purpose.

8.5.11 Standards and requirements for the transport of food

Food shall not be transported in a vehicle unless that part of the vehicle is clean, and contamination of the food is prevented. In addition, food may not be transported together with contaminated or waste food, with poison or harmful substances (for example, cleaning chemicals), with a live animal or anything that may spoil or contaminate the food.

The freight compartment of a vehicle used for transporting food must be made of a material that is easy to clean, dustproof and not used for transporting anything else at the same time. Food being transported must not be in contact with the floor or transported in such a way that it could be spoiled or contaminated in any way.

8.5.12 Exemptions, additional requirements and reservations

A person in charge of food premises may apply for exemption from any of the provisions of the regulations, except for exemption from the issuing of a certificate. The Health Officer will process the application and grant the exemption if it does not result in a health hazard. Exemptions may be subject to conditions imposed by the local authority, and may be withdrawn if the exemption is deemed likely to become a health hazard.

A local authority may set additional requirements to be met on any food premises where, despite compliance, a health hazard exists that is not provided for in the regulations.

The regulations are not applicable to private homes where food is prepared for domestic consumption or, without compensation, for a church, educational or welfare organisation for fund-raising. However, the person who receives that food must keep a record of the type of food and the address of the private residence for 30 days after receipt of the food. This is in case of any incidents of food poisoning occurring.

8.5.13 Offences

A person who contravenes the regulations, or allows a contravention to take place, shall be guilty of an offence.

8.6 Conclusion

A combination of adhering to the law, and practising good and effective principles of food, environmental and personal hygiene will assist in ensuring safe food preparation within your establishment.

Questions and exercises

1. Why is it important to comply with health and hygiene legislation?
2. How do SABS codes of practice interface with health and hygiene legislation?
3. Explain the need for municipal by-laws as separate from the food handling regulations.
4. Discuss the contents of Regulation R918.
5. Describe the differences in the duties and responsibilities of a person in charge of a food premises versus a food handler.
6. Write a brief to an architect regarding the minimum legal requirements for the kitchen of a restaurant that you are in the process of establishing. Include the expected number of staff and guests in the brief.

9

Tobacco legislation

Objectives of this chapter:

By the end of this chapter the learner will be able to:

- Determine the spatial requirements to be set aside for smokers and non-smokers in a hospitality environment
- Apply the provisions of the smoking legislation as required in hospitality establishments

The learner will know:

- The spatial and operational requirements imposed by law on hospitality operations with regard to the use and sale of tobacco products
- The responsibilities of the hospitality under the tobacco legislation with regard the health of their guests and employees

9.1 Introduction

The legislation controlling and regulating the sale, supply, promotion, advertising, product constituents and the smoking of tobacco products in public places was amended, requiring many employers, owners, licensees, lessees or persons in control of a public place or a workplace to effect physical and structural changes to their premises in order to accommodate smokers.

As the hospitality industry is operating, by the very nature of its business, in 'public places' as defined, the tobacco legislation has had a profound impact on the industry This is especially so in the case of small businesses. The Act and subsequent regulations have placed significant obligations on all hospitality operators in terms of the manner in which they are required to accommodate both employees and customers who smoke.

This chapter will consider the framework of the tobacco legislation, the actual provisions of the legislation, as well as the impact that these laws have on hospitality operations.

9.2 The framework of tobacco legislation

The Department of Health promulgated the framework of tobacco legislation as it is in the interest of public health, for which the department holds responsibility. The principal statute regulating the manufacture, production, sale, supply and consumption of tobacco products is the Tobacco Products Control Act 83 of 1993. This Act, the principal Act, prior to being amended by the Tobacco Products Control Amendment Act of 1999, was aimed mainly at regulating and controlling the production, manufacture, sale and supply of tobacco products.

The Tobacco Products Control Amendment Act 12 of 1999 resulted in significant changes to the Tobacco Products Control Act, particularly with regard to the consumption or use of tobacco products in public places.

The preamble to the Amendment Act sets out the reasons behind the amendments and the proposed objectives as follows:

- tobacco use is extremely injurious to the health of both smokers and non-smokers and warrants, in the public interest, a restrictive legislation. It is a widely accepted practice among adults, which makes it inappropriate to ban completely
- the association of smoking with social success, business advancement and sporting prowess through the use of advertising and promotion may have a particularly harmful effect of encouraging children and young people to take up smoking
- the extent of the effects of smoking on health calls for strong action to deter people from taking up smoking, and to encourage existing smokers to give up smoking; and to
- align the health system with the democratic values of the Constitution and to enhance and protect the fundamental rights of citizens by discouraging the use, promotion and advertising of tobacco products in order to reduce the incidence of tobacco-related illness and death

The provisions of this amending Act came into operation on 1 October 2000 and a month later the Minister published four sets of regulations, which dealt primarily with very specific requirements for implementation of the various provisions contained within each of the regulations.

The published regulations deal with, *inter alia*

- the point of sale of tobacco products
- smoking of tobacco products in public places

In effect, it was the promulgation of these regulations that led to significant changes having to be made in terms of the accommodation of smokers and non-smokers in public places, the sale of tobacco products by retailers, the physical manufacture of cigarette products and the manner in which the tobacco companies were required to go about their sales, advertising, promotion and marketing plans.

Figure 9-1: The framework of tobacco legislation

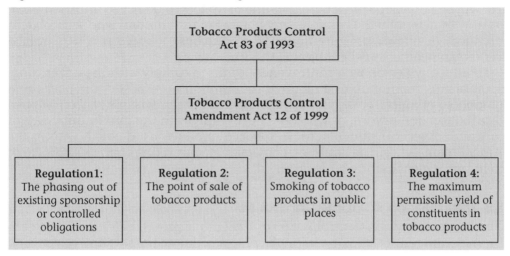

9.2.1 Draft amendments to the Tobacco Products Control Amendment Act of 1999

At the time of writing the Department of Health was looking to make further amendments to the Tobacco Products Control Amendment Act 12 of 1999 and the various regulations. The content of the proposed amendments, as they will apply to hospitality establishments, has been included at the end of the chapter. Being in draft format and as yet to be finalised, there is every possibility that they will change prior to promulgation. Readers should obtain clarity prior to implementing any changes to their current smoking arrangements and or policies.

9.2.2 Enforcement

Both the South African Police Services and the national, provincial and local health authorities have been given the power to lay charges against any person found to be in contravention of the requirements of either the principal or the Amendment Act. It should equally be noted that neither the principal Act nor the Amendment makes provision for a spot fine or a fine paid there and then by the guilty party. A criminal charge docket has to be opened, after which the offender has a choice between paying an admission of guilt fine or appearing in court.

9.2.3 Penalties

The Amendment Act makes provision for various levels of fines attached to specific offences.

First, any person who smokes outside of the areas declared and specified by the Minister as permissible smoking areas may be liable, on conviction, to a fine of up to R200 or to such penalties as may be determined.

Any person who contravenes or fails to comply with the provision concerning the sale of tobacco to persons under the age of 16 years and who fails to ensure that cigarette vending machines are not accessible to persons under the age of 16, will be liable, on conviction, to a fine of up to R10 000 or to imprisonment, as may be determined. Therefore, any hotelier or restaurateur who sells tobacco products, or allows someone under 16 to purchase tobacco products from a vending machine, may be subject to this fine.

Finally, any person who contravenes or fails to comply with the advertising, sponsorship, promotion and required information in respect of the packaging of tobacco products, or who fails to comply with the provisions concerning free distribution and reward, or who does not comply with the maximum yields of tar and other constituents in a tobacco product as defined within the Amendment Act, will be liable, on conviction, to pay a fine of up to R200 000 or to imprisonment as may be determined.

9.3 The Tobacco Products Control Act

The Tobacco Products Control Act 83 of 1993 made provision for the Minister to prohibit and restrict smoking in public places, regulate the sale and advertising of tobacco products in certain respects, and to prescribe what is to be reflected on packages. In effect the Act did not include much in the way of substance but made provision for the Minister to publish regulations covering the key objectives of the Act at some time in future.

The Act also made provision for the Minister, under the section dealing with smoking in public places, to grant certain powers to local authorities on request. Only the municipalities of Cape Town and Pretoria took up the offer and published by-laws controlling smoking in public places. Although these by-laws were adopted by the two above-mentioned local authorities, little if any enforcement took place.

In addition to the granting of certain powers to local authorities, the Act covers the requirement of health warnings being attached to any form of tobacco product, the restriction of the sale of tobacco products to persons under the age of 16 years, certain restrictions on the use of vending machines and offences and penalties.

The introduction of the Tobacco Products Control Amendment Act of 1999 sought to introduce into the principal Act provisions to control and regulate the use and/or consumption and advertising of tobacco products, and in doing so, even prohibiting the use and consumption of tobacco products in certain places and the advertising, sponsorship and promotion of tobacco products.

The Tobacco Products Control Act contains, amongst others, the prohibitions discussed below, which are only those particularly relevant to, and affecting the, hospitality industry.

9.3.1 Prohibition of smoking in public places

The principal Act defines 'smoke' to mean 'to inhale, exhale, hold or otherwise have control over an ignited tobacco product, weed or plant', and defines 'tobacco product' as 'any product manufactured from tobacco and intended for use by smoking, inhalation, chewing, sniffing or sucking.'

The principal Act prohibits the smoking of tobacco products in any public place. A 'public place' is defined as being 'any indoor or enclosed area which is open to the public, or any part of the public, and includes a workplace and a public convenience'. As a result of the definition, hospitality establishments were automatically required to comply with the relevant provisions contained within the Amendment Act of 1999.

The Act makes it equally clear that the restrictions do not only apply to those areas to which the public have access but to the workplace, which is defined as follows:

- 'any indoor or enclosed area in which employees perform the duties of their employment; and
- includes any corridor, lobby, stairwell, elevator, cafeteria, washroom or other common area frequented by such employees during the course of their employment; but
- excludes any private dwelling, and any portion of an area mentioned in paragraph *(a)* specifically designated by the employer as a smoking area and which complies with the prescribed requirements.'

This is a particularly important definition, as it is often misinterpreted when determining the amount of space to allocate to smoking areas in restaurants.

The principal Act provides that the Minister of Health may, by notice in the *Government Gazette*, declare specified public places as permissible smoking areas, subject to such conditions as are specified in such notices. The Tobacco Regulation R975 is one such notice relating to the smoking of tobacco products in public places, and forms the backbone of the provisions within which the hospitality industry is required to accommodate both their smoking and non-smoking guests.

9.3.2 Provisions regarding the sale of tobacco products

9.3.2.1 Sale of tobacco products by retailers
The principal Act permits a retailer of tobacco products to post or put up signs at points of sale that indicate the availability of tobacco products and their price. Such signs must comply with the regulations in terms of the Amendment Act, and may not advertise or promote the quality of the tobacco products sold, but may merely serve as notification to the public that tobacco products are sold at that particular establishment.

9.3.2.2 Requirements for the sale, and import for subsequent sale, of tobacco products
All tobacco products sold or imported for the purposes of subsequent sale must, in terms of the principal Act, be contained in a package bearing the prescribed warning concerning the health hazards incidental to the smoking of tobacco products and stating the quantities of constituents present in the tobacco product concerned.

This means that it is illegal to sell, for example, single or loose cigarettes to the consumer, as individual cigarettes do not have a health warning on them.

9.3.2.3 Sale of tobacco products from vending machines

The principal Act provides that vending machines from which tobacco products are sold, must be situated in such places that are inaccessible to persons under the age of 16 years.

The person in control, or responsible for, the premises (for example a hotel or restaurant) upon which tobacco vending machines are kept, has the responsibility to ensure that no person under 16 uses the vending machine. If someone under 16 years of age is found to have used the vending machine to buy a tobacco product, then the person in charge of the premises (for example the hotelier or restaurateur) in which that vending machine is located, will be held liable by law.

9.3.3 Regulation 1: Sponsorship or contractual obligations

Regulation R977 deals with the provision for exemption for unintended consequences and the phasing out of existing sponsorship or contractual obligations.

The regulation provides that any contract, undertaking or agreement concerning the advertising of tobacco products, and any organisation, sponsorship or promotion of any organised activity by a manufacturer, importer, distributor or retailer of tobacco product that existed and was binding on 23 April 1999 may continue for a period not exceeding two years from that date.

Furthermore, that copies of or sworn statements concerning such written and or verbal agreements and or contracts should be forwarded to the Director General of Health within one month from which the Act came into force.

Finally, the regulation requires that all advertising and promotional material that relate to organised activities must display the health message as required under the Act and that the space to be devoted to the health message must be at least one eighth of the total size of the advertisement or promotional item.

9.3.3.1 Applicability to the hospitality industry

As this particular regulation deals with undertakings, contracts and agreements concerning the advertising of tobacco products, it has had a relatively minor impact on hospitality establishments. The provision dealing with the promotion and sponsorship of tobacco products has resulted in a number of activities previously carried out in hospitality establishments having to cease. Unless a binding contract between a tobacco product manufacturer or supplier and a hospitality establishment was in place prior to 23 April 1999, all promotional, advertising and sponsorship activities are required to cease. Historically, many tobacco manufacturers and distributors held promotional activities in hotels, pubs and restaurants, which are no longer permitted.

9.3.4 Regulation 2: Point of sale of tobacco products

Regulation R976 deals with the point of sale of tobacco products. Any retailer of tobacco products may indicate the availability of the products together with the price by means of a sign that may not be more than one square metre and not more than one metre distant from the point of sale. In addition, every such sign must contain the prescribed health messages as provided for under the regulation.

9.3.4.1 Applicability to the hospitality industry

Contrary to the belief of many hospitality establishment owners, this particular regulation does impact on the manner in which they go about the sale of tobacco products on their premises, and does not solely apply to retail or traditional shopping outlets.

All owners of hospitality establishments that sell tobacco products to the public are required to ensure that signs, indicating the availability of tobacco products and prices are of the prescribed size and carry the prescribed warning as laid down in the regulation.

9.3.5 Regulation 3: The smoking of tobacco products in public places

Regulation R975 has by far the greatest impact on hospitality establishments, especially if they choose to accommodate smokers as well as non-smokers. It should also be noted that hospitality establishment owners have the right to totally prohibit smoking on their premises if they so choose.

Of equal significance, and commented on below, is that the regulation provides not only for the definition of a 'public place' but for the definition of a 'pub', 'bar' or 'tavern', a 'restaurant' and a 'smoking establishment' as well.

Regulation R975 provides for the type of establishments that may set aside an area for smokers, with examples being hotels, passenger trains and passenger liners, and furthermore, determines the portion of that specific public place that may be set aside for smoking. A hotel or restaurant or bar may set aside 25% of the public place for smokers.

In terms of the provisions of the regulation, smoking areas must be separated from the rest of the public place by a solid partition, and an entrance door must be sign-posted as a 'smoking area' using the required size of wording and must be ventilated in such a manner so as not to re-circulate smoke to any other area within the public place.

Two further signs are required – one covering the required health warning, and a second concerning the prosecution of those who smoke anywhere other in the designated areas within the public place. The specific signage requirements are covered a little later in this chapter.

In terms of the protection of employees, the employer is required to have a written policy on smoking in the workplace, must ensure that an employee who does not want to be exposed to tobacco smoke in the workplace is protected, and that employers are aware that employees have the right to object to tobacco smoke in the workplace without retaliation of any kind.

As this particular regulation specifically deals with the lawful manner in which hospitality establishments may accommodate smokers and non-smokers, a comprehensive and detailed explanation has been provided below.

9.3.5.1 The designated smoking area

The definition and meaning of a 'public place' as defined under the Act means 'any indoor or enclosed area which is open to the public or any part of the public and includes a workplace and a public conveyance'.

Indoor and enclosed areas therefore exclude, by definition, outdoor and un-enclosed areas. When considering the meaning of a particular definition it is not only important to understand the lawful interpretation but the practical interpretation as well. For example, if your establishment has an open-air terrace area adjacent to or leading off an indoor enclosed area, by definition the terrace would fall outside the 'indoor enclosed area'. If however, an operator decided to break down a wall in an area that was clearly intended to be indoor and enclosed and replaced it with sliding windows, claiming that the area would now be defined as an outdoor and unenclosed area, this would not meet the requirements. All attempts to get around the law, by creative or devious means, will result in difficulties with the authorities.

As the Act and regulations apply to 'public places', a number of hospitality owners decided that they would declare their establishments 'private places' by charging a membership fee and forming a club environment. Clearly they missed the point entirely. First, the definition of a 'public place' is quite specific in that it refers to the public, meaning any person other than a family member, and secondly, and more importantly, this hardly conveys a favourable impression to the non-smoking client base, which represents some 80% of the population of South Africa. A decision of this nature is certainly not lawful and clearly makes very little business sense.

The concept of a 'designated smoking area' requires further explanation. A key factor and one that is either missed or not understood by many hospitality establishment owners is the definition of a 'public place' as it applies to the area permitted to be set aside for consumers who wish to smoke. In addition, many establishment owners do not see the relevance of the separate inclusion, in the regulations, of definitions covering 'pubs, bars or taverns', 'restaurants' and 'smoking establishments'.

For the purposes of explaining the meaning of a permitted smoking area, a typical stand-alone restaurant or pub may be used as an example. The area of this restaurant or pub is divided 50/50 between that area set aside for use by the public, and that defined as the 'workplace' and used for the processing, production and storage of the food and beverage products required to meet the needs of the consumers. Therefore, 50% of the premises is accessible to the public, and comprises the reception, dining and bar area, while 50% comprises the back-of-house areas of kitchen, offices, storerooms, etc.

As mentioned above, but worth repeating, a public place means '*any indoor or enclosed area which is open to the public or any part of the public and includes a workplace and a public conveyance*'. Therefore, in our example, 25% of the *total* area may be set aside for smoking, not 25% of the public area.

In addition, it is important to note that a restaurant or a pub is defined as a single entity irrespective of the manner in which it may be designed or the area in which it may be located. Therefore, a restaurant or bar located inside a hotel is regarded as a single, separate entity, and must have the stipulated smoking/non-smoking allocation applied to it, separate from the allocations made for the hotel as a whole.

Understanding these two definitions is key to deciding on the actual square meterage of the area a restaurateur or publican may lawfully choose to set aside for smokers.

The regulation also states that the smoking of tobacco products is permitted in restaurants and pubs but subject to certain conditions, one of which is that the designated smoking area may not exceed 25% of the total floor area of the 'public place'.

Most operators assume therefore, that they can only consider that area frequented by consumers when deciding on the total area to be set aside for smokers but in fact, when the definition of a 'public place' is considered, it includes that area referred to as the 'workplace'. This confusion or misunderstanding results in many operators looking to set aside 25% of the 50% frequented by consumers only, resulting in most, if not all, believing the area to be too small to accommodate smokers. Those operators who looked to set aside 25% of the 100% available were clearly more able to accommodate both smokers and non-smokers in terms of the demographics of their client base.

As mentioned above, the inclusion of specific definitions within the regulation covering pubs, bars, taverns and restaurants has an impact on the manner in which certain other types of establishments would be required to comply with the law. A hotel, for example, in which there may be any number of varied products and services, ranging from bedroom accommodation, function facilities, lounges and in all probability both a restaurant and a pub, would be in a position to set aside 25% of the total hotel area, excluding those areas covering the pub and restaurant, as smoking areas. The restaurant and pub, because they are both provided for and defined as separate entities within the regulations, would each need to be subdivided/subtracted, i.e. 25% of that area that constitutes the restaurant and its workplace and 25% of that area that constitutes the pub and its workplace could be set aside for smokers. As far as the remainder of the hotel is concerned the smoking areas may be located or subdivided between the remaining products and services being the bedroom accommodation, the function facilities and lounges, etc, provided that they do not exceed 25% of the total indoor enclosed areas that comprise the hotel, but excluding both the restaurant and pub areas as mentioned above,

The following example may assist in applying this: the Grand Hotel consists of a total of 10 000 m². The restaurant and bar (and kitchens and cold-rooms) of the Grand Hotel occupies 1 000 m². The restaurant must be considered a separate entity that is subtracted from the total area of the hotel. Therefore, in the restaurant, 25% of the 1 000 m² may be allocated to smoking. For the remaining area of the hotel, 25% of the remaining 9 000 m² may be allocated to smoking.

With reference to function areas within a hotel, many operators and managers have chosen not to permit smoking at all. However, this should be seen as a business decision rather than a lawful requirement. Hoteliers may certainly set aside an area or areas within their function facilities, provided that the total area within the hotel allocated to smokers, excluding both the restaurant and pub areas, does not exceed 25% of the total indoor and enclosed areas of the hotel and provided that the required signage, ventilation and separation is in place. The 'smoking area' could change location on a day-to-day basis, provided that the signage is put in the correct place on each occasion. This would clearly assist owners who wish to accommodate smokers at various functions held within the establishment. A venue may be smoking today at the request of the client and non-smoking tomorrow, provided that the total areas set aside for smokers do not exceed the requirement.

One caution – if you decide to permit smoking in functions rooms ensure that the client requests smoking and that the client informs his/her delegates that the decision to permit smoking was his/hers and not that of the establishment.

9.3.5.2 The separation of the smoking area

Hospitality owners who intend to accommodate both non-smokers and smokers are required to separate non-smokers and smokers by means of a solid partition and an entrance door. Many operators have had to make building alterations and in many cases at significant cost owing to both the ventilation require-ments and the limit of 25% of the total floor area of the public place that is placed on the smoking area.

This provision is best viewed with the long-term business interests of the establishment in mind rather than the restrictive and costly impact of statute law. First, the smoking restrictions are not unique to South Africa and are spreading swiftly and being enforced in most countries around the globe. Consumer expectations have already changed and will continue to do so in the future. The effective accommodation of both non-smokers and smokers will therefore become a prerequisite for successful business. The need to offer products and services that meet the expectations of the client base makes good business sense. Any wise operator, taking a long-term business decision, will ensure that the establishment offers all of the products and services that attract business and clearly, the right to be accommodated in a healthy environment, is one of them.

When considering section 3(b) of the regulation, it is worth noting that a number of hospitality establishment have chosen to make use of air curtains rather than separate the non-smoking and smoking areas by means of a solid partition and a door. At the time of going to print, this point was under consideration by the Department of Health and they may outlaw the use of air curtains in future amendments to the regulations.

9.3.5.3 Ventilation requirements

Having now covered the areas permitted to be set aside for smoking, it is also important to note that each and every smoking area is required to comply with the ventilation provision.

The regulation states that 'the ventilation of the designated smoking area is such that air from the smoking area is directly exhausted to the outside and is not re-circulated to any other area within the public place'. Firstly, it is important to note that this provision does not necessarily require the installa-tion and the use of mechanical or automated air extraction. Normal airflow is permitted, provided that the air is not re-circulated to any other area within the public place. However, an operator would need to consider the effectiveness of the airflow within the smoking area in terms of the comfort of the smoking clients. When considering airflow requirements, bear in mind that it is somewhat of a specialist subject, and that it would be advisable to call in an expert before incurring any significant cost.

Many establishments, more especially pubs, coffee shops and restaurants located in indoor and enclosed areas such as hotels, shopping malls and entertainment complexes, often find themselves having to cope with a central air-conditioning system that automatically re-circulates a certain percentage of the air throughout the complex. In such cases a potential solution, should the establishment owner wish to accommodate smokers, would be to remove or close off the central system and install a separate system that is exhausted to the outside of the building. An alternative would be to look to opening up an outdoor unenclosed area should the establishment be located where this is possible, or should the operator be in a position to negotiate such costs or alterations with the landlord.

9.3.5.4 Signage requirements

All hospitality establishment owners are required to ensure that specific signage is displayed in terms of the regulation. However, it is fair to say that although the regulation specifies the size and colour of the wording, it would appear that the Department of Health has turned a blind eye where the prescribed signage does not fully comply. As long as the signage is located in the correct area, is clearly visible and easily read, the establishment owners have been allowed to retain the continuity of the décor in that particular area. The three signs required are:

SMOKING AREA

---

1. The designated smoking area is separated from the rest of the public place by a solid partition and an entrance door on which the sign 'SMOKING AREA' is displayed, written in black letters, at least 2 cm high and 1,5 cm wide, on a white background.

SMOKING OF TOBACCO PRODUCTS IS HARMFUL TO YOUR HEALTH AND TO THE HEALTH OF CHILDREN, PREGNANT OR BREASTFEEDING WOMEN AND NON-SMOKERS.
FOR HELP TO QUIT PHONE (011) 720 3145

---

2. The message: 'SMOKING OF TOBACCO PRODUCTS IS HARMFUL TO YOUR HEALTH AND TO THE HEALTH OF CHILDREN, PREGNANT OR BREAST-FEEDING WOMEN AND NON–SMOKERS. FOR HELP TO QUIT PHONE (011) 720 3145' is displayed at the entrance to the designated smoking area, written in black letters, at least 2 cm in height and 1,5 cm in breadth, on a white background; and
3. Notices and signs indicating areas where smoking is permitted, and where it is not permitted must be permanently displayed and signs indicating that smoking is not permitted must carry the warning: 'ANY PERSON WHO FAILS TO COMPLY WITH THIS NOTICE SHALL BE PROSECUTED AND MAY BE LIABLE TO A FINE'.

9.3.5.5 Employees

It must be noted that employees are afforded certain protections under the regulation. An employer must ensure that employees not wishing to be exposed to tobacco smoke are protected. It is recommended that, for the purposes of accommodating office and back-of-house employees, smoking is prohibited in these areas and that a designated smoking area is set aside for those who wish to smoke.

Before recruiting employees who will be required to work in designated public smoking areas, it would be wise to ensure that exposure to smoke is noted as a condition of service, that is unavoidable and that the contract of employment covers the requirement and that employment is therefore agreed to on this basis. Equally important however is that the employee agrees to this condition and is not forced to comply.

Employers are also required to ensure that a written policy on 'smoking in the workplace' is completed.

9.4 Draft amendments to the Tobacco Products Control Act

At the time of writing the Department of Health was looking to make further amendments to the Tobacco Products Control Act and the various regulations. Please note that the draft amendments listed below are only those likely to impact hospitality establishments.

9.4.1 Section 1. Definitions

'Public place' means any indoor, enclosed or **partially-enclosed area** which is open to the public and includes a workplace, a club and a public conveyance;

> 'Workplace' – (a) means any indoor, enclosed or **partially enclosed area** in which employees perform the duties of their employment;
> The Department has not provided a precise definition for the wording 'partially-enclosed.' Section 2: Control over Smoking of Tobacco Products
> (1)(a) No person may smoke any tobacco product in –
> (i) a public place;
> (ii) **any area within a prescribed distance from a window of, ventilation inlet of, doorway to or entrance into a public place.**

No definition for the words 'prescribed distance' was provided
(4) The owner of or a person in control of a place or area contemplated in subsection (1)(a), or employer in respect of a workplace, shall display the prescribed signs and shall make the **prescribed public announcements** in order to inform any person who enters or who is in or on such place or area of any prohibitions on smoking.

The Department has not provided clarity on whether or not the 'prescribed public announcements' would impact hospitality establishments.

(5) An employer must ensure that –

(c) **it is not a condition of employment, expressly or implied, that any employee is required to work in any portion of the workplace where smoking is permitted; and**

(d) employees are not required to sign any indemnity for working in any portion of the workplace where smoking is permitted.

(6) The owner of, or person in control of, a place or area contemplated in subsection (1)*(a)*, or employer in respect of a workplace, shall ensure that no person **under the age of 18 years is present in any portion of the workplace where smoking is permitted or in the area within a public place contemplated in subsection (1)*(b)* in or on which smoking is permitted.**

'Under the age of 18 years' has replaced 'under the age of 16' in the unamended Act. The meaning is such that no person under the age of 18 will be permitted to enter a designated smoking area.

9.4.2 Section 5: Restrictions on use of vending machines

The sale of tobacco products from vending machines shall be restricted to places in which purchases from such machines are inaccessible to persons under the age of sixteen years.

9.4.3 Section 7: Offences and penalties

All of the penalties have been increased significantly over those provided in the 1999 Act.

Readers are reminded that the amendments are in draft format and as yet to be finalised. There is every possibility that they will change prior to promulgation. Readers should obtain clarity prior to implementing any changes to their current smoking arrangements and/or policies.

9.5 Conclusion

The South African anti-smoking legislation is in line with world trends, and was motivated and supported by the World Health Organisation. It is certainly not going to go away and non-smokers have every right to dine or drink in a healthy environment. Compliance with the provisions of this legislation is a wise and long-term business decision and will ensure the future comfort of all of hospitality clients in a manner that promotes and increases business.

The anti-smoking laws are a part of public health protection, for both those sectors of the population who chose to smoke or make use of tobacco products, and those who do not. Both their rights are protected under this legislation. The hotelier or restaurateur is legally bound to make provision for the safe and legal use and sale of tobacco products to guests, minors and staff under this legislation, and therefore is bound to take the provisions of the legislation into account in hospitality operations, or face the penalties imposed by law.

Questions and exercises

1. Discuss the various options and costs for creating separate spaces for smoking and non-smoking in a restaurant consisting of one large room and an outdoor seating area.
2. List the specific provisions of anti-smoking legislation that a restaurant-pub must comply with, as well as the penalties for non-compliance.

10

Gambling legislation

Objectives of this chapter:

- By the end of this chapter the learner will be able to:
- Explain the background and regulatory framework for gaming legislation in South Africa
- Understand the penalties associated with money laundering activities, and the requirement to report any such activities to the authorities

The learner will know:

- The broad provisions of the National Gambling Act
- Application and licensing requirements for limited payout machines

10.1 Introduction

The democratisation of the Republic of South Africa in 1994 ushered in a completely new approach to gambling. Prior to 1994 gambling was prohibited in South Africa except in the so-called 'independent homelands'. However, betting on horseracing was legal in the Republic.

Following the release of a report by the Lotteries and Gambling Board, chaired by Professor Nic Wiehahn, the democratic government decided that the only way to deal with gambling was to regulate it. The government felt that regulating gambling could derive more benefits for the country.

The government has constructed a clearly defined policy framework for the gambling industry in South Africa which is designed to safeguard the community against the adverse effects of gambling, and to prevent an over-stimulation of the latent demand for gambling. The policy and legislative framework makes provision for three discrete components for the gaming industry (excluding horse racing and wagering), i.e. casinos, bingo and limited payout machines, with significant limits being imposed on the number of casinos in the country and the number of gambling machines (limited payout machines – LPM) that will be permitted to operate outside casinos. The objective is to prevent the unmitigated proliferation of gaming machines in the Republic. The regulation of bingo is bound by the same overall policy considerations and licensing commitments that apply to casinos and the LPM industry.

The National Gambling Act 33 of 1996 (as amended) was subsequently passed by Parliament. The Act defines the regulatory framework in South

Africa. For instance, it limits the number of casinos that can be licensed in the country to 40.

The regulation of gambling in South Africa was also expected to enhance the national policy of reconstruction and development. One of the policy objectives underlying the regulation of gambling is that the industry must leverage direct fixed investments, contribute towards the process of Broad-Based Black Economic Empowerment (BBBEE), create jobs, contribute to other infrastructural development, and promote tourism. These conditions, together with bid undertakings by prospective licensed operators must be satisfied before gambling licences are issued.

The gaming industry has realised investments of more than R12 billion, about 48% of equity in casinos belongs to BEE companies, infrastructural development such as the building of convention centres has taken place and employment opportunities continue to be created. While the ethical issue of gambling may be very contentious, these results prove the economic sense of the government policy in legalising gambling.

The National Gambling Act enjoins the National Gambling Board (NGB) to oversee gambling activities and protect the public from excessive gambling. It is recognised that a minority of gamblers can become addicted to gambling, with serious consequences to themselves, their families, their colleagues and communities. In order to fulfil this statutory obligation, and to promote the culture of responsible gambling, a body comprised of representatives from the National Gambling Board, all nine provincial gambling boards, civil society, the National Lotteries Board and the industry stakeholders, called the South African Advisory Council on Responsible Gambling (SAACREG), has been created. One of the objectives of this body is to ensure that there is a culture of responsible gambling in South Africa.

The National Responsible Gambling Programme (NRGP) was also established in 2000 in partnership with the government, the industry and the private sector as a way of redressing the challenges posed by problem gambling in South Africa. It is the first comprehensive programme of its type in the world in which prevention through public education, treatment, research and training initiatives are integrated in one institution. The South African Responsible Gambling Trust (SAGRT) supervises the NRGP in terms of reporting on its activities and policy. Both the industry and regulators are equally represented on the board of the Trust. The Trust directly reports to the SAACREG.

It should be emphasised that the only rational way to deal with gambling is to regulate it. Local and international experience has proved that any other approach is unworkable and unsustainable.

As such, South Africa has one of the most highly regulated gaming industries in the world.

Gaming legislation applies particularly to casino premises, but because these provide food and accommodation services as well as gambling activities, it is valuable for hospitality operators to be familiar with the legislation pertaining to gaming regulation.

Furthermore, the promulgation of the regulations for limited payout machines (December 2000) promulgated in terms of section 17 of the National

Gambling Act, makes provision for limited payout machines (LPMs) to be placed in a variety of outlets, including hospitality outlets, under licence from the provincial gaming authority. These regulations and processes are more important to the hotelier, restaurateur, or club operator who wishes to install limited payout machines on their premises.

10.2 Framework of the gaming industry

The Constitution (section 126) grants concurrent legislative powers to both the national and provincial legislatures regarding casinos, racing, gambling and wagering. Lotteries and sport pools are regulated nationally. The Department of Trade and Industry (DTI) controls the gaming and lottery industries in South Africa.

Two Acts, the National Gambling Act 33 of 1996 and the Lotteries Act 57 of 1997, established the following governance structures:

Figure 10–1: The governance structures in the gaming industry

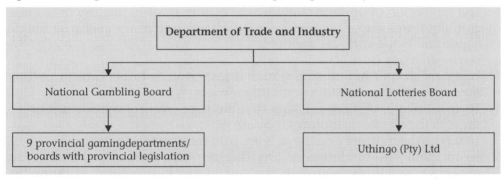

The Lotteries Act of 1997 regulates lotteries and sports pools. The only legal national lottery is the lottery operated by the Gidani empowerment consortium, which is supervised by the Lotteries Board.

The National Gambling Act 7 of 2004 repealed the National Gambling Act of 33 of 1996, which was the Act that legalised the gaming industry in South Africa.

The National Gambling Act of 1996 made provision for the establishment of the National Gambling Board, whose membership includes representation from relevant ministries (Environmental Affairs and Tourism, Safety and Security, Finance, and Trade and Industry), provincial representation and other interests. The Board continues under the new Act.

The original Act provided for the establishment and funding of the Executive Board (based in Pretoria), whose functions include the following:
1. Keeping track of provincial developments with regard to social, regional, economic and moral interests, as well as international developments in the field of gambling.
2. Promoting the underlying principles of gambling in South Africa.
3. Advising and guiding the provincial authorities on the regulation and control of gambling activities including:
    ◆ the granting, issuing, suspension, withdrawal and amendment of gambling licences

- the criteria to be complied with before any gambling licence is granted,
- the nature and manner of auditing the businesses of the licensees, and the documents and records that must be submitted to the provincial gambling authorities
- the imposition of taxes, levies and duties in respect of any gambling activities
- the types of games that may be played in a casino
- the types and minimum standards and qualities of gambling equipment that may be used by a licensee
- the control and restriction of the game of bingo or similar game
- other functions relating to advising the minister, measuring equity in the gambling industry, and allocating funds for rehabilitation programmes for persons who are addicted to obsessive gambling

10.2.1 Objectives of the board

The objectives of the board are stipulated as follows:
1. The promotion of uniform standards in certain matters relating to casinos, gambling and wagering, and to bring about uniformity in the gambling legislation in the various provinces,
2. To research any issue above,
3. To establish and maintain a national inspectorate to perform inspection services in respect of certain gambling services,
4. To monitor the existence of any dominant or over-concentrated market-share in the gambling industry in South Africa,
5. To advise the minister and the provinces on matters within its scope,
6. To facilitate the resolution of any disputes that may arise between the respective provinces regarding the regulation and control of gambling activities,
7. To liaise with any foreign or international body that has similar objectives to the Board.

10.2.2 General policy underlying gambling

The Act clearly states that the following principles apply to the regulation of gambling:
1. Gambling activities shall be effectively regulated, controlled, policed and licensed,
2. Members of the public who participate in any licensed gambling activity shall be protected from themselves in terms of addiction,
3. Society and the economy shall be protected against the over-stimulation of the latent demand for gambling,
4. Standardisation and the quality of equipment used by any licence holder shall be promoted and maintained,
5. The issuing of licences in respect of any gambling activity shall be transparent, fair and equitable,
6. The state (or organs of the state) shall have no interest in any gambling activity, apart from taxes or levies,
7. Licensing authorities with specific functions and powers relating to gam-

bling shall be established by the provinces for the regulation and control of gambling activities,

8. A maximum of 40 casino licences may be granted in South Africa:
   - Eastern Cape   5
   - Free State   4
   - Gauteng   6
   - KwaZulu-Natal   5
   - Limpopo   3
   - Mpumalanga   4
   - Northern Cape   3
   - North West   5
   - Western Cape   5

9. The maximum number of gambling machines other than in casinos (limited payout machines) is prescribed in regulations, and that these machines are linked to a central electronic monitoring system for the purposes of monitoring and detection of significant events associated with each gambling machine.

10. The South African Bureau of Standards (SABS) is appointed as the sole agent for testing, standardisation, analysis, calibration and certification of gambling machines.

11. In order to avoid monopolistic situations, no natural or juristic person may hold more than 16 casino licences in the country, or more than two in any province.

10.2.3 Inspectors

The board may appoint inspectors in terms of section 76 of the Act to perform the following functions:

1. Enter licensed or unlicensed premises where gambling activities are being conducted (he or she may be accompanied by an assistant, interpreter or police officer).
2. Require production of the authorised gambling licence of the premises/establishment.
3. Question any person on the premises or inspect any activity in connection with the conduct of any gambling activity.
4. Examine or inspect any gambling machine, equipment, device, book, record, or other document, and make copies thereof.
5. Require any person who is deemed to be in charge of such premises to:
   - point out any equipment or gambling devices or objects
   - produce any books, records or documents in connection with the gambling activity that they may have in their custody.
6. Seize and remove any gambling machine, equipment, device, object, books, documents and such that may furnish proof of contravention of the provincial law relating to gambling.

10.2.4 Offences

Any person who
- falsely represents himself or herself to be an inspector
- wilfully obstructs, hinders or delays an inspector in their functions

- removes, tampers with or destroys anything seized by an inspector
- refuses to comply with requests from an inspector
- contravenes or fails to comply with the Act

shall be guilty of an offence, and if proved guilty, may be fined, imprisoned for up to 10 years, or both.

10.2.5 Regulations
Section 87(1) of the Act grants the Minister of Trade and Industry with powers to make a determination of the number of machines to be made available for play, the minimum standards, the quality of gambling equipment operative, and to further guide against overstimulation of gambling activities within the Republic. The Minister may make regulations regarding:
1. The maximum number of any kind of licence relating to gambling to be granted in South Africa or in each province.
2. Norms and standards of gambling activities or equipment.

10.2.6 Gambling debts
Any gambling debt lawfully incurred by a person in the course of any gambling activity regulated by any law, and which is not in conflict with such a law, shall, notwithstanding provisions of common law or any other law, be enforceable by law.

10.3 Provincial regulation
Each of the provinces has promulgated its own gambling legislation to deal with the licensing processes of casinos and other forms of gambling allowed under national legislation. The legislation also created provincial gambling boards to license and supervise casinos in each province.

There is a general obligation on licence holders to act in accordance with the law. Any licensed operator that acts contrary to the legislation, regulations and rules is accountable to the relevant board, and could lose its licence because of such wrongdoing.

10.4 Legal requirements for casino staff
All people working in the casino industry have to be licensed by the provincial Gaming Board of the province in which they work. The requirements and process for this licence vary from province to province, but the general conditions on which a licence will be issued are the same. The process is called a 'probity' process, and the employer usually processes and forwards applications to the authority on behalf of the employee/trainee. The minimum legal requirements for obtaining a licence for working in a casino are as follows:
1. Must be over 18.
2. No criminal record.
3. No background of credit problems.
4. Must be up to date with tax returns, with no tax defaults.
5. Must be a South African citizen. Due to the problem of illegal immigrants into South Africa, fingerprints are now required as part of the probity

application, and identification papers are sent to the Department of Foreign Affairs for verification.

10.5 Limited payout machines

Limited payout machines (LPMs) are defined as gambling machines outside of a casino in respect of the playing of which the stakes and prizes are limited as prescribed by regulations made under section 17 of the National Gambling Act.

LPM Regulations R1425 of 21 December 2000 provide guidance on the requirements of sites, allocation and process for licensing of site and route operators, and other matters pertaining to the operation and regulation of LPMs in South Africa. The regulations state that each machine has a maximum wager of R5 and a maximum payout of R500, for every single game.

The LPM system in South Africa, from site level upwards, progresses as follows:

The *site operator*, who conducts that gambling activity with the LPM, is licensed by the *provincial gambling board*, and is either independent, or linked to a *route operator*, who provides and maintains the LPMs on that site. The Act states that all LPMs must be linked to a *central electronic monitoring* system operated under the appointment of the *National Gambling Board*.

Figure 10-2: Illustration of LPM monitoring system in South Africa

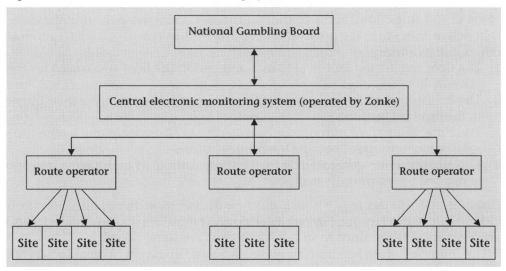

10.5.1 Licensing requirements for sites

A site may have a maximum of five machines, must be licensed by the provincial authority, and gambling must not be the core business of the site. The National Gambling Board may, on good cause shown, and upon application to it by the provincial licensing authority, approve the operation of LPMs in excess of five machines but not more than forty.

There are requirements and restrictions regarding the placement of the LPMs on the premises, and the site operator may not permit anyone under 18 to play the machines. The requirements, even pertaining to whom may qualify for site licences, and the control of the gambling activities are not dissimilar to the requirements of the Liquor Act.

Many hospitality operators will be involved in the provision of gambling activities through LPMs to the public. The following criteria apply to the evaluation of applications for site operator licences; again, these are the minimum requirements and there may be additional ones and these will vary from province to province:

1. Criteria on which suitable applicants will be assessed include
   ◆ character and integrity
   ◆ compliance with the law
   ◆ criminal history and prior convictions
   ◆ financial solvency
   ◆ record of associations with unsuitable persons
   ◆ previous licensing history
   ◆ taxation history and SARS compliance
2. Suitability of premises with regard to the proposed layout and the location of the site
3. The extent to which the applicant is able to demonstrate the achievement of Black Economic Empowerment through ownership and operation of the business.

An application for a site operator licence may be granted only if the operation of the LPMs is incidental to the primary business conducted at the premises.

In determining this, the provincial licensing authority will consider, amongst others, the following:

1. The floor space used for the LPM as compared to the floor space used for the primary business.
2. The investment of the operation of the LPM as compared to the investment in the primary business.
3. The time required to manage or operate the LPM as compared to the time required to manage or operate the primary business.
4. The gross revenue generated by the LPMs as compared to the gross revenue generated by the primary business.

Questions pertaining to the above must be answered in the application for a LPM Site Operator Licence. Further information regarding the requirements and processes may be obtained from the Provincial Gambling Board.

The number of LPMs that may be licensed in South Africa is 50 000, distributed provincially as follows:

◆ Eastern Cape   6 000
◆ Free State   4 000
◆ Gauteng   10 000
◆ KwaZulu-Natal   9 000
◆ Limpopo   3 000
◆ Mpumalanga   4 000
◆ Northern Cape   2 000
◆ North West   3 000
◆ Western Cape   9 000

The National Gambling Board has appointed Zonke Monitoring Systems to operate the central electronic monitoring system to which every LPM must be linked so that the activity of every machine can be recorded and monitored.

10.6 Prevention of Organised Crime Act

Legislation such as the Prevention of Organised Crime Act 121 of 1998 remains an important tool in the fight against serious economic crimes and organised crime. The Prevention of Organised Crime Act prescribes the procedure for confiscating the proceeds of crime, and also makes provision for dealing with money laundering and racketeering offences, among others.

This is of particular importance to operators within the casino and gaming industries. Should a casino operator or employee suspect that money laundering is taking place in their casino, he or she is required by law to report this to the authorities, or else they will be deemed to be aiding and abetting criminal activities. Failure to report suspicion regarding proceeds from unlawful activities is deemed an offence under the Act, with the penalty of a fine or imprisonment of up to 15 years.

Penalties for any activity involving the proceeds of racketeering, money laundering and related activities are prohibitively harsh: fines of up to R100 million or a prison sentence, with 30 years as the maximum.

10.7 Financial Intelligence Centre Act

The Financial Intelligence Centre Act 38 of 2001 (FICA) was promulgated in general to establish a Financial Intelligence Centre and a Money Laundering Advisory Council. Their duty is to combat money-laundering activities and to impose certain duties on institutions and other persons who might be used for money-laundering purposes. The Act requires institutions such as banks and casinos to fulfil certain requirements thereby making money laundering by criminals very difficult. The FICA also amended the Prevention of Organised Crime Act.

In terms of Schedule 1, any person who conducts a business in respect of which a gambling licence is required has to comply with the requirements of FICA unless there is an exemption from complying with particular sections.

The FICA makes the following provisions:
1. Accountable institutions listed in Schedule 1 to the Act must establish and verify the identities of the clients with whom they enter into business relationships or conduct single transactions.
2. Accountable institutions must keep a record of their clients' identities and the transactions entered into with their clients.
3. The period and the manner in which records are to be kept as well as the admissibility of those records in court proceedings and the Financial Intelligence Centre's access to those records.
4. Accountable institutions must develop and implement internal rules on their compliance with their obligations in terms of the Act and appoint compliance officers to ensure compliance with these obligations within the institutions.

5. A person convicted of any of these offences which underpin the enforcement of the provisions referred to above is liable to imprisonment for a period not exceeding 15 years or to a fine of up to R10 000.

In summary, the provisions that came into operation on 30 June 2003 placed accountable institutions under obligation to verify that they know who their clients are, and to keep proper records of their clients' identities. The coming into operation of these provisions results in clients of accountable institutions being asked for identification in different forms prior to transacting with the client. It may also result in requests for clients to update their records with institutions with which they have a relationship.

Accountable institutions are listed in a schedule to the Act and include a wide range of financial institutions such as banks, long-term insurance houses, securities brokers and investment advisers. Also included, are certain professions such as attorneys and estate agents, and non-financial institutions such as casinos.

The provisions referred to in the Act are aimed at, among others, establishing control measures within these institutions to protect them from abuse by criminals wishing to conceal or disguise their proceeds of crime. This forms part of a broader objective to combat money laundering and large-scale criminality.

Questions and exercises

1. Explain the process and requirements for obtaining a licence for limited payout machines in a restaurant.
2. Draw a diagram illustrating the relationship between site operators, route operators, the electronic monitoring system and the gaming authorities.
3. Discuss why South Africa legalised gambling.
4. Explain the motivation for the legislation that monitors and controls money-laundering activities, and why it may have an impact on the hospitality and related industries.

Section 3

Law for Employment

11

The Labour Relations Act

Objectives of this chapter:

By the end of this chapter you will be able to:

- define responsibilities under the Labour Relations Act
- distinguish between fair and unfair dismissals
- describe union security arrangements
- explain the mechanisms for centralised collective bargaining

You will know:

- types of industrial action
- the framework of industrial relations in South Africa
- labour implications in the transfer of a business
- basic procedures for the resolution of a labour dispute

11.1 Introduction

The Labour Relations Act 66 of 1995 (the LRA) aims to promote economic development, social justice and peace and democracy in the workplace. It sets out to achieve this by providing a framework for regulating the relationship between employees and their unions on the one hand, and employers and their organisations on the other hand. At the same time, it also encourages employers and employees to regulate relationships between themselves.

The Act promotes the right to fair labour practices, to form and join trade unions and employers' organisations, to organise and bargain collectively, and to strike and lock-out. In doing so, it reflects the vision of employees' and employers' rights contained in the Constitution.

The Act also promotes and provides for conciliation and negotiation as a way of settling labour disputes. It expects parties to make a genuine attempt to settle disputes through conciliation before going on to the next step, which could be arbitration, adjudication or industrial action. By providing for a more simplified dispute resolution process, through the Commission for Conciliation, Mediation and Arbitration (CCMA), the Act aims to provide for a quick, effective and inexpensive resolution of disputes.

In 2002 a number of amendments were made to the Act and these included, amongst others, provisions such as

- the right to strike against retrenchments and the facilitation of disputes around retrenchments
- increased powers for bargaining councils and their officials
- obliging bargaining councils to report to the registrar on the activities of small business
- better protection of vulnerable workers
- increased powers of the registrar in respect of bargaining councils, trade unions and employers' organisations
- one-stop conciliation and arbitration processes and one-stop final and binding disciplinary enquiries (called pre-dismissal arbitration)

11.2 Contents

The LRA as amended provides for the following:
Chapter 1: The purpose, application and interpretation of the Act
Chapter 2: Joining organisations
Chapter 3: Organising and collective bargaining
Chapter 4: Strikes and lock-outs
Chapter 5: Participating in workplace decision-making
Chapter 6: Registering and managing organisations
Chapter 7: Settling disputes
Chapter 8: Discipline and dismissals
Chapter 9: General provisions
LRA Schedules 1–8: The establishment of institutions, transitional arrangements, and codes of good practice

11.3 Who is covered by the Act?

11.3.1 Employees

Almost every employee and employer is covered by the Act. People who are considered to be genuine independent contractors are not employees and they are thus not protected by this Act (or by other labour legislation). However, it is important to note that the Labour Court has shown that it will not accept an independent contractor's contract at face value but will consider a range of factors to determine whether the person is in fact an independent contractor or an employee.

An amendment in 2002 clarified the issue further by providing that where a particular factor is present in the relationship between a worker and the person for whom he or she works, the worker is presumed to be an employee, unless the employer proves the opposite.

The factors that are considered are whether or not a person
- falls under the control or direction of the employer
- works hours that are subject to the control of another person
- forms part of an organisation
- has worked for another person for an average of at least 40 hours per month over the last three months

- is economically dependent on the employer
- is provided with the tools of trade or equipment
- only works for one employer

However, the assumption as to who is an employee does not apply to a person who earns in excess of an amount stipulated by the Minister in terms of the Basic Conditions of Employment Act, 1997.

11.3.2 Applicants for jobs

The Act not only protects people who are applying for a job from being discriminated against but also provides that no person may require a person seeking employment not to be a member of a trade union or workplace forum, or to give up his or her membership of the trade union or workplace forum.

11.3.4 Former employees

Former employees who are disputing an employer's failure to re-employ them when the employer has re-employed other former employees dismissed for a similar reason are also provided for under the Act. Likewise, if an employer fails to re-employ former employees in terms of an agreement to do so, this may also be challenged in terms of the Act.

11.3.5 Whom does the Act not cover?

The Act does not apply to members of the National Defence Force, the National Intelligence Agency and the South African Secret Service. Military and secret service personnel, who have a special duty towards the state, do not have the same employment rights as other public servants. However, these personnel have the right to protection against unfair labour practices in terms of the Constitution.

The Constitutional Court has held that this includes the right of Defence Force members to join trade unions.

11.4 Joining organisations

Strong trade unions and employers' organisations are necessary for effective collective bargaining as this process is an important way of regulating industrial relations and determining employees' wages and benefits.

As a result of organisational difficulties in the past the LRA attempts to strengthen trade union organisation in two ways:
- by supporting freedom of association rights that enable employees and job seekers to participate freely in union activities; and
- by supporting organisational rights that make it easier for unions to organise employees.

The LRA also supports the right of employers to join together to form employers' organisations.

11.5 Promoting and protecting employees' and employers' rights

11.5.1 Protecting employees, job seekers and employers

The Act prohibits employers from victimising employees or job seekers for their trade union activities both at their workplace and during their previous jobs. It also prohibits employers from offering some advantage to an employee or job seeker to prevent that employee or job seeker from joining a union. Employers may also not prevent employees or job seekers from exercising any right under the Act.

Employers cannot be placed under pressure not to join a particular employers' organisation or not to exercise any right conferred by the Act.

11.5.2 Registration of employers' organisations and unions

Employers' organisations and trade unions do not have to register with the Department of Labour, but they are advised to do so. If they do not register, there is no guarantee for members that there will be a proper constitution or control over finances. Registration provides some check on abuse, corruption and unconstitutional practices.

If unions or employers' organisations wish to be registered, their constitutions have to meet certain requirements. Two important criteria are as follows.

- There must be provision in the constitution for a ballot of members before a strike or lock-out is called.
- There must not be any provision in the constitution that discriminates on the grounds of race or sex.

The registrar of labour relations has the power to not register, or to withdraw the registration of, a trade union or an employers' organisation if the registrar is satisfied that the applicant is not a genuine trade union or employers' organisation.

11.5.3 Rights of registered unions

Registered unions have more rights than unregistered unions. These are:
- organisational rights awarded by the Commission for Conciliation, Mediation and Arbitration
- a right to be a member of a bargaining or statutory council, subject to the admission requirements of the council
- a right to enter into agency and closed shop agreements
- a right to establish workplace forums
- a right to conclude collective agreements as defined under the Act

If a trade union or employers' organisation is unable to continue functioning, it may be wound up by the Labour Court on the application of the registrar of labour relations or any member of the trade union or employers' organisation. A trade union or employers' organisation may also resolve to wind up its affairs, and it may apply to the Labour Court to give effect to that resolution.

11.6 Organisational rights

11.6.1 Organisational rights provided by the Act

The Act provides for a number of organisational rights – a trade union's right of access to a workplace in order to recruit or meet members, the right to hold meetings with employees outside their working hours at the employer's premises, and the right to conduct elections or ballots among its members on union matters.

Further rights include the deduction from employees' wages of trade union subscriptions by the employer on behalf of the trade union (stop-order facilities) and the election of trade union representatives at a workplace.

The trade union representative can assist and represent employees in grievance and disciplinary proceedings, monitor the employer's compliance with labour laws, and report any contravention to the employer, union or any responsible authority. They can also perform any other function agreed to between the union and the employer.

Union office bearers who are employees may take off reasonable time to perform their union duties. The amount of time to be taken, as well as the number of days' paid leave, is a matter for negotiation between the union and the employer.

The LRA specifically sets out procedures to be followed by a union wishing to gain organisational rights in a workplace that include, amongst others, writing to an employer requesting some or all of the organisational rights listed in the Act and attaching the relevant information regarding alleged membership and registration as required under the Act.

If no agreement is reached with the employer, the union or employer may refer the matter to the CCMA who will attempt to resolve the dispute, failing which either party can ask for the dispute to be settled by arbitration (a binding agreement between the parties). A trade union can, however, choose to strike rather than to follow the route of arbitration. If the union embarks on strike action, it has to wait one year before it can turn to the CCMA to obtain organisational rights. In other words, the union has a choice of using the CCMA procedure or the route of industrial action. However, it must live with the consequences of its choice for at least one year if it chooses strike action.

11.6.2 Organisational rights and union membership

If the applying union, or unions acting jointly, have majority membership in the workplace, they must be granted all the organisational rights provided for under the Act. If the registered union or unions are not representative of the majority of employees but are at least 'sufficiently representative' they can apply for:

- access to the workplace for union organisers
- deductions from employees' wages of trade union subscriptions by the employer for the trade union (stop-order facilities)
- time off for trade-union activities for union office bearers who are employees

The Act does not specify a fixed percentage of membership that will count as being sufficiently representative, as this can vary according to the circumstances of a particular workplace. Such circumstances will cover the type of workplace, the sector in which the workplace falls, the organisational history of that workplace or other workplaces of that employer, and the type of rights the union wants to exercise.

11.6.3 Disclosure of information
Unions that are members of a bargaining or statutory council automatically enjoy access, meeting and stop-order rights.

A registered majority union (or unions) has a right to disclosure of information by an employer on a range of workplace issues. Employers can be asked to disclose to a trade union and or a trade union representative, information that is relevant and may be required
* for grievance and disciplinary proceedings
* for monitoring of workplace-related provisions of the Act
* for monitoring any law concerning working conditions
* for monitoring any collective agreement
* for reporting alleged contravention's of collective agreements and labour laws
* for collective bargaining, for example wage negotiations
* for consultations, for example before retrenchments; and/or for performing any other function the employer agreed that the employees' representatives could do

11.6.4 Refusal of information
An employer may only refuse to give information if:
* it is legally privileged
* is such that a law or court order bans disclosure
* is confidential and would cause substantial harm to an employee or employer if disclosed
* is private and personal and the employee concerned does not agree to it being disclosed
* concerns the employer of a domestic worker

If there is a dispute about the disclosure of information, the employer or the trade union or trade union representative concerned may write to the CCMA to conciliate or arbitrate if necessary.

11.7 Union security arrangements

11.7.1 Agency shop agreements
The aim of an agency shop is to ensure that non-union employees, who would benefit from the union's bargaining efforts, make a contribution towards those efforts. An agency shop is a system that requires non-union employees to pay an amount into a special fund kept by the union. The amount may not be more than a union member's subscription.

11.7.2 Establishing an agency shop
Only a majority union (or unions) in a workplace or a sector can establish an agency shop by reaching an agency shop agreement with an employer or an employers' organisation.

The employer must pay the employees' agency fee into a separate account administered by the union and this account must be audited once a year. The auditor's report must be made available for inspection at the office of the registrar of labour relations.

Agency shop fees cannot be used to make contributions to political parties or political candidates, or used to pay affiliation fees to political parties. However, the fees can be used to advance or protect the socio-economic interests of employees.

11.7.3 Closed shop agreements

Closed shop agreements are similar to agency shop agreements, but provide a union with a more powerful way of strengthening its bargaining position with employers. Under a closed shop agreement, non-union employees must join the union or face dismissal. If a union expels a member or refuses to allow a new employee to become a union member and if this expulsion or refusal is in accordance with the union's constitution and is fair, then the employer will have to dismiss the employee.

There are two requirements for the establishment of a closed shop. These are:
- an agreement must be reached between the relevant employer and a majority union (or unions) in a workplace or sector
- a ballot must be held among the employees at the workplace where the closed shop will apply, and two thirds (66%) of the employees at the workplace who vote must support the establishment of a closed shop

Apart from the voting requirements, other democratic controls and protections for individuals are provided, namely:
- if one third of the employees covered by the agreement sign a petition calling for the ending of the agreement, and if three years have passed since the inception of the agreement or the last ballot was held, the union must hold a ballot to decide whether a closed shop agreement should end
- that the money deducted in terms of a closed shop agreement may only be used to advance or protect the socio-economic interests of employees and may not be used to make contributions to political parties or political candidates, or to pay affiliation fees to political parties
- a union that represents a significant grouping of employees covered by the closed shop can apply to join the closed shop agreement
- an employee who is unfairly expelled from a union and is subsequently dismissed can challenge the dismissal in the labour court if conciliation has failed

11.8 Centralised collective bargaining

Centralised collective bargaining occurs when employers in a sector get together and bargain with one or more unions representing the employees of those employers. Centralised collective bargaining can also occur at the level of a group of companies or at the national or regional level of a company.

The Act provides for three options.
- **Collective agreements:** Employers and a trade union (or unions) can negotiate a collective agreement, providing for joint negotiations. The terms and conditions of the collective agreement will apply only to the parties to the agreement and their members.

- **Bargaining councils:** Bargaining councils may negotiate agreements on a range of issues, including wages and conditions of work, benefits, training schemes, and disciplinary and grievance procedures. The agreements may be extended to all employers and employees in the council's registered scope of representivity, as long as certain requirements are met. However, the Minister may extend agreements even if these requirements are not met, and if the Minister believes that collective bargaining will be undermined if the agreement is not extended. Unions that are party to a bargaining council have organisational rights in all workplaces in that sector.
- **Statutory councils:** A statutory council is a weaker version of a bargaining council. While the parties to a statutory council can draw up agreements on wages and working conditions, these agreements cannot be extended to employers and employees outside the council. Unions that are members of a statutory council will enjoy the advantage of acquiring organisational rights of access, meetings, ballots and stop-order facilities for all workplaces in that sector.

11.8.1 Establishment of a bargaining council

To establish a bargaining council for a sector and an area, both the unions and the employers' organisations must be sufficiently representative of the sector and area. 'Sufficiently representative' is not defined in the Act. It could be determined by factors such as:

- the degree of union and employer organisation in the sector and area of the proposed council
- the nature of the sector
- the number of employees employed by members of the employers' organisation
- the ability of the unions and employers' organisations to represent the different interests of employers and employees to be covered by the proposed council

If the employers employ the majority of a sector's workforce and the union, or unions, have organised a majority of the workforce, they would be considered sufficiently representative to establish a bargaining council.

11.8.2 Enforcement of collective agreements by bargaining councils

Designated agents of bargaining councils can monitor and enforce compliance with any collective agreement concluded in the bargaining council. If a dispute about compliance remains unresolved, a council may refer the dispute to final and binding arbitration. An arbitrator may order the person to pay the amount owing, impose a fine, or confirm, vary, or set aside the compliance order.

The Minister has published a notice that sets out the maximum fines that may be imposed by an arbitrator for a breach of a collective agreement.

11.8.3 Establishment of a statutory council

In order to apply to the Minister of Labour for a statutory council, a registered union or unions must have organised at least 30% of the employees in the sector or area, or members of a registered employers' organisation or organisations must employ at least 30% of the employees in that sector or area. If the union or employers' organisation meets this requirement, the Minister will set in motion a process to establish a council even if some parties are not cooperative.

11.9 Workplace forums

Workplace forums are designed to encourage employee participation in the workplace with the goal of promoting the interests of employees and the efficiency of the business. These forums are committees of employees elected by employees in a workplace and they meet employers on a regular basis for consultation on workplace issues. The forums do not replace collective bargaining, but deal with matters that are better suited to resolution through consultation rather than through collective bargaining.

The general functions of workplace forums are to:
- promote the interests of all employees in the workplace – not only of trade union members
- enhance efficiency in the workplace
- facilitate consultation by the employer on certain matters
- encourage participation in joint decision-making on other matters

Unless the matters for consultation are regulated by a collective agreement with a representative trade union, a workplace forum is entitled to be consulted by the employer on the following general matters:
- restructuring the workplace
- changes in the organisation of work
- partial or total plant closures
- mergers and transfers of ownership
- dismissal of employees for operational reasons
- exemptions from any collective agreement or law
- job grading
- criteria for merit increases and bonuses
- education and training
- product development plans
- export promotion

The forum may present alternative proposals, which the employer must consider. If the employer, or a representative of the employer, rejects these alternative proposals and gives the reasons for doing so, he or she can then proceed to implement the original proposal. The consultation process is not a negotiation process, and the employer may unilaterally make decisions after genuine consultation with the forum.

However, in terms of the LRA and in terms of joint decision-making the employer must consult and reach consensus with the workplace forum before implementing any one or more of the following changes:
- disciplinary codes and procedures
- workplace rules not relating to employees' conduct
- affirmative action measures
- rules regulating social benefit schemes where these are controlled by the employer

An employer can refer a dispute over joint decision-making to the CCMA for conciliation. If it remains unresolved the employer may request that the dispute be resolved through arbitration. Because the matter will be resolved either through conciliation or by arbitration, the employees may not strike.

11.9.1 Workplace forums and their relationship with collective bargaining

Although the Act allocates certain matters for consultation and joint decision-making between employers and workplace forums, this does not mean that there is a rigid demarcation between this process and collective bargaining. The Act makes provision for an interaction between workplace forums and collective bargaining in two ways.

- A bargaining council may decide that certain matters are best referred to workplace forums to deal with rather than left to collective bargaining, and may refer these issues to such forums.
- The Act makes provision for a representative trade union and an employer to conclude a collective agreement giving the forum the right to be consulted or to participate in joint decision-making on other matters.

11.9.2 Establishing a workplace forum

A forum may be established in any workplace where there are more than 100 employees. Only a registered and representative trade union may initiate a workplace forum by applying to the CCMA.

The CCMA will appoint a commissioner to assist the parties to reach agreement on establishing the forum. If the parties cannot reach agreement on setting up a forum, then the CCMA must itself establish the forum following the Act's provisions.

The Act sets out certain requirements that the constitution of a workplace forum must meet. Most of these relate to the manner in which a forum should be elected. The commissioner must then facilitate the holding of the first election of members to the forum.

If a representative trade union is recognised by an employer in a collective agreement as the bargaining agent for all employees, that trade union may apply to the CCMA for the establishment of a trade union-based workplace forum. This allows the union simply to appoint the members of the forum without holding an election.

11.9.3 Operation of workplace forums

Forums operate by holding three kinds of meetings. These are:

- regular meetings of its representatives
- regular meetings with the employers at which meeting the employer must present a report on the company's performance and its financial situation and consult the forum on matters arising from the report
- the forum must also meet other employees in the workplace to report on its activities and on the consultation and joint decision-making between it and the employer

These meetings must take place during working hours without any loss of pay for the employees. Once a year at one of these meetings the employer must report on the company's financial and employment situation and future plans and prospects.

The Act specifies certain rights for workplace forums that the constitutions of forums must contain. The employer must allow each member of a forum reasonable time off with pay during working hours, and must allow members to perform the functions of a forum and to receive training regarding the performance of such functions. The employer must also provide facilities so that the forum can perform its functions. Office bearers and officials of the representative trade union may attend workplace forum meetings.

An employer may not dissolve a workplace forum unless the parties have a private agreement allowing for this. If there is no private agreement, a forum can be dissolved only if a representative trade union requests a ballot to dissolve a forum and the majority of those who vote, vote in favour of doing so. A trade union-based workplace forum may be dissolved by collective agreement or if the trade union is no longer representative of a majority of employees.

11.10 Industrial action

The Act regulates strikes, lock-outs and picketing, and it provides certain protections for employers and employees who embark on a lawful strike or lock-out.

11.10.1 Strikes and lock-outs

The Act gives effect to employees' constitutional right to strike. It also grants employers recourse to lock out employees. Strikes and lock-outs may be held over disputes that relate to a matter of mutual interest between employees and their employer. However, a strike or lock-out may not be held if the Act provides that the dispute may be resolved by way of arbitration or adjudication. An example would be the joint decision-making procedure mentioned in 11.9 above.

Some of the issues over which a strike or lock-out may be held are:
* wage increases;
* a demand to establish or join a bargaining council
* a demand to recognise a union as a collective bargaining agent
* a demand for organisational rights
* a demand to suspend or negotiate unilateral changes to working conditions
* an unprotected lock-out or unprotected strike by the other party

11.10.2 Strikes

A strike must involve two or more employees. Striking employees may work for the same or different employers but must Act with a common work-related purpose. The action can be a partial or complete refusal to work or the retardation or obstruction of work; for example, go-slows, work-to-rule, intermittent strikes and overtime bans. An overtime ban initiated by employees concerning voluntary or compulsory overtime constitutes a strike.

The reason must be to solve a grievance or dispute about a matter of mutual interest that concerns employees and employers. (A dispute between two unions does not constitute a strike nor does a non-work related grievance.)

Strike action can be protected or unprotected. Employees involved in protected strikes enjoy certain benefits that are denied to employees who engage in unprotected strikes.

Employees may not be dismissed as a result of a protected strike. Employees may, however, be dismissed for misconduct such as intimidation or violence during a strike. Employers may not get a court interdict to stop the strike, nor may they institute civil legal proceedings against employees. The employer can however, apply for a court interdict to prevent unlawful action, such as damage to machinery.

An employer does not have to pay an employee participating in a protected strike. If the employer provides food or housing as part of the employees' wages, then the employees can ask the employer to continue to provide these during the strike. The employer may not refuse this request. However, the employer may reclaim the money for the food and housing from the employees after the strike has ended by going to the Labour Court.

11.10.3 Procedures for a protected strike

The Act sets out certain procedures that must be followed for a strike to be protected.
- The issue in dispute must be referred in writing to the CCMA or to a bargaining or statutory council.
- The CCMA or council must try to settle the dispute by conciliation within 30 days.
- If this fails, the CCMA or council must issue a certificate saying that the dispute has not been resolved.
- At least 48 hours' notice in writing of the proposed strike must be given to the employer, or seven days' notice if the state is the employer.

The employees may then strike. It is not necessary to hold a ballot to make the strike protected, but union members may force a registered union to hold a ballot.

A strike will still be protected even if the procedures in the LRA have not been followed, if
- the parties to the dispute are members of a council and the dispute has been dealt with by that council in accordance with its constitution
- the strike conforms with the procedures in a collective agreement
- the strike is in response to an unprocedural lock-out
- the employer intends unilaterally to change the employees' employment conditions, or has changed them, and refuses to change them back again within 48 hours of a written request to do so

The Labour Appeal Court has held that if there is a collective agreement containing a dispute resolution procedure, compliance with either the procedure in the agreement or the procedures set out in the Act will render the strike as protected.

It is important to note, however, that if employees choose to follow the procedures in the Act rather than the procedures in a collective agreement, they may be in breach of that agreement, which may enable the employer to cancel the agreement or even claim damages from the employees or their union, depending on the wording of the agreement.

The Act sets out a special procedure to be followed where the dispute concerns a refusal to bargain. An advisory award must be obtained before a strike can take place over such a dispute. This award cannot force a party to bargain.

11.10.4 Limitations on strikes

A strike will not be protected if
◆ a collective agreement prohibits a strike in respect of the issue in dispute
◆ an agreement requires that the issue in dispute be referred to arbitration
◆ the issue in dispute is one that the Act says may be referred to arbitration or to the Labour Court
◆ the parties are bound by an arbitration award or collective agreement that regulates the issue in dispute
◆ the parties are bound by a sectoral determination that regulates the issue in dispute and the determination is less than one year old
◆ the parties are engaged in an essential service (see below)
◆ the parties are engaged in a maintenance service (see below)

11.10.5 Lock-outs

Employers can lock out employees by physically excluding employees from gaining access to the workplace. The action must be to force employees to accept a demand of the employer about a matter that concerns the employer and the employees. As in the case of strikes, employers can engage in a protected lock-out.

The following applies in terms of such a protected lock-out:
◆ Employees cannot apply to court to interdict the action.
◆ An employer does not commit a delict or breach of contract.
◆ Employees may not bring civil legal proceedings against an employer, for example, for loss of wages.
◆ An employer may not dismiss employees who have been locked out.
◆ The employer may use replacement labour only if the lock-out is in response to a strike. The employer may only do so until the lock-out ends; striking employees must then get their old jobs back.
◆ An employer does not have to pay wages to an employee participating in a protected lock-out. The same provisions apply with regard to food and housing as in the case of strikes (see above).

The Act sets out certain procedures that must be followed for a lock-out to be protected. These procedures are the same procedures that must be followed for a strike to be protected. They are as follows:
◆ The issue in dispute must be referred in writing to the CCMA or to a bargaining or statutory council.
◆ The CCMA or council has up to 30 days to try to settle the dispute through conciliation. If this fails, the CCMA or council must issue a certificate saying that the dispute has not been resolved.

- The employer must then give at least 48 hours' notice in writing of the proposed lock-out to the trade union, or employees if there is no union, or seven days' notice, where the state is the employer.

A lock-out will still be protected even if the procedures in the LRA are not followed by the employer, if:
- the parties to the dispute are members of a council and the dispute has been dealt with by that council in accordance with its constitution
- the lock-out conforms with the procedures in a collective agreement
- the lock-out is in response to an unprocedural strike

Employers or employees can claim compensation from the Labour Court if they suffer any loss as a result of an unprotected strike or lock-out, or as a result of any conduct connected to the strike or lock-out that does not comply with the Act. If a union wants to avoid being sued when its members engage in unprocedural strike action, that is, wildcat strikes, the union must inform the employer at the earliest possible opportunity that it disapproves of the strike, and must take steps to try to persuade its members to return to work.

11.10.6 Essential and maintenance services

Employees in essential and maintenance services may not strike, and employers may not lock out such employees. The Act defines an essential service as:
- one where interruption will endanger the life, personal safety or health of the whole or any part of the population
- the parliamentary service
- the South African Police Service

Disputes in essential services go to arbitration if conciliation has failed.

The Act defines a maintenance service as one where the interruption of that service will lead to the material physical destruction of the working area, plant or machinery. Where a service has been declared a maintenance service, employers may not employ replacement labour if non-maintenance service employees go on strike.

11.10.7 Picketing

The Act recognises the right of a registered union to authorise a picket. A picket may be held at any place to which the public has access outside the premises of an employer. Unions need the employer's permission to picket inside the workplace. If an employer refuses permission for a picket to take place inside the premises, the CCMA may overrule the employer if the refusal to grant permission is unreasonable, taking into account the conduct of the picketers, the duration of the picket, the number of employees taking part, and so on.

11.10.8 Secondary action

The Act makes specific provision for secondary action, and this happens when employees strike in support of a strike by other employees. It does not include a strike over a demand that has been referred to a council if the strikers are employed within the registered scope of the council, and they have a material interest in the demand of the main strikers.

A secondary action will be protected if the main strike is a protected strike, the secondary strikers give seven days' notice to their employer or the relevant employers' organisation, and the nature and extent of the secondary strike is reasonable in relation to the possible direct or indirect effect it may have on the business of the primary employer.

In other words, if dock-workers strike in support of striking mineworkers, their strike is unlikely to have any effect on the business of the mine owner who is the primary employer. If it has no effect, it will not be reasonable, and the dock-workers will be prohibited from holding their secondary strike.

11.10.9 Protest action to defend the socio-economic interests of employees

The Act also makes provision for protected stayaways in support of socio-economic issues. The issue must be raised at National Economic Development and Labour Council (Nedlac) or a similar forum and the action must be authorised by a registered union or federation. Even if these requirements are met, the Labour Court can remove protection against dismissal if participants do not comply with any order it issues to regulate the stayaway.

11.11 Unfair treatment in the workplace

The Act lists the following kinds of treatment as unfair labour practices:

* unfair conduct of an employer relating to the promotion, demotion, probation or training of an employee or the provision of benefits. For example: if all employees pass a test and all except one are promoted, the employer might be guilty of unfair conduct towards that employee
* unfair suspension of an employee or any other disciplinary action short of dismissal. For example: if an employee and her supervisor have an argument and the employer suspends only the employee, even though it is unclear who was to blame for the argument, this could be an unfair suspension
* failure or refusal of an employer to reinstate or re-employ a former employee in terms of any agreement. For example: if an employee was retrenched but it was agreed with the employer that the employee would be re-employed if a suitable job became vacant, and the employer disregards the agreement by employing another person when a suitable job does become vacant, the employer will be guilty of unfair labour practice
* occupational detriment, other than dismissal, in contravention of the Protected Disclosures Act 26 of 2000. This Act protects employees who 'blow the whistle' by disclosing wrongdoing or unlawful conduct taking place in the workplace. Employees who 'blow the whistle' may not be dismissed and may not be subjected to disciplinary action, suspended, demoted, harassed, intimidated, or be refused a transfer or promotion. For example: an employee informs the Department of Labour that an employer has been deducting UIF amounts from all the employees' wages in a hotel but has not been paying this money to the fund. If the employer discovers the employee's disclosure, the employer may not subject the employee to disciplinary action or in any other way prejudice the employee because of the disclosure.

11.11.1 Disputes about unfair labour practices

If there is a dispute about an unfair labour practice the aggrieved employee may refer the dispute to a council or to the CCMA. The referral must be made within 90 days of the alleged unfair labour practice and the council or CCMA must attempt to resolve the dispute through conciliation.

If the unfair labour practice concerns probation, the CCMA or council must deal with the dispute by 'con-arb'. This means that if conciliation is unsuccessful, the arbitration must start immediately. If the dispute does not concern probation then the employee must refer the dispute for arbitration within 30 days of the council or CCMA issuing a certificate that the dispute remains unresolved. The council or CCMA must then arbitrate the dispute.

The employee may refer a dispute concerning an alleged unfair labour practice to the Labour Court for adjudication if the employee has alleged that he or she has been prejudiced by his or her employer in contravention of the Protected Disclosures Act, 2000.

The remedies that an arbitrator may order include reinstatement, re-employment or compensation, which must be just and equitable and limited to a maximum of 12 months' remuneration.

11.12 Dismissals

An employer can dismiss employees for reasons of misconduct, for incapacity or for business-related reasons. A fair procedure must always be followed even in circumstances where there is a good reason for the dismissal.

11.12.1 What is a dismissal?

Under the Act an employee is regarded as dismissed when:

◆ an employer ends a contract of employment with or without notice to the employee
◆ an employee has a reasonable expectation that the employer will renew a fixed-term contract on the same or similar terms but the employer offers to renew it on less favourable terms, or does not renew it
◆ an employer refuses to allow an employee to return to work after maternity leave
◆ an employer selectively re-employs some employees after dismissal for the same or similar reasons but fails to re-employ others
◆ an employer makes the working environment impossible for the employee to tolerate, which forces the employee to leave (this is known as a constructive dismissal)
◆ the business is transferred as a going concern, and the new employer provides the employee with substantially less favourable terms and conditions of employment than the old employer, and as a result the employee resigns

A dismissal may be unfair or fair depending on the circumstances. The Act states that certain reasons for dismissal will always be unfair. Dismissal will be regarded as 'automatically unfair' if it is because:

◆ an employee takes part in the activities of a union or workplace forum
◆ an employee takes part in a protected strike or protest action

- employees refuse to accept an employer's offer on a matter of mutual interest between the employer and employees, such as a wage increase
- an employee refuses to do the work of someone who is on a protected strike or a lock-out, unless the work is necessary to prevent danger to life, personal safety and health
- an employee is pregnant (or any reason related to her pregnancy)
- the employee takes (or intends to take) action against an employer by exercising any right or by participating in any proceedings contained in the Act
- an employer dismisses an employee for a reason related to a transfer of the employer's business
- an employee makes a disclosure in terms of the protected disclosures Act of 2000
- the employee is dismissed on arbitrary grounds, such as the employee's race, age, religion, sex, sexual orientation or family responsibilities

However, there are two exceptions to this last class of automatically unfair dismissal. Firstly, an employer may retire someone who has reached the normal or agreed retirement age and, secondly, an employer may fairly dismiss someone if the reason for the dismissal is based on an inherent requirement of the job. For example, a teacher in a religious college who changes his or her faith could be justifiably dismissed.

11.12.2 Legal dismissal

An employer can dismiss an employee for a fair reason, which means that the dismissal is 'substantively' fair. If the employer has followed a fair procedure, the dismissal is 'procedurally' fair.

There are three fair reasons for dismissal:
- Misconduct – if an employee intentionally or carelessly breaks a rule at the workplace; for example, if he or she steals company goods.
- Incapacity – if an employee cannot perform duties properly owing to illness, ill health or inability.
- Operational reasons – if a company has to dismiss employees for reasons that are related to purely business needs and not because of some failing on the part of the employee.

A code of good practice published by the Department of Labour sets out the principles of substantive and procedural fairness to be followed in the case of dismissal for misconduct or incapacity.

The principles of a fair dismissal for operational reasons are contained in the Act itself and in a code of good practice on dismissals based on operational requirements, issued by Nedlac.

If there is a collective agreement on disciplinary procedures, the employer must comply with the procedures in the agreement.

11.12.3 Dismissal for misconduct

Dismissal for misconduct is the last resort of an employer when other measures to correct misconduct have failed, or are pointless. Principles of a proper disciplinary procedure are summarised below. The code of good practice on dismissals says that any person who has to decide on the fairness of a dismissal should consider whether or not

- the employee broke a rule of conduct in the workplace
- the rule was valid or reasonable
- the employee knew of the rule, or should have known of the rule
- the employer applied the rule consistently
- dismissal is the appropriate step to take against the employee for breaking the rule instead of less serious action like a final written warning or a suspension

Repeated offences could justify the final step of dismissal. Dismissal for a first offence may be appropriate if the misconduct is very serious, and makes the continued employment of that person intolerable.

Examples of serious misconduct are

- gross dishonesty (for example, theft)
- deliberate damage to the property of the employer
- deliberate endangering of the safety of others
- physical assault of the employer, a fellow employee, client or customer
- gross insubordination (for example, swearing at a supervisor in front of other employees)

Each case should be judged on its merits, and the employer should take into account other factors such as the employee's circumstances, for example, length of service, previous disciplinary record and personal circumstances, the nature of the job and the circumstances of the infringement itself, for example, if an employee was justifiably provoked to assault a colleague.

11.12.4 Procedural fairness

Even if there are very good substantive reasons for a dismissal, an employer must follow a fair procedure before dismissing an employee. This requires the employer to conduct an investigation into the alleged misconduct. This need not be a formal enquiry, but the following requirements should be met:

- The employer must inform the employee of the allegations in a manner the employee can understand.
- The union should be consulted before commencing an enquiry into the conduct of an employee who is a shop steward or union office-bearer.
- The employee should be allowed reasonable time to prepare a response to the allegations.
- The employee must be given an opportunity to state his or her case.
- The employee has the right to be assisted by a shop steward or other employee.

After the enquiry, the employer should inform the employee of the decision, preferably in writing. If the employer dismisses the employee, the employer must give reasons and inform the employee of his or her right to refer the dispute for resolution to a council or the CCMA. If the employee wishes to challenge the fairness of the dismissal by using a council or the CCMA, the matter must be referred to the correct body within 30 days of the dismissal.

Employers should keep records of disciplinary action for each employee, stating the nature of the misconduct, the disciplinary action, and the reasons for the action.

11.12.5 Fair disciplinary rules

Employers should adopt disciplinary rules that set out how employees must behave at work. The rules must be clear. All employees should be informed of them, unless they are so well known that everyone can be expected to know them.

The Act promotes the principle of progressive discipline. This means efforts should be made to correct employees' behaviour by means of graded disciplinary action. The most effective way for an employer to deal with minor problems is by informal advice and correction. Repeated misconduct will justify repeated and more severe warnings until a final warning is issued.

11.12.6 Dismissals during unprotected strikes

Although employees may not be dismissed for participating in a procedural strike, they can be dismissed if they participate in an unprocedural strike. Such action is regarded as misconduct, but will not always justify dismissal. Employers need to consider whether a dismissal would be substantively fair.

Factors to be taken into account would include how serious the breach of the Act was, whether attempts were made to comply with the Act, and whether or not the strike was in response to unjustified conduct by the employer.

Before dismissing striking employees, an employer should contact the union to discuss the employer's intention to dismiss strikers, give the striking employees a clear ultimatum that should state what is required of the employees and what will happen if they do not comply, give employees enough time to consider the ultimatum and allow the employees an opportunity to make representations, which the employer must consider.

The employer can ignore these steps if it is not reasonable to follow them. For example, if an unprocedural strike is accompanied by extreme violence, the employer might be forced in the interests of safety and security to dispense with these steps.

11.12.7 Dismissal for incapacity

The code of good practice on dismissals sets out guidelines on what is necessary for a dismissal for incapacity to be substantively and procedurally fair.

In terms of substantive fairness and before an employer can dismiss an employee for poor work performance, the employer must first give the employee appropriate evaluation, training or guidance and a reasonable time for improvement. The employer must hold an investigation into reasons for the poor performance. Only if the employee still continues to perform poorly thereafter, and the problem cannot reasonably be solved without dismissing the employee, will dismissal be fair.

If temporary incapacity causes an employee to be away from work for an unreasonably long time, it will be unfair to dismiss the employee unless the employer first investigates all possible ways of avoiding this step. If the incapacity is permanent, the employer should try to find alternative work for the employee, or adapt the work so that the employee is able to do it.

In terms of procedural fairness and when investigations relate to poor work performance and incapacity, the employee should be given an opportunity to state his or her case and to be assisted by a shop steward or co-worker.

11.12.8 Pre-dismissal arbitration

Instead of holding an internal hearing prior to dismissing an employee for misconduct or incapacity, the employer and employee can agree to hold a pre-dismissal arbitration paid for by the employer. This arbitration is conducted by a council, the CCMA or an accredited agency and is final and binding and subject only to review by the Labour Court.

Employees may agree to a pre-dismissal arbitration after receiving the charges brought against them. Higher-paid employees may agree to pre-dismissal arbitration in their contracts of employment. The purpose of a pre-dismissal arbitration is to avoid the duplication that often occurs when an internal hearing conducted at the workplace prior to dismissal is followed by an arbitration conducted by the CCMA or a council after the dismissal has taken place.

11.12.9 Dismissal for operational reasons

An employer may dismiss employees for operational reasons, but only if the employer has first attempted to avoid such an event by reaching an agreement with recognised representatives of employees. In terms of the 2002 amendments to the Act, a distinction is made between retrenchments of individuals, retrenchments at small-scale businesses, and retrenchments at large scale businesses.

The main changes introduced by the amendments are that individuals who are retrenched may refer a dispute either to arbitration by the CCMA or a council or to the Labour Court for adjudication. The consultation process in large scale retrenchments may be facilitated by a person appointed by the CCMA and employees involved in a large scale retrenchment may either strike or may refer a dispute over the substantive fairness of the retrenchments to the Labour Court.

11.12.10 The process in respect of small-scale and large-scale retrenchments

If an employer is considering dismissing employees for operational reasons, the employer must consult (in this order of preference) one of the following:

◆ any person whom the employer is required to consult in terms of a collective agreement

- a workplace forum and a registered trade union whose members are likely to be affected by the proposed dismissals
- any registered trade union whose members are likely to be affected by the proposed dismissals
- the employees likely to be affected by the proposed dismissals or their representatives nominated for that purpose

The employer and consulting parties must engage in a joint consensus-seeking process and attempt to reach consensus on the appropriate measures to avoid or minimise or change the timing of the dismissals, consider means to mitigate the adverse effects of the dismissals and agree the method for selecting employees and the severance pay for dismissed employees.

11.12.11 The written notice

When an employer contemplates a dismissal for operational reasons, the employer must issue a written notice inviting the other consulting parties to consult with it and must disclose all relevant information including:
- the reasons for the dismissals
- the alternatives considered
- the number of employees likely to be affected
- the proposed method for selecting the employees to dismiss
- when the dismissals are likely to take effect
- the severance pay proposed
- any assistance that the employer proposes to offer to the employees likely to be dismissed
- the possibility of future re-employment
- the number of employees employed by the employer
- the number of employees that the employer has dismissed for reasons based on its operational requirements in the last 12 months

The employer must allow the other consulting parties to make representations about these matters and any other matters. The employer must consider and respond to any representations that are made. If they were made in writing, the employer must respond in writing.

11.12.12 The process for large-scale retrenchments

The 2002 amendments to the Act introduced a new section to improve the effectiveness of consultations in large-scale retrenchments. This new section applies to workplaces where an employer employs more than 50 employees and where the number of retrenchments contemplated meets a certain minimum threshold. This threshold is reached if the employer contemplates the retrenchment of more than the specified minimum, or if the number of retrenchments that have taken place in the preceding 12 months plus the number contemplated, exceed the specified minimum.

Table 11.1: Provision for large-scale retrenchment of employees per size of organisation

Number of employees employed	Minimum number of dismissals contemplated by the employer
50 – 200	10 or more
201 – 300	20 or more
301 – 400	30 or more
401 – 500	40 or more
501 or more	50 or more

The employer or the consulting parties may request the appointment of a facilitator from the CCMA to assist the parties during the consultation process. If the employer makes the request, the request must accompany the notice calling on the other parties to consult. If the other consulting parties make the request, the request must be within 15 days of the employer issuing the notice to consult.

The Minister has made regulations dealing with the facilitation process. The facilitator may chair the meetings of the parties or direct them to meet on their own and must assist the parties to resolve disputes over the disclosure of information. He or she can arbitrate unresolved issues on this matter. The facilitator may meet up to four times with the parties.

When a facilitator is appointed, the employer may not issue notices of termination for 60 days after giving the notice to consult. If 60 days have passed from the date on which notice to consult was given, the employer may give notice terminating the contracts of employment and the registered trade union or the employees concerned may either give notice of a strike or may refer a dispute to the Labour Court concerning whether there is fair reason for the dismissal to the Labour Court.

If neither party requests the CCMA to appoint a facilitator, a party may not refer the dispute to a council or the CCMA for 30 days from the date of the notice to consult. Once the period for conciliation is finished (30 days or when a certificate is issued), the employer can give notice of termination and the union or employees can give notice of a strike.

In large-scale retrenchments, employees may elect to strike over their dismissals or to have the Labour Court adjudicate the substantive fairness of the dismissals. Employees may not do both, that is, refer a dispute to the Labour Court and strike.

11.12.13 The referral of a dispute by employees at a small-scale operation

Employees may refer a dispute over the substantive and/or procedural fairness of retrenchments to the Labour Court, if section 189A, which deals with large-scale retrenchments, is not applicable. This is the case if the employer has less than 50 employees or if the number of dismissals contemplated is less than the threshold figure set out above.

A single employee who has been retrenched may choose to refer a dispute either to arbitration or to the Labour Court.

11.12.14 Selection criteria

If one or more employees are selected for dismissal from a number of employees, the criteria for selection must be either agreed between the consulting parties or, if no criteria have been agreed, be fair and objective. Criteria that infringe a fundamental right protected by the LRA would be unfair, for example criteria based on union membership or pregnancy. Selection criteria that are generally considered to be fair include length of service, skills and qualifications. With regard to length of service, generally the last-in-first-out principle is regarded as fair but in some circumstances this principle may undermine affirmative action programmes.

11.12.15 Severance pay

Employees who are retrenched must receive at least one week's remuneration for every year of completed service from the employer. The consulting party may, however, reach agreement on a higher amount.

An employee who unreasonably refuses to accept an employer's offer of alternative employment with that employer or any other employer is not entitled to severance pay.

11.12.16 Disputes over dismissals

An employee may refer a dispute about a dismissal to the CCMA or a council for conciliation. If a dispute remains unresolved, the employee may refer the dispute to arbitration by the CCMA or a council or to adjudication by the Labour Court. The following dismissal disputes may be referred to arbitration:
- dismissals for misconduct or incapacity
- constructive dismissals, or where an employee resigns after being given less favourable terms and conditions of employment following a transfer of a business as a going concern or the transfer of an insolvent business

An individual employee who has been dismissed for operational reasons may refer a dispute either to the CCMA (or council) for arbitration, or to the Labour Court for adjudication. Automatically unfair dismissals, dismissals for participating in an unprotected strike, and operational requirement dismissals (other than those that only involve one employee) may be referred to the Labour Court for adjudication.

11.12.17 Remedies for unfair dismissals

Reinstatement is the first choice of remedy for an unfair dismissal, unless special circumstances exist.

These circumstances exist if the dismissed employee does not wish to return to work, the dismissal was only procedurally unfair, the working relationship between the parties has become intolerable, or it is not practical to do so.

For example, it may be excessively costly for an employer to adapt the workplace to the needs of an employee who was unfairly dismissed for incapacity.

An employee who is not reinstated is usually given compensation, which must be just and equitable and not more than the equivalent of 12 months remuneration. If the dismissal is automatically unfair, the maximum compensation that may be awarded is the equivalent of 24 months remuneration.

Evidence will need to be led on, for example, an employee's loss of earnings, to enable the court or arbitrator to decide what will be a just and equitable compensation. The compensation award is additional to monies owing for other reasons, such as outstanding holiday pay or bonuses.

In cases of automatically unfair dismissal or dismissal based on operational requirements, the Labour Court can make additional orders apart from reinstatement or compensation.

11.13 The transfer of a business

An employee's contract of employment automatically transfers when a business is transferred as a going concern or where a business is transferred in a situation of insolvency. In situations when a business is sold or transferred either as a going concern or because of insolvency, the Act seeks to prevent job losses and to ensure that employees' terms and conditions of employment remain the same.

11.13.1 The transfer of a business as a going concern

When a business is transferred as a going concern, the new employer takes over the employees' contracts of employment from the old employer. This happens automatically on transfer of the business unless there is an agreement to the contrary between the employers and the appropriate employee representative.

An employee's continuity of employment is not interrupted by the transfer of the business and the new employer must employ the employees on terms and conditions that are on the whole not less favourable than those which employees enjoyed with the old employer. However, if the terms and conditions of employment of the transferred employees are determined by collective agreement, the collective agreement continues to apply.

The purpose of the provision with respect to employees who are not covered by a collective agreement is to allow for flexibility in the total package provided by the new employer. For example, a white-collar employee may have received an allowance for a cellular telephone and a car allowance from the old employer, but does not enjoy those allowances with a new employer. However, he or she benefits from a housing subsidy instead.

Employees who do not wish to transfer to the new employer may resign and they will not be entitled to severance pay. If their new service conditions are substantially less favourable than their previous service conditions, they may resign and bring a claim for constructive dismissal.

11.13.2 Agreements between the parties

The old employer must reach agreement with the new employer as to a valuation on the date of transfer of the transferring employees in terms of accrued leave pay and severance pay, if the employees had been entitled to severance pay and any other accrued entitlements (for example, bonuses).

The agreement must also specify which employer is liable for paying these amounts and what provision has been made for the payment of those amounts. For a period of 12 months after the date of transfer both the old employer and the new employer are liable to any employee who becomes entitled to a payment as a result of being dismissed for operational requirements or as a result of the employer's liquidation or sequestration.

11.13.3 Obligations of the new employer
The old employer's obligations in respect of trade union organisational rights or recognition agreements are transferred to the new employer. This facilitates the continuity of collective bargaining. Unless the parties agree otherwise, the new employer is bound by any existing arbitration award or collective agreement.

The new employer becomes liable for any unfair dismissal, unfair labour practice or Act of discrimination committed prior to the transfer by the old employer. These provisions place a burden on the new employer and the new employer should factor into the purchase price the potential financial costs of transferring employees.

11.13.4 Dismissals and transfers of businesses
An employee cannot be dismissed merely because a transfer takes place, but an employee can be dismissed if the transfer creates operational requirements that justify dismissal. A dismissal due to a transfer that cannot be justified in terms of operational requirements is regarded as automatically unfair.

If an employee resigns because the new employer fails to provide employment conditions that are substantially as favourable as those provided by the old employer, then the employee may have a claim for a constructive dismissal.

11.13.5 The transfer of contracts of employment in circumstances of insolvency
Prior to the amendments to this Act, employees' contracts of employment would automatically terminate when a business became insolvent. Employees often lost severance pay and did not have a right to be reinstated if the business revived.

The Act deals with this problem by providing that when a business becomes insolvent and a scheme of arrangement is entered into to avoid the winding-up or sequestration of the business, employees' contracts of employment transfer from the old employer to the new.

The new employer is automatically substituted in the place of the old employer but all the rights and obligations between the old employer and its employee at the time of transfer remain with the old employer. This is in contrast to when a business that is not insolvent is transferred.

When an employer is facing financial problems that may result in the business becoming wound up or sequestrated, the employer must advise the employee representatives of that fact. An employer who applies to be wound up or sequestrated must provide the employee representatives with a copy of the application.

11.14 Resolution of disputes

The Act established the following dispute resolution institutions:

* the Commission for Conciliation, Mediation and Arbitration (CCMA), an independent body that seeks to resolve disputes through conciliation and arbitration
* the Labour Court and the Labour Appeal Court, which are the only courts that can hear and decide most labour disputes

11.14.1 Commission for Conciliation, Mediation and Arbitration (CCMA)

The CCMA is an independent body even though it is mainly state-funded. It is controlled by a governing body on which government, business and labour have three representatives each. The CCMA has an office in each province and a national office in Johannesburg.

The main functions of the CCMA are as follows:

* Resolving disputes: The CCMA must attempt to resolve, through conciliation, workplace disputes referred to it. If conciliation fails, the CCMA must settle the dispute by arbitration if the Act says that the next step is arbitration, or if any party to the dispute refers the dispute to arbitration.
* Assisting with the establishment of workplace forums.
* Giving advice, assistance and training: The CCMA can assist parties on a range of issues, including giving advice on dispute resolution design and collective bargaining structures.
* Accrediting councils and private agencies: The CCMA can accredit councils or private agencies to conciliate and arbitrate on certain disputes.

11.14.2 The Labour Court

The Labour Court has the same status as the High Court, and has exclusive jurisdiction over most labour matters. The Labour Court has concurrent jurisdiction with the High Court in constitutional matters that arise in an employment context, and in cases concerning contracts of employment. The Labour Court is a superior court, is second only to the Constitutional Court, and, as already stated, is of equal status to the High Court.

The Labour Courts are to be found in Johannesburg, Cape Town, Port Elizabeth and Durban. A Labour Court may make any appropriate order including granting urgent interim relief, an interdict, an order for specific performance, a declaratory order and an award of compensation or damages.

11.14.3 The Labour Appeal Court

Parties may apply to the Labour Court for leave to appeal to the Labour Appeal Court (LAC) against any final order or judgment of the Labour Court. The LAC is the final court of appeal against decisions of the Labour Court. The persons who hold the positions of judge president and deputy judge president in the Labour Court also hold the same positions in the LAC.

11.14.4 Basic procedures for the resolution of disputes

The Act tries to ensure that disputes are resolved as quickly as possible. It provides for a basic two-step procedure that will apply whenever the parties in dispute have not agreed to a private dispute procedure in a collective agreement that covers the issue in dispute.

Step one is conciliation. Step two is one of the following: arbitration, adjudication or industrial action, depending on the type of dispute. The second step is taken only if the first step fails. An important innovation in the 2002 amendments to the Act is that the CCMA may now resolve disputes by 'con-arb'.

In 'con-arb' the arbitration starts immediately after the end of the conciliation if the dispute is not settled. 'Con-arb' must be used in disputes about probation and dismissals for misconduct or incapacity, unless a party objects.

11.14.4.1 Step one: conciliation

Conciliation occurs when the parties in dispute get together with a third, neutral party, a conciliator. The conciliator does not decide who is right or wrong, but attempts merely to assist the parties to reach agreement. The Act states that conciliation can include mediation, fact-finding or the making of a recommendation to the parties. It is up to the conciliator to decide which is the most appropriate process.

Disputes may be conciliated either by a commissioner of the CCMA, a council (statutory council or bargaining council) or a private agency.

The general rule is that if a council has been established for a sector, then the council must conciliate the dispute and not the CCMA. To perform this role a council must either become accredited itself or use the services of an accredited agency.

The CCMA will normally only conciliate a dispute if there is no council covering the parties in dispute. However, certain disputes may be conciliated only by the CCMA, even if there is a council covering the parties in dispute; for example, disputes over picketing rights.

Where disputes relate to unfair dismissals, they must be referred for conciliation within 30 days of the dismissal or, if it is a later date, the employer's final decision to dismiss (for example, when the employer rejects the employee's appeal). Where disputes relate to unfair labour practices, they must be referred for conciliation within 90 days of the alleged unfair labour practice occurring or within 90 days of the employee becoming aware of the unfair labour practice. Once a dispute has been referred to conciliation, the commissioner must attempt to resolve the dispute within 30 days, although the parties may agree to extend this period.

11.14.4.2 Step two: arbitration or adjudication by the Labour Court or industrial action

If conciliation fails, parties can proceed to step two. At this second stage there are three alternative routes for dispute resolution: arbitration, adjudication by the courts, or industrial action.

The Act determines which process a particular type of dispute must follow. Parties must comply with the Act, unless they have agreed to follow their own private dispute resolution process.

Arbitration: In arbitration the dispute is referred to a neutral third party, called an arbitrator, who hears both sides of the dispute, and then makes a decision about who is right. The arbitrator will issue an arbitration award that is binding on the parties. There is no appeal against a decision of an arbitrator, but a review might be possible.

The Act specifies that certain disputes may be arbitrated by a commissioner of the CCMA, a council or a private agency. The body that conciliated the dispute should also arbitrate. If there is a council for the sector, the council will conciliate and then arbitrate if the dispute remains unresolved. If there is no council, then the CCMA will arbitrate the dispute after conciliation. Councils and private agencies must be accredited.

Disputes must be referred for arbitration within 90 days of the CCMA or council issuing a certificate that the dispute remains unresolved. Arbitrators must issue an arbitration award giving brief reasons for their decision within 14 days of the conclusion of the arbitration proceedings.

Adjudication (Labour Court disputes): Some disputes go to the Labour Court for a decision instead of arbitration. These disputes must be referred to the Labour Court within 90 days of the CCMA or council certifying that the dispute remains unresolved. It is also possible for parties to a dispute to agree that instead of referring the matter to the Labour Court, it will be referred to arbitration conducted by the CCMA.

A party can appeal against a decision of the Labour Court to the Labour Appeal Court, if leave to appeal is granted.

Industrial action: Parties can embark on industrial action (being strikes or lock-outs) only if the Act does not provide that the dispute may be referred for arbitration or adjudication, and specific restrictions in Chapter 4 of the Act do not apply.

The Act recognises private dispute resolution procedures. In other words, the parties themselves may reach agreement on procedures for the resolution of disputes. If they do this, they need not follow the procedures set out in the Act, provided the dispute is finalised.

11.15 Impact of the Act on particular employees

The Act aims to treat all employees the same. There are, however, some differences in the way the law might apply in certain sectors.

11.15.1 Small businesses with fewer than 100 employees

The Act requires a workplace to have at least 100 employees before a workplace forum can be established. Workplaces with fewer employees than this cannot have workplace forums. However, nothing prevents a registered union from reaching a collective agreement with the employer to establish a body like a workplace forum.

11.15.2 Small businesses with fewer than 10 employees

In such workplaces there is no automatic right of a majority union to trade union representatives (shop stewards). This can only be achieved by negotiation with the employer. However, employees in such a workplace still have the right to join unions. Unions may apply for access and meeting rights. Also, even if an employer refuses to recognise a shop steward, the employees may still rely on that shop steward to represent them in the capacity of a co-worker.

11.15.3 Small businesses under councils

Councils are compelled to make provision in their constitutions for the representation of small and medium businesses. The Act also requires councils to establish independent exemption committees to ensure that small businesses get a fair hearing in exemption applications from council agreements.

Each year councils must provide the registrar of labour relations with a report on small enterprises falling within their scope.

11.15.4 Retrenchments

Section 189A of the Act, dealing with large-scale retrenchments, does not apply to employers employing less than 50 employees. This means that workers in these businesses may not strike about impending retrenchments and do not have the right to request assistance from the CCMA to facilitate the retrenchment process.

11.15.5 Domestic workers

Domestic workers now have almost all of the same rights as other employees under the Act. The following exceptions are important to note:

◆ *No trade union access*: Unless an employer of a domestic worker agrees, no trade union official or office-bearer can demand the right of access to the home of such an employer.
◆ *No right to disclosure of information*: Unions of domestic workers have no right to disclosure of information from the employer (such as an employer's pay slips), unlike in other workplaces where a union has majority membership. This does not prevent an employer of domestic workers from agreeing to disclose relevant information to the union.

11.15.6 Workers employed by temporary employment services

A business may not employ people to perform its work directly but may instead pay a temporary employment firm to provide it with people to do its work. These people are not employees of the business, but of the temporary employment firm.

To ensure that employees in this situation are not exploited by either the business or the employment agency, the Act makes both responsible for complying with an employer's duties to the employee. Employees of temporary employment services can therefore make a claim either against the service itself or against the business where they perform their work. For example: Jacquie is employed as a waitress by Top Temps CC. Top Temps finds her banqueting work at a conference centre. Jacquie therefore has a claim against Top Temps or the conference centre if Top Temps does not pay her salary.

11.15.7 Probationary employees

New employees may be employed on probation to enable the employer to assess their performance. The period of probation must be reasonable. During the period of probation employees must be given feedback and guidance arising out of the employer's assessment of their performance.

If an employee on probation is not meeting the required standard, the employer must give the employee an opportunity to make representations and may then extend the probationary period or dismiss the employee. A dispute concerning the extension of a probationary period or the dismissal of an employee on probation may be referred to the CCMA or a council for conciliation and thereafter arbitration. In deciding whether the dismissal of an employee on probation for poor performance is fair, the arbitrator may accept less compelling reasons for the dismissal than would be required if the person had not been on probation.

Questions and exercises

1. Under what conditions may a trade union and its members engage in a lawful strike?
2. Under what conditions may employers and employees set up a bargaining council, and how do they go about it?
3. Give a brief description of the jurisdiction and responsibilities of the CCMA.
4. Briefly describe the differences between arbitration, conciliation and mediation.

12

Introduction to labour law

Objectives of this chapter:

By the end of this chapter the learner will be able to:
- Describe the foundation of labour legislation in South Africa
- Follow a simple process of fair labour practices
- Guide employees in the process of claims for UIF in the event of their becoming unemployed

The learner will know:
- Where to access and how to use codes of good practice
- The basic conditions of employment applicable in South Africa
- How to register for and pay unemployment insurance

12.1 Introduction

South Africa's system of labour relations revolves around various rules, processes, structures and procedures that are used by the state, business, trade unions, employers and employees to manage the workplace labour relationship.

The government supports freedom of association and free collective bargaining as a fundamental part of its labour relations policy. Labour legislation is introduced for the specific purposes of establishing parameters for the conduct of the labour relationship and to ensure the protection of employers and employees.

Chapter 3 of the Constitution sets out certain fundamental rights for all citizens of South Africa, and makes the content of the chapter binding on all legislative and executive organs of the state at all levels of government. This means that all forms of South African legislation, be they national, provincial and/or local, must give rise to these principles and that no law may contain any provisions which are deemed to be contrary to these rights:
- every person shall have the right to fair labour practices
- employees shall have the right to form and join trade unions
- employers shall have the right to form and join employer associations
- employers and employees shall have the right to organise and bargain collectively

- employees shall have the right to strike for the purposes of collective bargaining
- employers shall have the right of lock-out for the purposes of collective bargaining

As a direct result, the official labour relations policy of the government of South Africa is based on the following principles:
- the right to work
- the right to fair remuneration and conditions of service
- the right of access to training and retraining
- the right to organise and belong to a trade union
- the right to bargain and negotiate collectively
- the right to protection of safety and health
- the right to security against unemployment
- the right to security in the event of injury at work
- the right to job security and protection against unfair labour practices

In order to give rise to all of the labour principles adopted by the government, the Department of Labour has, over the last eight to ten years, introduced a significant number of new and amended legislative Acts and regulations.

Figure 12-1: The effect of the Labour Relations Act on legislation

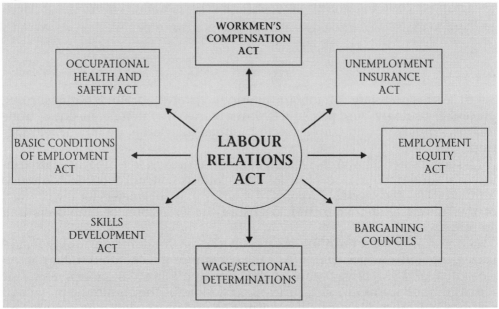

In effect, South African labour law revolves around the Labour Relations Act. The various labour enactments, as indicated in the diagram above, give rise to the key policies adopted by the Department of Labour, which are:
- to leave the regulation of labour relations to employers and employees as far as is possible
- to legislate only for minimum conditions of employment

- to provide adequate procedures to regulate collective bargaining and negotiation
- to provide for collective agreements and dispute resolution
- to ensure a negotiating balance between employers and employees
- to consult business, labour and the community representatives whenever changes to labour legislation are considered. This is primarily achieved through the National Economic Development and Labour Council (Nedlac)

12.1.1 National Economic Development and Labour Council

Nedlac, located in Rosebank, Johannesburg, is a forum at which government meets with organised business, organised labour and organised community groupings on a national level to discuss and try to reach consensus on issues of social and economic policy. The aim or objective is to make economic decision-making more inclusive, and to promote the goals of economic growth and social equity.

Nedlac is funded by the Department of Labour, which is the primary government representative. However, other departments such as Trade and Industry, Finance and Public Works are also predominantly involved in Nedlac. Other departments attend when there is an issue that relates to their portfolios.

Organised business is represented by Business South Africa, which is an umbrella body for 19 different employer organisations, such as the Chamber of Mines, the South African Chamber of Business, the Banking Council and the Steel and Engineering Industries Federation of South Africa.

Organised labour is represented by the three main labour federations in South Africa: Cosatu, Fedusa and Nactu.

Civil society is represented by the South African Youth Council, National Women's Coalition, South African National Civics Organisation, Disabled People of South Africa and the National Co-operatives Association of South Africa.

Nedlac's work is conducted in four chambers that discuss different aspects of social and economic policy. These are the Labour Market Chamber, the Trade and Industry Chamber, the Development Chamber and the Public Finance and Monetary Policy Chamber. Sub-committees and task groups of the chambers are formed to deal with specific issues. The chambers report to a management committee, which oversees the work programme and administrative issues.

12.2 Basic Conditions of Employment Act

This is a summary of the most important sections of the Basic Conditions of Employment Act 75 of 1997. Workers must be able to see a summary at their workplaces in the official languages that are spoken there.

The Act applies to all workers and employers, except members of the National Defence Force, National Intelligence Agency, South African Secret Service and unpaid volunteers working for charities. This Act must be obeyed even if other agreements are different.

12.2.1 Working time

This section does not apply to senior managers (those who can hire, discipline and fire), sales staff who travel and workers who work less than 24 hours a month.

12.2.1.1 Ordinary hours of work

A worker must NOT work more than:
- 45 hours in any week
- 9 hours a day if a worker works 5 days or less a week
- 8 hours a day if a worker works more than 5 days a week

12.2.1.2 Overtime

If overtime is required it must be agreed to by an employee and the employee may not work more than three hours' overtime a day or 10 hours' overtime a week. Overtime must be paid at 1,5 times the worker's normal pay or by agreement get paid time off.

More flexibility of working time can be negotiated if there is a collective agreement with a registered trade union. This can, for example, allow more flexible hours for working mothers and migrant workers.
- Compressed work week: You may agree to work up to 12 hours in a day and work fewer days in a week. This can help working mothers and migrant workers by having a longer weekend.
- Averaging: A collective agreement may permit the hours of work to be averaged over a period of up to four months. A worker who is bound by such an agreement cannot work more than an average of 45 ordinary hours a week and an average of five hours of overtime a week over the agreed period. A collective agreement for averaging has to be re-negotiated each year.

12.2.1.3 Meal breaks and rest periods

A worker must have a meal break of 60 minutes after five hours' work. But a written agreement may lower this to 30 minutes or do away with the meal break altogether if the worker works less than 6 hours a day.

A worker must have a daily rest period of 12 continuous hours and a weekly rest period of 36 continuous hours, which, unless otherwise agreed, must include Sunday.

12.2.1.4 Sunday work

A worker who sometimes works on a Sunday must get double pay. A worker who normally works on a Sunday must be paid at 1,5 times the normal wage. There may be an agreement for paid time off instead of overtime pay.

12.2.1.5 Night work

Night work is unhealthy and can lead to accidents. Night work refers to the hours between 6:00 at night and 6:00 in the morning and must afford workers extra pay or fewer work hours for the same amount of money.
Transport must be available but not necessarily provided by the employer.

Workers who usually work between 11:00 at night and 6:00 in the morning must be told of the health and safety risks. They are entitled to regular medical check-ups, paid for by the employer. They must be moved to a day shift if night work causes health problems to the workers concerned. All medical examinations must be kept confidential.

12.2.1.6 Public holidays
Workers must be paid for any public holiday that falls on a working day. Work on a public holiday is by agreement and paid at double the rate. A public holiday is exchangeable by agreement.

12.2.2 Leave

12.2.2.1 Annual leave
A worker can take up to 21 continuous days' annual leave or by agreement, one day for every 17 days worked or one hour for every 17 hours worked. Leave must be taken not later than six months after the end of the leave cycle.

An employer can pay a worker, instead of giving leave, only if that worker leaves the job.

12.2.2.2 Sick leave
A worker can take up to six weeks' paid sick leave during a 36-month cycle. During the first six months a worker can take one day's paid sick leave for every 26 days worked.

An employer may want a medical certificate before paying a worker who is sick for more than two days at a time or more than twice in eight weeks.

12.2.2.3 Maternity leave
A pregnant worker can take up to four continuous months of maternity leave. She can start leave any time from four weeks before the expected date of birth OR on a date a doctor or midwife says is necessary for her health or that of her unborn child. She also may not work for six weeks after the birth of her child unless declared fit to do so by a doctor or midwife.

A pregnant or breastfeeding worker is not allowed to perform work that is dangerous to her or her child.

12.2.2.4 Family responsibility leave
Full time workers employed for longer than four months can take three days' paid family responsibility leave per year on request when the worker's child is born or sick or for the death of the worker's spouse or life partner, parent, adoptive parent, grandparent, child, adopted child, grandchild or sibling.

An employer may want proof that this leave was needed.

12.2.3 Job information and payment

12.2.3.1 Job information
Employers must give new workers information about their job and working conditions in writing. This includes a description of any relevant council or sectoral determination and a list of any other related documents.

12.2.3.2 Keeping records

Employers must keep a record of at least:
- the worker's name and job
- time worked
- money paid
- the date of birth for workers under 18 years old

12.2.3.3 Payment

An employer must pay a worker:
- in South African money
- daily, weekly, fortnightly or monthly
- in cash, cheque or direct deposit

12.2.3.4 Payslip information

Each payslip must include:
- the employer's name and address
- the worker's name and job
- the period of payment
- the worker's pay
- the amount and purpose of any deduction made from the pay
- the actual amount paid to the worker

If appropriate, the payslip must also include:
- the ordinary pay rate and overtime pay rate
- the number of ordinary and overtime hours worked during that period of payment
- the number of hours worked on a Sunday or public holiday during that period
- the total number of ordinary and overtime hours worked in the period of averaging, if there is an averaging agreement

12.2.3.5 Approved deductions

An employer may not deduct any money from a worker's pay unless:
- that worker agrees in writing
- the deduction is required by law or permitted in terms of a law, collective agreement, court order or arbitration award

12.2.3.6 Adding up wages

- Wages are based on the number of hours normally worked.
- Monthly pay is 4 and 1/3 times the weekly wage.

12.2.4 Termination of employment

12.2.4.1 Notice

A worker or employer must give notice to end an employment contract of not less than:
- 1 week, if employed for four weeks or less

- 2 weeks, if employed for more than four weeks but not more than one year
- 4 weeks, if employed for one year or more

Notice must be in writing, except from a worker who cannot write.

Workers who stay in an employer's accommodation must be given one month's notice of termination of the contract or be given alternative accommodation until the contract is lawfully terminated.

An employer giving notice does not stop a worker from challenging the dismissal in terms of the Labour Relations Act or any other law.

12.2.4.2 Severance pay

An employer must pay a worker who is dismissed as a result of the employer's operational requirements pay equal to at least one week's severance pay for every year of continuous employment with that employer.

12.2.4.3 Certificate of service

When a job ends, a worker must be given a certificate of service.

12.2.5 Child labour and forced labour

- It is against the law to employ a child under the age of 15.
- Children under 18 may not do dangerous work or work meant for an adult.
- It is against the law to force someone to work.

12.2.6 Variation of basic conditions of employment

12.2.6.1 Bargaining council

A collective agreement concluded by a bargaining council can be different from this law as long it does not:
- lower protection of workers in terms of health and safety and family responsibilities
- lower annual leave to less than two weeks
- lower maternity leave in any way
- lower sick leave in any way
- lower protection of night workers
- allow for any child labour or forced labour

12.2.6.2 Other agreements

Collective agreements and individual agreements must follow the Act.

12.2.6.2.1 The Minister

The Minister of Labour may make a determination to vary or exclude a basic condition of employment. This can also be done on application by an employer or employer organisation.

12.2.7 Sectoral determinations

Sectoral determinations may be made to establish basic conditions for workers in a sector and area, an example being Sectoral Determination 14: Hospitality Sector effective 1 July 2007.

12.2.8 Employment Conditions Commission

This Act makes provision for the Employment Conditions Commission to advise the Minister of Labour.

12.2.9 Monitoring, enforcement and legal proceedings

Labour inspectors must advise workers and employers on their labour rights and obligations. They investigate complaints, question people and inspect, copy and remove records.

An inspector may serve a compliance order by writing to the Director-General of the Department of Labour, who will then look at the facts and agree, change or cancel the order. This decision can be challenged in the Labour Court. Workers may not be treated unfairly for demanding their rights in terms of this Act.

12.2.10 General

It is a crime to:

- hinder, block or try to wrongly influence a labour inspector or any other person obeying this Act
- get, or try to get, a document by stealing, lying or showing a false or forged document
- pretend to be a labour inspector or any other person obeying this Act
- refuse, or fail to answer fully, any lawful question asked by a labour inspector or any other person obeying this Act
- refuse or fail to obey a labour inspector or any other person obeying this Act

There are some other issues that are not regulated by the Basic Conditions of Employment Act – for example, transport allowances, bonuses, increases, afternoons off, weekends off, and so on. These issues can be negotiated with your employees.

12.3 Unemployment insurance

In 1967 the Unemployment Insurance Act 53 of 1946 was replaced by the Unemployment Insurance Act. Initially the Unemployment Insurance Act 30 of 1966 benefited only contributors who were registered as unemployed and who were capable and available for work and actively seeking employment.

Over the years many amendments to the Act were promulgated. In 2001, the Unemployment Insurance Act was totally rewritten and, after consultation with both business and labour, came into effect on 1 April 2002. This new Act provides a framework for an Unemployment Insurance Fund that is sustainable, efficient and gives extended benefits to workers at all levels, including domestic workers who were included from 1 April 2003.

All workers who work for more than 24 hours per month at a business have to contribute to the Unemployment Insurance Fund (UIF) in terms of the Unemployment Insurance Act 63 of 2001.

12.3.1 The Unemployment Insurance Act

The Unemployment Insurance Act 63 of 2001 sets out to establish the Unemployment Insurance Fund; to provide for the payment from the fund of unemployment benefits to certain employees, and for the payment of illness, maternity, adoption and dependant's benefits related to the unemployment of such employees; to provide for the establish-ment of the Unemployment Insurance Board, the functions of the board and the designation of the Unemployment Insurance Commissioner; and to provide for matters connected therewith.

The main purpose of the Act is to ensure that employees who are contributors have access to the Unemployment Insurance Fund and to financial aid under certain circumstances. Benefits may be paid to contributors as a result of:

♦ unemployment
♦ illness
♦ maternity
♦ adoption
♦ a deceased contributor (dependants only)

All employers who engage workers for more than 24 hours in a month are required to register with the fund, and are required to pay over contributions monthly to either the South African Revenue Service or the Unemployment Insurance Fund. Benefits are only paid out to contributors under the specific circumstances relating to the type of benefit being claimed. Employers should, whenever possible, assist employees when making an application under the Act.

This Act applies to all employers and employees, other than, amongst others, employees who work less than 24 hours a month and employees who receive remuneration under a learnership agreement registered in terms of the Skills Development Act 97 of 1998, and their employers.

12.3.2 Compliance and penalties

Any person committing an offence under the Act will be liable to a fine, imprisonment or both. The Labour Court has jurisdiction for offences commit-ted under the Act, whereas magistrates have jurisdiction for any criminal offences committed under the Act.

12.3.3 Practical application of the Act for employers

12.3.3.1 Registration

All employers that employ any person, and in return provide them with remuneration in either cash or in kind, must register with the fund. It is the responsibility of the employer to register the business and make the necessary contribution deductions from the earnings of the workers.

If any employer refuses to register with the fund and deduct contributions from the workers' salaries, the workers are advised to contact the nearest office of the Department of Labour, as the fund is there for their protection. Employers are required to comply with the provisions of the Act, as the fund provides relief to ex-workers who are left with limited means or no means of support owing to their services being terminated.

The employer may use the UIF website (www.uif.gov.za) to register, make declarations to the fund and also pay contributions to the fund.

In terms of Notice 850 of 15 September 2005 the Minister of Labour has set the rate of earnings threshold at R131,592. Employers are advised to check the threshold level with the UIF offices from time to time.

Employers must complete the following relevant forms:
- a UI 8 form for registration of commercial employers
- a UI 8D form for registration of domestic employers
- a UI 19 form for declarations

12.3.3.2 Declaring employees

Employers are required to furnish the UIF with details of all their employees as defined by the Act, which excludes non-natural persons and independent contractors. The employer's declaration must be submitted every month on or before the 7th of the following month. These details are added to the UIF employee database to maintain a record of each employee's employment history and forms the basis for the payment of benefits in terms of the Act.

Note that the details of all employees are required every month, irrespective of whether they are contributors or non-contributors.

Employers may make use of the following mechanisms:
- manual declarations
- electronic declarations
- declarations through the UIF website

For those employers who use an electronic payroll system, the fund, in conjunction with payroll service providers, has developed a system that accepts an extract from most payroll systems. If payroll declarations are made by e-mail, they must be in one of the specified formats, please refer to the Declaration Specification Document from the UIF in this regard. The subject of the e-mail must be DECLARATIONS in order to enable the fund's system to extract and read the e-mail. This facility and the e-mail address – declarations@uif.gov.za is to be used only for electronic declarations in the specified format.

An employer may also use the fund's website to make declarations. The on-line declaration facility is ideal for small and micro-enterprises who do not have an electronic payroll system but do have access to the internet. The user needs to have an authenticated username and password. To obtain this, please click on Online Declarations on the website.

12.3.3.3 Paying unemployment insurance

12.3.3.3.1 Employers of domestic workers and/or employers not registered with SARS for PAYE and SDL

Those employers who are not required to register with SARS for PAYE or SDL (Skills Development Levy) purposes must pay their contributions directly to the Unemployment Insurance Fund. The UI7 return form will be issued by the fund to all these employers. The return together with payment must be submitted to the fund not later than the 7th day of every month. Even if only one employee is liable for the payment of tax, the employer must register with SARS for PAYE, SDL and UIF purposes and the UIF contributions in respect of all employees must be paid to SARS.

Contributions can be paid at any provincial office or labour centre of the Department of Labour, or can be paid directly into the bank account of the fund. The employer reference number must be used for the deposit. Employers who have Internet banking facilities may also use this service to pay contributions to the fund. Please contact your bank for assistance in this regard.

12.3.3.3.2 Employers registered with SARS for PAYE and SDL
The new Unemployment Insurance Contributions Act 4 of 2002 came into operation on 1 April 2002 and brought considerable changes to the way employers interact with the fund.

All employers that are currently registered with SARS for PAYE and SDL purposes will receive their EMP 201 return from SARS and must pay their UIF contributions to SARS.

Included in the monthly EMP 201 return issued by SARS to employers, is an additional column for the declaration of UIF contributions.

Please note that PAYE, SDL and UIF contributions are payable not later than the 7th of the following month, i.e. contributions for May are payable no later than the 7th June.

The completed return together with payment for PAYE, SDL and UIF contributions must be submitted to SARS. Employers who are liable to pay contributions to SARS *may not* use the fund's website to pay their contributions.

SARS will receive these contributions on behalf of the fund and credit the employer's records accordingly.

12.3.4 Practical application of the Act for employees
12.3.4.1 Right to benefits
Subject to the provisions of the Act, a contributor or a dependant, as the case may be, is entitled to the following benefits:
◆ unemployment benefits
◆ illness benefits
◆ maternity benefits
◆ adoption benefits
◆ dependant's benefits

The scale of benefits may vary between a maximum rate of 60% of remuneration for lower income contributors and a lower rate of remuneration for higher income contributors as will be determined by thresholds as set out in Schedules to the Act.

12.3.4.2 Contributor not entitled to benefits under certain circumstances
A contributor is not entitled to benefits for any period that the contributor was in receipt of
◆ a monthly pension from the state
◆ any benefit from the compensation fund established under the Compensation for Occupational Injuries and Diseases Act 130 of 1993 as a result of an occupational injury or disease, which injury or disease caused the total or temporary unemployment of that contributor
◆ benefits from any unemployment fund or scheme established by hospitality bargaining councils

12.3.4.3 Right to unemployment benefits

An unemployed contributor is entitled to unemployment benefits for any period of unemployment lasting more than 14 days, if the reason for the unemployment is

- the termination of the contributor's contract of employment by the employer of that contributor, or the ending of a fixed term contract
- the dismissal of the contributor, as defined by section 186 of the Labour Relations Act in which fair, lawful and procedural dismissals by either the employer or employee are determined and defined
- insolvency in terms of the provisions of the Insolvency Act 24 of 1936

Application must be made in accordance with the prescribed requirements. The contributor must be registered as a work-seeker with a labour centre established under the Skills Development Act 97 of 1998; and must be capable of and available for work.

An unemployed contributor is not entitled to the benefits referred to in subsection (1) if the contributor

- fails to report at the times and dates stipulated by the claims officer in terms of the Act
- refuses without just reason to undergo training and vocational counselling for employment

A contributor who becomes ill while in receipt of unemployment benefits, remains entitled to unemployment benefits if the claims officer is satisfied that the illness is not likely to prejudice the contributor's chance of securing employment.

12.3.4.4 Application for unemployment benefits

The application must be made within six months of the termination of the contract of employment in the prescribed form at an employment office.

The claims officer will investigate the application and, if necessary, request further information regarding the applicant's continued unemployment. If the application complies with the provisions of the Act, the claims officer must

- *approve* the application
- *determine* the amount of benefits the applicant is entitled to, and authorise the payment of the benefits
- *stipulate* when the applicant must report to the employment office for purposes of confirming that the contributor has been unemployed for the period in respect of which the unemployment benefit has been claimed; and is capable of and available for work

If the application does not comply with the provisions of this chapter, the claims officer must advise the applicant in writing that the application is defective and the reasons why it is defective.

12.3.4.5 Right to illness benefits

A contributor is entitled to the illness benefits for any period of illness if

- the contributor is unable to perform work on account of illness

- the contributor fulfils any prescribed requirements in respect of any specified illness
- application is made for illness benefits in accordance with the prescribed requirements

A contributor is not entitled to illness benefits:
- if the period of illness is less than 14 days
- for any period during which the contributor is entitled to unemployment benefits
- or without just reason, refuses or fails to undergo medical treatment or to carry out the instructions of a medical practitioner, chiropractor or homeopath

12.3.4.6 Application for illness benefits

Application for illness benefits must be made personally in the prescribed form at an employment office. If the contributor cannot lodge the application personally, the claims officer may authorise any other person to lodge the application on behalf of the applicant.

The application for illness benefits must be made within six months of the commencement of the period of illness, but the commissioner may accept an application made after the six-month time limit has expired on good cause shown.

The claims officer will investigate the application and, if necessary, request further information regarding the applicant's continued unemployment. If the application complies with the provisions of the Act, the claims officer must
- *approve* the application
- *determine* the amount of benefits the applicant is entitled to and authorise the payment of the benefits
- *stipulate* how the benefits are to be paid

If the application does not comply with the provisions of this chapter, the claims officer must advise the applicant in writing that the application is defective, and the reasons why it is defective.

12.3.4.7 Right to maternity benefits

A contributor who is pregnant is entitled to maternity benefits for any period of pregnancy or delivery and the period thereafter.

The contributor must be paid the difference between the maternity benefit paid out by the Unemployment Insurance Fund and any benefit paid out in terms of any other law or any collective agreement, or contract of employment, for the period contemplated.

When taking into account any maternity leave paid to the contributor in terms of any other law or any collective agreement or contract of employment, the maternity benefit may not be more than the remuneration the contributor would have received if the contributor had not been on maternity leave.

The maximum period of maternity leave is 17,32 weeks.

A contributor who has a miscarriage during the third trimester or bears a still-born child is entitled to a maximum maternity benefit of six weeks after the miscarriage or stillbirth.

12.3.4.8 Application for maternity benefits

An application for maternity benefits must be made at least eight weeks before childbirth.

The commissioner may accept an application after the period of eight weeks, or extend the period of submission of the application up to a period of six months after the date of childbirth.

The claims officer will investigate the application and, if necessary, request further information regarding the applicant's continued unemployment. If the application complies with the provisions of the Act, the claims officer must
- *approve* the application
- *determine* the amount of benefits the applicant is entitled to, and authorise the payment of the benefits
- *stipulate* how the benefits are to be paid

If the application does not comply, the claims officer must advise the applicant in writing that the application is defective, and the reasons why it is defective.

12.3.4.9 Right to dependant's benefits

The surviving spouse or a life partner of a deceased contributor is entitled to the dependant's benefits if application is made and due process followed – similar to those mentioned above.

12.3.4.10 Benefits not subject to taxation

Benefits payable to contributors and dependants in terms of this Act are not subject to taxation in terms of the Income Tax Act 58 of 1962.

12.4 Disciplinary action/fair labour practices

12.4.1 Disciplinary procedures

All businesses should ensure that they formulate and implement a disciplinary policy and procedure in order to manage and administer employee discipline. The policy should include the procedures to be adopted and the levels of discipline that may be required. It is important to understand that more often than not, discipline is required in order to change behaviour rather than to punish it. The level of persuasion or discipline required must always equate with the severity of the employee error, omission or misconduct.

The disciplinary action that can be taken against an employee may take one of the following forms:
- verbal warning
- written warnings
- final written warnings
- dismissal with notice or summary dismissal

12.4.1.1 Verbal warning

This warning is usually given in the case of misconduct and poor performance; for example, late-coming or deliberate wastage of materials. Although it is verbal, it is often wise to briefly record the discussion in the employee's file for future reference.

12.4.1.2 Written warning (first, second, etc)

The first written warning is usually considered as the first formal disciplinary step taken against an employee. This warning is used for less serious offences and may cover breaches of discipline such as unauthorised absence or insolence being just two examples. A second written warning may be issued if a similar offence has been committed within a relatively short period of time. The fact that a second written warning is required clearly indicates that the first warning did not have the desired effect and did not correct the behaviour. A third written notice could follow the second, if a final warning is seen to be too severe a remedy, but the unacceptable behaviour has as yet not been corrected by the employee.

12.4.1.3 Final written warning

This warning is considered as the last step in endeavouring to improve the performance or behaviour of the employee. It could be the first step in the event of a serious offence as well as for less serious offences that are committed repeatedly. Bearing in mind that a final warning could, under certain circumstances, be a step away from dismissal it is important to ensure that it is not seen to be too severe a remedy.

12.4.1.4 Dismissal with notice or summary dismissal

Summary dismissal is justified only when the employee is guilty of a material breach of contract (for example, proven theft of business property or proven fraud) or when a final written warning for a similar offence is still in force.

12.4.1.5 Procedures to be followed in disciplinary action

A copy of all levels of written warning should be handed to the employee. The employee should acknowledge receipt in writing or, failing that, a third party should be requested to witness the event.

Employers must keep a record of any disciplinary action taken and this would best be retained in the employee's personal file. The record should specify the date, nature of the disciplinary transgression, the action taken and the reasons for the action.

Be cautious of taking disciplinary action against employees for poor work performance if an investigation into the reasons for the alleged poor performance has not been carried out. The breach of discipline may well be as a result of the lack of instruction or insufficient training, and may not necessarily be as a result of the inability of the employee to carry out the task.

If an employee is not capable of performing his or her duties, ensure that an investigation takes place and that the precise cause is established before taking disciplinary action. It may, for example, be as a result of a work-related injury in which case an entirely different course of action would be required. Making an assumption, when it comes to taking disciplinary action, can more often than not cause more difficulties for the employer than the employee.

12.4.1.6 Categories of dismissal

The Labour Relations Act 66 of 1995 as amended recognises three categories of dismissal, namely:
- Dismissal based on the employee's misconduct (for example wilful damage of property, assault of an employer, or gross subordination).
- Dismissal based on the employee's incapacity (for example poor work performance, inability to meet set standards, or physical disability).
- Dismissal based on the operational requirements of the employer (for example a downturn in the economy that may necessitate retrenchment and even the closure of a business).

When dismissing an employee for either misconduct or incapacity, the following two tests should be applied:
- the dismissal is fair and equates with the level of misconduct or incapacity and is not too severe a remedy
- the correct procedures have been followed throughout the course of the dismissal proceeding

The correct procedure must include the following:
- An enquiry takes place. The employee should be informed of the reason, date, venue and time of the proposed enquiry. Written notification should be given to the employee well before the date of the hearing in order to give him/her time to prepare. Four to five days notice, unless circumstances do not permit, would be deemed to be reasonable.
- The employee has the right to be assisted by another employee or a shop steward and has the right to be given a fair and reasonable opportunity to state his or her case in defence.
- The employee has the right of access to any and all of the evidence the employer intends to use, and must be given the opportunity to cross-examine persons who might testify. The employee may call witnesses in his or her defence.
- In the event that the employee is found guilty, and before deciding on the appropriate disciplinary action, the employee should be given an opportunity to advance any mitigating or personal circumstances that might result in a penalty, other than dismissal, being more appropriate.
- Inform the employee of the decision, and give the reasons in writing. The employee must then be informed of his or her right to refer the dispute for resolution to either the CCMA or a Bargaining Council Disputes Committee, if appropriate.
- Intended dismissal(s) for operational reasons will need to be handled in an entirely different manner. A comprehensive consultation process will need to take place with either all of the affected employees, a representative trade union or both. See Chapter 11 on the Labour Relations Act for all of the requirements.

12.5 Codes of good practice

Previously, a code of good practice issued under the LRA could be taken into account only when interpreting or applying that Act. Now, codes of good practice may be taken into account in interpreting or applying any employment law including:

- The Occupational Health and Safety Act, 1993
- The Compensation for Occupational Injuries and Diseases Act, 1993
- The Labour Relations Act, 1995
- The Basic Conditions of Employment Act, 1997
- The Employment Equity Act, 1998
- The Skills Development Act, 1998
- The Unemployment Insurance Act, 2001

As per the information provided in the section covering the Labour Relations Act, Nedlac and the Department of Labour have published seven codes of good practice. These cover:

- the arrangement of working time
- preparation, implementation and monitoring of an employment equity plan
- picketing
- the handling of sexual harassment cases
- protection of employees during pregnancy and childbirth
- dismissals based on operational requirements
- key aspects of HIV/Aids and employment

12.5.1 The arrangement of working time

The objective of this code is to provide information and guidelines to employers and employees concerning the arrangement of working time, and the impact of working time on the health, safety and family responsibilities of employees.

12.5.2 Preparation, implementation and monitoring of employment equity plan

The objective of this code is to provide guidelines on good practice in terms of the Employment Equity Act 55 of 1998 for the preparation and implementation of an employment equity plan.

12.5.3 Picketing

The code of good practice on picketing provides practical guidance on picketing in support of a protected strike or in opposition to a lock-out. It is a guide to those who take part in a picket and for employers, other employees or members of the public who may be affected by a picket. The code does not impose any legal obligations and a failure to observe it does not in itself render anyone liable.

12.5.4 The handling of sexual harassment cases

Sexual harassment is unwelcome conduct of a sexual nature and may include

- physical conduct
- unwelcome innuendoes
- sexual advances

- unwelcome gestures and indecent exposures
- *quid pro quo* treatment, where an employer or supervisor attempts to influence the process of employment or promotion or training or discipline and so forth in exchange for sexual favours

The code encourages the development and implementation of policies and procedures that will lead to workplaces that are free of sexual harassment, and where employers and employees respect one another's integrity, dignity and privacy. The application of the code goes beyond employers and their employees and may include clients and suppliers and other persons who have dealings with the business.

The code of good practice on handling sexual harassment cases aims at eliminating sexual harassment in the workplace. It defines sexual harassment as 'unwanted conduct of a sexual nature'. The unwanted nature of sexual harassment distinguishes it from behaviour that is welcome and mutual. The code further lists the following forms of sexual harassment:

- Physical conduct, ranging from touching to sexual assault and rape, and includes a strip-search by or in the presence of the opposite sex.
- Verbal conduct, which includes unwelcome innuendoes, suggestions and hints, sexual advances, comments with sexual overtones, sex-related jokes or insults or unwelcome graphic comments about a person's body made in his or her presence and directed toward him or her, unwelcome and inappropriate enquiries about a person's sex life and unwelcome whistling directed at a person or group of persons.
- Non-verbal conduct including unwelcome gestures, indecent exposure and the unwelcome display of sexually explicit pictures or objects.
- *Quid pro quo* harassment, which occurs when an owner, employer, supervisor, member of management or co-employee undertakes or attempts to influence the process of employment, promotion, training, discipline, dismissal, salary increment or other benefit of an employee or job applicant in exchange for sexual favours.

12.5.5 Protection of employees during pregnancy and childbirth

This code provides practical guidance on the management and protection of women during both pregnancy and while they are breastfeeding. It describes the type of work, workload and working conditions that a pregnant or breastfeeding woman should be protected from.

12.5.6 Dismissals based on operational requirements

The LRA defines a dismissal based on operational requirements as one based on the economic, technological, structural or similar needs of the employer. A dismissal based on operational requirements is regarded as a 'no-fault' dismissal. In other words it is not the employee who is responsible for the termination of the employment.

Because retrenchment leads to job losses, the LRA places particular obligations on an employer, most of which are directed to ensure that all possible alternatives to dismissal are explored and that the employees who are to be dismissed are treated fairly. The consultation process envisaged in the LRA between the employer and employee representatives is thus particularly important.

The Act provides for the disclosure of information by the employer on matters relevant to the consultation. The employer must disclose, for example

* the reasons for the proposed retrenchments
* the alternatives considered
* the number of employees likely to be affected
* the method for selecting which employees to dismiss
* the timing of the dismissal
* the possibility of future employment

If one or more employees are selected for dismissal from a number of employees the criteria for selection must be agreed upon either with the consulting parties or, if no criteria have been agreed upon, the criteria must be fair and objective. Criteria that infringe any fundamental right protected by the LRA would be regarded as unfair, for example criteria based on union membership or pregnancy.

The selection criterion that is generally considered to be fair includes length of service, skills and qualifications. Generally the last in and first out (LIFO) criteria is regarded as fair but may undermine affirmative action programmes.

Retrenched employees are entitled to one week's severance pay for every year of completed service. The consulting party may reach agreement on a higher amount. If any employee accepts, or unreasonably refuses to accept, an offer of alternative employment then the employee's rights to severance is forfeited. Dismissed employees should be given preference when it comes to new appointments if they have, within a reasonable time, expressed a desire to be rehired.

12.5.7 HIV/Aids and employment

The HIV/Aids epidemic is having a severe effect on the workplace, and is affecting productivity, employee benefits, occupational health and safety, production costs, and workplace morale.

The code's primary objective is to set out guidelines for employers and trade unions to ensure that employees infected with HIV are not unfairly discriminated against in the workplace.

The code must be taken into account when developing and implementing workplace policies or programmes in terms of employment-related legislation. The code makes the following points with respect to employees with HIV /Aids in the workplace:

* There is no general legal duty on an employee to disclose his or her HIV status to his or her employer or to other employees.
* No employer may require an employee or an applicant for employment to undertake a HIV test in order to ascertain that employee's or applicant's HIV status. Employers may however approach the Labour Court to obtain authorisation for HIV testing.
* The risk of HIV transmission in the workplace is minimal. However occupational accidents involving bodily fluids may occur, for example, in the health care profession. Where this happens, an employee may be compen-

sated in terms of the Compensation for Occupational Injuries and Diseases Act, 1993.

- Employees with HIV or Aids may not be unfairly discriminated against in the allocation of employee benefits. Employees who become ill with Aids should be treated like any other employee with a comparable life-threatening illness with regard to employee benefits.
- Employees with HIV or Aids may not be dismissed solely on the basis of their HIV status but, when they become too ill to perform their work, an employer will be obliged to follow the guidelines regarding dismissal for incapacity.

12.6 Aids governance and guidelines for employers

The Department of Health has drawn up guidelines to help employers deal with the growing numbers of workers who are HIV positive or have Aids. The guidelines include a step-by-step guide to drawing up an Aids policy and provide legal and practical advice on dismissals of employees with Aids, testing employees, benefits, managing workers with HIV and Aids, and Aids education.

The guidelines include the following key issues:

- People with HIV and Aids may not be discriminated against simply because they have the virus or the disease.
- Employers must prevent the transmission of HIV during accidents. They are required to create a safe working environment and must therefore ensure that the proper equipment is available and employees have been trained in how to prevent Aids transmission.
- People who become HIV positive through their work may claim compensation on application to the Workmen's Compensation Commissioner.

Further issues of dismissal, confidentiality, testing and so on, are also addressed, but the safety issues are important with regard to the content of this book. The guidelines are available from the Department of Health.

Questions and exercises

1. Describe in your own words how the labour legislation arises from the Constitution.
2. Access and file a disciplinary and grievance procedure from an existing organisation.
3. Draw up a list of responsibilities of an employer as outlined in this chapter.
4. Report on the process for a domestic worker to claim unemployment benefits.
5. Research and draw up an HIV/Aids policy for a hospitality establishment.

13

Hospitality employment law

Objectives of this chapter:

By the end of this chapter you will:
- be able to identify under which labour enactment a hospitality establishment falls
- know the framework of specific labour legislation that applies to the hospitality industry,
- know the content and area of jurisdiction of the sectoral determination
- know the content and area of jurisdiction of the two bargaining councils

13.1 Introduction

Labour legislation as it affects the hospitality industry in South Africa has at long last been simplified, and it is now a lot easier for an establishment owner to identify the specific employment conditions applicable to his or her business. The Department of Labour and the Employment's Condition Commission gazetted the new Hospitality Sectoral Determination No 14 in May 2007 which came into effect on the 1 July 2007.

Sectoral Determination 14: Hospitality Sector, makes provision for minimum conditions of employment and minimum wages for the South African Hospitality sector, and it will apply to every hospitality establishment across the country that falls outside of the two restaurant and catering bargaining councils currently operating in Johannesburg and Pretoria.

It is important to note that section 31 of the determination makes provision for the cancellation, effective 30 June 2007, of the following old wage determinations that governed hospitality employment conditions in the past:

Wage Determination 457 – Hotel Trade

Wage Determination 461 – Catering Trade Certain Areas

Wage Determination 479 – Accommodation Establishment Trade Certain areas.

The following legislation currently applies:
- Sectoral Determination 14: Hospitality Sector South Africa
- Bargaining Council for the Restaurant, Catering and Allied Trades – Gauteng

- Bargaining Council for the Restaurant, Catering and Allied Trades – Pretoria
- Basic Conditions of Employment Act 75 of 1997 as amended

The BCEA will apply only if and when the three labour enactments listed above are silent on a particular employment condition. The contents of the BCEA are covered in chapter 12. The following summary of each enactment is provided in order to assist in identifying the correct labour law and employment conditions applicable to a particular establishment. It is important to note that the information provided below is a guide, and all employers should obtain a copy of the latest or most up to date sectoral determination or bargaining council agreement applicable to their business.

13.2 Broad summary of the contents of Sectoral Determination 14: Hospitality Sector

13.2.1 Scope of application

This section defines the scope of the industry and the specific sectors covered by the agreement, and will assist employers in establishing whether or not the agreement applies to their particular hospitality business.

13.2.2 To whom does this apply

This determination applies to all employers and employees in the hospitality industry in South Africa. This includes any commercial businesses that make a profit from:
- providing accommodation in a hotel, motel, inn, resort, game lodge, hostel, guest house, guest farm or bed and breakfast establishment, including short-stay accommodation, self-catering, timeshares, camps and caravan parks
- providing food to the public, for example, restaurants, pubs, taverns, cafés, tearooms, coffee shops, fast food outlets, snack bars, industrial or commercial caterers, function caterers, contract caterers that prepare, serve or provide prepared food or liquid refreshments, other than drinks in sealed bottles or cans whether indoors or outdoors or in the open air, for consumption on or off the premises

13.2.3 Minimum wage levels

Since July 2007, employers must pay their employees the minimum wage prescribed in the determination. This amount does not include any gratuities that the employees may get, but may include commission payments. Therefore, any employee who works 45 ordinary hours of work per week must be paid:
- the minimum weekly or monthly wage specified in table 1 or 2 of the determination (which will be updated from time to time)
- at least the hourly rate set out in tables 1 or 2 of the determination for every hour or part of an hour that the employee works, but only if the employer and employee agree to this in writing

Two minimum wage schedules have been provided covering establishments with ten or less, and more than ten employees. The minimum wages came into effect on the 1st July 2007 and will run for a period of three years ending 30 June 2010. The minimum wage will increase annually by CPIX + 2% for each year covered by the agreement.

The minimum wages for period 2007 to 2010 are:

Figure 13-1: Minimum wages for employers with 10 or less employees

Minimum rate for the period			Minimum rate for the period			Minimum rate for the period		
1 July 2007 to 30 June 2008			1 July 2008 to 30 June 2009			1 July 2009 to 30 June 2010		
R.p.m	R.p.w	R.p.h	R.p.m	R.p.w	R.p.h	R.p.m	R.p.w	R.p.h
R1480–00	R341–60	R7–59	Previous Minimum Wage + CPIX + 2%			Previous Minimum Wage + CPIX + 2%		

Figure 13-2: Minimum wages for employers with more than 10 employees

Minimum rate for the period			Minimum rate for the period			Minimum rate for the period		
1 July 2007 to 30 June 2008			1 July2008 to 30 June 2009			1 July 2009 to 30 June 2010		
R.p.m	R.p.w	R.p.h	R.p.m	R.p.w	R.p.h	R.p.m	R.p.w	R.p.h
R1650–00	R380–80	R8–46	Previous Minimum Wage + CPIX + 2%			Previous Minimum Wage + CPIX + 2%		

13.2.4 Commission work
The determination permits the employers to make payment of commission, for example a percentage of their sales, to employees for as long as there is an agreement in writing, and the commission paid to employees is not less than the prescribed minimum wage levels.

13.2.5 Payment of wages
Employers are required to pay their employees by cheque or cash. This must be done during working hours, and the remuneration must be accompanied by a pay slip which provides information such as the employer's name and address, the employee's name and occupation, the employee's wage and overtime rate, the hours and overtime worked and the amount paid to the employee. The determination also outlines permissible deductions.

13.2.6 Employment particulars
It is important to note that an employer must supply an employee, when he or she commences work, with a letter of employment containing, amongst other matters, the full name and address of the employer, the name and job title of the employee, a brief description of the employee's work responsibilities, the date on which the employment began, the wage and overtime rate, and hours the employee is expected to work.

13.2.7 Hours of work and overtime
The determination makes provision for the ordinary hours of work of an employee, which is 45 hours a week. This translates into nine hours a day if the employee works for five days or less in a week and eight hours in any day if the employee works for more than five days in a week.

Overtime can only be worked by agreement with the employee, may not exceed 10 hours in a week, and the employee may not work more than 12 hours in a day. Overtime must be paid at one and a half times the normal wage. Alternatively, an employer must pay not less than the employee's ordinary wage for overtime worked and provide the employee with at least 30 minutes' time off on full pay for every hour of overtime

13.2.8 Compressed working week
An agreement may allow an employee to work up to 12 hours in a day, inclusive of the meal intervals, without receiving overtime pay for as long as she or he does not work longer than 45 hours in any week, does not work more than ten hours' overtime in any week and does not work on more than five days in any week.

13.2.9 Averaging of hours of work
By written agreement, the ordinary hours of work and overtime of an employee may be averaged over a period of up to four months for as long as the employee works an average of 45 ordinary hours a week and no more than an average of 5 hours overtime a week.

13.2.10 Sunday work
If an employee ordinarily works on a Sunday he or she is entitled to one and a half times the normal hourly rate. If the employee does not usually work on a Sunday he or she must receive double his or her normal hourly rate. An agreement between the employer and employee may permit paid time off equivalent to the difference in value between the pay received by the employee for working on the Sunday and the pay that the employee is normally entitled to. This time off must take place within one month from the date on which the overtime was worked.

13.2.11 Night work
Night work is defined as work carried out between the hours of 18h00 and 06h00 the next day. An employer may allow an employee to work nights for as long as there is an agreement and that the employee is compensated by an allowance decided upon between the employer and employee. Transportation must also be available between the employee's place of residence and the workplace and, if the cost is more than the usual daily cost of that particular transport, the employee should be reimbursed with the difference.

13.2.12 Meal intervals
If employees work continuously for more than 5 hours a day they are entitled to a meal interval of at least one continuous hour. The meal hour can be reduced to 30 minutes by written agreement between the employer and employee. The employer is not obliged to provide a meal.

13.2.13 Daily and weekly rest periods
An employer is required to give an employee a daily rest period of at least 12 consecutive hours between ending work and starting work the following day. For as long as there is an agreement in writing, the daily rest period can be

reduced to 10 hours for an employee who lives on the business premises, and whose meal interval lasts for at least three hours.

The weekly rest period is a minimum of 36 consecutive hours which must include a Sunday unless the employer and employee agree that it should be a different day.

13.2.14 Public holidays

Working on a public holiday must be by agreement between the employer and employee. If a public holiday falls on a day on which an employee normally works, an employer must pay the employee who does not work at least the wage that the employee would normally have received for work on that day.

If the employee does work on the public holiday then the employer must pay at least double the employee's daily wage.

If an employee works on a public holiday, on which the employee would not normally work, the employer must pay the employee an amount equal to the employee's daily wage plus the employee's hourly wage for each hour worked on that public holiday.

13.2.15 Annual leave

An employee is entitled to at least three weeks' leave on full pay for every twelve months of employment or, by agreement, at least one day's annual leave on full pay for every 17 days worked. Should a public holiday occur during the leave period, the employee will be entitled to an additional day's leave.

13.2.16 Sick leave

Sick leave is in line with the Basic Conditions of Employment Act. During every sick leave cycle of 36 months, the employee is entitled to an amount of paid sick leave equal to the number of days he or she would work during a six week period.

13.2.17 Family and maternity leave

At an employee's request an employer must grant at least three days' paid family leave when an employee's child is born, when a child is sick, or in the event of the death of an immediate family member.

An employee is entitled to at least four consecutive months' maternity leave at any time from four weeks before the expected date of birth, unless otherwise agreed, and she may not work for six weeks after the birth of her child, unless agreed to by a medical practitioner.

13.2.18 Other matters

The determination covers a number of other matters, provides a number of definitions and, in line with the Basic Conditions of Employment Act, makes reference to matters concerning the termination of employment, severance pay, temporary employment services and certificates of employment.

13.3 Hospitality bargaining councils

In terms of section 27 of the Labour Relations Act, one or more registered trade unions and one of more registered employer organisations may establish a bargaining council for a specified sector and area by adopting a constitution that meets the requirements of section 30 and by obtaining registration of the council in terms of section 29 of the Labour Relations Act.

There are currently two bargaining councils operating in the hospitality sector:

- Bargaining Council for the Restaurant, Catering and Allied Trades – Johannesburg area
- Bargaining Council for the Tea-room, Restaurant and Catering and Allied Trades – Pretoria area

Certain registered employer organisations representing the employers, and certain registered trade unions representing the employees meet either annually or every two years to negotiate, update and conclude a collective agreement that provides for conditions of employment and minimum wages in the sector, and in the geographical location covered by the scope of their agreement.

All employers are required by law to ensure that they have a copy of the agreement on the business premises, and that they allow employees access to the agreement should they be requested to do so.

Employers and or employees wishing to obtain copies of any one of the bargaining council agreements may contact the council offices directly.

13.3.1 Broad summary of the contents of a bargaining council agreement

Although specific details may differ, in the main, both of the agreements make provision for the following.

Scope of application: This section will define the industry, the specific sector and the magisterial or municipal areas covered by the agreement, and will assist catering and restaurant business owners in establishing whether or not the agreement applies to their particular business.

Period of the agreement: Each agreement, once published, will remain in force for a specified period until either cancelled by the Minister of Labour, or until renegotiated by the employer and employee representatives on the council. They usually run for a period of two years.

Special and general provisions: There are not necessarily included in every council agreement but, if and when provided, usually covers matters such as an extension of the agreement to non parties, or exclusions applicable to certain parties from specified parts of the agreement.

Definitions: A key requirement of all agreements in order to avoid varied interpretations, and to ensure a complete understanding and the correct application of the terms and provisions used in the agreement.

Remuneration/wages: A minimum wage schedule for each job category, usually covering a period of two to three years.

Payment of remuneration: This covers the manner in which payment should be made, and will include matters concerning casual, fixed term, function, part time and contract employees.

Ordinary hours of work, overtime and payment for overtime: This section will cover working days, ordinary hours of work, spread-over, meal intervals, overtime, a limitation to overtime and the payment of overtime and exclusions, if any, from one or more provisions of this section.

Paid holidays: This section covers the payment for employees who work or are given time off on a public holiday and how and when the remuneration should be made.

Uniforms and protective clothing: This section covers the specific supply, cleaning, replacement and costs concerning employee uniforms.

Prohibition of employment: This deals with child employment, aliens and the period before and after confinement for female employees granted maternity leave under the agreement.

Contracts of employment: Provide specific details that are required to be included in an employee's letter of employment and, in some cases, cover temporary and or probation period conditions.

Notice of termination of employment: This gives very specific and detailed requirements concerning the period, the payment, the conditions and the process of giving notice by either employer to employee or *vice versa*.

Maternity leave: As a requirement of the Basic Conditions of Employment Act, all council agreements will include a comprehensive provision covering the granting, notice period and the payment of maternity leave.

Annual leave: Provides annual leave requirements for the various categories of employees including the manner in which annual leave is requested, granted and remunerated, and covers the annual closing of businesses.

Sick leave: This covers aspects such as notification, medical certificates, aggregated entitlements and the payment of sick leave.

Meals and transport: Makes provision for the requirement, time period and permissible deductions for employee meals and transportation, and covers transportation requirements during certain periods for certain categories of employees.

Certificate of service: This requires that employers furnish departing employees with certificates of service under specified conditions.

Time/wage and attendance registers: These cover the register requirements and the recording of both the attendance and time worked by all categories of employees.

In addition to the above a number, but not all, of the council agreements include provisions covering designated agents, membership, rights and obligations of both the employer and employee representatives, dispute resolution functions of the council, conciliation functions, exemptions, codes of good practice, freedom of association, expenses of the council and copies of the required document types.

13.3.2 The scope and application of a bargaining council agreement

The following section will provide specific information covering the scope and geographical demarcations of each of the two bargaining councils applicable to the catering and restaurant trade in order to assist in identifying the correct labour conditions appropriate to a particular establishment.

13.4 Bargaining Council for the Restaurant, Catering and Allied trades

The scope of application of the agreement covers all employees who are members of the employer's organisation and all employees who are members of the trade unions in the magisterial districts of Alberton, Benoni, Boksburg, Brakpan, Delmas, Germiston, Johannesburg, Kempton Park, Krugersdorp, Randburg, Randfontein, Roodepoort, Springs and Westonaria.

Certain clauses of the agreement do not apply to employers and employees who are not members of the employer's organisation and trade unions respectively.

Parties to the agreement are:

The Restaurant and Food Services Association of South Africa representing the employers

and the

Catering Employees Union
Hotel & Allied Restaurant Workers Union of South Africa
Distributive, Catering, Hotels and Allied Workers of South Africa
South Africa Commercial, Catering and Allied Workers Union
all representing the employees.

13.5 Bargaining council for the Tea-room, Restaurant and Catering trades

The scope of application of the agreement covers all employers and employees who are members of the employers' organisation and the trade union respectively, in the magisterial districts of Pretoria, Brits, Bronkhorstspruit, Cullinan, Rustenburg, Warmbaths, Witbank and Wonderboom and in the municipal area of Midrand.

Certain clauses of the agreement do not apply to employers and employees who are not members of the employers' organisation and trade unions respectively.

Parties to the agreement are:

The Pretoria and District Caterers Association
representing the employers,

and the

General Industries Workers Union of South Africa.
South Africa Commercial, Catering and Allied Workers Union
Club, Caterers, Retail and Allied Workers Union

all representing the employees.

13.6 The Basic Conditions of Employment Act, as amended

The Basic Conditions of Employment Act (BCEA) 75 of 1997 as discussed in detail in the previous chapter, applies to all workers and employers except those who are party to a bargaining council agreement or a specific sectoral determination, members of the National Defence Force, National Intelligence Agency, and the South African Secret Service and unpaid volunteers working for charities.

It is important to note that where a bargaining council agreement and or a sectoral determination is silent or does not provide for a specific employment condition, the Basic Conditions of Employment Act would apply.

The Basic Conditions of Employment Act replaced the old 'Shops and Offices Act,' and was designed to make provision for minimum conditions of employment in those industries and sectors not governed by in-house collective agreements, sectoral determinations or bargaining councils. Unlike the bargaining council agreements and the wage determinations, the Basic Conditions of Employment Act does not make provision for minimum wages.

Questions and exercises

1. Identify the correct labour enactment applicable to the following establishments:
   (i) The Oasis hotel in Pretoria
   (ii) Jackies Restaurant in the centre of Cape Town
   (iii) The Grand Central hotel in Knysna
   (iv) The Travia Restaurant in Randburg.
2. Under what conditions may a group of employers and a group of employees form a Bargaining Council?
3. What is the minimum wage for a hospitality establishment that falls outside the two bargaining councils and that has more than ten employees?

14

Occupational health and safety legislation

Objectives of this chapter:

By the end of this chapter the learner will be able to:

◆ Contribute to upholding health and safety legislation
◆ Display an awareness of the consequences of unsafe practices in the workplace
◆ Describe which legislation governs occupational health and safety
◆ Access relevant SABS Codes of Practice when needed
◆ Access any relevant health and safety legislation when needed
◆ Report accidents and process claims for workplace injuries or diseases

The learner will know:

◆ The duties of health and safety representatives and committees
◆ The duties of employers and employees as stipulated by the OHS Act
◆ Penalties that may be incurred by any person who contravenes or fails to comply with the provisions of the OHS Act
◆ How the MOS Act and OHS Act have integrated
◆ The safety systems that are available in South Africa to assist with a health and safety maintenance programme
◆ Penalties for failing to observe occupational health and safety practices

14.1 Introduction

Every year, thousands of hours and days are lost due to accidents that occur in the workplace. This leads to a loss of productivity for the country as a whole, as a portion of the workforce is not able to work. Sometimes, in the case of serious injury, disablement or death can occur, which is a very high price to pay for not ensuring that safe work practices are always enforced.

The subject matters of occupational health and safety, and employees' compensation are closely linked. Occupational health and safety legislation aims at making the workplace as safe and healthy as possible for employees. If the provisions of such legislation are successfully implemented and adhered to, the risk of accidents in the workplace is decreased, and the demand on the compensation fund is reduced.

Workplace accidents can happen very easily in the hospitality industry, where many dangers abound in the workplace. Heat, steam, oils, electricity, gas, chemicals, machinery and dangerous implements are all found in our environment. Maintenance of safety practices and policies is therefore especially important in this environment of high risk.

14.2 Sources of occupational health and safety legislation

The Department of Labour has developed legislation that serves to protect employers and employees from accident and injury in the workplace. The Occupational Health and Safety Act 85 of 1993 (OHS) determines the responsibilities of the employer and the employee in the workplace, and primarily makes provision for the establishment and operation of safety committees and representatives.

In terms of this Act, any regulations made in terms of the original Machinery and Occupational Safety Act 6 of 1983 (MOS) will still be in force and in effect. The OHS Act and the regulations made in terms of the MOS Act therefore interface and cover different content and aspects of safety.

A range of laws, regulations and codes of practice govern workplace health and safety. The following diagram depicts the occupational health and safety regulatory framework:

Figure 14-1: Occupational health and safety regulatory framework

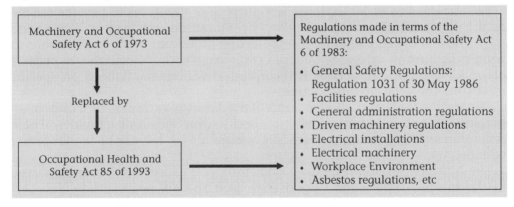

As can be seen above, the OHS Act replaced the MOS Act in 1993, but the regulations made under the MOS Act are still in effect, and are now governed by the OHS Act.

14.3 NOSA

The National Occupational Safety Association is an organisation that assists organisations to identify and control safety issues in the workplace. It has a safety system that gives a structure for applying the relevant safety laws needed in each organisation. Any branch of NOSA may be contacted for further information regarding safety systems and training.

14.4 ISO 9000

The SABS also governs quality management systems in the ISO 9000 series. The International Standards Organisation (ISO) has a range of systems for the quality assurance of various sectors of industry, and includes development of (safe) operational procedures. Although it is a voluntary system, the ISO series is becoming internationally recognised as a symbol of management (and safety) excellence. ISO 9000 information is available from any branch of SABS.

14.5 The Occupational Health and Safety Act

The OHS Act requires the employer to bring about and maintain, as far as is reasonably practicable, a work environment that is safe and without risk to the health of the workers.

However, it is not expected of the employer to take sole responsibility for health and safety. The Act is based on the principle that dangers in the workplace must be addressed by communication and cooperation between the workers and the employer. The workers and the employer must share the responsibility for health and safety in the workplace. Both parties must pro-actively identify dangers and develop control measures to make the workplace safe. Health and safety representatives may inspect the workplace regularly, and then report to a health and safety committee that, in turn, may submit recommendations to the employer.

To ensure that this system works, every worker must know his or her rights and duties as contained in the Act.

The Act consists of 50 sections. The purpose of the Act is to provide for the health and safety of persons at work, or in connection with the use of plant and machinery. It also provides for the protection of persons other than persons at work from hazards arising out of or in connection with the activities of persons at work. The Minister of Labour incorporates various regulations on specific topics into the Act from time to time.

The Minister of Labour may in terms of the Act issue various health and safety regulations and standards covering specific processes and activities. These regulations, as well as the General Safety Regulations, have to be read together with the Act.

The Act applies to all workplaces and employees except employees employed in the mining sector, who are covered by a specific health and safety Act designed for the mining environment, and certain aspects of workplaces and employees in aviation, which are covered by the Aviation Act.

14.5.1 Occupational Health and Safety Council

The Act makes provision for the establishment of the Occupational Health and Safety Council, consisting of 20 members representing a large range of stakeholders, including government. The duties of the council include the establishment of policy to protect employees from sustaining injury, illness or disease resulting from their work.

Its structure is designed to ensure that any hazards or potential hazards are investigated timeously, and necessary steps are taken to ensure that they are addressed in the best possible way.

Guidelines, policies, standards and regulatory changes and/or additions will be established and reviewed on an ongoing basis by the council. Notice will be given to employees and employers of changes and action(s) required to minimise the chance of accidents, and incidents by adequately addressing unsafe or hazardous conditions.

14.5.2 Health and safety policy

The Minister, acting on information that has been approved by the council, or submitted by a technical committee, may inform any employer of his or her decision that it is necessary for him or her to draw up and display a policy that is relevant to the potential hazards in their business.

The Chief Inspector of Health and Safety of the Department of Labour can call for a written policy on health and safety from the company or organisation. This policy must state the nature of activities, and the approach to the health and safety of the staff members.

This policy (which must be signed by the chief executive officer) must display appropriate guidelines, and any necessary steps, to inform its employees of action and procedures required by both parties to minimise health and safety risks in the workplace.

14.5.3 Enforcement and inspections

The OHS Act is predominantly a policing Act that aims at enforcement and regulation of workplaces in respect of safety and health issues. The Department of Labour and its officials are closely involved in the monitoring and implementation of the Act in the workplace.

The Chief Directorate of Occupational Health and Safety of the Department of Labour is the authority charged with the administration of the OHS Act. Provincial offices have been established in all the provinces to ensure the health and safety of employees nationally. To this end, occupational health and safety inspectors from these provincial offices have been appointed to carry out inspections and investigations at workplaces to ensure that the provisions of the Act are implemented and complied with.

There are two kinds of inspections: planned and unplanned inspections. Inspections are usually planned on the basis of accident statistics, the presence of hazardous substances, such as the use of benzene in laundries, or the use of dangerous machinery in the workplace. Unplanned inspections, on the other hand, usually arise from requests or complaints by workers, employers, or members of the public. These complaints or requests are treated confidentially.

14.5.3.1 Powers of inspectors

In order to fulfil their duties, inspectors have fairly far-reaching and broad powers. Inspectors may:

◆ enter a workplace or premises where machinery or hazardous substances are being used, at any reasonable time, and without notice
◆ request or serve a summons on persons to appear before them
◆ request that any documents be submitted to them
◆ investigate and make copies of such documents
◆ demand an explanation about any entries recorded in such documents

- inspect the working conditions, and any work performed on the premises
- inspect, or remove samples of, any substance or articles
- seize any article that may be used as evidence
- barricade, fence or restrict access to any area where danger exists
- investigate any serious incidents and report, if necessary, the outcome to the director of public prosecutions

These powers, although far-reaching, are not absolute, and anyone not satisfied with a decision made by an inspector may appeal this decision to the Chief Inspector: Occupational Safety.

If an inspector finds dangerous or adverse conditions at the workplace, he or she may set requirements to the employer.

14.5.3.1.1 Prohibition notice

In the case of threatening danger, an inspector may prohibit a particular action, process, or the use of a machine or equipment by means of a prohibition notice. No person may disregard the contents of such a notice, and compliance must take place with immediate effect.

14.5.3.1.2 Contravention notice

If a provision of a regulation is contravened, the inspector may serve a contravention notice on the workers or the employer. A contravention of the Act can result in immediate prosecution, but in the case of a contravention of a regulation, the employer may be given the opportunity to correct the contravention within a specified time limit, which is usually 60 days.

14.5.3.1.3 Improvement notice

Where the health and safety measures, which the employer has instituted, do not satisfactorily protect the health and safety of the workers, the inspector may require the employer to bring about more effective measures. An improvement notice, which prescribes the corrective measures, is then served on the employer.

14.5.3.2 Process of investigations

The processes of investigations, formal enquiries and appeals regarding incidents resulting in injury, illness or death of an employee are laid out. Employers and workers must comply with the directions, subpoenas, requests or orders of inspectors. In addition, no one may prevent anyone else from complying.

The inspector's questions should be answered, but no one is obliged to answer a question that may result in incriminating himself or herself. To incriminate oneself means that one is suggesting that one is responsible for a contravention.

When the inspector so requires, he or she must be provided with the necessary means and be given the assistance he or she may need to hold an investigation. The inspector may also request that investigations be attended. No one may insult the inspector, or deliberately interrupt the investigation.

14.5.4 Duties of employers towards workers

Section 8 of the OHS Act contains the general duties of employers to their employees, and outlines their safety obligations and responsibilities. An employer has obligations under law to provide a safe place for employees to work. The Act places the main responsibility to bring about and maintain a safe and healthy work environment on the employer. To this end the employer must ensure that the workplace is free from hazardous substances, articles, equipment and processes that may cause injury, damage or disease. Where this is not possible, the employer must inform workers of these dangers, how they may be prevented, and how to work safely, and provide other protective measure for a safe workplace.

Responsibility for the implementation of the Act is on the chief executive officer or most senior person in charge of the company.

14.5.4.1 Duties aimed at ensuring a safe and healthy workplace

To ensure that the workplace is safe and without risk to the health of the employees, the employer must provide and maintain all the equipment that is necessary to do the work, and all the systems according to which work must be done, in a condition that will not affect the health and safety of workers. Before personal protective equipment may be used, the employer must first try to remove or reduce any danger to the health and safety of his workers. Personal protective equipment should only be used when it is not practicable to remove or reduce any danger to the health and safety of employees.

The employer must take measures to protect his or her workers' health and safety against hazards that may result from the production, processing, use, handling, storage or transportation of articles or substances, in other words, anything that workers may come into contact with at work. Examples in the hospitality industry are numerous, especially in kitchens where heat, steam, cutting equipment, strong chemicals, and so on, are to be found. The employer must train employees in safe practices in this environment, and supply protective clothing (for example a chefs' uniform and gloves) for protection against hazards.

To ensure that these duties are complied with, the employer must:

- identify potential hazards that may be present while work is being done something is being produced, processed, used, stored or transported, and any equipment is being used
- establish the precautionary measures that are necessary to protect his or her workers against the identified hazards, and provide the means to implement these precautionary measures
- provide the necessary information, instructions, training and supervision while keeping the extent of workers' competence in mind. In other words, what they may do and may not do
- not permit anyone to carry on with any task unless the necessary precautionary measures have been taken
- take steps to ensure that every person under his or her control complies with the requirements of the Act
- enforce the necessary control measures in the interest of health and safety
- see to it that the work being done and the equipment used, is under the

general supervision of a worker who has been trained to understand the hazards associated with the work

* such a worker must ensure that the precautionary measures are implemented and maintained

The employer also has to ensure a safe work environment for contractors or visitors to the site, and their responsibility, in turn, is their responsible and safe conduct while on site.

Employers also have duties regarding listed work, namely any work and situations that have been listed as seriously hazardous, and that require special compliance. Duties include training, risk evaluation, identification of hazards, and so forth.

14.5.4.2 Duty to inform

The employer's duties extend to informing every employee about the health and safety hazards of any work being done. Every employee has a right and therefore must be informed of, and fully understand, all aspects relating to any possible risk, including exposure to any substance, plant, machinery or other hazards with which they may come into contact during work activities.

To this end the employer must:

* inform employees of their rights under the Act
* provide information about precautionary measures against any identified hazards
* appoint health and safety representatives and ensure that they receive the necessary training and perform their duties
* establish a health and safety committee where there is more than one safety representative, and ensure that this committee performs its duties
* inform health and safety representatives of the occurrence of an incident in the workplace.

Employees must fully understand all necessary precautionary measures required, and how to implement them. This is the right-to-know principle. This does not absolve the employers from responsibility under the Act.

14.5.4.3 Reporting duties

The employer also has the responsibility of informing the inspectors of any incidents. In this regard the employer must report to the local health and safety inspector any incident arising from a work activity.

The Act defines an incident as an event that occurs at the workplace where a person is killed, injured, or becomes ill. Injuries and illnesses requiring reporting in this regard include instances where the employee becomes unconscious, loses a limb or part of a limb, becomes so ill that he or she may die, or that he or she is unable to do his or her usual work for more than 14 days. Included in the definition of an incident is also the spillage of hazardous chemical substances, for example where a tank leaks chemical product due to a faulty valve, or where machinery runs out of control, even if these incidents do not result in injury or death.

An example could include a cook or kitchen attendant losing a finger on a slicing machine, or someone slipping while carrying a pot of hot soup, and sustaining serious burns that require hospitalisation.

14.5.5 Employees' rights and duties

Although the Act places primary responsibility for health and safety in the workplace on the employer, the employer is not expected to take sole responsibility. The Act is based on the principle that dangers in the workplace must be addressed by communication and co-operation between the employer and employees. To this end, employees also have certain duties.

14.5.5.1 Duties of the employee

While the employer must provide a safe work environment, and train employees and provide them with safety gear, the employee also has duties to ensure that they work in accordance with safe practices. It is the duty of the worker to

- know his or her rights and duties as contained in the Act
- take care of his or her own health and safety, as well as that of other persons who may be affected by his or her actions or negligence to Act. This includes playing at work. Many people have been injured and even killed owing to horseplay in the workplace, which is considered a serious contravention
- co-operate with the employer
- give information to an inspector from the Department of Labour if he or she should require it
- carry out any lawful instruction which the employer or authorised person prescribes with regard to health and safety
- comply with the rules and procedures that the employer gives him or her
- wear the prescribed safety clothing or use the prescribed safety equipment where it is required
- report unsafe or unhealthy conditions to the employer or health and safety representative as soon as possible
- report an accident that he or she is involved in that may influence his or her health or cause injury, to the employer, an authorised person, or the health and safety representative as soon as possible, but no later than by the end of the shift

Employees must:
- not act in such a way as to place themselves or others at risk
- inform the employer of a hazard
- report any incident within the same shift
- carry out instruction in accordance with the Act
- co-operate with the employer in complying with the Act

An employee has a duty not to interfere with, or misuse, any object that has been provided in the interest of health and safety. A person may, for example, not remove a safety guard from a machine and use the machine or allow anybody else to use it without such a guard.

14.5.5.2 Rights of the employee
The Occupational Health and Safety Act has extended workers' rights to include the following:

14.5.5.2.1 The right to information
The worker must have access to:
- the OHS Act and regulations
- health and safety rules and procedures of the workplace
- health and safety standards, which the employer must keep at the workplace

The worker may request the employer to inform him or her about:
- health and safety hazards in the workplace
- the precautionary measures which must be taken
- the procedures that must be followed if a worker is exposed to substances hazardous to health

14.5.5.2.2 The right to participate in inspections
If the worker is a health and safety representative, he or she may accompany a health and safety inspector from the Department of Labour during an inspection of the workplace and answer any questions the inspector may ask.

14.5.5.2.3 The right to comment on legislation and make representations
The worker may comment or make representations on any regulation or safety standard published under the Occupational Health and Safety Act.

14.5.5.2.4 The right not to be victimised
An employer may not dismiss a worker from his service, reduce a worker's salary or reduce a worker's service conditions as a result of the following:
- giving information to an authorised person in terms of the Act
- complying with a lawful instruction issued by an inspector
- giving evidence in court of law or the industrial court
- doing anything that he or she may do or be required to do in terms of the Act
- refusing to do anything that he or she is prohibited from doing in terms of the Act
- giving evidence before the Industrial Court or a court of law on matters regarding health and safety

14.5.5.2.5 The right to appeal
The worker may appeal against the decision of an inspector. Appeals must be referred in writing to the Chief Inspector, Occupational Health and Safety, Department of Labour, Pretoria.

14.6 Health and safety representatives
The OHS Act provides for the appointment of health and safety representatives and health and safety committees in the workplace. Every employer who has more than 20 employees in his employment at any workplace shall designate in writing health and safety representatives for that workplace.

Health and safety representatives are full-time workers nominated or elected and designated in writing by the employer after the employer and workers have consulted one another and reached an agreement about who will be health and safety representatives. Further they must at least be familiar with the circumstances and conditions at that part of the workplace for which they are designated. Agreement must also be reached on the period of office and functions of the health and safety representative and must be settled amongst the employer and the workers.

A representative must be designated for every workplace consisting of 20 or more workers. Therefore, where only 19 workers are employed, it is not necessary to designate a representative.

In the case of shops and offices, one representative must be designated for every 100 workers or part thereof. For example, one representative must be designated in the case of 21 to 100 workers. But two representatives must be designated where 101 to 200 workers are employed, and so forth.

In the case of other workplaces, one representative must be designated for every 50 workers or part thereof. For example, one representative must be designated in the case of 21 to 50 workers. But two representatives must be designated where 51 to 100 workers are employed.

14.6.1 Functions and duties of health and safety representatives

All activities regarding the designation, function and training of representatives must be performed during normal working hours. Health and safety representatives are entitled to do the following:

14.6.1.1 Health and safety audits

Representatives may check the effectiveness of health and safety measures by means of health and safety audits.

14.6.1.2 Identify potential dangers

Representatives may identify potential dangers in the workplace and report them to the health and safety committee or the employer.

14.6.1.3 Investigate incidents

Collaborate with the employer to investigate incidents, and also investigate complaints from workers regarding health and safety matters, and report about them in writing.

14.6.1.4 Make representations

Representatives may make representations regarding the safety of the workplace to the employer or the health and safety committee or, where the representations are unsuccessful, to an inspector.

14.6.1.5 Inspections

As far as inspections are concerned, representatives may
- inspect the workplace after notifying the employer of the inspection
- participate in discussions with inspectors at the workplace and accompany inspectors on inspections

- inspect documents
- with the consent of his or her employer, be accompanied by a technical advisor during an inspection

14.6.1.6 Attend committee meetings

Representatives may attend health and safety committee meetings.

14.7 Health and safety committees

The OHS Acts also makes provision for the establishment and duties of health and safety committees. These committees consist of the health and safety representatives, and any other employees as deemed necessary for the effective execution of its duties. Such other members may include the CEO (who has ultimate safety responsibility), or maintenance staff who will assist in attending to safety hazards. Each member must be appointed in writing for the designated time period that they will be members of that committee.

Health and safety committees are formed to initiate, promote, maintain and review measures of ensuring the health and safety of workers.

Health and safety committees must be established when there are two or more health and safety representatives designated in a workplace. The employer determines the number of committee members, based on the following:

- If only one committee has been established for a workplace, all the representatives must be members of that committee.
- If two or more committees have been established for a workplace, each representative must be a member of at least one of those committees.

Therefore, every representative must be a member of a committee. The employer may also nominate other persons to represent him or her on a committee, but such nominees may not be more than the number of representatives designated on that committee.

If, however, an inspector is of the opinion that the number of committees in a workplace is inadequate, he or she may determine the establishment of additional committees.

Committees are entitled to meet whenever it is necessary, but at least once every three months. The committee determines the time and place. The procedures adopted at a meeting are determined by the members of the committee who elect the chairperson and determine his or her period of office, meeting procedures, and so on.

Committees may co-opt persons as advisory members for their knowledge and expertise on health and safety matters. However, an advisory member does not have the right to vote.

14.7.1 Functions of health and safety committees

The committees only deal with health and safety matters at the workplace or sections thereof for which such committees have been established. Generally, health and safety committees have the following functions:

Making recommendations to the employer or to an inspector regarding any matter affecting the health or safety at the workplace for which that committee has been established.

- Discuss any incident at the workplace in which or in consequence of which any person was injured, became ill or died, and may in writing report on the incident to an inspector.
- Perform any other functions as may be prescribed.
- Keep records of any recommendations made to the employer, or report made to an inspector.
- Committee members must perform any other functions required of them by regulation.

14.8 Enforcement, prosecution and penalties

14.8.1 Prosecution

When a worker does something that, in terms of the Occupational Health and Safety Act, is regarded as an offence, the employer is responsible for that offence, and he or she could be found guilty and sentenced for it, unless the employer can prove that

- he or she did not give his or her consent
- he or she took all reasonable steps to prevent it
- the worker did not act within the scope of his or her competence, in other words, that the worker did something which he or she knew he or she should not have done

The same rule applies to an employer such as a sub-contractor unless there is an agreement in writing between employer and sub-contractor abut how the sub-contract will comply with the provisions of the Act. However, appointment of another person to ensure compliance with the Act does not absolve the employer of responsibility. The employer still has to monitor the situation in the workplace on a regular basis.

14.8.2 Penalties

If employers fail to ensure compliance in terms of the Act, or give false information, they may be fined R50 000 and/or imprisoned for one year. In cases where the employer's negligence leads to the death or injury of any person, the fine shall be as high as R100 000 and/or two years in prison.

If a medical practitioner examines or treats someone for a disease that he or she suspects arose from that worker's employment, the medical practitioner must report the case to the worker's employer and to the chief inspector. Failure to do so will result in a R50 000 fine and/or imprisonment.

14.8.3 Deductions

An employer may not make any deduction from a worker's remuneration with regard to anything he or she is required to do in the interest of health and safety in terms of the Act.

14.9 Workmen's compensation: the COID Act

The Workmen's Compensation Act was replaced by the Compensation for Occupational Injuries and Diseases Act 130 of 1993 (COID). The objective of the Act is to provide compensation for disablement caused by injuries and diseases sustained in the workplace, and as a result of the work and/or working conditions under which the person is placed. The COID applies to accidents arising out of and in the course of an employees' employment.

All employees, regardless of their earnings, are covered under this Act. The Act provides for loss of earnings and not for pain and suffering incurred. All full time and casual employees are covered by the Act, with the exceptions of:
* defence force members
* police
* domestic workers

14.9.1 Registration for the payment of compensation

Any employer who employs one or more employees at their business, is required to register with the Compensation Commissioner in Pretoria in terms of the COID.

Records must be kept of all employees' wages paid and time worked, and a statement setting out the wages paid to employees must be submitted to the commissioner before the end of March each year. Based on the information supplied to the commissioner, an amount is determined, which is to be paid to the compensation fund within 30 days of a date specified by the commissioner. These amounts cannot be recovered from the employees.

In terms of Government Notice No 84 dated 2 February 2007 the maximum amount of earnings on which the assessment of an employer is calculated is R201,984 per annum which came into effect from the 1 April 2007. Employers are advised to check the threshold level with the commissioner's office from time to time.

14.9.2 Reporting of accidents and occupational diseases

The General Safety Regulations, and section 24 of the OHS Act stipulate that injuries and accidents must be reported. The injuries and accidents to be reported are those of a serious nature in which professional medical attention is needed, and from which absence from work will occur. These injuries lead to workman's compensation in terms of the COID.

Employees must notify the manager of an accident on the same day. The accident report form must immediately be filled in and a copy sent with the person to the doctor.

Figure 14-2: Example of an accident report form

ACCIDENT REPORT FORM			
Details of person injured:			
Surname	First names	Age	Date of birth
Department:		Position:	
Date of accident:	Time:	Was the accident recorded in the accident book?	
How did the accident occur?			
Nature of injuries:			
Was first aid given?		By whom:	
Was the injured person sent to a doctor, medical centre or hospital? (Give details) If so, accompanied by whom?			
Name(s) of witness(es) of the accident:			
Any previous accident that may have been due to the same cause:			
Was the accident caused or contributed to by any defect in working conditions or premises, or the conditions of the equipment or utensils used?			
Signature of person reporting the accident:			
Date:			

Once the accident report form has been filled in, medical reports and claims forms should be completed by the responsible person. All incidents and injuries requiring formal attention, or on site first aid should be recorded in an accident book, usually kept by the supervisor or manager. This is to ensure that any recurring problems are dealt with, and prevented from happening again, and that first aid boxes are kept stocked. They also serve as a record of incidents should formal inquiries be held.

The report of the accident is followed by the following documents:
◆ first medical report

- progress/final medical report
- resumption (this must be completed and submitted before payment will be made)

The Compensation Commissioner must be contacted within seven days of the accident. This can be done by phoning your local office of the Department of Labour.

A claim for compensation in terms of this Act must be lodged within 12 months of the date of the accident. Employers are advised to make inquiries at the offices of the Compensation Commissioner regarding the procedures to follow when reporting an occupational injury. Workman's compensation claims may be made on forms WCL 1 and 2, which may be obtained from any Department of Labour that will provide instruction on all further procedures and documentation in the event of a compensation claim.

Delaying to report an accident, or alleged accident, is a criminal offence. The commissioner may also impose a penalty on the employer, which could be the full amount of the claim. The employer is liable for the payment of compensation for the first three months from the date of the occupational injury and will be refunded by the commissioner.

Copies of the Act and relevant forms are available from any office of the Department of Labour.

Questions and exercises:

Contact your local Department of Labour and acquire copies of the relevant forms needed for the reporting and further processing of an accident and compensation claim.

1. Explain in your own words how you understand the MOS Act and OHS Act have integrated
2. What safety systems are available in South Africa to assist with a health and safety maintenance programs?
3. Write an essay comparing the duties and responsibilities of employers and employees in terms of the OHS Act.
4. Describe the penalties that may apply to anyone who does not meet the requirements of the OHS Act.

15

Equal opportunities and anti-discrimination

Objectives of this chapter:

By the end of this chapter the learner will be able to:

- Follow a procedure to prepare and submit an employment equity plan
- Report on achieving employment equity as stated in the employment equity plan and report
- Identify designated employers, and identify designated groups of employees
- Explain the concept of affirmative action
- Comply with the Tourism BEE Scorecard if in scope

The learner will know:

- The principles of prohibition of discrimination in the workforce
- The sources and application of anti-discrimination law
- The basic provisions of the Employment Equity Act
- The duties of designated employers
- The process for developing, and the content of, an employment equity plan and report
- The requirement of reporting to the Department of Labour on implementation of employment equity plans
- The criteria and process for the Tourism BEE Scorecard

15.1 Introduction

South Africa had a legacy of discrimination on the basis of race, gender and disability, which prevented the majority of South Africans from obtaining access to opportunities for education, employment, promotion and wealth creation. In addition, the need for increased productivity and human resource development has required that organisations provide equal opportunities for all employees and, as a result, that the workforce reflects the demographics of the new democratic South Africa.

There are various benefits to employment equity; having a workforce that reflects the demographics of the country can improve market share and provide a better understanding of markets, which allows companies to service all current or prospective clients.

The legislation concerned with protecting the individual employee has so far adopted three protective mechanisms, namely protection against unfair dismissal, protection against unfair labour practices and the setting up of minimum standards and conditions of employment. Employment equity and unfair discrimination legislation essentially provides for a fourth protective mechanism, that is, protection against unfair discrimination.

15.2 Sources of employment equity and anti-discrimination law

Legislation is the main source of employment equity and anti-discrimination law, in addition to case law, which develops from how the courts interpret the legislation. The first piece of legislation dealing with discrimination in the workplace was the Labour Relations Act of 1995, which provides in section 187 that dismissal based on discrimination is automatically unfair. However, the fundamental principles for our employment equity and anti-discrimination legislation are contained in our Constitution.

15.2.1 The Constitution and employment equity

Chapter 2 of the constitution of the Republic of South Africa, 1996 contains the Bill of Rights, which entrenches certain fundamental rights for the citizens of the country. Section 9 of that chapter reads as follows:

'Equality –

(1) Everyone is equal before the law and has the right to equal protection and benefit of the law.

(2) Equality includes the full and equal enjoyment of all rights and freedoms. To promote the achievement of equality, legislative and other measures designed to protect or advance persons, or categories of persons, disadvantaged by unfair discrimination, may be taken.

(3) The state may not unfairly discriminate directly or indirectly against anyone on one or more rounds, including race, gender, sex, pregnancy, marital status, ethnic or social origin, colour, sexual orientation, age, disability, religion, conscience, belief, culture, language or birth.

(4) No person may unfairly discriminate directly or indirectly against anyone on one or more grounds in terms of subsection (3). National legislation must be enacted to prevent or prohibit unfair discrimination.

(5) Discrimination on one or more of the grounds listed in subsection (3) is unfair unless it is established that the discrimination is fair.'

From this section it is clear that the Constitution relies on two mechanisms to eliminate discrimination:

◆ Prohibition of discrimination, through which the principle of equality of treatment is reinforced. This is called formal equality and is protected in subsections (3) and (4) of section 9.

◆ Affirmative action, which is aimed at achieving equality in practice. Affirmative action aims at enshrining equality through the adoption of positive measures to empower previously disadvantaged persons. This mechanism is provided for in subsection (2) of section 9.

It is against this constitutional framework that the two main pieces of legislation aimed at achieving equality and eradicating discrimination, the Employment Equity Act 55 of 1998, and the Promotion of Equality and Prevention of Unfair Discrimination Act 4 of 2000, were developed.

15.3 Employment Equity Act

The Department of Labour introduced the Employment Equity Act 55 of 1998 (the EEA), which seeks to eliminate unfair discrimination in employment, and provides for affirmative action to correct the imbalances of the past with respect to access to employment, training, promotion and equitable remuneration, especially for black people, women and the disabled.

The Act also establishes an advisory and part-time Commission for Employment Equity, particularly to advise on the formulation of codes of good practice.

The Department of Labour has an extensive website on which reporting documents, formats and guidelines for the development and submission of employment equity forms may be found. Their website address is www.labour. gov.za.

The provisions and content of the Act are discussed below.

15.4 Chapter I: Definitions, purpose, interpretation and application

The purpose of the Act is to achieve workplace equity by promoting equal opportunity and fair treatment in the workplace through:
◆ the elimination of unfair discrimination
◆ the implementation of affirmative action measures to redress the disadvantages in employment experienced by designated groups (black [African, Coloured, Indian] people, women, and people with disabilities), in order to ensure their equitable representation in all occupational categories and levels in the workforce

The Act includes both the public and private sectors. However, it does not apply to members of the National Defence Force, the South African Secret Service and the National Intelligence Agency.

Employers who employ 50 or more workers are obligated to develop specific affirmative action plans, formulated in consultation with workers or their representatives, with voluntary targets, which are monitored by government through the submission of employment equity plans.

15.4.1 Definition of employee

An employee is regarded as any person, other than an independent contractor, who works for another person or for the state and who receives, or is entitled to receive remuneration. An employee also includes any person other than an independent contractor, who, in any manner, assists in carrying on or conducting the business of an employer. In terms of unfair discrimination, an applicant for a position is also regarded as an employee.

Temporary employment services: a person whose services are available to an employer who is required to submit an employment equity plan, by a temporary employment service (such as a company supplying casual banqueting staff to the hospitality industry) is considered to be an employee of that employer if the employment is of indefinite duration or for a period of three months or longer.

Where a temporary employment service, on the express or implied instructions of a client, commits an act of unfair discrimination, both the temporary employment service and the client are jointly and severally responsible.

15.5 Chapter II: Prohibition of unfair discrimination

Chapter II of the Act deals with the prohibition of unfair discrimination. All employers and employees are required to comply with this section of the Act.

No person may unfairly discriminate (directly or indirectly) against any employee, or an applicant for employment, on one or more grounds in any employment policy or practice, including race, gender, sex, pregnancy (or intended pregnancy, termination of pregnancy, or medical circumstances related to pregnancy), marital status, family responsibility (spouse or partner, dependent children, or immediate family members who need care and support), ethnic or social origin, colour, sexual orientation, age, disability, religion, HIV status, conscience, belief, political opinion, culture, language and birth.

Direct discrimination occurs where a person is disadvantaged simply because of the grounds listed above. Indirect discrimination is where broad rules create barriers to groups of individuals. For example, the requirement for matric as an entry criterion for higher education could be seen as indirect discrimination against anyone who does not have matric.

Medical testing, which includes any test, question, inquiry or other means designated to ascertain whether an employee has any medical condition, is prohibited. Medical testing may be conducted only under the following circumstances:

- If legislation permits or requires the testing.
- If it is justifiable in the light of medical facts, employment conditions, social policy, the fair distribution of employee benefits.
- The inherent requirements of the job demand it.

Medical testing of an employee to determine HIV status is prohibited unless determined to be justifiable by the Labour Court. Should the Labour Court deem testing for HIV status to be justified, the employer may be required to

- provide counselling
- maintain confidentiality
- adhere to a period during which the authorisation of any testing applies as determined by the Labour Court
- adhere to the category or categories of jobs or employees who can be tested, as determined by the Labour Court

Psychological testing and any similar assessments are prohibited unless the test or assessment can be scientifically shown to be valid and reliable, can be applied fairly to all employees and is not biased against any employee or group.

Harassment, including sexual harassment, of an employee is also regarded as a form of unfair discrimination.

Discrimination is not regarded to be unfair if affirmative action measures are taken, consistent with the purposes of the Act, or if distinctions, exclusions or preferences are based on the inherent requirements of the job. However, in any allegation of unfair discrimination, the burden of proof rests with the employer.

15.5.1 Disputes

The Act makes provision for an employee, or applicant for employment, to refer a dispute concerning alleged unfair discrimination (or medical or psychological testing) to the council for Conciliation, Mediation and Arbitration (CCMA) for conciliation. This must be done within six months of the alleged discriminatory action.

If a dispute is not resolved at conciliation, a party may refer it to the Labour Court for adjudication. The parties to a dispute may also agree to refer the dispute to arbitration.

Unfair dismissal disputes in which unfair discrimination is alleged must be dealt with in terms of the Labour Relations Act. The dismissal must be referred to the CCMA within 30 days.

15.6 Chapter III: Affirmative action

Chapter III contains all relevant guidance and regulation on affirmative action practices, including the duties of the parties, the processes to be followed, and the recording and submission of the EE plan.

15.6.1 Affirmative action measures

Affirmative action measures are intended to ensure that suitably qualified employees from designated groups have equal employment opportunities, and are equitably represented in all occupational categories and levels of the workforce.

These measures apply not only to the preferential appointment of members of designated groups, but also extend to preferential promotion, development and training of employees to increase their prospects of advancement. In aid of these measures, the employer must make 'reasonable accommodation', which means that the employer has to modify or adjust a job or the working environment in such a way so as to enable the person from a designated group to have access to or to participate or advance in employment.

Such measures must include:
- Identification and elimination of barriers with an adverse impact on designated groups.
- Measures that promote diversity.
- Making reasonable accommodation for people from designated groups.
- Retention, development and training of designated groups (including skills development).
- Preferential treatment and numerical goals to ensure equitable representation. This excludes quotas.

15.6.2 Designated groups

The beneficiaries of affirmative action are persons from 'designated groups' who are 'suitably qualified' to benefit from affirmative action measures. The EEA defines 'designated groups' as

◆ 'black people', which is defined to mean Africans, Coloureds and Indians,
◆ women
◆ people with disabilities, who are 'people who have a long-term physical or mental impairment which substantially limits their prospects of entry into, or advancement in, employment'

A 'suitably qualified person' is defined as someone who may be qualified for a job as a result of any one (or a combination) of that person's formal qualifications, prior learning, relevant experience or his or her capacity to acquire, within reasonable time, the ability to do the job.

Discrimination on the ground of lack of relevant experience alone is considered to be unfair discrimination.

15.6.3 Designated employer

A designated employer means an employer who employs 50 or more employees, or has a total annual turnover as reflected in Schedule 4 to the Act, municipalities and organs of state. Employers can also volunteer to become designated employers.

Figure 15-1: Schedule 4 to the EEA

Sector	Total annual turnover
Agriculture	R2 million
Mining and quarrying	R7,5 million
Manufacturing	R10 million
Electricity, gas and water	R10 million
Construction	R5 million
Retail and motor trade and repair services	R15 million
Catering, accommodation	**R5 million**
Finance and business services	R10 million
Community, society and personal services	R5 million

15.6.4 Duties of a designated employer

A designated employer must implement affirmative action measures for designated groups to achieve employment equity. In order to implement affirmative action measures, a designated employer must:

◆ consult with unions and employees in order to make sure that the EE plan is accepted by everybody
◆ assign one or more senior managers to ensure implementation and monitor-

ing of the employment equity plan, and must make available necessary resources for this purpose
◆ conduct an analysis of all employment policies, practices and procedures and prepare a profile of their workforce to identify any problems relating to employment equity (discussed in detail below)
◆ prepare and implement an employment equity plan setting out the affirmative action measures they intend taking to achieve employment equity goals (discussed in detail below)
◆ report to the director-general on progress made in the implementation of the employments equity plan
◆ display a summary of the provisions of the EEA in all languages relevant to their workforce

15.6.4.1 Consultation
Designated employers are required to take reasonable steps to consult with employees regarding workplace analysis, the preparation and implementation of an employment equity plan, and the submission and subsequent reporting on the employment equity plan to the director-general.
Consultation with employees must take place:
◆ with a representative of the trade union representing members at the workplace and its employees or representatives nominated by them
◆ if no representative trade union represents members at the workplace, with employees directly or representatives nominated by them

Employees or their nominated representative must include:
◆ employees across all occupational categories and levels in the organisation
◆ employees from designated groups
◆ employees not from designated groups

The designated employer is required to disclose to the consulting parties all relevant information that will allow those parties to consult effectively.

15.6.4.2 Transparency/duty to inform
All employers must display at the workplace, where it can be read by all employees, a notice, in the prescribed form, informing employees about the provisions of the Act.
In each of its workplaces, a designated employer must place in prominent, accessible places:
◆ The most recent employment equity report submitted.
◆ Any compliance order, arbitration award or order of the Labour Court concerning the provisions of this act in relation to the employer.
◆ Any other document concerning this act, as prescribed.

An employer that has an employment equity plan (EE plan), must make a copy of it available to its employees for copying and consultation.

15.6.4.3 Conducting of an analysis
A designated employer must conduct an analysis of employment policies, practices, procedures and working environment so as to identify employment

barriers that adversely affect members of designated groups. The analysis must also include the development of a workforce profile to determine to what extent designated groups are under-represented in the workplace.

The analysis must be conducted to:
- Identify employment barriers that adversely affect people from designated groups.
- Identify the degree of under-representation of people from designated groups in each occupational category and level in the workforce.
- Review employment policies and practices including, but not limited to:
  - recruitment procedures, advertising and selection criteria
  - appointments and the appointment process
  - job classification and grading
  - remuneration, employment benefits, and terms and conditions of employment
  - job assignments
  - the working environment and facilities
  - training and development
  - performance evaluation system
  - promotion
  - transfer
  - demotion
  - disciplinary measures other than dismissal
  - dismissal

A designated employer is required to establish and maintain records of its workforce, its employment equity plan, and any other matters relevant to compliance with the Act.

15.6.5 Preparing an employment equity plan

Figure 15-2: Employment equity plan

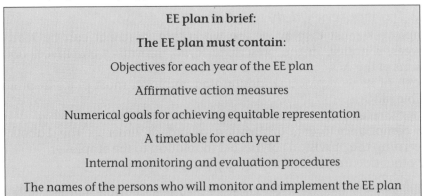

EE plan in brief:

The EE plan must contain:

Objectives for each year of the EE plan

Affirmative action measures

Numerical goals for achieving equitable representation

A timetable for each year

Internal monitoring and evaluation procedures

The names of the persons who will monitor and implement the EE plan

A designated employer must prepare and implement an employment equity plan that will achieve reasonable progress towards employment equity in the workforce. The EE plan must state:
- The duration of the EE plan, which may not be shorter than one year or longer than five years.

- The objectives to be achieved for each year of the EE plan.
- The affirmative action measures to be implemented, which would include
  - measures to identify and eliminate employment barriers, including unfair discrimination, that adversely affect people from designated groups
  - measures designed to further diversity in the workplace
  - making reasonable accommodation for people from designated groups to ensure that they enjoy equal opportunities and are equitably represented in the workforce
  - preferential treatment and numerical goals (not quotas) to ensure the equitable representation of suitably qualified people from designated groups in all occupational categories and levels in the workforce
  - measures to retain and develop people from designated groups, and to implement appropriate training, including any measures in terms of any legislation providing for skills development.
- Where an analysis reveals an under-representation of people from designated groups, the EE plan must state the numerical goals to achieve equitable representation of suitably qualified people from the designated groups within each occupational category and level, the timetable to achieve this desired state, and the strategies intended to achieve the goals. The Department of Labour includes factors to be taken into account in determining numerical goals in their published code of good practice. This analysis should be undertaken in accordance with the factors against which the Department of Labour will assess compliance, these being in relation to
  - the demographic profile of the national and regionally economically active population
  - the pool of suitably qualified people from designated groups from which the employer may reasonable be expected to promote or appoint employees
  - the economic and financial factors relevant to the sector in which the employer operates
  - the present and anticipated economic and financial circumstances of the employer;
  - the number of present and planned vacancies that exist in the various categories and levels and the employer's labour turnover.
- The procedures that will be used to monitor and evaluate the implementation of the EE plan, and whether reasonable progress is being made towards implementing employment equity.
- Internal dispute-resolution procedures regarding any dispute about the interpretation and implementation of the EE plan.
- The persons, including one or more senior managers with due authority and means, responsible for monitoring and implementing the EE plan (such persons do not relieve the designated employer of any duty imposed by the Act and, in addition, designated employers must take reasonable steps to ensure that such managers perform their functions).
- Any other prescribed matter.

A designated employer is not required to take any decision concerning employment policy or practice that would establish an absolute barrier to the prospective or continued employment or advancement of people who are not from designated groups.

15.6.6 Reporting

Designated employers must submit reports to the Department of Labour to portray their progress toward achieving their EE plan.

Designated employers employing fewer that 150 people must submit a report every two years on the first working day of October.

A designated employer employing 150 or more people has to submit a report annually on the first working day of October.

The first EE report to the Department of Labour deals with the detail of the initial development of, and consultation around, the EE plan. Subsequent reports detail the progress made in the implementation of the EE plan.

Figure 15.3: Submission schedule for employment equity reports

Employer	When to submit	How often
<150 employees	1 October	Every two years
>150 employees	1 October	Annually

Any hospitality company that is established, and grows in terms of its annual turnover and employment number, must be aware that once the requirements as a designated employer have been met, then they will have to meet the provisions of the EEA in terms of submission of an EE plan and subsequent EE reports on the implementation of the EE plan.

The EE report is a public document. The employer is therefore required to display a copy of the most recent EE report in all workplaces. Public companies are also required to publish a summary of the EE report in their annual financial reports.

15.6.7 Income differentials

A statement of remuneration and benefits received in each occupational category and level of the workforce must be submitted by a designated employer to the Employment Conditions Commission (ECC).

Where there are disproportionate income differentials, a designated employer must take measures to reduce it progressively. Such measures may include collective bargaining, compliance with sectoral determinations (section 51 of the Basic Conditions of Employment Act); the application of norms and benchmarks recommended by the ECC, relevant measures contained in skills development legislation, and any other appropriate steps.

15.7 Chapter IV: Commission for Employment Equity

This chapter of the Act established the Commission for Employment Equity. The commission advises the minister of Labour on any codes of good practice, regulations, policy and other relevant matters relating to the act. It may also make awards recognising the achievements of employers in furthering the purposes of this Act, research and report to the minister on matters relating to the application of the Act, including well-researched norms and benchmarks for the setting of numerical goals in various sectors, and perform any other prescribed functions.

15.8 Chapter V: Monitoring, enforcement and legal proceedings

15.8.1 Monitoring

Employee or trade union representatives can monitor contraventions of the Act and report to relevant bodies. Any employee or trade union representative may bring alleged contraventions of the Act to the attention of another employee, an employer, a trade union, a workplace forum, a labour inspector of the Department of Labour, the Director-General of the Department of Labour, or the Commission for Employment Equity.

15.8.2 Enforcement

The four ways in which compliance with the provisions of the EEA is ensured are discussed below:

15.8.2.1 Self-regulation

Every employment equity plan must include a dispute resolution procedure, and employers and employees are required to use this procedure to ensure that the provisions of the EEA are complied with.

15.8.2.2 Administrative procedures

Labour Inspectors are authorised to conduct inspections as provided for in sections 65 and 66 of the Basic Conditions of Employment Act. A labour inspector may enter any workplace, question employees and conduct an inspection. If the inspector has reasonable grounds to believe that a designated employer has failed to comply with its obligations in terms of the Act, the inspector will obtain a written undertaking from the employer to comply within a specified period.

15.8.2.3 Court action

If the designated employer refuses to comply with the written undertaking, the inspector will issue an order to comply. The compliance order, which must be prominently displayed in the workplace, would contain the maximum fine that may be imposed on the employer for failing to comply with the order. Schedule 1 to the Act sets out the maximum permissible fines that may be imposed for contravening the Act. These fines are highly punitive, and range up towards the R1 million mark.

Objection to a compliance order must be made in writing to the director-general of The Department of Labour within 21 days after receiving that order.

The Labour Court has ultimate jurisdiction to ensure compliance with the provisions of the EEA, and is empowered by section 50 of the Act to make a compliance order an order of court, to direct investigations by the CCMA, to hear appeals, and to impose fines upon employers who fail to comply with the provisions of the EEA.

15.8.3 Review by the director-general

The director-general may conduct a review to determine whether an employer is complying with the Act. On completion of the review, the director-general may make recommendations for compliance within certain time frames.

15.8.4 Protection of employee rights

The Act protects employees who exercise their rights and obligations under the act against victimisation, obstruction and undue influence.

No employee, including a former employee or an applicant for employment, may be discriminated against by any person for exercising his or her rights in accordance with the Act, and no person may do or threaten to do any of the following:

- Prevent an employee, former employee or applicant from exercising any right conferred by the Act or participating in any proceedings in terms of the Act.
- Prejudice an employee, a former employee or an applicant for employment as a result of the disclosure of information that the person is lawfully required or entitled to provide to another person.
- Favour, or promise favour, to an employee, former employee, or applicant in exchange for such person not exercising any right conferred by the Act or for not participating in any proceedings in terms of the Act.
- Disputes relating to the interpretation or application in respect to the protection of employee rights may be referred, in writing, to the CCMA. The CCMA must attempt to resolve the dispute through conciliation, but if it remains unresolved, any party may refer the dispute to the Labour Court or all parties may consent to arbitration by the CCMA.

15.9 Chapter VI: General provisions

15.9.1 Awarding of State contracts

A less direct method of enforcement is contained in section 53 of the Act, which provides that designated employers who want to enter into commercial contracts with organs of the state must comply with the provisions of the EEA. Commercial contracts can include supplies or services, such as catering to correctional facilities, state hospitals or educational institutions, or contracts for accommodating or providing travel services to civil servants. A non-designated company must comply with the section relating to unfair discrimination only.

The Minister of Labour will issue a time-limited certificate confirming the relevant compliance, which the employer may attach to the offer. Alternatively, the employer may attach to an offer a declaration of compliance that has been verified by the director-general. Failure to comply in this area is sufficient ground for rejection of any offer to conclude an agreement, or for cancellation of the agreement.

15.9.2 Liability of employers

Should employees contravene any provision of this Act, while performing their duties, the employer will be liable unless the employer can prove that it did everything in its power to prevent the undesired act.

15.10 Codes of good practice

The Minister of Labour may issue any code of good pr̶
employers with information and guidance that may ̶
implementation of the Act. Such codes are available from̶
Labour, or may be found on their website. These may inclu̶

- preparing employment equity plans
- advertising, recruitment procedures and selection criteri̶
- special measures to be taken in relation to persons with famiʎy ̶
  ties and to persons with disabilities, including benefit schemes
- practice on key aspects of HIV/AIDS and employment
- sexual and racial harassment
- internal dispute-resolution procedures regarding the interpretation or application of the Act, and sector specific issues
- guidelines to employers on the prioritisation of specific designated groups.

Other aspects covered in Chapter VI include stipulations relating to:

- publication of further regulations to the Act
- delegation of power by the Minister
- temporary employment services
- designation of organs of the state
- breaches of confidentiality and related fines
- liability of employers for contravention of this Act by employees
- obstruction, undue influence and fraud with related fines for such offences
- application of the Act when in conflict with other laws

15.10.1 Implications for business/required action

The Department of Labour has, using a variety of existing data sources, compiled a national database of all employers from whom it expects to receive reports. This database will be updated on an ongoing basis. The Department will follow up on employers from whom reports are expected, and who do not report.

The preparation and implementation of an employment equity plan may be conducted in three sequential phases as discussed below.

Figure 15-4: Employment equity planning process

Phase 1: PREPARATION	Phase 2: IMPLEMENTATION	Phase 3: MONITORING
Step 1: Assign Responsibility	Step 5: Corrective measures and objectives	Step 9: Monitor, evaluate and review
Step 2: Communication, awareness and training	Step 6: Time frames established	Step 10: Report
Step 3: Consultation	Step 7: Allocation of resources	
Step 4: Analysis	Step 8: Plan communication	

...nformation on this 10-step approach may be downloaded from the ...ment of Labour website.

...0.2 Phase 1: preparation

...he preparation phase contains the relevant steps that an employer needs to take in order to produce an employment equity plan.

Step 1: Assigning responsibility

The first step in the process is to assign responsibility for the development, implementation, and monitoring of the EE plan to one or more senior managers.

Step 2: Communication, awareness and training

This step should focus on the better utilisation of human resources, the creation of a more diverse and productive workforce, and a workforce that reflects the relevant labour market. Creating awareness and sensitivity among employees of the requirements of the EEA is also part of this step.

Step 3: Consultation

Consultation should start as early as possible in the process. A consultative forum should be established – or an existing forum used if this is appropriate, for example, an existing diversity committee, affirmative action or employ-ment equity forum.

All stakeholders, such as representative trade unions, employee representa-tives from designated groups, non-designated groups, and all occupational categories and levels as well as senior management, including the managers assigned with responsibility, should take part in the consultative process.

Meetings should take place regularly and employers should allow time off for these meetings.

Step 4: Conducting an analysis

This entails conducting an analysis to assess all employment policies, practices, procedures, and the working environment. The aim is to identify barriers that may contribute to the under-representation or under-utilisation of employees from the designated groups.

The analysis also aims to determine the extent of under-representation of employees from the designated groups in the different occupational categories and levels of the employer's workforce.

15.10.3 Phase 2: implementation

The second phase contains all the steps that an employer needs to take to implement the EE plan.

Step 5: Setting objectives and formulating measures

This step entails setting realistic and achievable objectives and goals by utilising the information obtained in the preparation phase together with the employ-er's business plan. It is important to develop an affirmative action measure to counter each unacceptable practice that has been identified in Phase 1. For example, if pre-employment psychological tests are found to be culturally biased, employers need to consider introducing acceptable competency-based tests, or where there is an unusually high resignation rate of members of designated groups, reasons should be investigated, and action taken to address these problems.

Step 6: Establishing a time frame
As specified in the Act, the duration of a plan should be between one and five years.

Step 7: Allocate resources
Resources such as financial budgets, human resources, infrastructure, training and other appropriate resources required to implement the EE plan must be allocated.

Step 8: Communicate the EE plan
This step requires that the EE plan be communicated to all stakeholders so that they know who is responsible for its implementation, where information regarding the plan may be obtained, what the objectives and duration of the plan are, and what the proposed dispute resolution procedures are.

15.10.4 Phase 3: monitoring
Phase 3 contains the steps that an employer takes to monitor and review the implementation of the employment equity plan.

Step 9: Monitoring and evaluating the EE plan
This step entails the internal monitoring of the implementation of the EE plan and the evaluation thereof by means of keeping records of the EE plan, reporting to the consultative forum, evaluating progress at structured and regular intervals and, where progress is not satisfactory, by reviewing and revising the EE plan to eliminate flaws.

Step 10 : Reporting to the Department of Labour
EE reports on the progress made in implementing the EE plan must be submitted to the Department of Labour. The format (EEA2) for the EE report is available from the Department. Reports must be submitted to the Employment Equity Registry, Department of Labour, Pretoria, or to the provincial office or labour centre in an envelope clearly marked 'Employment Equity Registry'.

It is advisable to keep a copy of the report, as well as a record that the report was sent, as the onus is on the employer to prove that the report has been submitted if the report is mislaid or goes astray.

Employers must, *at the same time* as reporting, complete and submit an Income Differential Statement Form EEA4.

Designated employers whose operations extend across different geographical areas, functional units, workplaces or sectors may elect to submit either a consolidated or a separate report for each of these. This decision should be made by employers after consultation with the relevant stakeholders.

15.10.4.1 Other uses of the EE Report:
Employers can use the report form to provide them with an information framework to assist them with their employment equity plans. The form requires information from employers regarding recruitment, promotions,

terminations, disciplinary action, and skills development. Interpretation of this type of information can alert employers to employment equity barriers, and so assist them with their analysis of employment policies and practices.

The Department of Labour has established a database of employers from which it expects to receive reports. Once initial reports have been received from employers, the department will be able to identify those employers who have not reported. These employers will be issued with a written demand to comply. The routine inspections conducted by the Department of Labour will also include a checklist of employer obligations for the Act.

Figure 15-5: Employment equity compliance table

Who	What	When
Department of Labour	Enforcement and inspection	Continuous, planned and unplanned
Designated Employers	◆ consult with unions and employees in order to make sure that the EE plan is accepted by everybody ◆ assign one or more senior managers to ensure implementation and monitoring of the employment equity plan, and make available necessary resources for this purpose ◆ conduct an analysis of all employment policies, practices and procedures, and prepare a profile of their workforce to identify any problems relating to employment equity; (discussed in detail below) ◆ prepare and implement an employment equity plan setting out the affirmative action measures they intend taking to achieve employment equity goals (discussed in detail below) ◆ report to the Director-General on progress made in the implementation of the EE plan ◆ display a summary of the provisions of the EEA in all languages relevant to their workforce.	◆ Continuous and annually
Designated Employers	**Less than 150 employees:** ◆ develop and submit an EE plan to Department of Labour – duration 1 to 5 years ◆ submit EE Implementation Report Plan to Department of Labour to report on the implementation of the plan as stipulated	◆ Submit EE plan when previous plan expires ◆ Submit EE report every two years on the 1st working day of October
	More than 150 employees ◆ develop and submit EE plan to Department of Labour – duration 1 to 5 years. ◆ submit EE plan to Department of Labour – report on the implementation of the plan as stipulated	◆ Submit EE plan when previous plan expires ◆ Submit EE Report every year on 1st working day of October

15.11 The Promotion of Equality and Prevention of Unfair Discrimination Act

The Promotion of Equality and Prevention of Unfair Discrimination Act 4 of 2000 supplements the EEA in so far as equality and anti-discrimination legislation in South Africa is concerned. The difference being that the EEA has application specifically in the workplace, the Promotion of Equality and Prevention of Unfair Discrimination Act applies generally.

15.11.1 Purpose of the Act

The objectives of this Act, as outlined in section 2, are specifically to:
- Enact legislation required by section 9 of the Constitution, the equality clause.
- Give effect to the letter and spirit of the Constitution, in particular:
  - the equal enjoyment of all rights and freedoms by every person
  - the promotion of equality
  - the values of non-racialism and non-sexism
  - the prevention of advocacy of hatred based on race, ethnicity, gender or religion
- Provide for measures to facilitate eradication of unfair discrimination, hate speech and harassment, particularly on the grounds of race, gender and disability.
- Provide for procedures for the determination of circumstances under which discrimination is unfair.
- Provide for measures to educate the public, and raise public, awareness on the importance of promoting equality and overcoming unfair discrimination, hate speech and harassment.
- Provide for remedies for victims of unfair discrimination, hate speech and harassment, and persons whose right to equality has been infringed.
- Facilitate further compliance with international law obligations in terms of specified conventions, which focus on the subject matter of this Act.

15.11.2 Application of the Act

Section 5 provides that the Act binds the state as well as all persons, but that it does not apply to any person or situation covered by the Employment Equity Act.

This clearly confirms that the Promotion of Equality and Prevention of Unfair Discrimination Act is an Act of general application in contrast to the EEA, which is focused specifically on the workplace.

The two pieces of legislation are meant to complement each other, rather than this Act overriding or substituting the EEA in any way.

15.11.3 Provisions of the Act

15.11.3.1 Prohibitions

Chapter 2 generally prohibits unfair discrimination. In section 6 the state, and any person, is prohibited from unfairly discriminating against any person. The act imposes a burden on all citizens as well as the state not to discriminate unfairly on the grounds of race, gender or disability, and at the same time, protects everyone against hate speech, harassment, and the publication and dissemination of information that is unfairly discriminatory.

Chapter 5 then places on the state and all persons a duty to promote (and in the case of the state, achieve) equality. Further, a social duty is imposed on all persons, non-governmental organisations, community-based organisations and traditional institutions to promote equality in their relationships with other entities and in their public activities.

15.11.3.2 Procedure and enforcement

The key mechanism to enforce the provisions of the Act is by means of legal action on the part of the aggrieved party in special courts, which are established in terms of section 16 of the Act. This does not mean that there are separate equity or equality courts, but that existing magistrates' courts and high courts will adjudicate matters related to the Act.

This Act has a unique feature in the provisions regarding a person's right to institute legal action in a particular matter. The normal rule is that a person can only institute legal action in respect of his or her own right, and not for anyone else, unless they have power of attorney for another person. However, the Act provides that proceedings may be instituted by

- any person acting in his or her own interest – the normal rule
- any person acting on behalf of another person who cannot act in their own name
- any person acting as a member of, or in the interest of, a group or class of people – a so-called class action
- any person acting in the public interest – a so-called public action, which was previously not available in our law
- The South African Human Rights Commission or the Commission for Gender Equality

Equity, or equality, courts have broad powers, and can make a variety of orders in judgment in matters before them, including orders to pay damages, restraining orders or interdicts, orders to suspend or revoke licences, or orders referring the matter to public prosecution or criminal prosecution.

Appeals may be lodged to the High Court or the Supreme Court of Appeal.

In a case of discrimination, the complainant has to provide evidence or proof of the discriminatory act or conduct, and the responding party must prove that it did not take place.

15.11.4 Illustrative list of unfair practices

The schedule attached to the Act contains a list of practices to illustrate what would be considered as unfair practice in terms of the Act. The following examples would all be regarded as unfair:

- **Labour and employment**: for example, failure to respect a principle of equal pay for equal work.
- **Health care services and benefits**: subjecting people to medical experiments without their informed consent
- **Education**: failure to reasonably and practicably accommodate diversity

- **Housing, accommodation, land and property**: arbitrary eviction of people on one or more prohibited grounds
- **Insurance services**: disadvantaging a person, including unfairly and unreasonable refusing to grant services to persons solely on HIV/AIDS status
- **Partnerships**: imposing unfair and discriminatory terms or conditions under which a person is invited to become a partner
- **Professional bodies**: unfairly limiting or denying members access to benefits or facilities on the basis of a prohibited ground
- **Provision of goods, services and facilities**: the practice of unfairly limiting access to contractual opportunities for supplying goods and services
- **Clubs, sport and associations**: failure to promote diversity in selection of representative teams

15.12 The Black Economic Empowerment Act

The President signed the Broad-Based Black Economic Empowerment Act 53 of 2003 into law in January 2004. The objectives of the Act are to facilitate broad-based black economic empowerment by:
- promoting economic transformation in order to enable meaningful participation of black people in the economy
- achieving a substantial change in the racial composition of ownership and management structures, and in the skilled occupations of existing and new enterprises
- increasing the extent to which communities, workers, cooperatives and other collective enterprises own and manage existing and new enterprises, and increasing their access to economic activities, infrastructure and skills training
- increasing the extent to which black women own and manage existing and new enterprises, and increasing their access to economic activities, infrastructure and skills training
- promoting investment programmes that lead to broad-based and meaningful participation in the economy by black people in order to achieve sustainable development and general prosperity
- empowering rural and local communities by enabling access to economic activities, land, infrastructure, ownership and skills
- promoting access to finance for black economic empowerment

15.12.1 The role of the Department of Trade and Industry

The Department of Trade and Industry (DTI) has been tasked with setting up, administrating and implementing the black economic empowerment legislation.

It is intended that the Act and the codes of good practice will promote the economic empowerment of all black people, including black women, black workers, black youth, black people with disabilities and black people living in rural areas, through diverse but integrated socio-economic strategies. These will include:
- increasing the number of black people who manage, own and control enterprises and productive assets

- facilitating ownership and management of enterprises, and productive assets by communities, workers, co-operatives and other collective enterprises
- human resource and skills development
- achieving equitable representation in all occupational categories and levels in the workforce
- preferential procurement
- investment in enterprises that are owned or managed by black people

15.12.2 The Balanced BEE Scorecard

In order to monitor the progress of the Black Economic Empowerment legislation and the various strategies, the DTI has introduced what is referred to as a 'balanced scorecard' that will assess and measure the progress being made by enterprises and sectors in achieving BEE. The scorecard is used to rate a business or enterprise in the event that the sector has not introduced its own BEE Charter and appropriate scorecard.

The generic DTI scorecard measures three core elements of BEE:
- direct empowerment through ownership and control of enterprises and assets
- human resource development and employment equity
- indirect empowerment through preferential procurement and enterprise development

Government will use the total score to rank enterprises according to their progress in achieving broad-based BEE. The following are the categories for ranking:
- total score of 80% and above – excellent contributor to broad-based BEE
- total score of 65% to 79.9% – good contributor to broad-based BEE
- total score of 40% to 64.9% – satisfactory contributor to broad-based BEE
- total score of 25% to 39.9% – limited contributor to broad-based BEE
- total score of below 25% – unsatisfactory contributor to broad-based BEE

15.12.3 Measuring black economic empowerment

All BEE initiatives must be measurable, as this is critical in determining the progress made by businesses, sectors and the economy as a whole, towards the BEE objectives.

There are seven key elements that are the pillars to broad-based BEE. These elements provide a common base for measuring the impact of BEE across different entities and sectors with the economy.

15.12.3.1 Ownership

Ownership recognises and measures the entitlement of black people to the voting rights and economic interest associated with equity holding.

15.12.3.2 Management

Management refers to the effective control of economic activities and resources. This involves the power to determine policies as well as the direction of economic activities and resources within a business.

15.12.3.3 Employment equity

Employment equity is the promotion of equal opportunities through the elimination of unfair discrimination in order to redress the disadvantages in employment experienced by black people.

15.12.3.4 Skills development

Skills development refers to the development of core competencies of black people to facilitate their interaction in the mainstream of the economy.

15.12.3.5 Preferential procurement

Preferential procurement is a measure designed to widen market access for entities in order to integrate them into the mainstream of the economy.

15.12.3.6 Enterprise development

Aims to assist and accelerate the development of the operational and financial capacity of small and medium black-owned and -controlled entrepreneurial enterprises.

15.12.3.7 Residual or industry-specific factors

Residual or industry-specific factors allow for other factors that may accelerate broad-based empowerment, and will include industry-specific initiatives as well as social development factors.

15.12.4 Tourism BEE Charter and Scorecard

Tourism industry stakeholders need to develop the sector to make it accessible, relevant and more reflective of the population of South Africa.

As a result of this imperative, the Tourism BEE Charter and Scorecard was launched at Indaba in May 2005.

The scorecard is a measurement tool to help participants in the tourism industry ascertain their current levels of BEE, spot gaps in their profile, and identify how their profiles can be improved.

The scorecard sets five-year milestones (2009 and 2014) with attached targets to be achieved by the end of each five-year period. It is based on the generic BEE Scorecard published by the DTI.

The last indicator on the scorecard is industry-specific. The two indicators that have been identified by the tourism sector relate to the ability of the industry to create jobs, and to market South Africa as a preferred tourism destination. These indicators are:

- Recruitment of employees with no prior working experience
- The status of the tourism enterprise as a TOMSA levy collector. In this regard the Tourism Charter will urge marketing bodies benefiting from TOMSA funds to ensure that these funds are used to further the interests of black people in al aspects of tourism.

15.12.5 Tourism BEE Council

The Tourism BEE Charter Council has been established to drive the implementation of the Tourism Charter. The council develops and implements a number of initiatives to help companies comply with the charter, to grow emerging companies and to attract innovation and growth in the sector.

The council is based at the DEAT offices in Pretoria, and their website address, for further information and support is www.tourismbeecharter.co.za

15.12.5.1 Exemptions and Compliance

After debate and consultation with key tourism stakeholders, it was established that the scorecard would exempt certain businesses from specific key elements.

The exemptions will be based on the turnover of the business, which gives an indication of the size of the business. As such, small businesses that will battle to comply with the requirements of the scorecard will be exempt.

If your company is not exempt, and you need to comply with the charter and scorecard, you will need to determine your company's BEE status using the charter and scorecard:

- by using the self-assessment tool provided by the Tourism BEE Charter Council
- by conducting an internal evaluation yourself
- by appointing an external BEE verification agency to conduct an external evaluation or rating

Once your BEE score has been determined, you will be able to categorise your company according to its contribution to BEE.

The following ratings are applied to BEE-compliant companies:

- excellent BEE contributor
- good BEE contributor
- satisfactory BEE contributor
- BEE-compliant SMMEs
- black-women-owned SMMEs

Questions and exercises

1. Draw up a plan for the development and submission of an employment equity plan for a game lodge employing 58 staff. Include all steps and procedures in a chart that clearly indicates the length of time for each process, the actions and stakeholders involved. The plan must be submitted to the Department of Labour by the required date; all actions must therefore be completed in time for this date.
2. Debate the difference between discrimination and affirmative action.
3. Explain the process of reporting on the achievement of employment equity.
4. Name two examples of direct discrimination and two examples of indirect discrimination, and explain why these are examples of discrimination.
5. An international hotel chain has employed you as a consultant to brief them on legislative requirements pertaining to employment in South Africa. Write a report to them in which the following are explained:
   - the need for employment equity in South Africa

- the instruments by which the government intents to achieve employment equity, and
- their prospective responsibilities as employers in South Africa toward employment equity.
6. Visit the Tourism BEE Scorecard website and list the tools that you will find useful to develop both yourself and your hospitality business.

16
Skills development legislation

Objectives of this chapter:

By the end of this chapter the learner will be able to:

+ Register for levy payments with SARS
+ Determine if their establishment falls within scope of THETA
+ Claim grants from THETA
+ Explain the role of the Department of Labour and the National Skills Development Strategy in skills development for South Africa
+ Describe the NQF and the qualifications available to employees in the hospitality industry.

The learner will know:

+ Functions and duties of a skills development facilitator
+ The process for levy payments
+ The process for grant claims from THETA

16.1 Introduction

South Africa needs world-class skills to be able to compete in a global market and to make the domestic economy grow. Also, there is a need to develop the skills of those people who were historically denied access to training and development.

South Africa has developed a national Human Resources Development (HRD) Strategy that is drawn from the Reconstruction and Development Programme (RDP) where the development of human resources is identified as one of the five key programmes of the RDP.

The purpose of the HRD Strategy is to provide the people of South Africa with a solid educational foundation for social participation, and also to be empowered to develop relevant and marketable skills at further and higher education levels. At the same time, employers will contribute to the identification and development of skills for the economy, and government will promote and support policies that target employment growth in key industrial sectors.

According to the strategy, the government has two roles to play. One is to ensure that the various components of the state work together in a co-ordinated way to deliver opportunities for human development. The second is to ensure that those people who have suffered from discrimination in the past are put at the front of the queue in terms of the identified national priorities. It is therefore important to view the Skills Development Strategy and legislation as complimentary to employment equity legislation, as they work together to achieve the same purpose.

The strategy is underpinned by a set of institutional arrangements, including sector education and training authorities (SETAs) under the Department of Labour, and the reshaping of Further and Higher Education by the Department of Education. The Department of Labour has developed and implemented the National Skills Development Strategy toward achieving the HRD Strategy.

The South African Government's commitment to promote active labour market policies is well demonstrated in the Skills Development Act 97 of 1998 and the Skills Development Levies Act 9 of 1999. These two pieces of legislation introduced new institutions, programmes and funding policies designed to increase investment in skills development.

Regulations promulgated under both of these Acts provide the operational and logistical means of achieving the objectives of these Acts.

16.2 Skills Development Act

The Skills Development Act (SDA) seeks to establish a high quality workplace education and training system that is cost effective and accountable, meets training needs and complements employment and economic growth.

Specifically the SDA provides for:

- A research and strategic planning unit to gather and disseminate information on labour market skills trends, and promote planning for, and prioritisation of, skills development
- Employment services that will promote people's active participation in the labour market
- Learnerships and other training programmes that will result in registered qualifications signifying work readiness, and that respond to the needs of the labour market
- Co-ordination of the skills development strategy through SETAs working with the National Skills Authority and the Minister of Labour; and for these to co-ordinate with the financing of skills development through a skills development levy of one percent

The SDA consists of 8 chapters, which are briefly summarised as follows:

Chapter 1 contains definitions, purpose and interpretation of the Act.

Chapter 2 deals with the National Skills Authority (NSA), its establishment, functions, compositions, constitution and remuneration and administration. The main function of the NSA is to develop and implement a national skills development policy and strategy with the Department of Labour, and the SETAs.

Chapter 3 makes provision for Sector Education and Training Authorities (SETAs), and outlines their establishment, functions, composition, chambers, constitution and finances, as well as taking over the administration of SETA in the event of maladministration or incapacity. SETAs are established for any national economic sector. They must:

- develop and implement a skills plan for their sector
- promote learnerships
- be accredited by the South African Qualifications Authority to accredit training providers in its sector
- collect and disburse the skills development levies in its sector
- liaise with the NSA on national skills issues
- report to the Director General of Labour, and other sections of the Department of Labour

Chapter 4 addresses learnerships, which are training programmes that replace the apprenticeship system in South Africa. Learnerships must lead to a recognised qualification for a learner, and consist of a structured learning component and practical work experience of a specific type and duration. The terms and conditions of employment contracts are sketched in the Act, and further detailed in regulations attached to the Act.

Chapter 5 addresses skills programmes, which are smaller than learnerships, but contribute credits towards full qualifications. They are occupationally specific, for example, in reception work, in bar tending, fast-food cookery, and so on.

Chapter 6 makes provision for various institutions in the Department of Labour to support the Act. These include a Skills Development Planning Unit, employment services, registration of persons that provide employment services, cancellation of registration of employment services and appeals against decisions of the Director-General.

Chapter 7 addresses financial issues, including the National Skills Fund (NSF), the use of money in the fund, control and administration of the fund, and budget for training by public service employers. Twenty percent of levies collected go into the NSF, and this money will be used for projects that support the National Skills Development Strategy.

Chapter 8 deals with general issues such as the jurisdiction of the Labour Court, monitoring, enforcement and legal proceedings, offences, penalties, delegation, regulations, repeal of laws, and the short title of the Act if there is an abbreviated title of the Act. The SDA repeals the Manpower Training Act 56 of 1981, the Guidance and Placement Act 62 of 1981, the Local Government Training Act 41 of 1985, and certain sections of the Telecommunications Act 106 of 1996.

16.3 Skills Development Levies Act

The short supply of skilled staff is a serious obstacle to the competitiveness of industry in South Africa. The levy grant scheme aims to expand the knowledge and competencies of the labour force resulting in improvements in employability and productivity.

The payment towards this levy grant scheme is legislated in terms of the Skills Development Levies Act (SDLA). The intention is to stimulate skills development by enabling employers to reclaim some expenditure on skills development initiatives.

The SDLA provides a funding mechanism for incentivising skills development. This is achieved by collecting a levy from all employers designated in the Act. This levy is 1% of gross remuneration cost, and is collected by the South African Revenue Service (SARS). The levies paid to SARS are deposited into a special fund from where 80% of it is distributed to the relevant SETAs as indicated on the employer registration forms, and the balance (20%) is paid into the National Skills Fund. SETAs in turn pay levy grants to qualifying employers as percentages of their levy paid, in accordance with certain legislative requirements set by the Department of Labour.

The National Skills Fund has been established to provide funding for the training of unemployed people, and for special skills development projects not within the scope of SETAs.

The process that is created by the SDLA is represented in figure 16–1 as follows:

Figure 16-1: Levy and grant process established by Skills Development Levies Act

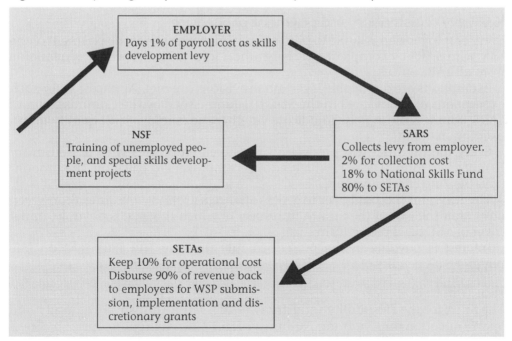

The Skills Development Levies Act was promulgated to provide the financial structure to implement the Skills Development Act. The three chapters of the Act address the following:

Chapter 1 addresses the administration, imposition and recovery of the levy. Every employer must pay a skills development levy, which is a percentage of the total amount of remuneration (as defined in the Act) paid by the employer. Exemptions are listed, as well as the process of registration for payment of the levy. It further describes the methods of collection, distribution of levies, collection costs and penalties of not paying the levy. The penalty is in the form of interest being added to unpaid levies.

The levy must be paid by every employer in South Africa who is registered with SARS (South African Revenue Services) for PAYE, or who has an annual payroll in excess of R500,000. This levy payment was increased from R250 000 by the Minister of Finance and became effective as from 01 July 2006 in an effort to reduce the tax and administrative burden on SMMEs.

Chapter 2 covers the recovery of the levy by a SETA, the role of inspectors and general issues of compliance. The Department of Labour and SARS have drafted a Skills Development Levy guideline containing comprehensive details in this regard.

Chapter 3 covers general provisions that relate to offences, penalties for offenders and proof of accuracy of information provided by employers. It also covers a provision for the publication of regulations in support of the Act, makes provision for amendments, and stipulates the date of commencement of the Act.

16.4 Levy registration and payment procedure

Every employer who is liable to pay the levy must register for the payment of the levy with SARS by completing a registration form SDL 101 which is available from all SARS offices.

Exemptions are applicable if certain provisions are met. Application for such exemptions are contained in the SDL 101 form issued by the Commissioner of SARS, who will ultimately adjudicate whether the employer will qualify for an exemption or not.

Every month SARS will provide all registered employers with a 'Return for Remittance' form SDL 201, which enables employers to calculate the amount payable, and effect payment.

The levy must be paid over to SARS (after registration), not later than seven days after the end of the month in respect of which the levy is payable, under cover of a SDL 201 return form.

Interest is payable at the prescribed rate (Income Tax Purposes) on late payments. A penalty of 10% will be levied on the unpaid amount.

16.5 THETA

The SETA for the Hospitality Industry is THETA – the Tourism, Hospitality and Sport Education and Training Authority. THETA has a broad scope of business types that fall under its jurisdiction for skills planning. All businesses falling under the scope of THETA as listed below will have their levies, as collected by SARS, paid to THETA. They will also have to interact with THETA when claiming for grants against the levies that they have paid.

THETA has five chambers, as follows:

16.5.1 The Tourism and Travel Services Chamber

The tourism and travel sector consists mainly of travel services, tourism services, car hire and airline operators. Employers that fall within the scope of this chamber are as follows:

- Retail and general travel operations, including
  - travel agencies, tour operators and tourist guides
  - destination management operators
  - venue management,
- Tourism services, including
  - tourism marketing and development agencies and companies
  - tourism authorities, commissions and boards
  - tourist information centres
  - tourism industry associations,
- Motor car rental services
- Inbound international airline operators,
- Business tourism operators, including
  - event and conference organisers
  - convention and conference centres.

16.5.2 The Hospitality Chamber

Hospitality is offered at many venues, and includes the broad services of providing food or accommodation to the consumer.

The Hospitality Chamber of THETA comprises:

- Accommodation services, including
  - hotels, motels, hostels, guest houses, guest farms and bed-and-breakfasts
  - self-catering, timeshares, camps and caravan parks
  - resorts and game lodges
- Food preparation, catering and food and beverage services, including
  - restaurants, licensed clubs and fine dining establishments
  - bars, pubs and taverns
  - fast food outlets, snack bars, canteens and kiosks
  - industrial and contract caterers
  - function and outside caterers
  - club administration operations

16.5.3 The Gambling and Lotteries Chamber

The Gambling and Lotteries Chamber of THETA comprises Gaming and gambling, including:

- licensed casinos and other licensed table, electronic and slot machine gaming outlets
- licensed clubs and other slot gaming outlets,
- licensed gambling, betting, bingo and bookmaking operators

◆ totalisators and lottery operations
◆ horseracing events, clubs and academies

16.5.4 The Conservation and Guiding Chamber

Conservation is often closely linked with tourism and hospitality, and for the purposes of clarifying what it is all about, it comprises the following:
◆ natural resource management: the conservation of flora and fauna and the core business of conservation
◆ natural resource security, controlling crime such as poaching and illegal trade in wildlife
◆ ecological management, where most scientists are based, for example ornithologists, entomologists
◆ regional management strategy, which includes determining assets, environmental impact assessment and so forth
◆ community conservation
◆ permaculture: progressive ways of farming, for example using organic waste to enrich soil

The Conservation and Guiding Chamber of THETA therefore includes:
◆ **Wildlife conservation**, including
  ▶ wildlife parks, game reserves and zoological establishments
  ▶ camp and conservation park management
  ▶ trekking and safari operators
  ▶ botanical gardens
◆ **Heritage and cultural conservation**, including
  ▶ management of museum, cultural and heritage activities
  ▶ preservation of monuments, historical sites and buildings
◆ **Hunting, trapping, taxidermy** and related services
◆ **Tourist guides. There are four types of tourist guides**
  ▶ local guides ('site guides') who are registered for and operate in a specific area
  ▶ regional guides who operate in a specific region or province.
  ▶ national guides who operate in all regions
  ▶ specialist guides who have specialised knowledge of an area or subject, for example museums, safaris

16.5.5 The Sport, Recreation and Fitness Chamber

The Sport, Recreation and Fitness Chamber of THETA comprises:
◆ sport or recreation services to or facilities for sporting bodies, universities, sports persons or the public at large
◆ event management, sponsorship, sports media and allied activities
◆ any kind of sports and recreation events, outdoors or indoors, for professionals or amateurs, and the operation of the facilities in which these are performed
◆ the operation of facilities for all sports, arenas and stadiums
◆ sporting events and the activities of sports people, sponsors, athletes, judges, umpires, referees, timekeepers, instructors, teachers, coaches, other technical officials and administrators

- gymnasiums, health and well-being centres, including but not limited to hydros, spas, lifestyle clubs, aerobics and fitness centres and activities
- sport and game schools
- parks and beaches, fairs and shows of a recreational nature
- recreational transport activities such as cable-way transport at sightseeing places

16.6 THETA Functions

16.6.1 Qualifications

While a process of development of qualifications and unit standards for qualifications is undertaken by a Standards Generating Body, once these are registered with the South African Qualifications Authority (SAQA) on the National Qualifications Framework (NQF), THETA becomes the custodian of these qualifications.

THETA may register certain identified qualifications as learnerships or parts of qualifications – skills programmes – with the Department of Labour. Learnerships are a structured way to achieve a qualification on the NQF, and consist of both an on- and off-job learning component.

THETA will approve grants to enable employees to gain qualifications or credits that are recognised on the NQF. For further information on the NQF and the qualifications available for the hospitality industry, visit the SAQA website on www.saqa.org.za.

The following examples of each of these components will illustrate how they build on each other:

Figure 16-2: Types of qualifications available

Unit standard	Skills programme	Learnership	Qualification
FP23: Prepare and cook meat, poultry, game and offal dishes (8 credits)	Cook: Convenience cook (14 credits) Assistant chef (35 credits)	Certificate in professional cookery (120 credits)	Certificate in professional cookery (120 credits)
AS03: Service guest bedroom areas (1 credit)	Room attendant: (13 credits) Assistant housekeeper (54 credits)	Certificate in accommodation services (120 credits)	Certificate in accommodation services (120 credits)
FH15: Maintain the front office service (3 credits)	Receptionist (58 credits)	Certificate in hospitality reception (120 credits)	Certificate in hospitality reception (120 credits)
FS14: Serve bottled wines (3 credits)	Table attendant (48 credits) Drink service attendant (16 credits)	Certificate in food and beverage services (120 credits)	Certificate in food and beverage services (120 credits)

16.6.2 Quality assurance

Under the SDA, THETA must establish an Education and Training Quality Assurance body (ETQA) to provide for the accreditation of training providers in its sector. This means that any entity – training institution, college or employer-provider (a hospitality establishment e.g. restaurant or hotel) that undertakes to train against qualifications of which THETA is the custodian, must be accredited by the THETA ETQA to do so.

16.6.3 Learner records and certification

Once the hospitality establishment is accredited by THETA, it may register its employees with THETA for skills programmes or qualifications. Once the learner, who THETA tracks on a learner database, has completed the qualification and achieved all the unit standards required, THETA will provide a certificate to the learner for the qualification that they have achieved.

16.7 Levies and grants

The Minister of Labour has published regulations about the skills grants to be paid by SETAs; the Minister also determines levy and grant values. THETA will inform the employers of these values once they are determined. Late submissions of plans and reports will impact directly on grant payments, and may result in delays in payments. In extreme cases, forfeiture may result.

To qualify for a grant, the Work Place Skills Plan (WSP) and implementation reports must be submitted and approved by THETA.

There are six types of grants that an employer might claim. These are shown in figure 16–3

Figure 16–3: Types of skills grants and grant payments by THETA

Type of grant	Payment of grant by THETA
◆ Workplace skills grant ◆ Workplace skills implementation grant	**Mandatory Grants**: THETA *must* pay grant to employer provided specific conditions are met
◆ Grant towards the costs of learnerships and learner allowances ◆ Grant towards the costs of skills programmes ◆ Grant towards the costs of providing apprenticeship training ◆ Grant towards a programme, project or research activity that helps the relevant SETA to implement its sector skills plan	**Discretionary Grants**: THETA *may* pay these grants on application from an employer, subject to various conditions such as funds available, alignment to sector skills needs, and so forth.

Figure 16-4:THETA submission requirements and grant payments

Requirements	Submission Date	Grant payment date	Grant value
Submit SDF details Submit WSP	Date stipulated in the funding regulations issued by the DOL from time to time. (Currently 30 June 2007 annually) Communicated by THETA to the industry	Must be paid to the employer at least quarterly.	50%
Submit WSP implementation report	By 30 June 2007 annually From 2006/2007 and in subsequent years, submit an Annual Training Report (in respect of the previous years' WSP) simultaneously.		
Discretionary grants	Date to be stipulated by THETA and communicated to the industry		20%

16.7.1 Grant values

1.7.1.1 Mandatory grants:

Payment of mandatory grants will be made by Theta:

◆ upon nomination of a skills development facilitator and

◆ upon receipt, submission and approval of your workplace skills plan (WSP) and annual training report (ATR) for the preceding year

The payment of the mandatory grant is 50% of the total levy value received by THETA from SARS.

The grant must be paid to the employer by THETA at least quarterly.

If a grant claim is not submitted by the 30th June, THETA must transfer the employer's unclaimed mandatory grant into the Discretionary Grant Fund.

16.7.1.2 Discretionary grants

Twenty percent of the Skills Development Levy contribution will be pooled and utilised for discretionary training activities as determined by THETA. These activities, as well as grant values and claims procedures, must comply with one or more of the '13 funding windows' prescribed by the Department of Labour and which are published and updated by THETA from time to time.

16.8 Claiming grants

16.8.1 Workplace skills planning grant

Each up-to-date levy-paying employer may expect a grant from THETA, if:

◆ Levy contributions have been forwarded by SARS and received by THETA (grant payments will be pro-rated and based on levies received).

◆ Levy contributions are up to date.

◆ At least one skills development facilitator (SDF) has been designated by the employer, and the name has been submitted to THETA.

◆ A workplace skills plan has been submitted and approved by THETA.

- The employer has submitted a training report of performance in respect of the previous years' WSP
- All required supporting documentation (proof of training, signed authorisation form, cancelled cheque) are provided

Remittance advices confirming grant payments will be faxed or e-mailed by THETA to the employer at least two weeks after the grant payment has been made.

16.9 Skills development facilitator

Each employer, after consultation with the workforce, must designate at least one Skills Development Facilitator (SDF). For multi-site or large organisations, more than one facilitator might be appropriate. Small employers, with less than 50 employees, or with a sales turnover less than that specified in Schedule 4 to the Employment Equity Act 55 of 1998, may wish to designate a SDF jointly. Employers should provide the SDF with the resources, facilities and training to enable him or her to perform the role.

Figure 16–5: Schedule 4 to the EEA

Sector	Total annual turnover
Agriculture	R2 million
Mining and quarrying	R7,5 million
Manufacturing	R10 million
Electricity, gas and water	R10 million
Construction	R5 million
Retail and motor trade and repair services	R15 million
Catering, accommodation	**R5 million**
Finance and business services	R10 million
Community, society and personal services	R5 million

The SDF not only processes forms and develops the WSP for the employer, but should also be in a position to advise and guide the employer on skills development issues such as the selection and choice of relevant training programmes or qualifications for employees. The SDF should be able to:
- provide the company with information regarding all aspects of the National Qualifications Framework (NQF)
- provide advice on selecting and implementing national qualifications that are registered on the NQF
- provide advice and support for learnership implementation
- conduct a skills audit and/or a training needs analysis to determine training gaps and needs for the organisation
- develop and draft the workplace skills plan

- monitor the implementation of training and development interventions and related assessment against the workplace skills plan
- draft the required implementation reports
- assist and provide advice regarding accreditation
- complete and submit any other necessary paperwork as required by THETA
- assist the employer and employees to develop the WSP
- advise the employer and employees on the implementation of the WSP
- assist the employer to draft the annual training report (ATR) on the implementation of the WSP
- advise the employer of any quality standards set by THETA
- act as a contact person between the employer and THETA
- serve as a resource with regard to all aspects of skills development

If a SDF leaves the organisation, or for any other reason ceases to perform the role, the employer should designate another SDF and inform THETA.

16.10 Workplace training committee

It is a legislated requirement in terms of the various skills development legislation that employers of 50 or more persons constitute a workplace training committee representing both owner/employer and labour/employee interests. This forum must fairly include members that represent both interests.

The committee is to meet regularly to collectively determine training priorities, agree on skills gaps, training interventions to be implemented, etc.

Many large employers combine the functions and objectives of an employment equity committee and training committee as the issues discussed overlap considerably. This arrangement makes it more practicable for employers by minimising time away from work for participating members.

16.10.1 The role of an SDF in constituting a training committee

A very important function of the SDF is to establish a training committee for the enterprise or company.

Where a workplace is unionised, trade unions or management structures could fulfil this function. It is important that workplace consultative structures be consulted in the appointment of a skills development facilitator.

16.10.2 Functions of the training committee

- Development and approval of a training policy.
- Ensuring that the development and implementation of the workplace skills plan is aligned to the strategic mission and vision of the company.
- Keeping the envisaged training and development of employees in the company abreast with the long-term transformation objectives of the company.
- Ensuring that the workplace skills plan is aligned to the employment equity plan and business plan of a company.
- Establishing training priorities for the company, based on its short and long term needs.
- Aligning training to the sector skills plan, learnerships, career pathways, registered national qualifications, etc.

- Supporting the SDF in communicating the completed workplace skills plan to other employees in the company.
- Monitoring the implementation of the workplace skills plan.
- Periodic revision of the workplace skills plan. This will in most cases be carried out in conjunction with the training committee.
- Compiling the annual training implementation report

16.10.3 THETA requirements regarding a workplace training committee

THETA organisations that employ 50 persons or more must:
- Ensure that a workplace training committee is properly constituted to adequately represent the interests of both management and labour.
- Ensure committee members are capacitated on the role, function and objectives of the forum.
- Ensure the committee meets regularly to deliberate relevant issues and make decisions on all skills development issues.
- Keep detailed minutes of all meetings held.
- Keep signed copies of attendance registers from said meetings.

THETA does not require this information to be submitted with grant applications but employers may have to produce this evidence for grant claim monitoring and auditing visits.

16.11 Workplace skills plan

Based on the analysis of business requirements, and the skill needs of current staff, the WSP must define the skills priorities that each workplace will pursue, the training programmes that are required to meet and deliver those priorities and the staff who will be targeted for training – 'the beneficiaries'.

THETA uses a standard form for all employers, large and small. This form can be accessed, filled in and submitted electronically on the THETA website: www.theta.org.za.

16.11.1 Source documents to complete the WSP

To enable the SDF to draw up a meaningful plan, he/she should have access to
- the company business plan
- any other priorities set
- human resource records: THETA requires educational data, age profiles of employees and information on BEE compliance, training spend, and other such information.
- the employment equity plan
- a completed skills audit and/or training needs analysis
- details of staff earmarked for progression
- details of employee career paths
- copies of all EMP201 forms (remittance advices submitted to SARS on a monthly basis) for the period in question.

16.11.2 WSP/ATR processing by THETA

Once the WSP has been completed and submitted to THETA, the plan will be reviewed. If the plan is approved the organisation will automatically qualify to receive the portion of the grant available for the submission of workplace skills plan and annual training report. No additional paperwork is required.

If the plan is rejected, it will be returned to the organisation for correction and/or amendment. It should then be resubmitted. If the (amended) plan is accepted, the organisation will automatically qualify to receive the mandatory grant portion, and no additional paperwork will be required.

The establishment will receive a fax or e-mail acknowledging and confirming receipt of the WSP/ATR. The establishment is advised to ensure that an acknowledgement of receipt is obtained to avoid potential delays later on. Once the WSP has been reviewed by THETA, notification advising of approval or rejection of the WSP will also be given.

16.11.3 System to maintain accurate record keeping

A system to maintain accurate records should be devised and maintained for
- all training interventions implemented (copies of invoices, attendance registers, and so forth)
- all assessments completed (information may also be verified against information held for learners in the THETA database)
- all training committee meetings.

Copies of this documentation must be submitted to THETA in hard-copy format by the 30th June every year. These documents cannot be attached to the ATR as the report is submitted electronically on the THETA website. Therefore all supporting documentary evidence must be submitted in hard copies separate from the ATR.

16.11.4 Workplace skills plan implementation report grant

Employers who are up-to-date with their levy payments can claim a grant from THETA if they (through their SDF) submit a report each year on the implementation of their workplace skills plan before the date stipulated by THETA.

As from the 2006/2007 levy year, and for all subsequent years, a SETA may not pay a mandatory grant to an employer who has not submitted an ATR. Thus, employers are required to submit a WSP (upcoming year) and ATR (previous year) simultaneously by no later than 30th June to qualify for the 50% mandatory grant.

This grant amount is therefore paid out in quarterly payments for the submission of both the plan and report. The regulations are quite strict on this as they state 'may not' and '. . . who fail to meet the . . . criteria . . . will forfeit the grant'.

Implementation reports must be supported by proof of training interventions implemented during the period (refer the section above on *Maintain record keeping systems* to confirm the type of proof that will be required).

Establishments are also advised to include and submit copies of EMP201 forms (the remittance advices submitted monthly to SARS) for the period (1 April to 31 March) with the implementation report.

THETA will send a fax or e-mail acknowledging and confirming receipt of the implementation report (ATR). The establishment is advised to ensure that an acknowledgement of receipt is obtained to avoid potential delays later on.

Once the implementation report has been received by THETA, a desk evaluation will be completed. A sample number of implementation reports, selected on a random basis, will then be subject to an on-site audit for verification of data. Once this has been completed, notification advising approval or rejection of the implementation report will be given.

If the implementation report is approved, the information is captured by THETA, and the organisation will automatically qualify to receive the portion of the grant available for the implementation of training and development interventions. No additional paperwork is required.

16.11.4.1 Conditions for payment of implementation grants

THETA will only pay grants for WSP implementation if the following conditions are met:

◆ A workplace skills plan must have been submitted and approved by THETA.
◆ Verifiable proof of training interventions must be submitted with the implementation report.
◆ The planned training indicated in the workplace skills plan must have taken place. Variances must be clearly identified and motivated.
◆ Levy contributions must be up to date.
◆ Levy contributions must have been forwarded by SARS and received by THETA (grant payments will be pro-rated and based on levies received).

16.11.5 Discretionary grants

Twenty percent of the skills development levy contribution, plus all unclaimed mandatory grants, will be pooled and utilised for discretionary training activities as determined by THETA. These will be identified activities that will assist THETA to achieve its sector skills plan by addressing training and development priorities in the sector.

16.11.5.1 Learnerships

Any employer may seek a grant from THETA to support the implementation of learnerships. THETA will determine the level of the grant, and details of the grant will be registered with the Department of Labour when each learnership is registered.

There are two possible types of grants to support learnerships. The first is a grant to offset the costs of implementing a learnership, (for example, off-the-job education and training provider fees). The second is a grant that may be paid to subsidise the learner's allowance if the learner was unemployed immediately before starting the learnership. The learner allowance will be in terms of the Learnership Determination published by the Minister of Labour.

It is a matter for THETA to decide how many and what applications it will support. THETA will need to make its decisions in the light of:

◆ the priorities of its sector skills plan
◆ the amount of money it has available to support learnerships
◆ the suitability of the applicant employer (capacity to provide appropriate experiential learning opportunities, learner support, mentor/coach capacity, and employment prospects for unemployed learners on completion of the programme)

- the accreditation and programme approval status of the training provider

THETA must inform an employer whether or not it will make a grant before the learnership starts. THETA will agree with the employer when the grant will be paid, for example if this will be in staged payments or only once the learnership is successfully concluded.

16.11.5.2 *Sector priorities*

A major function of THETA is the implementation of its sector skills plan. In order to do this THETA may make a grant to an employer, to a training provider or to an individual. For example, a grant might be to finance research or to develop the training infrastructure in the sector. The grants will be determined by THETA, which will also publish details of how to apply.

16.12 Standard industry categories

Figure 16-6: Definitions: standard industry categories (SIC) for THETA

Chamber	SIC CODE	Type of Business/Activities
Hospitality	64101	Hotels, motels, boatels and inns registered with the SA Tourism Board
	64102	Caravan parks and camping sites
	64103	Guest houses and guest farms
	64104	Hotels, motels, boatels and inns not registered with the SA Tourism Board
	64105	Bed and breakfast
	64106	Management and operation of game lodges
	64201	Restaurants or tearooms with liquor licence
	64202	Restaurants or tearooms without liquor licence
	64203	Take-away counters
	64204	Caterers
	64205	Take-away restaurants
	64206	Fast food establishments
	64207	Other catering services n.e.c. including pubs, taverns, night clubs
	64209	Other catering services n.e.c.
	84111	Timesharing
	88994	Bioscope cafes

Chamber	SIC CODE	Type of Business/Activities
Gaming & Lotteries	96419	Operation and management of horse racing events and clubs and academies
	96494	Gambling, licensed casinos & the National Lottery incl but not limited to bookmakers, totalisators, casinos, bingo operators
Travel & Tourism Services	71214	Tour operators (inbound and outbound tour operators)
	71222	Safaris and sight seeing bus tours
	71223	Safaris and sightseeing trip operators
	73002	Inbound international flights
	74140	Travel agency and related activities
	85110	Renting of land transport equipment
	85111	Renting of land transport equipment including car rentals
	8899A	Event and conference management
	96195	Operation and management of convention centres
	96336	Tourist info centres
	99028	Car hire
	99048	Tourism authorities incl. but not limited to tourism marketing, tourist information centres, publicity associations
Sport, Recreation & Fitness	93195	Operation and management of health and well-being centres including but not limited to hydros, spas, fitness centres etc
	96000	Recreational, cultural and sporting activities
	96002	Recreational, leisure and outdoor adventure activities incl. management and operation of facilities, Government departments
	96196	Amusement parks
	96410	Sporting activities
	96411	Operation and management of sporting facilities and clubs
	96412	Operation and management of sport academies
	96413	Promotion and management of sporting events and activities

Chamber	SIC CODE	Type of Business/Activities
	96415	Management and operation of non-motorised sporting activities
	96417	Sporting activities incl. but not limited to sport federations etc
	96418	Management and operation of motorised sporting activities
	96491	The operation and management of recreation parks & beaches, fairs and shows of a recreational nature and recreational transport activities
Conservation & Tourism Guiding	11520	Hunting and trapping including related services
	96320	Museum activities and preservation of historical sites and buildings
	96322	Provision for management and operation of monuments, historical sites and buildings
	96323	Management and operation of museum, cultural and heritage activities
	96333	Game parks, reserves incl. but not limited to wildlife, parks, zoological or animal parks and botanical gardens
	96334	Activities of conservation bodies
	96335	Wildlife conservation incl. wildlife, game, parks, game reserves, zoological establishments, botanical gardens etc
	99049	Guides incl. tourist river, mountain etc.

Questions and exercises

1. Write a job specification and job description for a skills development facilitator.
2. Design a process for the development of a workplace skills plan.
3. Describe how skills development and employment equity are complimentary principles and processes.
4. Explain the rationale and process of the levy-grant system to a new hospitality operator.

Appendix: BASIC CONDITIONS OF EMPLOYMENT ACT 75 OF 1997

SECTORAL DETERMINATION 14: HOSPITALITY SECTOR, SOUTH AFRICA

SCHEDULE

PART A: APPLICATION

1. Scope of application

(1) The determination applies to employers and employees engaged in the Hospitality Sector activities in the Republic of South Africa.

(2) Hospitality Sector means any commercial business or part of a commercial business in which employers and employees are associated for the purpose of carrying on or conducting one or more of the following activities for reward:

(a) providing accommodation in a hotel, motel, inn, resort, game lodge, hostel, guest house, guest farm or bed and breakfast establishment, including short stay accommodation, self-catering, timeshares, camps, caravan parks;

(b) restaurants, pubs, taverns, cafés, tearooms, coffee shops, fast food outlets, snack bars, industrial or commercial caterers, function caterers, contract caterers that prepare, serve or provide prepared food or liquid refreshments, other than drinks in sealed bottles or cans whether indoors or outdoors or in the open air, for consumption on or off the premises; and

(c) includes all activities or operations incidental to or arising from any of the activities mentioned in paragraphs (a) and (b).

(3) This determination does not apply to employers and employees who are:

(a) involved in the trade of letting of flats, rooms or houses;

(b) covered by another sectoral determination in terms of the Basic Conditions of Employment Act 75 of 1997; or

(c) covered by a collective agreement of a bargaining council in terms of the Labour Relations Act of 1995.

(4) The provisions of the Basic Conditions of Employment Act apply to all employees covered by this determination and their employers in respect of any matter that is not regulated by this sectoral determination.

(5) The provisions of the Ministerial Determination for Small Business apply to those employers employing less than 10 employees in respect of overtime, averaging of working hours, and family responsibility leave.

PART B: MINIMUM WAGES

2. Minimum wage levels

(1) With effect from 1 July 2007, an employer must pay an employee at least the minimum wage, excluding any gratuity or tips, prescribed in this clause.

(2) An employer must pay an employee who works 45 ordinary hours of work per week –

(a) at least the weekly or monthly wage set out in table 1 or 2; or

(b) by written agreement between the employer and the employee, at least the hourly rate set out in Table 1 or 2 for every hour or part of an hour that the employee works.

(3) An employee who works for less than four hours on any day must be paid at least for four hours work on that day.

Table 1: Minimum wages for employers with 10 or less employees

Minimum rate for the period			Minimum rate for the period			Minimum rate for the period		
1 July 2007 to 30 June 2008			1 July 2008 to 30 June 2009			1 July 2009 to 30 June 2010		
R.p.m	R.p.w	R.p.h	R.p.m	R.p.w	R.p.h	R.p.m	R.p.w	R.p.h
R1480–00	R341–60	R7–59	Previous Minimum Wage + CPIX + 2%			Previous Minimum Wage + CPIX + 2%		

Table 2: Minimum wages for employers with more than 10 employees

Minimum rate for the period			Minimum rate for the period			Minimum rate for the period		
1 July 2007 to 30 June 2008			1 July 2008 to 30 June 2009			1 July 2009 to 30 June 2010		
R.p.m	R.p.w	R.p.h	R.p.m	R.p.w	R.p.h	R.p.m	R.p.w	R.p.h
R1 650-00	R380–80	R8–46	Previous Minimum Wage + CPIX + 2%			Previous Minimum Wage + CPIX + 2%		

3. Commission work

(1) An employer and employee may agree in writing that the employee will perform commission work on a regular basis.

(2) An employer must pay an employee the rates applicable for commission work as agreed to, provided that irrespective of the commissioned earned; the employer shall pay such employee not less than the prescribed minimum wage for the period worked.

(3) An agreement to perform commission work in terms of this clause must be concluded before the work commences and must include –

(a) the employee's wage and rate;

(b) the basis for calculating commission;

(c) the period over which the payment is calculated which may not be longer than one month;

(d) when the employer must pay the commission to the employee which may not be longer than seven days after the end of the period in which the commission is earned; and

(e) the type, description, number, quantity, margin, profit, or orders (individual, weekly, monthly or otherwise) for which the employee is entitled to earn commission.

(4) The employer must supply the employee with a copy of the agreement to perform commission work.

(5) If during any calculation period the employee does not earn an amount equivalent to at least the prescribed minimum wage, excluding any gratuity or gift received from a customer for service rendered, because of any act or omission by or on behalf of the employer or the employer has restricted the employee's ability to earn commission in terms of the agreement, the employer must pay the employee at least the applicable minimum wage as prescribed.

(6) An employer who intends to cancel or amend the agreement entered into relating to commission work which is in operation or the rates applicable thereunder, shall give the affected employee not less than four weeks notice of such intention.

4. Calculation of wages or remuneration

(1) The wage or remuneration of an employee is calculated by reference to the employee's ordinary hours of work.

(2) For the purposes of any calculation in terms of this determination –

(a) the hourly wage or remuneration of a worker is obtained by –
  (i) dividing the weekly wage or remuneration by the ordinary number of hours worked in a week;

(b) the daily wage or remuneration of an employee is obtained by –
  (i) multiplying the hourly wage or remuneration by the number of ordinary hours worked in a day; or
  (ii) dividing the weekly wage or remuneration by the number of days worked in a week;

(c) the weekly wage or remuneration of an employee is obtained by –
  (i) multiplying the hourly wage or remuneration by the number of ordinary hours worked in a day multiplied by the number of days worked in a week; or
  (ii) multiplying the daily wage or remuneration by the number of days worked in a week; or
  (iii) dividing the monthly wage or remuneration by four and one-third;

(d) the monthly wage or remuneration of an employee is obtained by multiplying the weekly wage or remuneration by four and a third.

5. Payment of remuneration

(1) An employer must pay an employee –

(a) in South African currency;

(b) daily, weekly, fortnightly or monthly; and

(c) in cash, by cheque or by direct deposit into an account designated by the employee.
 (2) Any payment in cash or by cheque must be given to each employee –
(a) at the workplace;
(b) during the employee's working hours; and
(c) in a sealed envelope which becomes the property of the employee.
 (3) An employer must pay an employee on the normal pay day agreed to in writing by the employee.

6. Information concerning pay

 (1) On every pay day, the employer must give the employee a statement showing:
(a) the employer's name and address;
(b) the employee's name and occupation;
(c) the period in respect of which payment is made;
(d) the employee's wage rate and overtime rate;
(e) the number of ordinary hours worked by an employee during that period;
(f) the number of overtime hours worked by the employee during that period;
(g) the number of hours worked by the employee on a paid holiday or on a Sunday;
(h) the employee's wage;
(i) details of any other pay arising out of the employee's employment;
(j) details of any deductions made;
(k) the employer's registration number with the Unemployment Insurance Fund and the employer's contribution to the Fund; and
(l) the actual amount paid to the employee.
 (2) An employer must retain a copy or record of each statement for three years.

7. Deductions and other acts concerning remuneration

 (1) An employer may not make any deduction from an employee's remuneration unless:
(a) subject to subsection (2), the employee in writing agrees to the deduction in respect of a debt specified in the agreement; or
(b) the deduction is required or permitted in terms of a law, collective agreement, court order or arbitration award.
 (2) A deduction in terms of subsection (1)(a) may be made to reimburse an employer for loss or damage only if –
(a) the loss or damage occurred in the course of employment and was due to the fault of the employee;
(b) the employer has followed a fair procedure and has given the employee a reasonable opportunity to show why the deductions should not be made;
(c) the total amount of the debt does not exceed the actual amount of the loss or damage; and
(d) the total deductions from the employee's remuneration in terms of this subsection do not exceed one-quarter of the employee's remuneration in money.

(3) A deduction in terms of subsection (1)(a) in respect of any goods purchased by the employee must specify the nature and quantity of the goods.

(4) An employer who deducts an amount from an employee's remuneration in terms of subsection (1) for payment to another person must pay the amount to the person in accordance with the time period and other requirements specified in the agreement, law court order or arbitration award.

(5) An employer may not require or permit an employee to:

(a) repay any remuneration except for overpayments previously made by the employer resulting from an error in calculating the employee's remuneration; or

(b) acknowledge receipt of an amount greater than the remuneration actually received;

(c) Pay the employer or any other person in respect of –
    (i) the employment or training of that employee
    (ii) the supply of any work equipment or tools; or
    (iii) the supply of any work clothing.

(6) An employer may not require an employee to purchase any goods from the employer or from any person, shop or other business nominated by the employer.

(7) An employer may not levy a fine against an employee.

An employer may not make any deduction from remuneration or require or permit an employee to make any payment to the employer or any other person in respect of anything that the employer is required to do in the interests of the health and safety of an employee (section 23 of the Occupational Health and Safety Act 85 of 1993.

7A. Payment of contributions to benefit funds

(1) For the purposes of this section, a benefit fund is a pension, provident, retirement, medical aid or similar fund.

(2) An employer that deducts from an employee's remuneration any amount for payment to a benefit fund must pay the amount to the fund within seven days of the deduction being made.

(3) Any contribution that an employer is required to make to a benefit fund on behalf of an employee, that is not deducted from the employee's remuneration, must be paid to the fund within seven days of the end of the period in respect of which the payment is made.

(4) This section does not affect any obligation on an employer in terms of the rules of a benefit fund to make any payment within a shorter period than that required in subsection (2) or (3).

PART C: PARTICULARS OF EMPLOYMENT

8. Written particulars of employment

(1) An employer must supply an employee, when the employee commences work, with the following particulars in writing –

(a) the full name and address of the employer;

(b) the name and occupation of the employee, or a brief description of the work for which the employee is employed;

(c) the place of work, and where the employee is required or permitted to work at various places, an indication of this;
(d) the date on which employment began;
(e) the employee's ordinary hours of work and days of work;
(f) the employee's wage or the rate and method of payment;
(g) the rate of pay for overtime work;
(h) any other cash payments that the employee is entitled to;
(i) any food or accommodation that the employee is entitled to and the value of the food or accommodation;
(j) any other payment in kind received by the employee;
(k) how frequently wages will be paid;
(l) any deductions to be made from the employee's wages;
(m) the leave to which the employee is entitled to;
(n) the period of notice required to terminate employment, or if employment is for a specific period, the date when employment is to terminate.

(2) If an employee is not able to understand the written particulars, the employer must ensure that they are explained to the employee in a language and in a manner that the employee understands.

(3) The employer must revise the written particulars if there is any change in the employee's terms of employment.

(4) An employer must retain a copy of the written particulars of employment while the employee is employed and for three years thereafter.

PART D: HOURS OF WORK

9. Ordinary hours of work

(1) An employer may not require or permit a employee to work more than –
(a) 45 hours in any week; and
(b) nine hours on any day if the employee works for five days or less in a week; or
(c) eight hours in any day if the employee works for more than five days in any week.

10. Overtime

(1) An employer may not require or permit an employee –
(a) to work overtime except in accordance with an agreement concluded by the employer and the employee;
(b) to work more than 10 hours' overtime a week; or
(c) to work more than 12 hours, including overtime, on any day.

(2) An agreement concluded in terms of subclause (1)(a) with an employee when the employee commences employment, or during the first three months of employment, is only valid for one year.

11. Payment of overtime

(1) An employer must pay an employee at least one and one-half times the employee's wage for overtime worked.

(2) Despite subclause (1), an agreement may provide for an employer to –

(a) pay an employee not less than the employee's ordinary wage for overtime worked and grant the employee at least 30 minutes' time off on full pay for every hour of overtime worked; or

(b) grant an employee at least 90 minutes' paid time off for each hour of overtime worked.

(3) An employer must grant an employee paid time off in terms of subclause (2) within one month of the employee becoming entitled to it.

(4) An agreement in writing may increase the period contemplated by subclause (3) to twelve months.

12. Compressed working week

(1) An agreement in writing may require or permit an employee to work up to twelve hours in a day, inclusive of the meal intervals required in terms of clause 16, without receiving overtime pay.

(2) An agreement in terms of subclause (1) may not require or permit an employee to work –

(a) more than 45 ordinary hours of work in any week;

(b) more than ten hours' overtime in any week; or

(c) on more than five days in any week.

13. Averaging of hours of work

(1) Despite clause 9(1) and (2) and 10(1)(b), the ordinary hours of work and overtime of an employee may be averaged over a period of up to four months in terms of a written agreement.

(2) An employer may not permit an employee who is bound by a written agreement in terms of subclause (1) to work more than –

(a) An average of 45 ordinary hours of work in a week over the agreed period;

(b) An average of 5 hours overtime in a week over the agreed period.

(3) An agreement in terms of subclause (1) lapses after 12 months.

(4) Subclause (3) only applies to the first two agreements concluded in terms of subclause (1).

14. Work on Sundays

(1) An employer must pay an employee who works on a Sunday at double the employee's wage for each hour worked, unless the employee ordinarily works on a Sunday, in which case the employer must pay the employee at one and one-half times the employee's wage for each hour worked.

(2) If the payment calculated in terms of subclause (1) is less than the employee's daily wage, the employer must pay the employee, for the time worked on that Sunday , the employee's daily wage.

(3) Despite subclauses (1) and (2), an agreement may permit an employer to grant an employee who works on a Sunday paid time off equivalent to the difference in value between the pay received by the employee for working on the Sunday and the pay that the employee is entitled to in terms of subclauses (1) and (2).

(4) Any time worked on a Sunday by an employee who does not ordinarily work on a Sunday is not taken into account in calculating the ordinary hours of work of the employee in terms of clause 9.

(5) If a shift worked by an employee falls on a Sunday and another day, the whole shift is deemed to have been worked on the Sunday, unless the greater portion of the shift was worked on the other day, in which case the whole shift is deemed to have been worked on the other day.

(6)(a) An employer must grant paid time off in terms of subclause (3) within one month of the employee becoming entitled to it.

(b) An agreement in writing may increase the period contemplated by paragraph (a) to 12 months.

15. Night work

(1) In this clause, 'night work' means work performed after 18:00 and before 06:00 the next day.

(2) An employer may only require or permit an employee to perform night work if so agreed and if –

(a) an employee is compensated by the payment of an allowance, which may be a shift allowance, or by a reduction of working hours; and

(b) transportation is available between the employee's place of residence and the workplace at the commencement and conclusion of the employee's shift.

(c) if the transport cost is more than the daily cost to the employee, an employer who requires such an employee to perform night work must subsidise such employee for transport expenses.

(3) An employer who requires an employee to perform work on a regular basis after 23:00 and before 06:00 the next day must:

(a) inform the employee in writing, or orally if the employee is not able to understand a written communication, in a language that the employee reasonably understands –

(i) of any health and safety hazards associated with the work that the employee is required to perform; and

(ii) of the employee's right to undergo a medical examination in terms of paragraph (b);

(b) at the request of the employee, enable the employee to undergo a medical examination, for the account of the employer, concerning those hazards –

(i) before the employee starts, or within a reasonable period of the employee starting, such work;

(ii) at appropriate intervals while the employee continues to perform such work; and

(c) transfer the employee to suitable day work within a reasonable time if:

(i) the employee suffers from a health condition associated with the performance of night work; and

(ii) it is practicable for the employer to do so.

(4) Subclause (3) applies to an employee who works after 23:00 and before 06:00 at least five times per month or 50 times per year.

16. Meal intervals

(1) An employer must give an employee who works continuously for more than five hours a meal interval of at least one continuous hour.

(2) During a meal interval, an employee may be required or permitted to perform only duties that cannot be left unattended and cannot be performed by another employee.

(3) An employee must be paid:

(a) for a meal interval in which the employee is required to be available for work;

(b) for any portion of a meal interval that is in excess of 75 minutes, unless the employee lives on the premises at which the workplace is situated.

(4) For the purpose of subclause (1), work is continuous unless it is interrupted by a meal interval of at least 60 minutes.

(5) An agreement in writing may –

(a) reduce the meal interval to not less than 30 minutes;

(b) dispense with a meal interval for an employee who works fewer than six hours on a day.

17. Daily and weekly rest period

(1) An employer must grant an employee –

(a) a daily rest period of at least twelve consecutive hours between ending work and starting work the next day;

(b) weekly rest period of at least thirty-six consecutive hours which, unless otherwise agreed, must include a Sunday.

(2) A daily rest period in terms of subclause (1)(a) may, by written agreement, be reduced to 10 hours for an employee –

(a) who lives where the workplace is situated; and

(b) whose meal interval lasts for at least three hours.

(3) Despite subclause (1)(b), an agreement in writing may provide for a rest period of at least sixty consecutive hours every second week.

18. Public Holidays

(1) An employer may not require an employee to work on a public holiday, except in accordance with an agreement.

(2) If a public holiday falls on a day on which an employee would ordinarily work, an employer must pay –

(a) an employee who does not work on the public holiday, at least the wage that the employee would ordinarily have received for work on that day;

(b) an employee who does work on the public holiday at least double the employee's daily wage.

(3) If an employee works on a public holiday on which the employee would not normally work, the employer must pay the employee an amount equal to –

(a) the employee's daily wage; plus

(b) the employee's hourly wage for each hour worked on the public holiday.

(4) An employer must pay an employee for a public holiday on the employee's normal pay day.

(5) If a shift worked by an employee falls on a public holiday and another day, the whole shift is deemed to have been worked on the public holiday, but if the greater portion of the shift was worked on the other day, the whole shift is deemed to have been worked on the other day.

(6) In accordance with section 2 (2) of the Public Holidays Act, 1994 the parties may exchange a public holiday for any other day.

PART E: LEAVE

19. Annual leave

(1) An employer must grant an employee –

(a) at least three weeks (21 consecutive days) leave on full pay in respect of each twelve months of employment (the 'annual leave cycle'); or

(b) by agreement, at least one day of annual leave on full pay for every 17 days on which the employee worked or was entitled to be paid; or

(c) by agreement, one hour of annual leave on full pay for every 17 hours on which the employee worked or was entitled to be paid.

(2) An employer must grant an employee an additional day of paid leave if a public holiday falls on a day during an employee's annual leave on which the employee would otherwise have worked.

(3) An employer may reduce an employee's entitlement to annual leave by the number of days of occasional leave on full pay granted to the employee at the employee's request in that annual leave cycle.

(4) An employer must grant:

(a) the annual leave not later than six months after the end of the annual leave cycle in which leave was earned;

(b) the leave earned in one year over a continuous period, if requested by the employee.

(5) Annual leave must be taken –

(a) in accordance with an agreement between the employer and the employee; or

(b) if there is no agreement in terms of paragraph (a), at a time determined by the employer in accordance with this section.

(6) An employer may not require or permit an employee to take annual leave during –

(a) any other period of leave to which the employee is entitled in terms of this Part E; or

(b) any period of notice of termination of employment.

(7) An employer may not require or permit an employee to work for the employer during any period of annual leave.

(8) An employer may not pay an employee instead of granting paid leave in terms of this clause except on termination of employment in terms of clause 26.

(9) An employer must pay an employee leave pay at least equivalent to the remuneration the employee would have received for working for a period equal to the period of leave, calculated at the employee's wage immediately before the beginning of the period of leave.

(10) An employer must pay an employee leave pay before the beginning of the period of leave or, by agreement, on the employee's usual pay day.

20. Sick leave

(1) For the purpose of this clause 'sick leave cycle' means the period of 36 months employment with the same employer immediately following –

(a)   when the employee commenced work; or

(b)   the end of the employee's prior sick leave cycle.

(2) During every sick leave cycle, the employee is entitled to an amount of paid sick leave equal to the number of days the employee would normally work during a period of six weeks.

(3) Despite subclause (2), during the first six months of work, the employee is entitled to one day's sick leave for every 26 days worked.

(4) An employer may, during the employee's first leave cycle, reduce the employee's entitlement to sick leave in terms of subclause (2) by the number of days' sick leave taken in terms of subclause (3).

(5) Where an employer, at the request of the employee, pays fees for an employee's hospital or medical treatment, the fees paid may be set off against the employee's pay.

(6) An employer is not required to pay the employee in terms of this clause if the employee has been absent from work for more than two consecutive days or on more than two occasions during an eight-week period and, on request by the employer, does not produce a medical certificate stating that the employee was unable to work for the duration of the employee's absence on account of sickness or injury.

(7) The medical certificate in terms of subclause (6) must be issued and signed by a medical practitioner or any other person who is certified to diagnose and treat patients and who is registered with a professional council established by an Act of Parliament.

(8) If it is not reasonably practicable for an employee who lives on the employer's premises to obtain a medical certificate, the employer may not withhold payment in terms of subclause (6) unless the employer provides reasonable assistance to the employee to obtain the certificate.

21. Family responsibility leave

(1) This clause applies to an employee –

(a)   who has been employed by an employer for longer than four months; and

(b)   who works on at least four days a week for that employer.

(2) An employer must grant an employee, during each 12 months of employment, at the request of the employee, three days' paid leave, which the employee is entitled to take –

(a)   when the employee's child is born;

(b)   when the employee's child is sick; or

(c)   in the event of the death of –

  (i) the employee's spouse or life partner; or

  (ii) the employee's parent, adoptive parent, grandparent, child, adopted child, grandchild or sibling.

(3) An employee may take family responsibility leave in respect of the whole or part of the day.

(4) Subject to subclause (5), an employer must pay an employee for a day's family responsibility leave –

(a)   the wage the employee would normally have received for work on that day; and

(b) on the employee's usual pay day.

(5) Before paying an employee for leave in terms of this clause, an employer may require reasonable proof of an event contemplated in subclause (2) for which the leave was required.

(6) An employee's unused entitlement to leave in terms of this clause lapses at the end of the annual leave cycle in which it accrues.

22. Maternity leave

(1) An employee is entitled to at least four consecutive month's maternity leave.

(2) An employee may commence maternity leave –

(a) at any time from four weeks before the expected date of birth, unless otherwise agreed; or

(b) on a date from which a medical practitioner or a midwife certifies that it is necessary for the employee's health or that of her unborn child.

(3) An employee may not work for six weeks after the birth of her child, unless a medical practitioner or midwife certifies that she is fit to do so.

(4) An employee who has a miscarriage during the third trimester of pregnancy or bears a stillborn child is entitled to maternity leave for six weeks after the miscarriage or stillbirth, whether or not the employee had commenced maternity leave at the time of the miscarriage or stillbirth.

(5) An employee must notify an employer in writing, unless she is unable to do so, of the date on which the employee intends to –

(a) commence maternity leave; and

(b) return to work after maternity leave.

(6) Notification in terms of subclause (5) must be given –

(a) at least four weeks before the employee intends to commence maternity leave;

(b) if it is not reasonably practicable to do so, as soon as is reasonably practicable.

(7) No employer may require or permit a pregnant employee or an employee who is nursing her child to perform work that is hazardous to her health or the health of her child, including operating dangerous machinery or handling and/or using spray chemicals.

(8) During an employee's pregnancy, and for a period of six months after the birth of her child, her employer must offer her suitable, alternative employment on terms and conditions that are no less favourable than her ordinary terms and conditions of employment, if –

(a) the employee is required to perform night work, as defined in clause 15 or her work poses a danger to her health or safety or that of her child; and

(b) it is practicable for the employer to do so

PART F: PROHIBITION OF CHILD LABOUR AND FORCED LABOUR

23. Prohibition of child labour and forced labour

(1) No person may employ a child –

(a) who is under 15 years of age; or

(b) who is under the minimum school leaving age in terms of any law, if this is 15 or older.

(2) No person may employ a child in employment –

(a) that is inappropriate for a person of that age;

(b) that places at risk the child's well-being, education, physical or mental health, or spiritual, moral or social development.

(3) An employer must maintain for three years, a record of the name, date of birth and address of every employee under the age of 18 years employed by them.

(4) Subject to the Constitution of the Republic of South Africa, all forced labour is prohibited.

(5) No person may, for his/her own benefit or for the benefit of someone else cause, demand or impose forced labour in contravention of subclause (4).

(6) A person who employs a child in contravention of subclauses (1) and (2) or engages in any form of forced labour in contravention of subclauses (4) and (5) commits an offence in terms of sections 46 and 48 of the Basic Conditions of Employment Act respectively, read with section 93 of that Act.

PART G: TERMINATION OF EMPLOYMENT

24. Notice of termination of employment

(1) A contract of employment terminable at the instance of a party to the contract may be terminated only on notice of not less than –

(a) one week if the employee has been employed for six months or less;

(b) two weeks, if the employee has been employed for more than six months but not more than one year;

(c) four weeks, if the employee has been employed for one year or more.

(2) The employer and employee may agree to a longer notice period, but the agreement may not require or permit an employee to give a period of notice longer than that required of the employer.

(3) Notice of termination of contract of employment must be given in writing except when it is given by an illiterate employee.

(4) If an employee who receives notice of termination is not able to understand it, the notice must be explained orally by, or on behalf of, the employer to the employee in an official language the employee reasonably understands.

(5) Notice of termination of a contract of employment given by an employer must –

(a) not be given during any period of leave to which the employee is entitled to in terms of this determination;

(b) not run concurrently with any period of leave to which the employee is entitled in terms of this determination, except sick leave.

(6) Nothing in this clause affects the right –

(a) of a dismissed employee to dispute the lawfulness or fairness of the dismissal in terms of Chapter VIII of the Labour Relations Act, 1995, or any other law; and

(b) of an employer or an employee to terminate a contract of employment without notice for any cause recognized by law.

25. Payment instead of notice

(1) Instead of giving an employee notice in terms of this clause, an employer may pay the employee the wages the employee would have received, if the employee had worked during the notice period.

(2) If an employee gives notice of termination of employment, and the employer waives any part of the notice, the employer must pay the wages referred to in subclause (1), unless the employer and the employee agree otherwise.

26. Payments on termination

(1) On termination of employment, an employer must pay an employee all monies due to the employee including –

(a) any remuneration that has not been paid;

(b) any paid time off that the employee is entitled to in terms of clause 11(2) or 14(3) that the employee has not taken;

(c) remuneration calculated in accordance with clause 19(9) for any period of annual leave due in terms of clause 19(1) that the employee has not taken; and

(d) if the employee has been in employment longer than four months, in respect of the employee's annual leave entitlement during an incomplete annual leave cycle as defined in section 19(1) –

    (i) one day's remuneration in respect of every 17 days on which the employee worked or was entitled to be paid; or

    (ii) remuneration calculated on any basis that is at least as favourable to the employee as that calculated in terms of subparagraph (i).

27. Severance pay

(1) For the purpose of this clause, 'operational requirements' means requirements based on the economic, technological, structural or similar needs of an employer.

(2) An employer must pay an employee who is dismissed for reasons based on the employer's operational requirements, severance pay equal to at least one week's remuneration for each completed year of continuous service with that employer.

(3) An employee who unreasonably refuses to accept the employer's offer of alternative employment with that employer or any other employer is not entitled to severance pay in terms of subclause (2).

(4) The payment of severance pay in compliance with this clause does not affect an employee's right to any other amount payable according to law.

(5) If there is a dispute only about the entitlement to severance pay in terms of this clause, the employee may refer the dispute in writing to the CCMA.

28. Certificate of service

(1) On termination of employment, an employee is entitled to a certificate of service stating –

(a) the employee's full name;

(b) the name and address of the employer;

(c) the date of commencement and date of termination of employment;

(d) the title of the job or brief description of the work for which the employee was employed at the date of termination;

(e) any relevant training received by the employee;

(f) the pay at date of termination; and

(g) if the employee so requests, the reason for termination of employment.

29. Keeping of Sectoral Determination

(1) Every employer on whom this sectoral determination is binding must keep a copy of the sectoral determination or an official summary, available in the workplace in a place to which the employee has access.

30. Temporary employment services

(1) In this clause, 'temporary employment service' means any person who, for reward, procures for or provides employees to a client if that person remunerates the employees.

(2) For the purpose of this Determination, an employee whose services have been procured for, or provided to, a client by a temporary employment service is employed by that temporary employment service, and the temporary employment service is that person's employer.

(3) The temporary employment service and the client are jointly and severally liable to comply with this determination in respect of its employees.

(4) If the temporary employment service is in default of its obligation to make any payment in terms of this determination to an employee for a period of thirty days, the client concerned becomes liable to make payment.

(5) A client that in terms of this clause makes any payment that is owing to an employee is entitled to recover such amount from the employment service.

31. Cancellation of wage determinations

(1) Wage determination 457: Hotel Trade, Certain Areas; Wage determination 461: Catering Trade, Certain Areas; and Wage determination 479: Accommodation Establishment Trade, Certain Areas, is [sic] cancelled with effect from the date that this determination becomes binding.

32. What words mean in this determination

(1) Any expression in this determination, which is defined in the Basic Conditions of Employment Act (the Act) and is not defined in this clause, has the same meaning as in the Act and –

'agreement' includes a collective agreement;

'Basic Conditions of Employment Act' means the Basic Conditions of Employment Act, 1997 (Act 75 of 1997)

'child' means a person who is under 15 years of age;

'day' means, for the purposes of measuring hours of work, a period of 24 hours, measured from the time when an employee normally commences work;

'**dispute**' includes an alleged dispute;

'**employee**' means –

    (a) any person, excluding an independent contractor, who works for another person or for the State and who receives, or is entitled to receive, any remuneration; and

    (b) any other person who in any manner assists in carrying on or conducting the business of an employer;

'**incapacity**' means inability to work owing to sickness or injury;

'**Minister**' means the Minister of Labour;

'**month**' means a calendar month;

'**monthly wage**' means an employee's weekly wage multiplied by four and a third;

'**night work**' means work performed after 18:00 and before 06:00 the next day;

'**ordinary hours of work**' means the hours of work permitted in terms of clause 9;

'**overtime**' means the time that the employee works during a day or in a week in excess of ordinary hours of work;

'**paid leave**' means any annual leave, paid sick leave or family responsibility leave that an employee is entitled to in terms of Part E of this determination;

'**public holiday**' means any day that is a public holiday in terms of the Public Holiday Act, 1994 (Act 36 of 1994);

'**remuneration**' means any payment in money or in kind, or both in money and in kind excluding any gratuity or gift received from a customer for service rendered, made or owing to any person in return for that person working for any other person, including the State;

'**trade of letting of flats, rooms or houses**' means the trade carried on by persons who carry on the business of letting flats, rooms or houses and includes the agents to who such persons entrust the letting of flats, rooms or houses and the employees of such agents who are employed exclusively in connection with such flats, rooms or houses;

'**wage**' means the amount of money paid or payable to a employee in respect of ordinary hours of work or, if they are shorter, the hours a employee normally works in a day or week, excluding any gratuity or gift received from a customer for service rendered;

'**week**' in relation to an employee, means the period of seven days within which the working week of that employee falls;

'**worker**' has a corresponding meaning as 'employee';

'**workplace**' means any place where an employee works.

Glossary of Latin legal terms

actio empti – an action upon the purchaser, brought by the purchaser against the seller to enforce performance of the contract of sale or to claim damages

actio iniuriarum – action for pain and suffering

actio legis Aquiliae – Acquilian action (action brought by the lessor against the lessee to enforce the contract of hire

actio quanti minoris – an action for the reduction of price

actio redhibitoria – an action to cancel a sale; for the recission of a sale (purchase); redhibitory action

aedilitian actions – remedies for breach of the implied warranty against latent defects

constitutum possessorium – transfer of possession where A with the intention of transferring his ownership in a thing to B declares that he will be henceforth hold the thing for B

culpa – negligence

dolus – intention

edict de nautis cauponibus et stabularis – in respect of goods brought on to property by guests, strict liability will be imposed

essentialia – essential elements of a legal act

exceptio non adimpleti contractus – exception of an unfulfilled contract; exception on the ground that the plaintiff, too, is in default (and therefore cannot demand performance)

incidentalia – non essential elements or components of a contract

merx – the thing to be sold

mora – delay or default

mora debitoris – default by the debtor

mora ex persona – default by after notice given

mora ex re – default resulting from the expiry of the term set in the contract (default through mere lapse of the term agreed upon)

naturalia – natural elements or components of a contract

pactum de non petendo in anticipando – agreement not to sue (the creditor will not enforce his claim)

stare decisis – courts bound by previous decisions

Index